Expanding Boundaries

This book challenges the common European notions about African migration to Europe and offers a holistic understanding of the current situation in Africa. It advocates a need to rethink Africa-Europe relations and view migration and borders as a resource rather than as sources of a crisis.

Migrant movement from Africa is often misunderstood and misrepresented as invasion caused by displacement due to poverty, violent conflict, and environmental stress. To control this movement and preserve national identities, the EU and its various member states resort to closing borders as a way of reinforcing their migration policies. This book aims to dismantle this stereotypical view of migration from Africa by sharing cutting-edge research from the leading scholars in Africa and Europe. It refutes the flawed narratives that position Africa as a threat to European societies, their economies, and security, and encourages a nuanced understanding of the root causes as well as the socioeconomic factors that guide the migrants' decision-making. With chapters written in a concise style, this book brings together the migration and border studies in an innovative way to delve into the broader societal impacts of both. It also serves to de-silence the African voices in order to offer fresh insights on African migration – a discourse dominated hitherto by the European perspective.

This book constitutes a valuable resource for research scholars and students of Border Studies, Migration Studies, Conflict and Security Studies, and Development Studies seeking specialisation in these areas. Written in an accessible style, it will also appeal to a more general public interested in gaining a fuller perspective on the African reality.

Jussi P. Laine is an associate professor of multidisciplinary border studies at the University of Eastern Finland and holds the title of Docent of Human Geography from the University of Oulu, Finland. Currently, he also serves as the President of the Association for Borderlands Studies.

Inocent Moyo is a senior lecturer and Head of Department of Geography and Environmental Studies, University of Zululand, South Africa. His research interests include migration and development, migration politics, cross-border trade, regional integration in the Southern African Development Community, borders and urban informality, and governance.

Christopher Changwe Nshimbi is Director at the Department of Science and Technology and a National Research Foundation Research Fellow at the Centre for the Study of Governance Innovation, University of Pretoria. His current research focuses on migration, borders, regional integration, the informal economy, and water resources management.

Border Regions Series
Series Editor: Doris Wastl-Walter
University of Bern, Switzerland

In recent years, borders have taken on an immense significance. Throughout the world they have shifted, been constructed and dismantled, and become physical barriers between socio-political ideologies. They may separate societies with very different cultures, histories, national identities, or economic power, or divide people of the same ethnic or cultural identity.

As manifestations of some of the world's key political, economic, societal, and cultural issues, borders and border regions have received much academic attention over the past decade. This valuable series publishes high quality research monographs and edited comparative volumes that deal with all aspects of border regions, both empirically and theoretically. It will appeal to scholars interested in border regions and geopolitical issues across the whole range of social sciences.

Community, Change and Border Towns
H. Pınar Şenoğuz

Borderless Worlds for Whom?
Ethics, Moralities and Mobilities
Edited by Anssi Paasi, Eeva-Kaisa Prokkola, Jarkko Saarinen and Kaj Zimmerbauer

African Borders, Conflict, Regional and Continental Integration
Edited by Inocent Moyo and Christopher Nshimbi

Expanding Boundaries
Borders, Mobilities and the Future of Europe-Africa Relations
Edited by Jussi P. Laine, Inocent Moyo and Christopher Changwe Nshimbi

For more information about this series, please visit: www.routledge.com/ Border-Regions-Series/book-series/ASHSER-1224

Expanding Boundaries

Borders, Mobilities and the Future
of Europe-Africa Relations

**Edited by
Jussi P. Laine
Inocent Moyo
Christopher Changwe Nshimbi**

Routledge
Taylor & Francis Group

LONDON AND NEW YORK

First published 2021
by Routledge
2 Park Square, Milton Park, Abingdon, Oxon OX14 4RN

and by Routledge
52 Vanderbilt Avenue, New York, NY 10017

Routledge is an imprint of the Taylor & Francis Group, an informa business

British Library Cataloguing-in-Publication Data
A catalogue record for this book is available from the British Library

Library of Congress Cataloging-in-Publication Data
A catalog record has been requested for this book

ISBN: 978-0-367-53921-4 (hbk)
ISBN: 978-1-003-08372-6 (ebk)

DOI: 10.4324/9781003083726

Typeset in Times New Roman
by Newgen Publishing UK

Contents

Illustrations

Figures

Maps

Table

Contributors

Disney Andreas is an environmentalist by profession and an advocate for sustainable living. She is a self-driven social entrepreneur who has co-founded two start-ups and found her passion in finding ways to celebrate the Namibian entrepreneurial and creative scene through communicating their stories to the rest of the world.

Rodrigo Bueno Lacy is a political geographer at the Nijmegen Centre for Border Research at Radboud University, the Netherlands. He studies the interaction among geopolitics, representation, and borders, with a distinct interest for the ways in which visual, textual, and media discourses exert power over territory by establishing spatial and ideological borders.

Anna Casaglia is an associate professor in political geography at the University of Trento, Italy. She works on the relationship between conflict and space and the embodied character of bordering processes within a structural frame of power, inequality, and violence.

Felix Kwabena Donkor is post-doctoral at the College of Agriculture and Environmental Sciences at the University of South Africa. His research interests include sustainable rural livelihoods, climate change and migration, sustainable agriculture, and indigenous knowledge systems. He serves on Future Earth's Knowledge Action Networks and as the deputy of the South African Adaptation Network.

Lena Englund currently works on her postdoctoral research project which is financed by the Kone Foundation. She is affiliated with Åbo Akademi University in Turku, Finland. Forthcoming publications include a chapter on Doris Lessing's autobiographical writing and an article on Petina Gappah's short story collection *Rotten Row*.

Olukayode A. Faleye is a lecturer in Edo University, Nigeria. His research focuses on Environmental History, Borderlands, and Global Studies. He is the author of "Plague and Trade in Lagos, 1924–1931". *IJMH* (2018) and "Border Securitization and Politics of State Policy in Nigeria, 2014–2017". *IOA* (2019).

Henk van Houtum is a professor of Geopolitics and Political Geography at Radboud University, co-founder of the Nijmegen Centre for Border Research, and part-time research professor of Border Studies, University of Eastern Finland. He has written extensively on the auto-immunity of EU external borders, nationalism, b/ordering and othering, (undocumented) immigration, visa-policies, and the cartography of borders.

Omotomilola Ikotun is an early stage researcher of the Time, Space, and the Environment in Society Doctoral Programme at the University of Eastern Finland, Joensuu. Her research analyses the impact of conflicts on borders, access to natural resources, access to water supply, infrastructure development, and agriculture market access development in Nigeria.

Jussi P. Laine is an associate professor of multidisciplinary border studies at the University of Eastern Finland and holds the title of Docent of Human Geography from the University of Oulu, Finland. Currently, he also serves as the President of the Association for Borderlands Studies and in the Steering Committee of the IGU's Commission on Political Geography.

Kevin Mearns is a full professor in the College of Agriculture and Environmental Sciences at the University of South Africa. His research interests include Environmental Management, Ecology, and Ecotourism. He is involved in a number of community projects including sustainability benchmarking for the South African Tourism Industry and climate change and tourism, amongst others.

Tomasz Milej is a professor at Kenyatta University, Nairobi. He specialises in public international law, regional integration law, and comparative constitutional law. Recent publications include "Legal Framework for Free Movement of People Within Africa – A View from the East African Community" (2019) and "Human rights protection by international courts – What role for the East African Court of Justice?" (2018).

Calvin Minfegue is a geographer and political scientist. He has just completed a thesis in co-supervision between the Catholic University of Central Africa (Cameroon) and the University of Grenoble-Alpes (France). His work focuses mainly on border processes and the dynamics to which they give access: conflicts, migration issues, questions of belonging, and experiences of hospitality.

Anna Moraczewska is an assistant professor in the Department of International Security, Faculty of Political Science and Journalism, Maria Curie-Sklodowska University of Lublin, Poland. Research interests include international security, EU borders, border management, and new technologies in border control, as well as risk analysis and management.

Inocent Moyo is a senior lecturer and Head of Department of Geography and Environmental Studies, University of Zululand, South Africa. His research interests include migration and development, migration and immigration politics, cross-border trade, regional integration in the Southern African Development Community (SADC), borders and urban informality, and governance

Quivine Ndomo is a PhD student of Social Policy at the University of Jyväskylä, Finland. She has a Master's Degree in Development and International Cooperation. Her research focuses on labour market segmentation and migrant division of labour with a focus on skilled African migrants in European labour markets.

Christopher Changwe Nshimbi is Director of the Centre for the Study of Governance Innovation (GovInn) and senior lecturer in the Department of Political Sciences, University of Pretoria. He researches migration, regional integration, borders, the informal economy, and water. Chris also sits in on international advisory panels on migration, the water sector, social protection, and well-being.

Juliet Ogbodo is a doctoral researcher of Commercial Law at the School of Law, University of Eastern Finland. Her research interest and previous publications are on regional integration, legal transplants, and impacts of intellectual property regimes and international trade on West African countries.

Okechukwu Richard Oji is the director of research and policy analysis at the National Boundary Commission in Abuja, Nigeria. He has degrees from the University of Ibadan, Enugu State University of Science and Technology, University of Nigeria and the Nigerian Law School. He has acted as the Director of ESUT Social Science Research Institute and as a special assistant to the Hon. Minister of State Foreign Affairs.

Mika Raunio is senior researcher at the Migration Institute of Finland. He has been working on research and policy development for over twenty years in the field of knowledge-based regional development and migration in both global North and South, and has over sixty publications on the field.

Laura Sumari is a doctoral candidate at the EuroStorie centre for excellence at the University of Helsinki, Finland. She is working on her doctoral dissertation on migration from sub-Saharan Africa towards Europe and on how Europe is experienced during different stages of the migratory and asylum processes. Her research interests include postcolonial power dynamics, human security, and narratives of Europe.

Leon Mwamba Tshimpaka is a research Fellow at the Centre for the Study of Governance Innovation at the University of Pretoria, South Africa. His works on alternative regionalism, political transnationalism of African migrants, decolonialism, and political transformation. His publications include "Curbing inequality through decolonising knowledge production in higher education in South Africa" (ARAS 2018).

Introduction

Migration and border politics amidst the Europe-Africa relations

Jussi P. Laine, Inocent Moyo, and
Christopher Changwe Nshimbi

Africa and Europe seem increasingly interconnected, yet divided. Apart from the commonly mentioned factors of history and geographical proximity, both continents face a growing number and a broader variety of shared challenges, interests, and goals. As these cover various political domains from economy to security and from culture to mobility, relations can justifiably be regarded as of high strategic importance: "Africa needs Europe; Europe needs Africa" (Marchetti, 2020, p. 4). However, the nature of this interconnectedness often remains more assumed than comprehensively analysed. The balance may not be even, but more importantly, it may not lead us in the direction a shared understanding of the past would lead us to believe. The time has come to reassess the deep-seated belief that Africa remains dependent on European aid and offers little in return. Such a misunderstanding leads to misrepresentations, which are not only unfortunate and misleading on their own but lead to a significant loss of opportunities. The future of the continents is one of mutual dependence. The dynamics which simultaneously bind and separate the continents deserve proper examination and reappraisal.

Recently, relations have been undergoing a process of gradual institutionalisation. The European Union (EU) and the African Union (AU) have worked together in a series of joint summits and declarations towards a new partnership agreement. Following the tenth meeting between the European Commission and African Union Commission in Addis Ababa in February 2020, at which future cooperation was discussed, the European Commission President Ursula von der Leyen affirmed that "Africa is the European Union's natural partner and neighbour" and that "a more prosperous, more peaceful, and more sustainable future for all" could only be built together. Her perspective was supported by the High Representative of the European Union for Foreign Affairs and Security Policy, Josep Borrell, who confirmed that Europe's future was at stake in Africa. "To face our common challenges, we need a strong Africa, and Africa needs a strong Europe," he asserted. He underlined that both continents needed "each other to strengthen themselves, to strengthen each other, and to achieve a common ambition: a better world based on a rules-based international order" (European Commission, 2020a).

DOI: 10.4324/9781003083726-1

The European Commission's and the European External Action Service's vision of the future EU–Africa partnership, as elucidated in the joint Communication to the European Parliament and the Council (JOIN/2020/4 final), proposed a more comprehensive strategy for the EU's engagement with Africa, "our twin continent" (European Commission, 2020b). While the high-level expressions of the political will to broaden the collaborative agenda must be appreciated, they can also be seen as adopting a somewhat traditional stance on causes and responsibilities. The proposal acknowledges that to benefit both continents, the new partnership should be based on a clear understanding of respective and mutual interests and responsibilities, "reflecting the comprehensiveness and maturity of our relationship". Interestingly, however, the challenges to stability, security, democracy, equality, sustainability, social cohesion, and good governance that the document lists all seem to stem from the African side; nowhere in the document is the European struggle with these fundamental concepts mentioned. It is the economic, political, social, technological, demographic, climate, and environmental changes in Africa with which Europe is concerned, and which its leaders see as necessary to tackle together. Thus, it can be seen that the EU has co-opted the AU and many individual African states into cooperation; the unevenness of the relations gets upheld by the EU remaining the one that sets the tone and the collaborative agenda (Staeger, 2015; Ndlovu-Gatsheni, 2018). In addition to the challenges, the communication acknowledges that Africa also holds great potential that is now attracting increased interest from many players globally (ibid.). Although it is disconcerting that it was only on realising that its competitive edge was at stake that it was acknowledged that "Europe, with the EU and its Member States working together in unison, must adapt the way it engages with Africa", it is nonetheless imperative that such a realisation has been reached.

The proposed strategy identifies five key areas for the EU's deepened strategic alliance with Africa to be discussed with African partners, including: (1) green transition and energy access; (2) digital transformation; (3) sustainable growth and jobs; (4) peace and governance; and (5) migration and mobility (European Commission, 2020b). Although the efforts made to broaden the scope of the relations beyond mere migration matters must be warmly welcomed, the governance of human mobility, as Mbembe (2019, p. 16) suggests, rises above the rest as the most important challenge of the twenty-first century. Rather than a mere phenomenon of its own or one item out of five, this volume advances the notion that the various patterns with which migration and mobility are inherently linked describe a broad spectrum of structural factors, developments, and challenges. These require a holistic perspective to better understand the complex drivers of migration and find appropriate ways to manage it safely and effectively. It is imperative to attempt to debunk tenacious false narratives about migration and provoke debate in a manner that will lead to a nuanced understanding of not merely the root causes and motivating factors behind the migrant flows and their broader social impacts, but of the impact of broader social and economic forces in shaping migrant decision making.

A problem with numbers?

Migration from Africa continues to be fundamentally misconstrued and misrepresented, both in relation to its core dynamics and the implications it is asserted to have for European economies and societies (Ardittis, 2017). Migration – and the commonplace fears associated with it – has become effectively politicised, which in itself is a global phenomenon, but has nevertheless been particularly evident in the case of Europe (Czaika and de Haas, 2017, p. 894). Fuelled by sensationalist media images and narratives as well as alarmist and opportunistic right-wing politicians seeking to capitalise on the purported immigrant invasion (Laine, 2018), Africa is now portrayed as a "continent on the move" (Flahaux and de Haas, 2016: 1) – a continent of mass exodus. Characteristic of the debate has been the depiction of millions of migrants, assumed to consist predominantly of those of an irregular kind, looming at the gates of Europe and waiting for the first opportunity to cross. The depiction of immigration as something to be contained, controlled, and even combated has resulted in it being addressed largely through a security nexus, thereby enforcing the perception of borders as protective yet vulnerable defences against the various "ills" seeking to infiltrate and paralyse the very body of our European and "national" societies (Laine, 2020a). The good news from the perspective of this volume is that polls[1] have indicated that immigration has lost ground as the long-term key concern for the EU in the eyes of Europeans, while the severity of climate change has been an increasing concern. The bad news, as Donkor and Mearns discuss in their chapter, is that the two are inherently connected. Climate change causes displacement because of habitat destruction and biodiversity loss. Yet it facilitates migration by allowing an expansion of human activity into previously uninhabitable and less favourable areas.

The main suppositions underlying such a vision tend to be that African migration is excessive and increasing, mainly directed towards Europe, and driven by poverty and violence. In contrast to popular perception and wide-ranging misconceptions and myths about African migration, the first destination for immigrants from Africa is not Europe but Africa itself (Alaoui M'hamdi, 2015, p. 5). Africa is the region of the world with the least migration, and most African migrants and refugees move within the region to neighbouring countries, never leaving the continent (McAuliffe and Kitimbo, 2018; Parshotam, 2018). This is especially the case in sub-Saharan Africa, where the vast majority of international migrants (89%) move between countries located within the same region (UN DESA, 2019). African outmigration has certainly increased significantly: it has more than doubled since 1990 in tandem with the general population growth, and cannot be dismissed as inconsequential. Yet intra-regional migration continues to outpace extra-regional migration: for example, between 2015 and 2019, the number of international migrants living in Africa grew from seventeen to more than twenty-one million, whereas the number of Africans moving outside the continent increased more moderately, from around seventeen to nearly nineteen million. More than half (10.6 million) live in Europe (IOM 2019, pp. 54–55; UN DESA, 2019). Notably, however, IOM statistics reveal that migration both within and from Africa occurs largely along particular migration corridors, many of which are related to geographical proximity and historical ties, as well as displacement factors. Although more than half the main migration corridors occur within Africa, the largest migration corridors between the continents are from Algeria, Morocco, and Tunisia to France, Spain, and Italy, in part reflecting postcolonial connections and proximity (IOM 2019, p. 58). The number of migrants to Africa has remained virtually unchanged (at around two million). Most are from Asia and Europe (IOM, 2019, p. 54).

The total number of international migrants worldwide had reached nearly 272 million by 2019 (IOM, 2019). The forty million African migrants, more than half of whom remain in Africa, cannot be considered a particularly noteworthy share of the total migrant stock that is used to support the claims of a continent on the move. The total number of international migrants comprises 3.5 percent of the global population, compared to 2.8 percent in 2000 (IOM, 2019). While the share of migrants has indeed grown slightly, the more evident conclusion from the statistics is that the vast majority of people continue to live in the country in which they were born. Europe continues to hosts the largest number of international migrants (eighty-two million), yet migrant populations are growing fastest in Africa (IOM, 2019, p. 24; UN DESA, 2019). Non-European migration to Europe is effectively mitigating an otherwise decreasing population. The number of non-European migrants in Europe has increased slightly. It now totals around thirty-eight million. A majority is of Asian origin, and slightly more than ten million come from Africa (IOM, 2019, pp. 85–86).

However, by far the most striking increase has been witnessed in the number of those forcibly displaced by war, persecution, and other violence, which reached a disconsolate all-time record of 70.8 million worldwide at the end of 2018. Of them, 25.9 million were refugees, while 3.5 million were asylum seekers (UNHCR, 2019). Nevertheless, Czaika and de Haas's (2017, p. 894) earlier observation that despite the extensive media and scholarly attention paid to irregular and other forms of "unwanted" migration, the great majority of migrants seem to abide by the rules and regulations holds true. According to the UNHCR (2019) some eighty-five percent of all refugees and asylum seekers are hosted by developing countries; two-thirds in North Africa and Western Asia (13.1 million), and sub-Saharan Africa (5.9 million). Europe as a whole hosted 3.6 million refugees and asylum seekers, less than Turkey (3.7 million) alone (UN DESA, 2019; UNHCR, 2019).

Most refugees and asylum seekers in Africa are hosted in neighbouring countries within the region. South Sudan continues to produce the largest number of refugees in Africa (2.3 million in 2018) and is ranked third in the world, behind the Syrian Arab Republic and Afghanistan (IOM, 2019, p. 59). However, while Syrians and Afghans have consistently formed the largest citizenship groups of first-time asylum applicants in the EU since 2013 (Eurostat, 2020), the vast majority of South Sudanese are hosted in neighbouring countries – especially in Uganda, but also in Sudan, Ethiopia, and the Democratic Republic of the Congo (UNHCR, 2019).

The big picture reveals that the general perspective on migration in Africa differs from what has become prevalent in Europe. While making broad continental generalisations and reinforcing binary divisions must be avoided, the basic premise holds that far from being seen as something threatening, migration on the African side is considered above all as a phenomenon with the potential to trigger socioeconomic development. As the African Union's Revised Migration Policy Framework for Africa and Action Plan (African Union Commission, 2018) and the earlier African Common Position on Migration and Development demonstrate, the management and governance of migration is approached from the perspective of development (Nshimbi and Moyo, 2016). At the policy level, therefore, the AU and EU seem to be on different tracks. However, discussing Africa or Europe as coherent blocks and pitting them against each other obscure more than they illuminate. In addition to commission-to-commission relations, there is a multitude of bilateral, regional, and highly networked relationships between the EU, its member states, and the various African countries that defies convenient generalisation.

To reduce this complexity yet develop a perspective that opens spaces for a productive engagement with potential for and challenges to increased cooperation, this volume will dig deeper, going beyond mere policies and official rhetoric. The chapters that follow highlight some of the specific nuances and regional differences and propose alternative framings that will allow us to move beyond past perspectives and practices. They are written at a time when, despite the common rhetoric and symbolic depictions of unity, both continents remain – and have become increasingly – divided in various ways. Under the pressures of migration, Europe especially, but not exclusively, has become increasingly torn, with the very foundations of its unity being tested (see Laine in this volume). On the African side, there are also disconcerting developments that depart from the conventional African frame, the understanding of which requires a more regionally specific approach.

The countries of North Africa form a unique region that has more in common in terms of ethnic, cultural, and linguistic ties with the Middle East and West Asia than with sub-Saharan Africa. These relations to the north and east, developed over several decades, continue to be a defining feature of the migration dynamics of the subregion (IOM, 2019, p. 66). Given its geographical proximity to Europe, the countries of North Africa fall under a broader spectrum of EU policies, most notably the European Neighbourhood

Policy (ENP). However, these countries face many challenges associated with irregular migration from the rest of Africa to Europe, functioning as a transit zone – and getting stranded, as captured in the notion of limboscape, in which migrants' trajectories towards the "European EU" are spatially and temporally suspended (Ferrer-Gallardo and Espiñeira, 2015; Ferrer-Gallardo and Albet-Mas, 2016). They also increasingly reflect the influence of the externalisation of European migration and bordering policies on African soil. Dubbing this practice, addressed in detail in Minfegue's chapter, as the "hallmark of European anti-African migration policy", Mbembe (2017) explains that "brutal and corrupt African regimes are entrusted with the task of locking up potential African migrants and warehousing asylum seekers" in exchange for money.

This volume takes the discussion beyond mere Euro–Mediterranean and Europe–North African relations. The aim here is not to reduce the apparent significance of the Mediterranean as a space of interaction and regional cooperation, or as a backdrop for poignant human drama and tension, nor do we aim to distract attention from its realities. While acknowledging that in the last couple of decades the EU as a political project has sought to expand its policies and sphere of influence especially to the northern part of the African continent, the overall relations between Europe and Africa cannot be confined to this immediate neighbourhood.

Extending the investigation further also reveals more specific migration patterns. In East Africa, perverse conflicts and political and communal violence have resulted in the displacement of millions. The region has also become an increasingly important source of migrant workers in Gulf Cooperation Council (GCC) states. Southern Africa has long been a major destination for migrants from within Africa, as well as from other continents. Together, migration in East and Southern Africa continues to involve large numbers of irregular migrants. The drivers of migration include socioeconomic factors, conflict, and political instability, but environmental change and disasters, as well as xenophobic attacks, have become increasingly important in influencing human movement and displacement. Intraregional migration is particularly momentous in West and Central Africa, where irregular migration remains prevalent despite the free movement agreements in the subregion that have been put in place to facilitate migration and reduce irregularity. Conflict, violence, communal and ethnic tension, and extremism are major causes of internal and cross-border displacement, yet increasingly severe environmental changes are impacting the livelihoods and thus mobility of many (IOM, 2019, pp. 62–66).

These dynamics suggest that despite the perseverance of the far from perfect colonially imposed state boundaries, Africa thrives on mobility. Although borders did exist in Africa before the colonial era, they were not static lines but fluctuating zones of various width, which often served more as points of contact for cultural and political groups to coexist (Ajala, 1983, p. 179) instead of lines of separation and delimitation. Where they existed, borders were always porous and permeable (Mbembe, 2017). The concept of the territorial delimitation of political control – statehood – was a European import (McEwen, 1971, p. 8). Because they were generally "culturally alien" to Africa (Engelbert, Tarango, and Carter, 2002, p. 1095), these imposed borders have played a mainly deconstructive role in perpetuating conflict (Silberfein and Conteh, 2006). Nevertheless, while mobility continues to be an important part of everyday life for many Africans, border controls have become increasingly stringent. Despite the common illustration of the shape of the continent without internal demarcations – for example, used symbolically to signify African unity in the emblem of the African Union – the reality of the continent is more divided.

Various disputes between African states have resulted in border closures, and increasingly robust border security responses have been put in place following the escalation of smuggling and other cross-border activities considered illegal, as well as fears of uncontrolled migration. In their "fetishisation of the nation state", postcolonial African states have failed to articulate a common legislative framework and policy initiatives in relation to border management, visa liberalisation, or the treatment of third-country nationals residing legally in member states (Mbembe, 2017). The aspiration for state sovereignty has done "untold damage to Africa's destiny in the world" (ibid.) and continues to trump the earlier visions of pan-African unity and ease of travel and doing business – and even the much anticipated and heralded African Continental Free Trade Area (AfCFTA), originally intended to commence in July 2020 (Oneko, 2019). However, far from being the year of open borders in Africa (Steinwehr, 2020), the COVID-19 global pandemic postponed the launch of the AfCFTA and derailed the plans to broaden the introduction of a common African Union passport also beyond the elite. It urged many African states, just as in Europe, to close their borders and regress into state-centric thinking. The "thousands of internal borders in the continent", Mbembe (2019, p. 17) argues, prevent rational movements and development within the continent by making the costs of mobility prohibitive and thereby encouraging Africans to migrate to "Europe, where they know nobody, where nobody is waiting for them, and where they are not welcome".

Bordering crisis and the state of exception

Migration from Africa to Europe has been at the top of the European political and public agendas since the sudden peak in migration flows to the EU in 2015. While the numbers and the pace at which the event unfolded were certainly notable, framing the overall situation as a "refugee crisis" was questionable. Rather than the refugees, the wider socio-politics, geographies, and economies contributed to producing the "crisis" (Pallister-Wilkins, 2016, p. 311), which has more accurately been relabelled as "Europe's border crisis" (Vaughan-Williams, 2015) and a "crisis of modern humanism" (Squire, 2017), describing it as a crisis management crisis. This reflected the European authorities' lack of political will and ability to manage the situation with respect to fundamental rights (Laine, 2018). To an extent, the entire talk of "the crisis" in Europe has been banalised, even as invocations of a veritable "crisis of Europe" have proliferated (Tazzioli and de Genova, 2016; de Genova, 2017). The way in which the events of 2015 has come to be used in framing African migration to Europe has also been questionable: after all, the majority of arrivals came from the war-ravaged societies of Afghanistan, Syria, and Iraq, not Africa.

In the ensuing debate, rational assessments have been overshadowed by emotional outbursts and short-sighted standpoints. Irregular migration to Europe has become a field in which estimations often prevail over researched actualities, and hearsay and myths govern concrete evidence (Laine, 2020a). Bordering – understood as the politics of difference – has become an increasingly affectual, rather than factual, practice. Mbembe (2019, p. 15) contends that as far as the question of borders and migration is concerned, facts no longer seem to matter. Yet facts exist. Migration policy has become symbolic politics (de Genova, 2013, p. 1183), producing security, stability, and order amidst paralysing anxieties. Most EU member states, with much of the global north, are working on a number of initiatives to attract more highly skilled migrants at the same time as they have adopted more measures to keep the unwanted out. Thus, rather than closing state spaces, bordering is ultimately about filtering flows and enhancing mobility for those deemed welcome, while impeding it or denying it to the unwanted (Laine, 2020b). The sad realisation that "there is hardly any country in the world that does not consider migrants from Africa undesirable", Mbembe (2017) postulates, leads to Africa increasingly resembling "a massive open-air prison". From this perspective, borders appear as both frontiers of fear (d'Appolonia, 2012) and a protective skin (Cash, 2017) that help to maintain a secure and healthy interior – a notion that has only been reinforced by the ongoing COVID-19 pandemic.

The rhetoric of crisis is in itself tied tightly to the rhetoric of an emergency (Neocleous, 2008) that necessitates a security response (Laine, 2020b). However, this response has been "neither appropriate nor effective" (Adepoju, 2020). The hardening of the border through new security practices, Jones (2016, p. 5) asserts, is the *source* of the violence, not a *response* to it. Borders will not make the ostensible problem go away because they are themselves a fundamental part of the problem (Laine, 2018, p. 300). A common framing throughout Europe was to depict the growing number of refugee arrivals as something unprecedented. An exceptional situation requires exceptional measures. On the flipside, such a state of exception creates circumstances, Agamben (2005) explains, whereby the legal order is no longer valid, and there can be deviation from customary rules and norms. As this turbulent era has been characterised by constant and multiple crises, the state of exception is no longer an exception, but a rule. Brambilla and Jones (2019, p. 9) assert that the routinisation of emergency accompanies the routinisation of violence that the sovereign authority is entitled to exercise to manage crisis or emergency situations. Together, they cultivate an indifference to the deaths at Europe's borders (see Bueno Lacy and van Houtum's chapter) and nurture an interpretation that sees them as merely a necessary evil that must be tolerated for a greater good to result. However, the result appears to be the "troubling situation whereby death becomes a norm through which migration is governed" (Squire, 2017, p. 528).

While the humanitarian approach, often depicted as balancing the security approach, is more compelling, it also comes with flaws of its own. According to Walters (2011, pp. 138–9) it "crystallizes as a way of governing this new and alarming situation, and tries to compensate for the social violence embodied in the logic of controlling migration", ultimately making it more acceptable. Humanitarianism at the border, Cuttitta (2018) explains, is also a factor of the depoliticisation of the border and naturalisation of death. The integration of the "exception" in border normalcy endlessly reproduces the need for intervention, which leads Gazzotti (2020, p. 410) to reason that "humanitarianism becomes a tool for the ordinary maintenance of migrants' degraded life, transformed by the border into a less-than-citizen, less-than-human form of existence".

This volume advances the premise that our moral obligation towards others stems not only from a mere humanitarian principle but rests on the realities of today's interconnected world. As Mbembe (2019, p. 16) stresses, we cannot speak about migration without addressing the presence and actions of the west in the rest of the world. He justifiably observes that "Europe's and America's violence abroad is a key reason why people are forced to run away from places where they were born and raised, but which have become uninhabitable". He posits an injustice whereby the colonisers, having first destroyed African living environments by "extracting their oil, gas, timber, diamonds, and gold, shipping it all home, leaving nothing behind, turning their cities into rubble", then bring "to an end the possibilities of life in faraway places, and expect those affected by such upheavals to survive in the midst of the ruins" (ibid., p. 16).

Mbembe's captivating account may have been sparked by the common European postulation that Europe is not involved in what drives people to leave their homes, and that "we" do not have the resources to deal with and solve the entire world's problems. The "refugee crisis" has been sensationalised across the European mediascape, with plastered images of desperate Africans on overcrowded boats bound for Europe (Laine, 2018, p. 289), yet the interpretation which gained the most prominence insinuated that Europe was external to the exposed suffering. While direct causalities are not always easy to demonstrate, there is no escaping the fact that Europe itself produces the conditions that cause migrant deaths. As Benhabib (2004) noted, we are no longer simply part of isolated communities; by virtue of an interconnected world when other people suffer, we are complicit in that suffering. We are all in the same boat.

Towards more balanced relations

The centuries of interaction between the two continents have been characterised by a prolonged period of colonialism and a difficult postcolonial period (Marchetti, 2020, p. 3). This framing is important, yet it also makes relations unmistakeably lopsided and burdened. Generally speaking, on the European side colonial legacies tend to be easily forgotten; on the African side the tendency to blame colonial mistakes remains strong. Of course, these cannot be equated, because the latter would not exist without the former. As Udeze (2009, p. 85) puts it, European colonisation left an indelible mark on Africa, and the continent will never be what it was, "no matter the benefits or disadvantages it brought to the continent these years [sic]". Nevertheless, this premise, burdened as it is by the past, does not provide the most fertile ground for fashioning a mutually beneficial collaborative agenda. To paraphrase the Nigerian writer and novelist Adaobi Tricia Nwaubani (2018), blaming colonial miscalculations and subsequent neo-colonial manipulations for Africa's numerous conflicts will not help bring them to an end. Victimisation itself serves to confirm a sense of inferiority and maintain uneven and unequal relations. The argument here is not that history should be belittled or that it has lost its meaning, but that Africa–Europe relations need to go beyond the enduring blame game and change with the times if emerging opportunities are to be grasped. For the relationship to be more balanced and mutually beneficial, a fresh framing might be of use.

Reasons for European collective amnesia are likely to be multiple; reducing them to a mere disparagement of the era seems superficial. Instead, individuals and communities alike cope with the traumatic events and painful memories of their past by seeking to forget them, yet this may not necessarily be, as Tanesini (2018, p. 195) suggests, simply to memorialise a new version of their history. Amnesia may also function as an ontological coping mechanism amidst the unfortunate realisation that little can be done to change the past and undo its inherent injustices. While intellectual self-trust is a prerequisite for the exercise of any epistemic capacity (Tanesini, 2018, p. 196), it is also sensitive to social power (Jones, 2012, p. 245), which promotes the miscalibration of self-trust towards inflation in those who occupy positions of dominance, and deflation in those who are subordinated (Tanesini, 2018, p. 215). "We cannot truly know who we are or where we are going," McCullough (2008) writes, "unless we know where we have been". Collective ignorance may indeed be harmful, as Tanesini (2018) suggests; since some of these harms are also wrongs, they can be seen to contribute to causing and furthering epistemic injustices. Yet looking to the future with fresh eyes should not be seen as an attempt to ignore or disparage the past.

Challenges aside, Africa and Europe are and will remain neighbours. It is also likely that despite the current prominence of deterrent migration and border policies, their interconnectedness will only increase. Hence, following Mbembe (2017; 2019), the management of human mobility appears as the key issue of the twenty-first century. To manage these mobilities properly – balancing legal commitments and regulations with ethical and moral concerns, and without jeopardising our core values in doing so – new and alternative perspectives and proposals are needed that challenge the old taken-for-grantedness. As Marchetti (2020) has underlined, it is necessary to go beyond pure intergovernmentalism and adopt a pluralist understanding from a multi-stakeholder perspective of the relationship between Africa and Europe. One of the main reasons relations between the continents have remained lopsided is that the situation in Africa remains poorly understood, meaning many decisions are made based on outdated information or outsiders' perspectives. African voices are still seldom heard. There is a need to gain more knowledge and understanding of the perspective, concerns, and interests of the other, and thus prevent myths and misconceptions from spreading. This volume aims to provide concrete evidence for debunking unfounded commonly held myths and counter the narratives promoted by the widespread populist agendas, fake news, and alternative facts.

The fundamental problem is that we still do not know each other, and a lack of knowledge has led to a lack of trust – a trust that is desperately needed to prepare for mutual future challenges and tap into the obvious synergies. Nor can the security concerns be dismissed, yet tackling them would, perhaps more than anything else, benefit from the recognition that the threats do not occur somewhere in between but are increasingly global. Terrorism, cyberattacks, climate change, and pandemics are among the obvious challenges that require a mutual approach and broad international collaboration, instead of more borders and exclusionary policies. While Europe is struggling with low growth, a declining population, and brain drain – among other things – Africa boasts the youngest, fastest-growing middle-class in the world and has experienced sustained high economic growth over the past decade. Sub-Saharan Africa's population is set to double over the next thirty years. It will account for more than half the global population growth between now and 2050. With more than 1.3 billion people, Africa currently accounts for about sixteen per cent of the world's population, yet this population is expected to double by 2100 (UN DESA, 2019). However, the debate about African futures should not be confused with European fears of a great exodus (Mbembe, 2019, p. 16). While challenges remain and conflicts persist, Africa is a massive continent with a great potential that is waiting to be fully activated (Nshimbi, 2019), which Europe should seek to tap into rather than ignore or exclude.

As Marchetti (2020, p. 3) points out, Africa and Europe are developing in divergent yet reciprocally dependent paths: Europe is growing older, Africa younger; Africa has seen rapid economic growth, Europe has stagnated. Apart from people, Africa has many other resources Europe needs. Europe, in turn, remains the leading aid provider to Africa. Europe also remains an important market for Africa's primary goods, and as a major supplier of finished products to the continent. Although these observations point towards obvious synergies, capitalising on them is less straightforward.

Africa has twice as many countries and people as Europe, meaning many continental dynamics are of a different scale. Mere size apart, their migration and bordering dynamics are also inherently different because they have evolved through entirely different processes (Silberfein and Conteh, 2006, p. 344; Ndlovu-Gatsheni and Mhlanga, 2013), a realisation which demands "the dialectical and inextricable links of geography and history" (Matereke, 2013, p. 25) to be brought into the light. The lack of understanding of the African context and the migration situation has led the EU to implement policies aimed at preventing migration rather than capitalising on it. This seems paradoxical, and it seems that Europe will simply not manage without migrants. "If you think about migration in marketing terms," Adepoju (2020) postulates, "Africa is selling, but Europe isn't buying". As the following chapters aim to show, the reason the supply does not match the demand is hardly a question of numbers alone.

The lop-sidedness of relations is also evident in that most Europeans provide most of the information and analysis, inevitably reflecting a European perspective. Concerning policies, the European institutions issue most of the referenced official documents and reports. We set out to balance this discrepancy by exploring the question of migration and stressing the need to rethink the entirety of relations between the continents from both sides. In offering analyses by scholars from both Africa and Europe, this volume provides a more holistic picture of the current migration conundrum. Importantly, it also advocates for the setting of relations on a broader premise for the mutually beneficial development of the relationship.

Each chapter highlights the role of borders. We do not thereby restrict ourselves to traditional territorial boundaries but expand the concept of "border" to integrate its *relational* political, social, and cultural dimensions, and multiscalar nature (Laine, 2016). As Bigo and Guild (2005) have argued, the traditional border narrative has proven largely fictional, often only living in the ambitions and imaginations of political and security actors. Challenging the conceptualisation of fortress Europe, Carrera and Stefan (2020, p. 3) point to the EU and its Schengen scheme as "perfect illustrations of the inherently unstable, geographically inconsistent, and politically dynamic nature of frontiers, as well as of the difficulty in identifying them neatly along the territorial lines of national and EU administrative entities nicely drawn in maps". Much more than as a specific line or demarcation, we see borders as dynamic processes which define and constrain, but also empower and facilitate, interaction.

Structure of the book

This volume is divided into three parts, all of which shed light on the various aspects of the borders, mobilities, and future of Europe–Africa relations. The first part, providing a critical perspective on border management and regimens, is by Calvin Minfegue, who argues that the externalisation of

European borders into Africa has led to outcomes far from their initial objectives. He sees these measures, designed to act as a deterrent, as having had the opposite effect in that they encourage movement instead by redefining migration trajectories and generating new desires to leave. Focusing on Cameroon, an important country of emigration, he describes how the idea and imaginary associated with this externalisation are paradoxically appropriated by migrant actors, who see it as a way of constituting a point of attraction that encourages movement – a call for movement, indeed. Furthermore, the measures implemented represent the effective politics of difference in their ambition to sort and select those considered to deserve entry into Europe from those who are seen as unwanted.

Anna Moraczewska sees the externalisation of EU border management as an attempt to extend the spatial range of the Union beyond its territory. It thus contradicts the idea of "fortress Europe". She explains that instead of erecting a fortress, the assumed approach establishes multiple filters outside the EU's external borders. However, this is not done following the classical "control at a distance" model. Frontex strategy represents a type of networked multilateral relations in which state actors cooperate with a non-state actor in collecting what she defines as information of social and criminal value. Her chapter explores whether the cooperation between Frontex and the African countries provides an actual opportunity to understand the root causes and motivations of the migrant flows, or is only a European obligation imposed on Africa to prevent migration before it reaches the shores of the EU.

Okechukwu Richard Oji, speaking from his perspective as the director of the Department of Research and Policy Analysis of the Nigerian National Boundary Commission, sees the witnessed migration challenges as stemming from poorly managed borders and policies that fail to meet their objectives. The problem is not the deficiency of knowledge concerning how to solve the challenges, he asserts, but West Africa's lack of enhanced border security management and intelligence gathering and sharing. The problem lies in the lack of political will: should the region's various governments become committed to building an invincible West African border security architecture, this could, Oji claims, be achieved in record time. Until this happens, migration and border security mismanagement on the African continent will continue to have remote implications for Europe as well.

In their chapter, Rodrigo Bueno Lacy and Henk van Houtum discuss the recent authoritarian turn in the EU's bordering policies and its fatal consequences. The power to decide who lives and who dies, they argue, is inherent to this deadly border architecture, highlighting the banality of the evil of our age. They describe how migrants have become all-purpose punchbags in the contemporary EU political discourse, the constant bunching of which serves to hide the EU's own inability to articulate a response true to its own values and principles. Although the EU's supranational and national bureaucracies have veered into uncharted waters, they see hope in individual European citizens willing to challenge unconscionable laws and spearhead the moral revolt that will be needed to overpower the deadly return of history into which the EU's political elites seem to be sleepwalking.

In the last chapter of Part I, Anna Casaglia discusses the Euro–African border regime by critically analysing the humanitarian corridors established by Italian non-profit and religious organisations with the Italian government. With the explicit aim of deterring dangerous journeys and combating trafficking, humanitarian corridors grant legal entry to Italian territory with a humanitarian visa to people in "conditions of vulnerability". Her study demonstrates that these projects have direct consequences for migrants because they constitute a safe way to migrate while entailing a process of selectivity and therefore categorisation of people according to their "deservingness" to be part of the programme. To this end, she discusses the very definition of vulnerability in relation to the categorisation of people on the move and related discourses in the context of the shifting Mediterranean border regime.

Tomasz Milej opens Part II of the volume, which explores political transnationalism and policy impact, with an analysis of the legal instruments regulating migration, their evolution, and implementation. He contends that the rejection of African migrants by the EU has deep roots. Over decades – if not centuries – European identity has been largely constructed in opposition to outsiders, and more specifically to Africans. This is precisely what needs to be completely rethought in moving forward. He advocates an Afro–European integration scheme which would break with the prevailing identity narratives stigmatising migrants. Borrowing from the best practices in both the EU and Africa, such a scheme – unlike the current Cotonou regime – should adopt a rule-based approach, linking migration with trade, conferring individual rights enforceable in a court of law, and encompassing lower- and higher-skilled workers. To be successful, he underlines the need to move away from addressing migration through the prism of security risks alone and focus instead on the many opportunities it creates.

Leon Mwamba Tshimpaka focuses on the under-studied topic of the transnational political activities of Europe-based African migrants. Concentrating on Central African migrants, he explains that they have entered into a solidarity nurtured by shared tragedies during their perilous mobility from various smuggling routes to Europe. Apart from their individually exercised transnational political activities, Tshimpaka clarifies, Europe-based Central African migrants strengthen their exercised intercontinental citizenship on arrival in Europe by entering into solidarity to contest homeland authoritarian regimes. Given the misleading narrative on African migration to Europe, and that African voices are still seldom heard, he posits, Europe-based combatants from Central Africa unite to create alternative avenues to combat the perceived authoritarian regimes of their homelands.

In her chapter, Quivine Ndomo claims that recent migration processes are characterised by stringent regulation within nation state territories. She calls this a pervasive internal bordering that is illustrative in capturing the extent of interference with migrants' daily lives. Her chapter, based on a study of

African students' experiences in Finland, presents a narrative of "chronic" exclusion enforcing temporality, and which pits migrants' agency against ubiquitous structures in a protracted struggle that models migration trajectories for settlement. She demonstrates that such regulation misses the point of contemporary migration, resulting in socioeconomic loss for both the migrants and their host countries. Furthermore, pervasive internal bordering reinforces the tendency to settle and incentivises migrants' longer, and even permanent, stays in their host country.

In their chapter, Omotomilola Ikotun and Juliet Ogbodo argue that in seeking to move away from the EU's usual aid and conditionality approach and to genuinely address the root causes of migration, intense advocacy for youth engagement in agribusiness value chains would be instrumental. They demonstrate that the return to agribusiness and trade-related activities for agricultural products creates youth employment, offering the potential to harness their creative and innovative abilities, diminishing in so doing the push factors of emigration. However, to achieve sustainable results, this solution necessitates the revision of the current EU–Africa trade agreements by incorporating specific, measurable, achievable, realistic, and timely (SMART) development objectives. Achieving economic growth would contribute to stability and thus reduce the appetite for migration of a significant proportion of young people.

Mika Raunio and Disney Andreas argue that African development has serious consequences not only for the continent but globally. Rapid population growth, the lack of economic opportunities, and the several impacts of climate change are among the usual causes of anticipated migration pressures from Africa to Europe. However, they also note that many African economies are the fastest growing in the world. With a young and growing population, this offers prospects of significant economic opportunity. They introduce a specific governance approach that aims to foster the emergence of transnational business and innovation ecosystems with strong local anchors in Africa to build mutually beneficial relations between Europe and Africa, and connect their economies and businesses. They suggest that the relationship cannot be developed at the expense of the other party. Europe and Africa are destined either to prosper or fail together.

The third and final part of the volume proposes alternative framings for Europe–Africa relations. Lena Englund extends the analytical angle beyond the social sciences by addressing literature as a reflection and representation of society. Literature provides an illuminating interpretative frame through its political dimension, which takes issue with ongoing societal shifts and events. This becomes evident in her chapter, which examines how African writers present migration in contemporary texts. She explains that migrants have often been seen as either victims of oppression and injustice or as opportunists hoping to ensure a better life elsewhere. Englund's study shows that both these views are problematic. Literary texts offer a possibility to investigate representations of migration from a variety of perspectives. The novels she analyses inspire new views of migration that do not focus on departure, arrival or return, homesickness, assimilation, and culture clash but on movement and the need to stay mobile. Paradoxically, she contends, arrival in a new location implies mobility because it allows individuals to carry on with their lives and move forward. Arriving, she concludes, means moving on.

Building on her multi-sited ethnographic fieldwork in East Africa, Laura Sumari turns the discussion to the impacts of the controversial EU and Schengen security measures on sub-Saharan African refugees and migrants. She explains that Europe's security measures produce multiple forms of suffering, fear, hate, uncertainty, and insecurity in the people at whom they are targeted. This not only affects their everyday lives but shapes how migrants understand and perceive Europe. She argues that securitising discourses and the related bordering practices that see migration as a security threat over-shadow the multiple benefits of migration, contending that migrants are an important but underused resource of knowledge and information whose voice should be heard in seeking to find solutions to the issues linked with migration.

Third, Jussi P. Laine underlines that it is only by first looking inwards that we may see outwards clearly and build an honest basis for Europe–Africa relations. He suggests migration has become an issue that sharply divides the European and national political arenas. He shifts the discussion of migration as a phenomenon in its own right and with its own dynamics to its broader societal implications. The interpretation he advances is that the widespread, less-than-welcoming mindset towards immigration cannot be taken explicitly as a manifestation of an anti-migrant attitude but as a symptom of the much broader insecurities many Europeans have felt. He describes how reactions to immigration have become increasingly emotional no matter which angle is taken, and more rational arguments have been pushed aside. The attempts to manage migration by setting aside Europe's core values, he posits, are paving the way to its own downfall, with considerable social and political repercussions.

Felix Kwabena Donkor and Kevin Mearns argue that Euro–African relations have been widely misrepresented, and that the time has come to rethink them. Now more than ever it is important to foster a new relationship that embraces the EU and African nations as partners in crucial issues of common concern. Of these, combating climate change is critically important not only as a phenomenon in its own right but for its influence on the migra-tion patterns between the continents. They also reflect on the ongoing COVID-19 pandemic, which has fostered the need for locally tailored and resilient policy frameworks and infrastructure. While Africa is one of the regions likely to suffer most from the impacts of climate change, the policies that would address its multidimensional impacts are lagging behind. Donkor and Mearns assert that good governance, communal resilience, and robust conflict reso-lution mechanisms are needed to act in concert in effectively addressing the complexity of climate-induced migration.

Finally, before the editors' concluding remarks, Olukayode A. Faleye examines migration as an engine of interregional mutual development within the framework of EU–Africa relations that has remained under-studied. The argumentation he advances stems from the premise that interregional relations are inevitable in a world characterised by resource scarcity and inequality, yet the contestation of human and material resources across socially constructed state-centric boundaries has led to theoretical multiplicity in explaining the operationalisation of the international system. The reconstruction of Afro–European identities for mutual development, he suggests, offers an alternative way forward that unveils the complementarity of the EU and African geo-cultural space within the global world system. By adopting an interregional framework built on what he calls the reality of global citizenry, the EU could right the wrong of European imperialism in African history by setting out a mutual developmental journey towards an EU–Africa geo-cultural economic union.

Note

1 Standard Eurobarometer 92 survey (autumn 2019).

References

Adepoju, A. (2020) After the "Migration Crisis": The Many Faces of African Migration. (online) Available at: www.opendemocracy.net/en/beyond-trafficking-and-slavery/after-migration-crisis-many-faces-african-migration/ (Accessed 22 May 2020).

African Union Commission. (2018) *Migration Policy Framework for Africa and Plan of Action (2018 – 2030): Migration for Development in Africa.* Addis Ababa: African Union Commission.

Agamben, G. (2005) *State of exception*, trans. K. Attell. Chicago, IL: University of Chicago Press.

Ajala, A. (1983) The Nature of African Boundaries. *African Spectrum*, 18(2) pp. 177–89.

Alaoui M'hamdi, N. (2015) The Relations between the European Union and Africa. *Atlantic Future Policy Papers,* 3.

Ardittis, S. (2017) African Migration to Europe: How can Adequate Data Help Improve Evidence-Based Policymaking and Reduce Possible Misconceptions? *Global Migration Data Analysis Centre Data Briefing Series*, 11.

Benhabib, S. (2004) *The Rights of Others*. Cambridge: Cambridge University Press.

Bigo, D. and Guild, E. (2005) Policing at a Distance: Schengen Visa Policies. In: D. Bigo and E. Guild, eds. *Controlling Frontiers. Free Movement into and within Europe*. London, Ashgate, pp. 233–63.

Brambilla, C. and Jones, R. (2019) Rethinking Borders, Violence, and Conflict: From Sovereign Power to Borderscapes as Sites of Struggles. *Environment and Planning D: Society and Space*, 38(2), pp. 287–305.

Carrera, S and Stefan, M. (2020) Justicing Europe's Frontiers: Effective Access to Remedies and Justice in Bordering and Expulsion Policies. In: S. Carrera and M.

Stefan, eds. *Fundamental Rights Challenges in Border Controls and Expulsion of Irregular Immigrants in the European Union: Complaint Mechanisms and Access to Justice*. London: Routledge, pp. 3–22.

Cash, J. (2017) The Dilemmas of Ontological Insecurity in a Postcolonising Northern Ireland. *Postcolonial Studies*, 20(3), pp. 387–410.

Cuttitta, P. (2018) Repoliticization through Search and Rescue? Humanitarian NGOs and Migration Management in the Central Mediterranean. *Geopolitics*, 23, pp. 632–60.

Czaika, M. and de Haas, H. (2017) The Effect of Visas on Migration Processes. *International Migration Review*, 51(4), pp. 893–926.

d'Appolonia, A. C. (2012) *Frontiers of Fear: Immigration and Insecurity in the United States and Europe*. Ithaca, NY: Cornell University Press.

de Genova, N. (2013) Spectacles of Migrant "Illegality": The Scene of Exclusion, the Obscene of Inclusion. *Ethnic and Racial Studies*, 36(7), 1180–98.

de Genova, N., ed. (2017) *The Borders of "Europe": Autonomy of Migration, Tactics of Bordering*. Durham, NC: Duke University Press.

Engelbert, P. S., Tarango, S., and Carter, P. (2002). Dismemberment and Suffocation: A Contribution to the Debate on African Boundaries. *Comparative Political Studies*, 35(10): pp. 1093–118.

European Commission. (2020a) Press Release: EU Paves the Way for a Stronger, more Ambitious Partnership with Africa, IP/20/373.

European Commission. (2020b) Joint Communication to the European Parliament and the Council. Towards a comprehensive Strategy with Africa. Brussels, 9 Mar. 2020. JOIN(2020) 4 final.

Eurostat. (2020). Asylum Statistics (online) Available at: https://ec.europa.eu/eurostat/statistics-explained/index.php/Asylum_statistics (Accessed 18 Apr. 2020).

Ferrer-Gallardo, X. and Albet-Mas, A. (2016) EU-Limboscapes: Ceuta and the Proliferation of Migrant Detention Spaces across the European Union. *European Urban and Regional Studies,* 23(3), pp. 527–30.

Ferrer-Gallardo, X. and Espiñeira, K. (2015) Immobilized between Two EU Thresholds: Suspended Trajectories of Sub-Saharan Migrants in the Limboscape of Ceuta. In: T. van Naerssen and M. van der Velde, eds. *Mobility and Migration Choices. Thresholds to Crossing Borders*. London: Ashgate, pp. 251–63.

Flahaux, M.-L. and de Haas, H. (2016) African Migration: Trends, Patterns, Drivers. *Comparative Migration Studies*, 4(1): 1–25.

Gazzotti, L. (2020) Deaths, Borders, and the Exception: Humanitarianism at the Spanish–Moroccan Border. *American Behavioral Scientist*, 64(4): 408–35.

IOM. (2019) *World Migration Report 2020*. Geneva: International Organization for Migration.

Jones, K. (2012) The Politics of Intellectual Self-Trust. *Social Epistemology*, 26(2), pp. 237–52.

Jones, R. (2016) *Violent Borders: Refugees and the Right to Move*. London: Verso.

Laine, J. (2016) The Multiscalar Production of Borders: An Introduction. *Geopolitics*, 21(3), 465–82.

Laine, J. (2018) The Ethics of Bordering: A Critical Reading of the Refugee "Crisis". In: G. Besier and K. Stoklosa, eds., *How to Deal with Refugees? Europe as a Continent of Dreams*. Berlin: LIT Verlag, pp. 278–301.

Laine, J. (2020a) Ambiguous Bordering Practices at the EU's Edges. In: A. Bissonnette and É. Vallet, eds., *Borders and Border Walls: In-security, Symbolism, Vulnerabilities*. London: Routledge, pp. 69–87.

Laine, J. (2020b) Reframing African Migration to Europe: An Alternative Narrative. In: I. Moyo, C. C. Nshimbi and J. P. Laine, eds., *Migration Conundrums, Regional Integration and Development: Africa-Europe Relations in a Changing Global Order*. London: Palgrave Macmillan, pp. 93–116.

Marchetti, R. (2020) A More Encompassing Understanding of the African-European Relationship. In: R. Marchetti, eds. *Africa–Europe Relationships: A Multistakeholder Perspective*. London: Routledge, pp. 3–13.

Matereke, K. (2013) Space Matters Rethinking Spatiality in Discourses of Colonial and Postcolonial "Boundaries". In: S. J. Ndlovu-Gatsheni and B. Mhlanga, eds. *Bondage of Boundaries and Identity Politics in Postcolonial Africa: The 'Northern Problem, and Ethno-Futures*. Oxford: African Books Collective, pp. 24–44.

Mbembe, A. (2017) Scrap the Borders that Divide Africans. M&G 17 Mar 2017. (online) Available at: mg.co.za/article/2017-03-17-00-scrap-the-borders-that-divide-africans/ (Accessed 22 May 2020).

Mbembe, A. (2019) Bodies as Borders. *From the European South* 4, pp. 5–18.

McAuliffe, M. and Kitimbo, A. (2018) African Migration: What the Numbers Really Tell Us. World Economic Forum 07 Jun 2018. (online) Available at: www.weforum.org/agenda/2018/06/heres-the-truth-about-african-migration (Accessed 22 May 2020).

McCullough, D. (2008) History and Knowing Who We Are. *American Heritage*, 58(1).

McEwen, A. C. (1971) *International Boundaries of East Africa*. Oxford: Clarendon Press.

Ndlovu-Gatsheni, S. J. (2018) *Epistemic Freedom in Africa: Deprovincialization and Decolonization*. Abingdon: Routledge.

Ndlovu-Gatsheni, S. J. and Mhlanga, B., eds. (2013) *Bondage of Boundaries and Identity Politics in Postcolonial Africa: The 'Northern Problem, and Ethno-Futures*. Oxford: African Books Collective.

Neocleous, M. (2008) *Critique of Security*. Montreal: McGill-Queen's University Press.

Nshimbi, C. C. (2019) Pan-African Aspirations Drive a New Free Trade Area Pact. *Current History*, 118(108): 188–94.

Nshimbi, C. C. and Moyo, I. (2016) Visible and Invisible Bordering Practices: The EU-African Migration Conundrum and Spatial Mobility of Borders. *World Journal of Science, Technology and Sustainable Development*, 13(4), pp. 300–14.

Nwaubani, A. T. (2018) Letter from Africa: Complaining about Colonialism Makes Us the Victims. BBC 8 July 2018. (online) Available at: www.bbc.com/news/world-africa-44741772 (Accessed 22 May 2020).

Oneko, S. (2019) Africans Want Open Borders, But Can They Overcome Stumbling Blocks? DW 18 Dec 2019. (online) Available at: p.dw.com/p/3UzwA (Accessed 22 May 2020).

Pallister-Wilkins P (2016) Interrogating the Mediterranean Migration Crisis. *Mediterranean Politics*, 21(2): pp. 311–5.

Parshotam, A. (2018) *Sliding Towards Disaster: Migration in European–African Relations*. Cape Town: Heinrich-Böll-Stiftung.

Silberfein, M. and Conteh, A. (2006) Boundaries and Conflict in the Mano River Region of West Africa. *Conflict Management and Peace Science*, 23(4), pp. 343–61.

Squire, V. (2017) Governing Migration through Death in Europe and the US: Identification, Burial, and the Crisis of Modern Humanism. *European Journal of International Relations*, 23(3), pp. 513–32.

Staeger, U. (2015) Africa–EU Relations and Normative Power Europe: A Decolonial Pan-African Critique. *Journal of Common Market Studies*, 54(4), pp. 981–98.

Steinwehr, U. (2020) Africa: When Closed Borders Become a Problem. DW 2 May 2020. (online) Available at: p.dw.com/p/3bgnd (Accessed 18 May 2020).

Tanesini, A. (2018) Collective Amnesia and Epistemic Injustice. In: J. A. Carter, A. Clark, J. Kallestrup, S. O. Palermos, and D. Pritchard, eds. *Socially Extended Epistemology*. Oxford: Oxford University Press, pp. 195–219.

Tazzioli, M. and de Genova, N. (2016) *Europe/Crisis: Introducing New Keywords of "The Crisis" in and of "Europe"*. Near Futures Online 1. New York: Zone Books.

Udeze, B. (2009) Why Africa? A Continent in a Dilemma of Unanswered Questions. Xlibris US. (online) Available at: www.bbc.com/news/world-africa-44741772 (Accessed 18 May 2020).

UN DESA. (2019) *International Migrant Stock 2019*. New York: United Nations, Department of Economic and Social Affairs, Population Division.

UNHCR. (2019) Global Trends. (online) Available at: www.unhcr.org/globaltrends 2018/ (Accessed 18 Apr. 2020).

Vaughan-Williams, N. (2015) *Europe's Border Crisis: Biopolitical Security and Beyond*. Oxford: Oxford University Press.

Walters, W. (2011) Foucault and Frontiers: Notes on the Birth of the Humanitarian Border. In: U. Bröckling, S. Krasmann and T. Lemke, eds., *Governmentality: Current Issues and Future Challenges*. New York: Routledge, pp. 138–64.

Part I

Critical perspectives on border regimes

Part I

Critical perspectives on
border regimes

1 Pushing the boundaries forwards

Shifting notes on the implications of European border control externalisation beyond the Sahel region

Calvin Minfegue

The issue of geographical mobility and the challenges it poses is a significant feature of our contemporary condition today (Mbembe, 2020). It is not that the phenomenon is new, but the "terms" in which it appears today and its reception by societies set it on a new trajectory. The latter consists of tension, fear, threat, political and military injunctions, as well as disillusionment, despair, torture, and death (Perocco, 2019; Cuttitta and Last, 2020). Of course, this global trend differs from one area to another and from one country to another, without always removing them from the hegemonic hold (especially the European) of the ways of governing migration.

This is the case with many African countries, including Cameroon. Cameroon is an important country of emigration to Africa and other continents relative to the size of its population, while being a country of immigration for nationals from Central and West Africa. The country is also connected to the global logics that characterise contemporary migration governance. It serves as an interesting site for observing the articulation between the internal migration dynamics of the African states and global migration processes, not necessarily for generalisation but for indicative purposes. Cameroon, which has a long history of migration, now faces some challenges, mainly due to crises on a regional scale. Since the early 2000s, the East Region of Cameroon has hosted many Central Africans fleeing the devastation resulting from the sociopolitical crises that the Central African Republic (CAR) is experiencing. The Boko Haram attacks affecting the northern part (Far North Region) of the country have resulted in an influx of Nigerian refugees and many internally displaced persons. Since 2016, the separatist crisis known as the "Anglophone crisis" has turned the English-speaking Northwest and Southwest Regions into areas where life has slowed down, if not serving to exemplify "empty countries" (*pays vides*) (Delpla, 2019). This has caused the displacement of many persons moving to other parts of the country and Nigeria. In addition to these endogenous dynamics, the country has not escaped the orbit to which many African states are subject in connection with European migration policy. It is on this last point – that is, how the externalisation of European borders is taking shape and producing multiple effects – that this chapter will focus. It thus intends to contribute to

DOI: 10.4324/9781003083726-2

a better understanding of African migration dynamics and their connections with global processes far from the many clichés that simultaneously hinder the possibilities of a more serene relationship between Africa and Europe.

I therefore propose to discuss an ambiguous idea: the possibility that European border control externalisation in Africa may have serious effects beyond the Sahel region, which is supposed to be its main front. This process and the mechanisms that support it consist of the acts, practices, and figures by which Europe (in this particular context) extends its borders to the countries of the Sahel region, and subjects them to management and control by third-party countries (Morocco, Niger, or Libya, for example). Like other border systems, this meta-border extends beyond its supposed "formal" boundaries. It has an unexpected impact in countries further south, like Cameroon. European border control externalisation produces effects in Cameroonian territory. It does so through the diffusion of a specific imaginary functioning under the duality of attraction – repulsion and hidden incentives

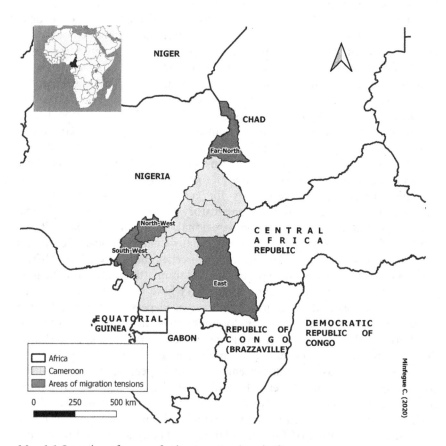

Map 1.1 Location of areas of migratory tensions in Cameroon.

and institutional measures. These effects are multi-scale and seem to take at least two forms. First, they belong to the cooperation modalities between the EU and the Cameroonian state on the one hand, and collaboration between the EU and civil society on the other. Second, they concern individuals by influencing how they define the trajectory of their migration.

To discuss these two aspects at a theoretical level, I have chosen to reinvest the notion of "banality" and all the potential that can be extracted from it by mobilising some of the work of sociologist Jean-Marc Ela and historian (and political scientist) Achille Mbembe. Ela's banality directs the gaze towards things – hidden situations – often considered insignificant, but which constitute the true encyclopaedia of ordinary social life. Indeed, "by studying ordinary life, the attentive observer finds a host of clues that provide analysis with a vast repertoire for understanding the 'ways' of doing things that testify to the creativity of social actors" (Ela, 1999, p. 104, *translation by the author*). There is an idea that it is sometimes more productive to look at people's practices to understand how they "capture" or what they do with things that are supposed to be beyond their reach, such as the issue of border control externalisation here. Mbembe's perspective is useful because it also allows us to see something that reveals banality in dominant processes or orders. Banality is mainly located in situations where the dominant power creates a representational system, or system of meaning. This power (*pouvoir*) seeks to make it "fully real, turning it into a part of people's common sense not only by instilling it in the minds of the *cibles*, or 'target population' but also by integrating it into the consciousness of the period" (Mbembe, 1992, p. 3). Power is thus explicitly oriented towards the control of the imagination (Ela, 1999). As far as they are concerned, the "dominated" subjects often demonstrate an ability to play with all the fetishised order that constitutes the dominant *dispositif*. By trying to impose its domination, the power paradoxically allows others (those who suffer it) to do something else by investing the ordinary in challenging and subverting it. This possibility of doing something else with this powerful order is undoubtedly linked to the fact that all power (and its declinations) must, in order to persist, be part of individuals' ordinary situations. If this is not the case, it exposes itself to being engraved in the order of the ordinary by ("dominated") individuals. They thus give meaning to this dominant dynamic and enter into a relationship with it. The effects of such relationships can be instructive for grasping the trajectories of devices referring to an order of power, as is the case with the externalisation of European borders.

To give substance to this reflection, I will combine data from ethnographic surveys conducted in eastern and southern border areas of Cameroon with documentary material providing information about recent trends in the nature of collaboration between the EU, the Cameroonian state, and Cameroonian civil society organisations (CSOs). The discussion will be organised around three main points. The first task will consist of tracking and identifying institutional dynamics, particularly those related to cooperation and collaboration – elements that indicate some considerations for Europe's positioning (in the Cameroonian context) in terms of migration/border policy. The second task will discuss the idea of creating and disseminating an imaginative incentive in how "externalisation" is recorded, discussed, "appropriated", and disseminated in specific places in Cameroon. The last task will examine the issue of the trivialisation ("banalisation") of the externalisation of European borders. It will also address their link to the possible constitution of the counter-geographies of the European migratory order.

Do with them to fix them at home

To gain a broad overview of cooperation between the EU and Cameroon on migration, a historical review of public action in this sector is necessary. This point will be followed by a discussion of the contemporary development of the migration and co-development nexus (and the role of the EU) and the place that is given to civil society in this cooperative framework.

The evolution of public action on migration in Cameroon

Historically, Cameroon's migration policy was based on the intersection of three cognitive cues. These are the idea of national preference, the challenge of regional and continental solidarity, and the connection with international concerns. As early as the 1960s, *govern the mobility* consisted, for the young Cameroonian state, of ensuring the protection of national subjects and the integrity of the national territory. In the turbulent context of the 1960s and early 1970s, this issue of national preference took on a security dimension. The struggle against the nationalists of the "Union des populations du Cameroun" (UPC) party was played out intensely on the migration field and more specifically on the control of (geographical) mobility. The aim was to control the mobility of individuals deemed "subversive" or "nationalist". The latter sometimes found refuge in British Cameroon (before 1961) and later in Congo – Brazzaville, then under communist rule (Sourna Loumtouang, 2015). National preference also meant protecting the territory from an unstable regional environment. Neighbouring territories such as Chad and the CAR were experiencing conflict. Migration policy was a border policy projected onto the national territory to be controlled and secured. This border policy was projected and concerned bodies – those of individuals deemed subversive, and who in their way constituted a threat to the national ideal. These two dimensions were often combined to give both political and security density to borders.

At the same time, the country has been part of a continental solidarity movement also linked to a pan-Africanist ideology. This regional solidarity has found consistent expression in the country's migration policy: the reception of refugees since the 1960s, visa exemption agreements with countries such as Mali, contributions to integration efforts (sub-regional and continental). Having been based on a humanitarian activity requiring external resources, this anchoring in regional solidarity has also fostered a growing internationalisation of the migration issue. It has materialised in collaboration with international humanitarian actors: the UNHCR (formally since 1965) and the International Committee of the Red Cross (since 1969), among others. The border was somehow presented as a solidarity and connection mechanism, shaped by what was then migration policy.

The connection with international issues was built in the wake of the Cameroonian state's commitment to the African scene. It has grown since the 2000s because of two significant changes. The first is regional and geopolitical. It concerns the multiplication of crises around Cameroon. Since 2003, the CAR has been experiencing a political crisis with obvious military effects. The extremist Boko Haram movement's actions, which had been limited to the northeast of Nigeria, have extended since 2014 to the Lake Chad Basin. These actions now affect Cameroon (particularly the far north region), Niger, and Chad. Cameroon has itself been facing a separatist crisis since 2016, with armed clashes in the Southwest and Northwest Regions (referred to as "Anglophone" areas). These crises and conflicts have had considerable migration effects on Cameroon. At the beginning of 2020, the country was home to 292,787 Central African refugees and 110,627 Nigerian refugees, and it had registered more than 976,773 internally displaced persons (UNHCR, 2020). The care of these displaced, deprived, and vulnerable bodies required resources provided mainly by international actors under the leadership of the UNHCR.

The second change is global, and of a political and geopolitical nature. It has something to do with the growing reconfiguration of public action in Africa (Eboko, 2015). After the glorious years of the 1960s and 1970s, when the "developing" and "strategic" state intervened in every sector, the 1980s saw a retraction of the state. The structural adjustment programmes imposed on states to "improve" their governance were the main motivations for this. Since 2000, the state has returned, but under the supervision of various international actors. The latter intervene in national public action by investing in its cognitive frameworks and operational mechanisms (Eboko, 2015). Subnational actors, in this case CSOs, are stakeholders in this new configuration. As an international actor, the EU is particularly involved in this collaborative framework in Cameroon. It is especially involved in the popularisation and dissemination at the national level of ways of doing and seeing the migration issue. Let us now focus on this actor and its involvement in Cameroon's migration policy.

The migration and co-development couple in the light of Cameroon–EU cooperation

Cooperation between Cameroon and the European Union is longstanding. It has focused on specific issues related to the development of the critical sectors of national socioeconomic life: health, education, port and road infrastructure, etc. Beyond these immediate effects, this cooperation can be presented as a political–institutional complex for the dissemination of the neoliberal capitalist order and later for the consolidation of its political counterpart, the nation state. As such, it has articulated economic (commercial and financial cooperation) and political (consolidation of democratic governance) issues.

Cooperation between Cameroon and the EU dates back to 1958 within the broader framework of cooperation between the EU and the countries of the African, Caribbean, and Pacific Group of States (ACP). It therefore already took shape in the colonial era. It continued, based on the Yaoundé Conventions of 1963 and 1969, and later the Lomé Convention of 1975 and its subsequent Conventions. Although trade and financial issues have always been at the heart of Cameroon–EU cooperation, there was a shift in 1989 concerning the issue of human rights in the Lomé IV Convention. At the turn of the 2000s the issue of migration gradually became part of the cooperation between Cameroon and the EU. Judging by the guidelines of the latest calls for projects for non-state actors, the issue of migration has become a vital issue in this cooperation in the last ten years.

One of the latest examples is the establishment of a European Trust Fund in 2015 to deal specifically with migration issues. This fund involves Cameroon[1] and is called "*Fonds fiduciaire d'urgence en faveur de la stabilité et de la lutte contre les causes profondes de la migration irrégulière et du phénomène des personnes déplacées en Afrique*". Addressing the issue of migration for the EU has consisted of guiding the government in the fight against illegal migration. The aim was to discourage any desire to leave Cameroon illegally for Europe. Such a stance amounts to making Cameroonian territory a vanguard post on the European border, and not only symbolically. The border thus extends further south in a configuration of meta-border points (corresponding to northern and sub-Saharan African countries with the classic functions of sorting control or even selection specific to the traditional border). This concern for migration has been politically and institutionally accentuated by what has been considered the "refugee crisis" (Wihtol de Wenden, 2016). As is well known, this crisis has taken shape more around public rhetoric emphasising protectionist and even populist issues. The consequence has been a strengthening of the security management of the migration issue, justified by the increase in the arrival of refugees and asylum seekers in Europe. Far from being a refugee crisis, we are strictly speaking facing a political crisis ("a management crisis") concerning the options for dealing with the migration issue (Laine, 2018; 2020). Beyond this, the most palpable effect of the importance taken by the migration issue is its insertion in a paradigmatic framework that reinvests the notion of co-development.

Historically, co-development has been part of the need to refresh French cooperative action. It has aimed to improve the effects ("effectiveness") of official development assistance by linking the development of the countries receiving aid with the export needs of the countries providing it – France in this case (Gubert, 2008). Co-development refers to joint actions to support and facilitate the development of various sectors of socioeconomic activity to create employment and resources "locally" in migrants' countries of departure. This resource creation is thus a factor in retaining potential candidates for clandestine migration to Europe. It is above all a question of creating the conditions for keeping *in their own country* all those whom we would not always like to have in our own country.

Co-development appears as a "local solution" to clandestine migration. Co-development is thus part of an incentive for the return of migrants with the promise or assurance of facilitating socioeconomic and therefore socio-professional integration. It is therefore based on the creation and facilitation of conditions for professional integration in countries of origin (mostly African) to motivate the greatest number of migrants in returning home. It is thus an incentive to return home (Gubert, 2008). The effectiveness and scope of such options remain problematic, particularly in their ability to reduce emigration (Mouhoud, 2018). Today, the idea of co-development is indicative of the more structural junctions, officially assumed, between migration and development with, for example, an emphasis on the contribution of diasporas to the development of their countries of origin[2]. The evolution of Cameroon–EU cooperation on migration issues has also seen the growing involvement of CSOs.

CSOs at the forefront

Limiting clandestine migration also requires additional work to convey messages to populations and potential candidates for irregular departure. This work at ground-level must be carried out by specific actors close to the populations. In many respects, the plethora of actors (associations, trade union structures, religious organisations, etc.) acting as civil society is especially mobilised. For many years, Cameroon–EU cooperation has included civil society organisations in its operations. They are therefore likely to be supported by funding. This "eligibility" gives them access to resources enabling them to act in the fight against illegal migration. The term "fight" [*lutte*] itself reflects the metaphors or imaginative indications underlying such action: clandestine migration is seen as an "enemy" and perhaps a "disease" that must be "fought". Such a conception undoubtedly departs from the fundamental nature of the issue of "irregular" migration. In essence, it is the product of a system that is both global (reflecting the interconnection between regions of the world) and multifaceted (social, political, and economic).

However, this reference to "the struggle" or "fight" must be understood as constituting all the (particular) historical logics that have led to the popularisation of a certain idea of the border (migratory action is in many respects a border action). This proximity between border and "struggles" (a reference to conflict) is valued in the discursive and political infrastructure underlying the externalisation of Europe's borders. The involvement of Cameroonian civil society in this public European migration action has also been achieved by appropriating or aligning itself with the discourse of "struggle". In the case of Cameroon associations at the forefront of this "struggle" have or had already positioned their actions in favour of the "fight against illegal migration", as is the case for an association such as "*Solutions aux Migrations Clandestines*" (SMIC)[3]. We can also mention organisations such as the "*Association de Luttes contre les migrations clandestines*" (ALCEC) and the "*Association des Rapatriés et de Lutte Contre l'Émigration Clandestine*" (ARECC).

CSOs working on migration issues are supported and intervene in this field according to relatively common operational modalities, which consist of informing, educating, and raising public awareness of the risks associated with leaving for Europe through "clandestine", "irregular", or "illegal" channels. For example, between 2012 and 2014, with Belgian cooperation, SMIC organised awareness-raising campaigns against clandestine migration[4]. More recently, in March 2020, awareness raising was conducted in towns like Foumban (west Cameroon) as part of another campaign funded by the European Union Delegation in Cameroon. This action also takes the form of "accompaniment" and "support" for those wishing to emigrate regularly. The idea is to ensure that they respect all the conditions required for this purpose. CSOs are involved in a selection or at least an upstream conditioning of the candidates eligible to migrate to Europe.

These civil society activities are therefore both anticipatory and essential operations of European migration policy. These operations extend beyond the Sahel Strip, and specifically to countries like Cameroon. However, two reasons should lead to a better consideration and analysis of the place and action of Cameroonian CSOs in this global migration pattern. Civil society investment still seems to be based on a restricted circle of organisations, which is evidence of the compartmentalisation of this action around particular organisational figures. Yet, contrary to other sectors, such as health or education, the mobilisation of civil society in the field of migration justifies a smaller experiential liability. Moreover, it is concerned with structural and organisational difficulties that have often been associated with civil society in Cameroon (Abéga, 2007). While these European measures are positioned as a bulwark against irregular migration by an operational, discursive, and dissuasive framework, they are variously "received" by potential candidates for departure to Europe.

Thinking and dreaming of elsewhere

The actions and discourses that give substance to the process of externalising European borders in Cameroon are varied. They consist of a series of cooperation and collaboration agreements, and the establishment of financial support funds for specific initiatives, just as they take shape in precise public discursive positions. Compared with the regional scale, the way this process unfolds in Cameroonian territory is not comparable with what is observed in countries like Mali or Niger. The logic has been more advanced in the latter countries, making them hotspots: vanguard points in the migration selection of those wishing to go to Europe; and the first bulwark in the fight against irregular migration to the old continent. However, it is possible to discuss the other effects of how this process has enveloped Cameroon. These effects consist mainly of the production of a specific imaginary which, far from dissuading candidates for travel (be it irregular/illegal), incites them to take the risk of setting off on an adventure.

All measures that are taken to deter travel prove unproductive and generate effects contrary to those expected. The structural scale is somewhat inappropriate to account for these countereffects. They can be understood at the individual level by examining the sinuosity of certain micro-geographies. I will therefore start from empirical situations involving Central African refugees in Garoua-Boulaï (a local council located in the east of Cameroon and bordering the CAR) and West African migrants in Kye-Ossi (a local council located in the south, bordering Gabon and Equatorial Guinea). The cases briefly described here will enable us to discuss the diffuse or contrasting effects of the measures taken in the wake of this outsourcing. Emphasis will also be placed on the logic by which these measures are appropriated, deconstructed, or re-appropriated by potential candidates for departure.

The East Region of Cameroon had about 200,000 Central African refugees at the beginning of 2020. At the end of 2018, the commune of Garoua-Boulaï registered about 50,000 refugees, nearly half of whom were settled in the village of Gado Badzere, where a camp was established in 2014 by the UNHCR (Minfegue, 2020). Many of these refugees in the region, most of whom have been there since 2014, have registered for durable settlement. The living and security conditions in their countries of origin, which they still consider deplorable, do not encourage them to return. Repatriation operations were carried out in 2019 but involved fewer than 10,000 refugees. Many refugees consider the option of moving to the northern Sahel Strip. Access to countries such as Niger or Libya is often seen as a stepping stone to Europe by applying for refugee status or using clandestine routes.

Two factors play an essential role here. The first is the return or dissemination of the experiences of refugees or relatives of refugees who have already used these routes (especially clandestine ones). These experiences are then considered a reference point to encourage departure, despite the awareness-raising activities against clandestine migration often carried out among these refugees. To give them consistency, these experiences are linked to the situation in the Central African Republic, the country of origin, which is still not improving.

> The situation there (in the CAR) is not changing too much, although it's a little bit better there. We sometimes think we'll go back to Niger or Libya to see if we can take our chances. Some of us have already left…
>
> (A CAR refugee, August 2017, in Garoua-Boulaï)

The second factor refers to the circulation within refugee communities of information that "applying" for refugee status in European countries is easier in Sahelian countries like Niger or Mali. Going there "by all means" would be a migration step extending the "regular" or "formal" possibilities of access to Europe. We can see the attraction that sometimes constitutes the status of "refugee" *elsewhere* (in European countries) compared to the status that can be enjoyed *here* (Cameroon).

> (…) It would be nice to go to these countries, and it seems that there you can easily apply for refugee status in France, Europe…
>
> (A CAR refugee, April 2018, in Garoua-Boulaï)

We see these empirical indications as one of the modalities of appropriation of the discourses and actions related to this process of externalisation. Some potential candidates for travel reinterpret them as factors that encourage movement. Faced with initiatives that were intended to limit movement or deter it as much as possible, it emerges that these deterrent or limiting measures are being redefined for some. The limiting or even repulsive functions of outsourcing are subverted by these actors, who see it rather as factors of attraction – of appeal to movement. They divert the initial objectives of this externalised control of European borders. They then make this process part of a specific trajectory of trivialisation (Mbembe, 2001).

Kye-Ossi, a Cameroonian locality, connects Cameroon with Gabon and Equatorial Guinea. The scientific and institutional literature about this locality has focused on its economic dynamics (Fodouop, 1987; Bennafla, 2002; INS, 2014). However, through this economic dynamism, based mostly on the oil boom in Gabon and later in Equatorial Guinea, intense migration dynamics take place there. One of the characteristics of these dynamics is to make Kye-Ossi a transit territory for many West African migrants to Gabon and especially Equatorial Guinea. The main countries of origin of these West African migrants are Mali, Burkina-Faso, Côte d'Ivoire, Niger, Guinea-Conakry, and Nigeria. On the way to Gabon and especially Equatorial Guinea, Kye-Ossi has proved to be a stage of preparation for the adventure. Taking into account the migration projects of some West Africans, Kye-Ossi is part of a migration project to access Gabon or Equatorial Guinea. These two countries are places where the capital required to facilitate a trip to Niger or Morocco is collected. They are considered places from which the European migration adventure can easily be envisaged.

> Kye-Ossi is the step for those who don't have the money. They stay here first until then. If you decide to go out, you have to go out (in Equatorial Guinea). After that, when you have something, you can see if you can go to Niger or Morocco. There are possibilities there…"
>
> (migrant from Burkina-Faso, May 2018, in Kye-Ossi)

This indication paves the way for an interesting hypothesis: some spaces may be places for the constitution of the *capital* indispensable for the start of a move towards African countries that are considered African gateways to Europe (Libya, Morocco, and Niger). Such an option reinforces a known reality which indicates that the tightening of entry into European territory results in an increased selection of migrants. One of the criteria for this selection is having the means to assume the "psychological" and more importantly "financial" cost of the move (Mouhoud, 2018). Of course, in the overall migration picture, a minority of African migrants head for Europe (Duwicquet, Mouhoud, and Oudinet, 2014). The continent's migration needs are met by turning towards the continent itself. In other words, these needs from elsewhere can hardly be presented as a total figure. Yet the empirical reference above suggests that the deterrent measures taken by Europe are counterproductive or at least inoperative.

These measures focused on countries presented as vanguard points of European migration policy constitute a basis from which illegal or non-legal departures to Europe can be envisaged. Libya, Morocco, Niger, and even Mali can thus be presented as key points of the European meta-border. Travelling to these countries with capital accrued elsewhere is therefore seen as presenting oneself at the gates of Europe. We can argue that an imaginary, or at least incentive representation is developed around or because of the investment made by Europe. We can see that this high-stakes process has been re-appropriated in the sense of its trivialisation (*banalisation*) by actors. This trivialisation is located in "ordinary choices" (the choice to migrate or the decision to save money), and how the process's initial aims are redefined.

In both cases one point stands out: it is the role played by circuits and other information networks that feeds migration dynamics. Taking an alternative approach to European migration measures, and the institutional and practical incentives that accompany them, is based on the availability of and access to information. This availability of information is a key determinant of people's migratory trajectories. Information flows between migrants. It is present in the places where they stop and through which they transit. Even refugee camps are irrigated by these flows of information, as Michel Agier (2008) has pointed out.

Banality and counter-geographies of European measures: "Lines of resistance"[5] in minor mode?

The idea of European border control externalisation has a structuring capacity to impose itself in various imaginary and action plans, particularly those of states or those guiding the framework for action and collaboration with CSOs. This appears in the specific logics of cooperation in which, over the last five years or so, migration has gradually become both a key issue in cooperation between the EU and Cameroon and a key theme in the collaboration and support for Cameroonian CSOs. It expands the idea of migration control with its point zero, which is raising awareness of the dangers of certain forms of migration and proposing (imposing) a model of co-development designed as a bulwark against illegal and clandestine migration.

The idea and imaginary associated with this externalisation are paradoxically appropriated by migrant actors, who see them as a way of constituting a point of attraction that encourages movement. In other words, the limiting, even repulsive, function of this externalisation is subverted by these actors, who seem to see it as a factor of attraction, a call for movement. It seems that they are doing *something different* from the initial objectives of border control externalisation. On the eastern borderlands of Cameroon, this is reflected in the willingness of Central African refugees to rely on countries such as Niger. The same observation is made concerning West African migrants, for whom the Cameroonian stage (in the southern border area between Cameroon, Gabon, and Equatorial Guinea) represents a point of the constitution of a useful *capital* for the migration adventure towards these places (Libya, Morocco, Niger), which are key points of the European meta-border. These two levels of effect (institutional and individual) are articulated and form a basis for the debate on the impact of this process of European border control externalisation beyond the Sahel region.

These effects of European migration policies are based mainly on their trivialisation: banality is at the heart of dominant power and the multiple forms of its expression. The salient points of European migration policy are set out materially or concretely, forming the basis of its gradual trivialisation. The latter can be seen, for example, in activities that are commonplace in how certain actors do things (such as awareness raising and educational activities among civil society actors). What symbolises the dominant power, its partners, and other targets (including possibly those who are dominated) is an inscription in a common imaginative (and therefore banal) framework, which constitutes its share of banality (Mbembe, 1992; 2001). The dominant power or process creates a representational system, a system of meaning, and seeks to make it "fully real, turning it into a part of people's common sense not only by instilling it in the minds of the targets, or 'target population' but also by integrating it into the consciousness of the period" (Mbembe, 1992, p. 3). It is also everyday activities that constitute the core of the implementation of the European migration policy in the Cameroonian situation – evidence that these movements and ordinary activities are indicative of more important issues (Ela, 1999). This should not allow us to forget that this banality at the heart of the externalisation of European borders is also constitutive of local and individual reactions to these policies. These reactions can be read in the capacity of individuals in Garoua-Boulaï or Kye-Ossi to do something else with these European policies and to give them different purposes from those imposed by Europe. In any case, the migration issue is one of the most perennial means of the international integration of African countries, as well as those of the global south (Mouhoud, 2018).

On the scale of the effects of the externalisation of European borders, these situations of banality seem to remain marginal. However, they seem to outline the counter-geographies of these European measures. I borrow this notion of "counter-geography" from Saskia Sassen, who has mobilised it in the context of reflections on the alternative circuits of globalisation, for example, by seeing a greater involvement of women. Such involvement is also commitment (or engagement) but remains minor in the analysis of global flows (Sassen, 2000). In the present reflection, I place it within a more political construction, whose framework is the power structure represented by the process of externalisation of European borders and the attributes of domination that characterise it. These counter-geographies refer here to spaces, places, and above all to socio-spatial situations where European migration policies are reinterpreted according to logics different from their initial objectives. They should not be seen as binary opposites of European migration processes. However, they should be considered one possibility among others in the range of effects or trajectories they may cause or take. These counter-geographies, carried by the target actors of European measures, sometimes consist of inserting the activities and aims of these measures into the ordinary course of their lives.

This insertion has a subversive purpose, especially in its capacity to produce counterproductive effects concerning the initial aims of this European policy. *Thinking far away* for the Central African refugee in East Cameroon is often synonymous with inserting the possibilities and flaws of European policy into their migration projects. This can sometimes mean getting closer to the countries at the heart of this European migration system – Libya, Mali, and Morocco. For the West African migrant, *access to the desired location* involves detours, returns, expectations, and the rush to new destinations that may correspond to these same key countries of European policy. These counter-geographies represent the marginal and dark side of these measures, as well as how potential migrants and other populations grasp or at least identify with them. They then make it possible to grasp the externalisation of borders at their least expected ends.

These counter-geographies can be seen as the unexpected and underestimated face of the dominant processes embodied by the willingness of Europeans to push their borders further south in the Mediterranean. They constitute an unspoken externality which, no doubt and by all means, is the basis of their banality. As such, these counter-geographies are first linked to these dominant dynamics with an externalising vocation, especially by subverting them in their forms and projections. Second, they have the particularity of not always being their visible face (in the way the effects of these measures are placed in the discourse). However, they are intimately linked to these measures. Finally, they must be considered in their large dimension – that is, in their capacity to depend on the experiential liabilities and longstanding historical practices of actors and communities (migration dynamics, an imaginary of mobility, movement). In this respect, these counter-geographies must be understood for what they are in the context of the present chapter: a hypothesis of the marginal (and invisible) effects of the externalisation of European borders, which additional studies could confirm.

Conclusion

The European will and action in pushing back the borders of the "old" continent further south in the Mediterranean aims to limit migration flows onto its soil. They represent a willingness to sort and select profiles deserving entry into Europe. At the same time, they are synonymous with a ban on access to the European area for specific categories of people. Throughout this chapter, the aim has been to pave the way for reflection on the minor effects of these measures. As in other countries, this European border policy is reflected in institutional readjustments. The latter consists of popularising the co-development model, and using civil society to convey its ideas and practices.

Yet these measures, acting as a deterrent, have the opposite effect, consisting instead of encouraging movement by redefining migration trajectories or generating new desires to leave (oriented towards new destinations). These effects in the latter case are perceptible at the level of individuals. They thus draw the contours of counter-geographies (relating to the policy of externalisation of European borders). Not far from totally generating socio-spatial situations where departures (especially illegal ones) to Europe are discouraged and reduced, we can see the development of situations where these departures are explicitly envisaged at a far remove from legal circuits. I have sketched the hypothetical contours of these situations based on data that is somewhat inconsistent and does not allow for generalisations. These counter-geographies therefore merit more detailed exploration. This perspective needs to be further explored to refine our understanding of Euro–African migration dynamics.

Notes

1 The other countries concerned are Burkina Faso, Chad, Gambia, Mali, Mauritania, Niger, Nigeria, and Senegal. These are countries "located on African migration routes to Europe" (CAONFED 2018).
2 One of the highlights of this new orientation in Cameroon was the holding of a forum on the diaspora in June 2017 in Yaoundé, the Cameroonian capital. The event was aimed at "creating a platform for the promotion and strengthening of actions of Cameroonians abroad in favour of the country" (see www.journalducameroun. com/yaounde-accueille-premier-forum-de-diaspora-camerounaise-juin/).
3 For more information on this association, which presents itself as a "pioneer" in terms of reflection and action in the field of migration, see the website www.ong-smic.org.
4 See the website ong-smic.org/blog/.
5 I borrow this notion of "lines of resistance" from the work of the philosopher Fabien Eboussi Boulaga, published in 1999.

References

Abéga, S. C. (2007) *Le retour de la société civile en Afrique*. Yaoundé: Presses Universitaires Catholiques d'Afrique Centrale.

Agier, M. (2008) *Gérer les indésirables. Des camps de réfugiés au gouvernement humanitaire*. Paris: Flammarion.

Bennafla, K. (2002) *Le commerce frontalier en Afrique centrale. Acteurs, espaces, pratiques*. Paris: Karthala.

Cuttitta, P. and Last, T. (2020) *Border Deaths. Causes, Dynamics and Consequences of Migration-related Mortality*. Amsterdam: Amsterdam University Press.

Delpla, I. (2019) Vivre au pays vide? *Critique*, 2019/1 (860–1), pp. 123–35.

Duwicquet, V., Mouhoud, E., and Oudinet, J. (2014) International Migration by 2030: Impact of Immigration Policies Scenarios on Growth and Employment. *Foresight*, 6(2), pp. 142–64.

Eboko, F. (2015) *Repenser l'action publique en Afrique. Du Sida à l'analyse de la globalisation des politiques publiques*. Paris: Karthala.

Ela, J-M. (1999) Vers une économie politique des conflits au ras du sol. *Africa Development*, XXIV(3–4), pp. 103–33.

Fodouop, K. (1987) Le commerce frontalier dans le département du Ntem au Cameroun, *Cahiers d'outre-mer*, 158(june), pp. 127–48.

Gubert, F. (2008) (In)cohérence des politiques migratoires et de codéveloppement françaises. Illustrations maliennes, *Politique Africaine*, 109, pp. 42–55.

Institut National de la Statistique (INS). (2014) *Monographie des échanges transfrontaliers de marchandises au Cameroun*. Rapport d'étude. Yaoundé: Institut National de la Statistique.

Laine, J. (2018) The ethics of bordering: a critical reading of the refugee "crisis". In: G. Besier and K. Stoklosa, eds., *How to Deal with Refugees? Europe as a Continent of Dreams*. Berlin: LIT Verlag, pp. 278–301.

Laine, J. (2020) Reframing African migration to Europe: an alternative narrative. In: Moyo, I., C. C. Nshimbi & J. P. Laine, eds. (2020). *Migration Conundrums, Regional Integration and Development: Africa-Europe Relations in a Changing Global Order*. London: Palgrave Macmillan.

Mbembe, A. (1992) Provisional Notes on the Postcolony, *Africa: Journal of the International African Institute*, 62, (1), pp. 3–37.

Mbembe, A. (2001) *On the Postcolony*. Berkeley, Los Angeles, London: University of California Press.

Mbembe, A. (2020) *Brutalisme*. Paris: La Découverte.

Minfegue, C. (2020) *Espaces (trans)frontaliers, territorialités et conflictualités en Afrique centrale. Cas des bassins frontaliers Est et Sud du Cameroun*. Phd thesis in Geography and Political science University of Grenoble-Alpes and Catholic University of Central Africa (unpublished).

Mouhoud, E. (2018) Les frontières visibles et invisibles des migrations internationales. *Pouvoirs*, 165(2), pp. 99–112.

Perocco, F. (2019) *Tortura e migrazioni/ Torture and Migration*. Venezia: Ca'Foscari.

Sassen, S. (2000) Women's burden: Counter-geographies of globalisation and the feminisation of Survival. *Journal of International Affairs*, 53(2), pp. 503–24.

Sourna Loumtouang, E. (2015) Frontières de l'Etat et état des frontières au Cameroun: esquisse d'analyse de la gouvernance des périphéries de l'Etat réunifié

(1961–2011). *Revue Internationale des Sciences Humaines et Sociales / International Review of Human and Social Sciences*, pp. 31–52.

UNHCR. (2020) *Fact Sheet. Cameroon.* [S. l.]: UNHCR.

Wihtol De Wenden, C. (2016) L'Europe et la crise de l'accueil des réfugiés. *Revue des juristes de Sciences Po*, 12, pp. 41–8.

2 The Africa-Frontex Intelligence Community

The EU-African information sharing platform on migration and border issues

Anna Moraczewska

Migration in Africa has been a feature of everyday life for centuries and the vast majority of it occurs within the continent. It differs from region to region, and postcolonial borders only deepen this phenomenon. Historically, in West Africa, migrants consist of refugees, cross-border traders, professionals, and clandestine workers. In Eastern Africa, forced migration to neighbouring stable countries (Kenya or Tanzania) continues, stemming from the conflicts in Burundi, Somalia and South Sudan. The migration flows in Southern Africa are primarily motivated by economic pursuits. Thus, poverty, post-independence conflicts, and population growth are regular push factors for people's movement across and outside Africa. (Nshimbi and Lorenzo, 2016, pp. 8–9.) Processes of internal migration within the African continent are less regulated and more spontaneous compared to those that take place in the European Union (EU). Hence, the different experiences of these two political and geographic areas cannot be considered in isolation, but in tandem, according to their determinants.

Since the colonial period, Europe has never been more interested in gaining situational awareness about migratory processes in African countries than it is today. Processes of migration between African countries and the efficiency of state borders have become the apple of the European Union's eye in the face of the migration crisis. Specialized EU agencies have increased their activity on the African continent to analyse social, economic, and human factors that shape the push and pull factors of migration. The Africa-Frontex Intelligence Community (AFIC) represents a new type of multilateral relationship where state actors cooperate with a non-state actor in monitoring the flow of people across borders and combating crimes related to it. AFIC was set up in 2010 to provide a framework for regular knowledge and intelligence sharing in the field of border security between the European Border and Coast Guard Agency (Frontex) and African countries. The initial geographical focus of AFIC on West Africa, parts of the Sahel region, and Morocco is being gradually extended to the east and north of the continent.

DOI: 10.4324/9781003083726-3

Frontex has been active as an autonomous EU agency since 2004 and its competences have been extended several times during the ensuing period. From the very beginning, the Agency was responsible for managing the external borders of the EU member states and developing and strengthening common principles governing the crossing of these borders – the so-called Integrated Border Management approach. Leaving states their sovereign power over borders, Frontex coordinates operational cooperation among them and promotes its universalised external borders model. One of its crucial tasks is conducting risk analysis concerning the situation at the external borders and beyond them, with a specific focus on the migration process.

> The agency also carries out vulnerability assessments to evaluate the capacity and readiness of each member state to face challenges at its external borders, including migratory pressure. (…) [It] coordinates and organises joint operations and rapid border interventions at the external borders, including in humanitarian emergencies and rescue at sea.
>
> (Frontex, 2020a)

However, Frontex does not possess the authority to decide which person is entitled to international protection. Instead, this power lies within the remit of the member states. On the other hand, the Agency assists member states and independently organises return operations for illegal migrants and overstayers.

The EU member states, initially sceptical toward sharing their border prerogatives with Frontex, have agreed to extend its power twice, in 2016 and 2019. Undoubtedly, accompanying circumstances at the EU's external borders impacted states' responses and their move toward tightened security measures. Frontex was expected to enhance its operations against irregular migration, monitor the situation at the borders and outside the EU, and investigate states' vulnerability and efficiency in external border control. With the 2016 amendment, Frontex was named the European Border and Coast Guard Agency. Since 2019, it has been able to interact with third countries and begin recruiting guards to the European Border and Coast Guard standing corps. This direction of change indicates a trend toward constructing an expanded defence system against all kinds of perceived threats affecting the body of "national" societies. On the other hand, Frontex, using its new power, engages in numerous interactions with authorities in third countries responsible for border control and security. The aim is to control the "insecurities" defined by its own methodology outside the external borders of the EU. Across these transformations, we can observe a combination of the re-emergence of state-centric thinking in protecting state borders and the supranational activity of Frontex outside the EU external borders.

AFIC can be seen as an example of the externalisation of EU border management based on a regional network approach to risk analysis and an expert-based community providing crucial information. Risk analysis is a key tool in the international cooperation mechanisms used by Frontex and its results are expressed in the Agency's reports. The chapter will begin with a theoretical section focusing on the concept of externalising border management within the domains of maintaining a regional risk analysis network as well as expert cooperation on migration and the border situation in Africa. The second section will be devoted to the origins of AFIC. The third section will discuss empirical information provided by the AFIC network and delve into what can be learnt from AFIC reports and how it can be used.

The idea of the externalisation of EU border management contradicts the concept of "fortress Europe". Instead, the EU is continuing to extend its spatial range beyond its territory by establishing cooperation with its neighbours using different tools and implementing associated measures outside its territory. In this context, externalisation refers to the dissemination of some practices rooted in Europe among its neighbours, including methods of border control, collecting data about travellers, using IT during controls, promoting respect for human rights, etc. Levy (2011, pp. 165–7) calls this practice "a remote border management", naming the European Border Assistance Mission (EUBAM) as an example. Instead of erecting a fortress, this approach establishes and multiplies filters outside the EU's external borders, which perform tasks directed by the "management centre" in Europe. One alternative lens through which to look at this is that it can pre-empt border and migration management based on risk management to identify a potential threat before it reaches the shores of Europe.

Notwithstanding the above, the type of management in question is not a classical type of "control at a distance", seeing as Frontex's liaison officers have become permanent and mobile fixtures in some third countries, including Bosnia and Herzegovina, Serbia, Montenegro, Libya, Niger, and Turkey. The Agency has developed a network of Frontex Liaison Officers (FLOs) in non-EU countries, who are part of a broader network deployed outside of the EU. This category encompasses the European Migration Liaison Officers (EMLOs), European Return Liaison Officers (EURLOs) and Immigration Liaison Officers (ILOs) of EU Member States. Frontex deployed FLOs to Turkey in 2016, to Niger in 2017, and to the Western Balkans in 2018 (the latter were based in Serbia). Moreover, Frontex experts support the EU Border Assistance Mission in Libya (EUBAM) and have established two risk analysis cells in Niger and Senegal. This strategy represents a type of networked multilateral relation where state actors cooperate with a non-state actor in monitoring the flow of people across borders and combating crimes based on cooperative intelligence. I define this last term as the collection of information of social and criminal value conducted by representatives of one country concerning the situation in his/her country, and coordinated by envoys of another state. The existence of this kind of cooperation is not classified, but access to information is limited. Since May 2016, the AFIC has been issuing a monthly report and has given an additional impetus to information exchange, helping to promote the Frontex concept of a regional approach to risk analysis.

The aim of this chapter is to study whether cooperation between Frontex and African countries is an opportunity to understand the root causes and motivations of the flow of people from Africa to Europe or just an obligation imposed on neighbouring countries to stop migration on their continent before it reaches the shores of the European Union. This will allow us to better understand whether more information obtained at the source by Frontex can provoke a constructive debate between both sides and lead to the realignment of many EU countries' misshapen attitudes toward and perceptions of Africa.

Externalisation of border management

The concept of externalisation, as applied to borders, reflects the changing nature of the border in a globalising world. It indicates a course that consists of abandoning the state-centred and territorial paradigm of the border towards dispersed bordering as a consequence of socio-political practices outside the state's territory (Scott, 2017). The externalisation of border practices can be perceived as a symptom of globalisation and technological development that creates new channels and instruments for interactions between different actors. Bialasiewicz (2011; 2012) views this concept as the out-sourcing and off-shoring of border practices as a strategy of sub-contracting border control to local security authorities or private companies. Other equivalents of the term include "translated borders" (Sloterdijk, 1994), "virtual border practicing" (Bigo, 2001), "securing the external" (Bialasiewicz, 2009), or "border work" (Laïdi, 2005), which occur far beyond external borders of the EU.

Different dimensions of externalisation can be found in both academic literature and political documents. Lavenex (2011, p. 374) considers external governance as a disaggregation of the processes of re-bordering and de-bordering in different dimensions of political order, and this is exemplified with the EU's regulatory shift to third countries as a full projection of the EU's *acquis communautaire*, or selective norm transfer. This form of norm transfer often "involves specialised transgovernmental networks, including, where available, cooperation with EU agencies" (Lavenex, 2011, p. 386). Casas-Cortes, Cobarrubias, and Pickles (2012, p. 45) point to signs of externalisation under the European Neighbourhood Policy as an example of "... different forms of governance emerging at the crossroads between regional economic integration on the one hand and border policy on the other". The strategy of externalising security management is nothing new and could be found in many political documents of the eventual European Union member states at the beginning of the twenty first century. In the EU's new Global Strategy, one may read that some security problems inside the Union have their roots outside its territory and the concept of "concentric circles" is aimed at managing these problems in neighbouring countries. This concept is implemented by a four-tier border security model and consists of border checks at the EU's external borders, measures inside the Schengen area, cross-border cooperation with neighbouring countries, and measures taken in the third states. It shifts the EU's functional borders beyond its territorial frontier (Lavenex, 2004). This sphere of policy is part of the Common Security and Defence Policy (CSDP), but Frontex is a key player when it comes to implementing the externalisation of border management.

Within several years and in the face of the migration crisis, the Agency's mandate has broadened significantly. At the same time, the security management of the ring of neighbouring states has proven insufficient. Most of these countries have been at the end of the chain of movement of persons or participants of larger organized cross-border criminal activities. In October 2016, improving the EU's management of migration was hot on the agenda of the EU institutions and the notion of shifting the spotlight to distant territories was widely accepted. Parkers (2016) named this a "plasma ball" that replaced the idea of ordered concentric circles and transformed them into disordered peripheral hotspots. This situation sparked further discussions regarding the entity in charge of managing migration and crises within the third countries from which they ultimately originate. Did Frontex have the authority to formulate and implement a new strategy, or did CSDP? Generally, both entities are responsible for the promotion of European integrated border management standards and for the situational awareness and risk analysis on the external borders and beyond them. While this is not the subject of this chapter, time has shown that Frontex has emerged as a key entity implementing the externalisation of border and cross-border threat management, with accompanying political agreements with several third countries concerning migration management.

The Frontex Regulation (Frontex, 2019a) states that high-level border security must be accompanied by the proactive management of migration, including the implementation of necessary measures in third countries. Within the framework of the external action policy of the EU, the Agency is supposed to provide technical and operational assistance to third countries which have been identified through risk analysis as being a point of origin or transit for illegal immigration (Frontex, 2019a, Art 3, 71). The Agency, acting within its expanded mandate, has started to export several elements that make up the externalisation of border management. These include: delegating experts and liaison officers to third countries, trainings for border guards, and cooperation in regional risk analysis with third countries. This last activity is connected with information sharing, which is also used by Frontex to prepare external border vulnerability analysis.

Frontex's coordination function, which had been primarily applied to member states, subsequently expanded beyond the EU's external borders. Today, the Agency provides technical and operational assistance to third countries as an additional measure of implementing European integrated border management. It may carry out actions on the territory of a third country on the basis of an operational plan formulated between the Agency and the third country, in accordance with international agreements (Frontex, 2019a, p. 74.) Drawing on its standing corps, Frontex deploys its staff as members of border or migration management teams, return teams in joint operations, and rapid border interventions or any other relevant operational activities, not only in the member states but in third countries as well (Frontex, 2019a, p. 54). Since 2019, a new recruitment drive to a European Border and Coast Guard standing corps has been under way and is aimed at increasing total staffing from today's 1,500 to 10,000 by 2027. The Agency is responsible for the development and organisation of the command and control structures for the deployment of the standing corps on the territory of third countries. This means that Frontex will become more operational in third countries classified as risky and its presence there will become more feasible – and ultimately permanent. The Agency corps is getting more and more engaged in supporting border staff in cooperating countries that share European models of border management.

Moreover, within the Liaison Officers Networks Unit, which is a part of Frontex's International and European Cooperation Division, the Agency is delegating experts to non-EU countries to improve border management skills among staff via training and monitoring. The Frontex Liaison Officers (FLOS) are part of a network of other European liaison officers deployed outside the EU, such as the European Migration Liaison Officers, European Return Liaison Officers, and Immigration Liaison Officers of EU Member States as well as future LOs from other EU agencies. Since 2017, Frontex experts have supported the EU Border Assistance Mission in Libya (EUBAM) on the ground (Frontex, 2020b). A few FLOs operate in Turkey (Ankara), Niger (Niamey), and the Western Balkans (Belgrade, Serbia), but Frontex expects to have ten LOs by the end of 2020. The shared experiences of European and non-European staff both inform and reveal the differences in their approaches. On the one hand, Frontex aims to implement European border control standards and increase the efficiency of third-country border services, which in effect serves to decrease the flow of migrants to the EU. Non-European border guards have strong situational awareness of their own states and neighbouring countries, but the fight against crime and curbing the intensive movement of people is not always their priority.

Risk analysis is the last instrument of externalisation of border management by Frontex. It is also one of the main tasks of the Agency and remains crucial for strategic and operational decisions concerning the EU's external border management. Risk analysis refers to developing a pre-warning mechanism in the context of migratory flows towards the Union, their volume and routes, trends and possible challenges at the external borders, and analogous issues related to migrants' return routes. Risk is defined as a function of threat, vulnerability, and impact, and Frontex has elaborated a common integrated risk analysis model – CIRAM – which is applied by the Agency, Member States, and cooperating third countries (Frontex, 2020b). Frontex risk analysis structure consists of a Risk Analysis Unit (RAU) that provides several types of risk analysis – the annual risk analysis (ARA), quarterly reports (FRAN) and risk analysis of neighbouring regions for the Western Balkans, Eastern Europe, and Africa.

Short, ad-hoc analyses are also prepared on individual, emerging risks. A risk-based approach to border management aims to, first, rationalise a decision-making process, and second, standardise a methodology of border management. Paul (2020) additionally considers Frontex risk analysis as a remedy for the institutionalisation of EU border control as well as a risk regulator. On the other hand, Ekelund (2014, pp. 111–12) questions the scientific approach of Frontex to border control with regard to risk assessment methodology. The risk-based approach adapts migration to the concept of risk and brings it under its particular lens. This connects with an approach anchored in critical security studies that identifies migration as a threat and a destabilising agent for European societies, in line with the Foucauldian securitisation discourse (Huysmans, 2000, p. 753). From this perspective, Frontex tries to transfer this perception of migration to third countries, along with the methodologies used to manage it. By establishing regional risk analysis networks in a surrounding area – the Eastern Partnership Risk Analysis Network (EaP-RAN), the Western Balkans Risk Analysis Network (WB-RAN), the Turkey-Frontex Risk Analysis Network (TU-RAN) and the Africa-Frontex Intelligence Community (AFIC) – the Agency has created a risk-regulating system that applies both its threat construct and the tools to manage it. Since Frontex is not a regulatory agency, it relies on information gathering and sharing, then the analysis of said information, followed by coordinated operations in member and third states once the information is processed (Paul, 2020). Training organised by the Agency, among many topics, aims to present migration as an assessable phenomenon that can be managed with precise analytical techniques. This constructive approach to defining migration risk can contrast with the alternative perception of migration, which is treated in Africa as an everyday practice.

It should be noted, however, that migration is not the only phenomenon that poses a threat and is affected by training. Above all, Frontex focuses on the essence of irregular migration and its accompanying crimes, such as human trafficking and smuggling as well as the activities of organised criminal groups that prey on individuals and societies, promising them a happy life in the European Union. Thus, there are tailored risk analysis mechanisms that are based on information provided by member and third states, focusing on areas such as the efficiency of border control, return operations, the unauthorised secondary movements of third-country nationals within the Union, migratory routes, facilitation of unauthorised border crossings, terrorism, and hybrid threats (Frontex, 2019a, point 40). Continuous monitoring of border areas and their immediate vicinity is also crucial in rescue operations and actions taken to limit the risk of death and bodily harm. The EUROSUR system (which became an integrated element of Frontex in 2019) is based on the common application of surveillance tools, including the provision of the

Copernicus Earth Observation Programme's satellite services, and provides the member states and the Agency with information to detect small vessels and to improve collective rapid response capabilities (Frontex, 2019a, points 37–38). Hence, the externalisation of risk analysis and management must be perceived in two ways: first, it imposes the subject of the risk on third countries via Frontex, and second, it involves evaluating actual cross-border threats to further assess, manage, and neutralise them. The goal of this externalisation is to introduce and deepen the EU-led model of risk management in non-EU countries, which as a result makes outside risks less uncertain, more predictable, and better manageable.

The idea of the Africa-Frontex Intelligence Community

Based on the desirability of the FRAN at the member state level, the European Union and Frontex have found it appropriate to establish similar platforms based on this concept for joint analytical work with some of its non-EU partner countries. Regional risk analysis networks represent a bridge for mutual information and knowledge sharing between the EU and the cooperating countries on a continuous and structured basis. Africa was not first in line but became a key point of attention after 2015 and the migration crisis that escalated that year. The Africa-Frontex Intelligence Community (AFIC) was established in 2010 to provide a framework for regular information sharing about migrants' movements and border security threats across the continent.

Cooperation has been expanding within Africa, starting with a number of states along the main smuggling routes and reaching 28 participating members in 2019 – the largest regional risk analysis network. The initial geographical focus was on West Africa, parts of the Sahel region, and Morocco, and gradually extended to the eastern and northern parts of the continent. Today, the participating countries include (in alphabetic order): Angola, Benin, Burkina Faso, Cameroon, Cape Verde, Chad, Democratic Republic of Congo, Ivory Coast, Egypt, Eritrea, Gambia, Ghana, Guinea, Kenya, Liberia, Libya, Mali, Mauritania, Morocco, Niger, Nigeria, Senegal, Sierra Leone, Somalia, South Sudan, Sudan, Togo and Tunisia. The main instruments of cooperation include workshops, field visits, regular information exchange, and replies to Requests for Information. Three AFIC workshops took place in 2017, two of which were in Africa. During the second meeting, 65 experts from 25 African countries discussed criminal networks operating in Africa with representatives of the EU and international organisations (Frontex, 2017). In October 2019, Frontex launched a two-week risk analysis course, this time at the National Police Academy in Spain. This course was organised as part of the Strengthening of Africa Frontex Intelligence Community project and aimed to "…improve the capacity of AFIC countries to produce risk analysis and to enable effective cooperation by introducing common standards. Students [discussed] topics ranging from integrated border management

[and] fundamental rights to statistical analysis and report writing" (Frontex, 2019c).

Frontex perceived AFIC as a key element in battling cross-border crime and security threats affecting African states and the EU (AFIC Report, 2017). In the case of Africa, the primary fields of cooperation do not differ from those of the Western Balkans or the Eastern European risk analysis networks and include a series of training activities, setting up integrated border management systems, and the collection, sharing, and analysis of relevant data. The primary stated aim is to develop national and regional strategies to fight cross-border crimes (AFIC Report, 2017).

Moreover, basing on bilateral agreements with third countries, Frontex has established risk analysis cells in Africa: a first cell in 2018 in Niamey, Niger and a second in 2019 in Dakar, Senegal, with six more planned in Gambia, Ghana, Guinea, Kenya, Mali, and Nigeria. Niger was Frontex's first choice because it is the main corridor for migration and migrant transfer. The cells are run by local risk analysts who have been trained by Frontex and whose mission is to support relevant authorities tasked with border management. They collect and analyse data concerning flows of migrants, the activity of organised crime groups dealing with human trafficking, the efficiency and effectiveness of border infrastructure and border control, etc. Information is shared with states' authorities and Frontex together with policy recommendations (Frontex, 2019b). AFIC issues an annual report, but also makes ad-hoc statements. Frontex uses information from different African states to create external border threat and vulnerability maps, which inform the Agency's operational actions and the European Commission decisions.

Since AFIC is the largest regional network in terms of both territorial range and number of participants, it absorbs much of Frontex's activity and engages much of its staff. To a great extent, the decision to develop the standing corps was predicated on the shifting range of the network. Different kinds of Frontex liaison officers are on a temporary secondment on the African continent, while representatives of participating states participate in visits and workshops in the European Union. Among the AFIC states, there are out-migration countries, transit countries, and countries hosting refugee camps, all of which create a discrete migration network. Hence, additional emphasis must be placed on strengthening regional cooperation between AFIC partner countries. A holistic approach is necessary to investigate the intricate links and conflicting actors within the African continent, which influence the push factors of irregular migration and cross-border crimes.

Information platform on migration and border issues

Frontex treats risk analysis as an "intelligence cycle" that consists of information collection, evaluation, and sharing. Data gathered from different sources – member states and external actors – are validated and interpreted. As its name indicates, AFIC was conceived as an intelligence community, which places it at the heart of Frontex's risk analysis process. There are multiple similarities between the traditional duties of an intelligence agency and those of the intelligence community; the difference lies largely in the latter's structure. The community is coordinated by an institution (in this case, Frontex), while maintaining the supremacy of state authorities. By exporting its framing of the intelligence cycle, the Agency harmonises the security activities of countries participating in risk analysis networks. As Horii (2016, p. 246) notes using the example of member states, this practice incorporates the intelligence culture into migration and border management.

Studying information provided in AFIC reports creates an impression that much of it concerns the push factors of irregular migration and changes in the intensity of migrant flows. Both of them, together with information from other regional risk analysis networks, allow us to paint a situational picture for the EU external borders and judge the vulnerability of these borders, as presented in the annual risk analysis reports. The reports contain information about migrant routes, migration centres, a particular migrant's or smuggler's profile, the situation at some African borders, and prices charged by smugglers. Moreover, the collected information allows Frontex to distil general risk trends and react accordingly. However, some deficiencies can be observed. First, the last official AFIC report was published by Frontex in 2017, whereas the most up-to-date analysis for the Western Balkans and Eastern Partnership was issued in 2019; second, the AFIC reports were issued annually, while the two others were published on a quarterly basis. Most data are classified and Frontex is not willing to share them with outsiders.

On the other hand, much information can be gleaned from these operations about criminal networks in Africa that deal with smuggling and trafficking human beings. Figure 2.1 presents a visual of these issues, based on data from Niamey risk cell. It shows a process flow as well as the entities involved in the smuggling operation.

Niger is considered a transit country, with the city of Agadez serving as a hub and many networks that provide infrastructure and services for migrants. Agadez is a centre of large-scale smuggling practices in the corridor from the Sahara Desert to the North African coast. Cities with a similar role include Niamey and Tahoua in southern Niger, which is mainly used as a connection point with Algeria. As Figure 2.1 shows, there are several pieces to the puzzle – bus operators, chasseurs, ghettos, ghetto bosses, fixers, and drivers – who together form the interconnected vessels of a large-scale smuggling system. The ghettos in Agadez are meant to serve travellers with basic accommodation and gather groups of them to dispatch later, either in large weekly convoys or smaller daily ones, bound for Libya. Many drivers, who frequently use Toyota Hilux cars or large military-style trucks, are former tour guides and handle transportation between the city and the border crossings. They carry not only migrants but smuggled goods as well. Since demand has increased, more

Border crossing

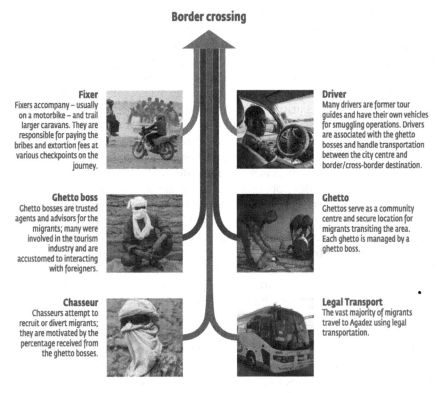

Fixer
Fixers accompany – usually on a motorbike – and trail larger caravans. They are responsible for paying the bribes and extortion fees at various checkpoints on the journey.

Driver
Many drivers are former tour guides and have their own vehicles for smuggling operations. Drivers are associated with the ghetto bosses and handle transportation between the city centre and border/cross-border destination.

Ghetto boss
Ghetto bosses are trusted agents and advisors for the migrants; many were involved in the tourism industry and are accustomed to interacting with foreigners.

Ghetto
Ghettos serve as a community centre and secure location for migrants transiting the area. Each ghetto is managed by a ghetto boss.

Chasseur
Chasseurs attempt to recruit or divert migrants; they are motivated by the percentage received from the ghetto bosses.

Legal Transport
The vast majority of migrants travel to Agadez using legal transportation.

Figure 2.1 Smuggling operations in Agadez, Niger.
Reproduced with the permission of Frontex.

and more bus operators – private and government-owned – have been identified as involved in smuggling schemes. They transport people to different
destinations, which creates additional contact points in the smuggling system.
Every part of the service is paid; even upon reaching the Libyan border, each
migrant has to pay a bribe to be allowed into Libya (AFIC Report, 2017).
Hence, many migrants have to stay in transit countries for several months, or
even years, to collect money in order to continue their journey. They take jobs
on a temporary basis that are offered by local employers, often in very poor
conditions. Some migrants earn a low salary, which they subsequently use to
pay the smugglers; some are not paid and have to stay with the employer until
he decides that they have earned enough money for their passage to the EU
(AFIC Report, 2016).

Information from participating countries – usually from police or border
officers and national authorities – is collected and analysed, with varying
points of focus. These institutions provide information about migrant routes,
migrant hubs and profiles of persons involved in the smuggling process.

People are transported further north to Algeria, Libya, and Morocco, where they continue their journey in rubber dinghies or wooden boats toward the EU. This provides information about border corridors and calls Frontex's attention to the state of different national borders. After further investigation, the Agency notifies the authorities of any shortcomings or lack of necessary standard operating procedures regarding border checks and data collection. As a result of this kind of investigation, Frontex has pointed out the limited presence of Internal Security Forces at the border checkpoint at Labbezanga at the Malian-Nigerien border, limited coordination and contact between border checkpoints and central-level authorities in many African countries, and the perpetual lack of IT equipment for border surveillance, among others.

On the other hand, Frontex identified the efforts of the Ghana Immigration Service (GIS) toward developing a preventive strategy aiming to curb pernicious migration trends as a positive precedent for managing migration. A Migration Information Bureau was established by the GIS to organise information campaigns across the country to warn potential migrants of the dangers of irregular travel and smugglers' deceptive promises (AFIC Report, 2017). This activity is crucial for the whole migration process because it targets the source – people who are lured to leave their country in search of a better life but often condemn themselves to a perpetual wandering, with no notion of how, where, and when their journey will actually end. Unfortunately, this is not a widespread practice in other African countries.

Basing on data gathered from participating countries, Frontex also assesses the push and pull factors of migration. In Africa, economic underdevelopment and all of its consequences, ongoing conflicts in many regions, and extremist religious activity (e.g. Boko Haram) are the most commonly recorded push factors mentioned during interviews with migrants. Moreover, on the example of Niger, ethnic boundaries and the tribal landscape extend beyond national borders and are said to be a crucial facilitator for cross-border criminal activities (AFIC Report, 2017). In terms of pull factors, the asylum policy of the EU states, social benefits for asylum seekers, the language spoken in the country of destination (especially among Francophone or Anglophone migrants), and contact with relatives who are already in Europe are the most prominent factors. This information illustrates the complex situation in many African states, for which there are no quick or effective solutions. Frontex's competences are not broad enough to control these factors. However, the results of the risk analysis prepared by the Agency are forwarded to EU institutions, which can make decisions that affect these factors to some extent. Considering that this is a difficult and complex process, it is much easier to point out the deficits of the borders and border services and constantly assess the situation in African countries. By exporting its approach to border management and risk analysis to third countries and gathering data and information from different regions, the EU may consider itself to be more in control of the situation outside its external borders.

Conclusion

In light of its access to an enormous amount of information on the conditions of migration processes in Africa, Frontex has a chance to play an important role in building new relations between Africa and the European Union. Collecting and analysing information can result in all parties gaining a better understanding of the determinants of both positive and negative processes taking place on the African continent. This cannot be a unilateral strategy of cooperation but rather a multilateral network of equal partners. Frontex uses three elements of externalisation in its border management mechanisms: delegating experts and liaison officers to third countries, trainings for border guards, and cooperation in regional risk analysis based on information sharing. In these ways, the European agency exercises a direct impact on the decisions of national authorities responsible for border management in Africa. By training border service staff, it frames their perception of some concepts and processes, including migration and the porosity of borders, using securitisation discourse. This draws from the Copenhagen School of security studies in international relations, which defines these objects through a threat-security discourse (Buzan, Wæver, and De Wilde, 1997). Migration – a daily reality in Africa – has been identified as a threat that has to be managed using the European Union's methods. Moreover, in a way that is reminiscent of Donald Trump's interpretation of migrant flows on the southern border of the United States, the EU makes African states responsible for stopping this process, which threatens primarily the EU.

The complicated status of African borders, combined with the EU's forceful approach, has reignited the subject of European intervention. Investigating the porosity of national borders and the efficiency of border protection services creates the impression that Frontex is attempting to transplant the standards that the EU applies to its external borders onto the borders of participating states in order to filter and stop risky movements and flows. To accomplish this, the Agency "exports" its common integrated risk analysis model (CIRAM), accompanied by the methodology and terminology of risk and risk management. Using these tools, Frontex promotes a rational approach to border practices and migration that treats risk as an assessable and manageable object. Paul (2017) analyses this approach toward the EU member states and examines a successful application of Frontex's risk analysis calculations in the decision-making process at the institutional level within the EU. As for the cooperation with African countries, the rational approach, with its emphasis on risk analysis and risk management, became a keystone in building an information sharing platform between partner countries and Frontex. The autonomous Agency interacts with national authorities responsible for border security, which partly de-politicised this cooperation. The EU uses its institutional envoy to investigate the state of risk in a given environment, mitigate it if possible, and provide a synthetic analysis that will

help to prepare preventive actions. Risk analysis is meant to show participating countries the shortcomings of their border system and to provide a
technical framework for how it should work in light of the EU's needs. Risk
and risk management have become a new sphere of foreign affairs where the
EU actively tries to introduce its security strategy. However, problems appear
when the process of migration is treated as assessable and manageable. Can
migration be perceived as a homogenous phenomenon when different people
from different countries are motivated or pressed to move for a variety of
reasons? A refugee's decision to leave their country is often very risky, the flow
of people from one migration hub to another is risky, and violence and uncertainty constitute risks for people on the move. It is thus almost impossible to
accurately calculate risk for every individual. This may lead us to ask who
benefits the most from AFIC's information sharing platform when, as Horii
observes, "information has been translated into knowledge that shapes social
reality and prompts action" (Horii, 2016, p. 255).

AFIC's annual reports provide a large amount of unique information that
is still not used adequately. While the creation of such a platform was a positive development in the relations between the European Union and African
states, it is still too strongly rooted in the stereotype of the superiority of
European solutions over their African counterparts. If Frontex is to promote
integrated border management among the EU member states, it can also try
to reframe and reshape the negative perspective toward African migrants
as a positive one and encourage a universal attitudinal shift. Undoubtedly,
AFIC's crucial role is to assist in fighting human trafficking and smuggling
on the African continent rather than fighting migration *per se*. This process
can be supported by IT equipment transfer and coordinated actions between
European and African states' border or police forces. Another major short-
coming is the very limited number of open and publicly available publications
concerning the migration situation in Africa compared to reports from other
regional networks. Publishing AFIC's quarterly reports, much like what is
already done for the Eastern Partnership Risk Analysis Network, would provide analysts and scientific researchers with an important source of data. If
Frontex succeeds in transforming its role from that of a supervisor to that of
a partner, it would create a great opportunity for the Agency to establish a real
partnership between Europe and Africa.

References

AFIC Report. (2017) Frontex webpage. (online) frontex.europa.eu/publications/afic-
2017-ktLwW1 (Accessed 8 Mar. 2020).

AFIC Report. (2016) Frontex webpage. (online) frontex.europa.eu/publications/afic-
2016-Xj6uSE (Accessed 8 Mar. 2020).

Bialasiewicz, L. (2012) Off-shoring and out-sourcing the borders of Europe: Libya
and EU border work in the Mediterranean. *Geopolitics*, 17 (4), pp. 843–66.

Bialasiewicz, L. (2011) *Europe in the World. EU Geopolitics in the Making of European Space*. Farnham: Ashgate.

Bialasiewicz, L. (2009) The new political geographies of the European "neighbourhood". *Political Geography*, 28 (2), pp. 79–89.

Bigo, D. (2001) The Möbius Ribbon of International and External Security(ies). In: M. Albert, D. Jacobson and Y. Lapid, eds., *Identities, Borders, Orders: Re-Thinking International Relations Theory*. London and Minneapolis: University of Minnesota Press, pp. 91–116.

Buzan, B., Wæver, O., and De Wilde, J. (1997) *Security: A New Framework for Analysis*. Boulder, Colorado: Lynne Rienner Pub.

Casas-Cortes, M., Cobarrubias, S., and Pickles J. (2012) Re-bordering the neighbourhood: Europe's emerging geographies of non-accession integration. *European Urban and Regional Studies*, 20(1), pp. 37–58.

Ekelund, H. (2014) The establishment of FRONTEX: A new institutional approach. *Journal of European Integration*, 36(2), pp. 99–116.

Frontex. (2017). News Release: Frontex launches capacity building project for Africa during AFIC meeting (online). https://frontex.europa.eu/media-centre/news-release/frontex-launches-capacity-building-project-for-africa-during-afic-meeting-g3JfQJ (Accessed 8 Mar. 2020).

Frontex. (2019a) Regulation (EU) 2019/1896 of the European Parliament and the council of 13 November 2019 on the European Border and Coast Guard and repealing Regulations (EU) No 1052/2013 and (EU) 2016/1624, Official Journal of the European Union L 295/1.

Frontex. (2019b) News release. (online) frontex.europa.eu/media-centre/news-release/frontex-opens-risk-analysis-cell-in-senegal-6nkN3B (Accessed 7 Mar. 2020).

Frontex. (2019c) News release (online) frontex.europa.eu/media-centre/news-release/africa-frontex-intelligence-community-risk-analysis-course-held-in-spain-HpOyJZ (Accessed 8 Mar. 2020).

Frontex. (2020a) Frontex origin & tasks. (online) frontex.europa.eu/about-frontex/origin-tasks/ (Accessed 16 Apr. 2020).

Frontex. (2020b) Frontex liaison officers to non-EU countries. (online) frontex.europa.eu/partners/liaison-officers-network/ (Accessed 1 Mar. 2020).

Horii, S. (2016) The effect of Frontex's risk analysis on the European border control. *European Politics and Society,* 17(2), pp. 242–58.

Huysmans, J. (2000) The European Union and the securitization of migration. *Journal of Common Market Studies*, 38(5), pp. 751–77.

Laïdi, Z. (2005) *La Norme Sans la Force*. Paris: Presses de la Fondation Nationale des Sciences Politiques.

Lavenex, S. (2011) Concentric circles of flexible "European" integration: A typology of EU external governance relations. *Comparative European Politics*, 9(4/5), pp. 372–93.

Lavenex, S. (2004) EU external governance in "wider Europe". *Journal of European Public Policy*, 11(4), pp. 688–708.

Nshimbi, C. C. and Lorenzo F. (2016) *Regional Migration Governance in the African Continent. Current State of Affairs and the Way Forward*. Bonn: Stiftung Entwicklung und Frieden (sef:)/Development and Peace Foundation.

Parkers, R. (2016) Managing migration abroad. Why, where, what and how? *Brief Issue,* 31 November 2016, European Institute for Security Studies, pp. 1–4.

Paul, R. (2020) Risk Analysis as a Governance Tool in European Border Control. In: A. Weinar, S. Bonjour, and L. Zhyznomirska, eds. *The Routledge Handbook on the Politics of Migration in Europe*. London: Routledge.

Paul, R. (2017) Harmonisation by risk analysis? Frontex and the risk-based governance of European border control. *Journal of European Integration*, 39(6), pp. 689–706.

Sloterdijk, P. (1994) *Falls Europa erwacht*. Frankfurt am Main: Suhrkamp Verlag.

Scott, J. W. (2017) *Globalisation and the Study of Borders*. *Cross-Border Review,* Budapest: European Institute of Cross-Border Studies – Central European Service for Cross-border Initiatives, pp. 5–30.

3 Mainstreaming intelligence and information technology in border governance

A transcontinental mechanism for migration flow

Okechukwu Richard Oji

Introduction

On 22 August 2019 the Nigerian government launched a security operation code-named *Ex-Swift Response*. It was a robust border security exercise, intended to secure Nigeria's international land border with the Republic of Benin following a recent escalation of smuggling across its borders. The exercise featured men and women from the relevant branches of the armed forces and was coordinated by Nigeria's Office of the National Security Adviser (ONSA).

Nigeria is no stranger to transnational migration and its security challenges. The country's vast array of resources – tangible and intangible – makes it an ideal and constant target for the activities of cross-border criminal elements, most of whom operate between Nigeria and her less economically vibrant neighbours like Benin, Chad, and the Republic of the Niger. From the perspective of Nigeria's import-dependent economy, the situation is not only perpetuated but inevitable. Further compounding these problems are Nigeria's vast land and maritime borders, totalling 923,768 kilometres – humanly impossible to secure with manpower alone. This requires state-of-the-art security equipment and intelligence gathering – skills and technology Nigeria is yet to acquire or master. It was in recognition of this gap in border security management that the African Union Border Programme (AUBP) outlined the following among its other objectives between July 1964 and June 2007: a) the promotion of cross-border corporation between Regional Economic Countries (RECs), African countries, and other regional integration mechanisms and local border region communities; b) encouraging capacity building in border management through research and special education. These objectives were further narrowed to three action points: demarcation and delimitation, cross-border cooperation, and capacity building. This chapter focuses on capacity building as it relates to intelligence gathering and

DOI: 10.4324/9781003083726-4

information technology as mechanisms for controlling the outcome of trans-continental migration flows.

This chapter is divided into three sections. The first is a retrospective study of West Africa's history of cross-border security challenges, ranging from trafficking in goods, arms, and people to terrorism and robbery. The section justifies not only the serious nature of the security challenges but the dire need for improved security and intelligence. Discussions of the role of policy in con-tinental efforts geared towards improving border security follow in the second section, emphasising the ECOWAS Protocol on Free Movement, Right of Residence and Establishment, and the African Union Border Programme. The final section uses the American model to highlight best practice in the areas of intelligence and information technology in securing the border.

Cross-border security challenges in West Africa

Context

The movement and settlement of goods and people are essential to the regional integration of countries in the West African sub-region. Lamine (2006) reports that between four and five million people travel through the ECOWAS corridor every month. However, regardless of the socioeconomic prospects this holds for the region, a major challenge remains: West Africa's porous borders continue to breed cross-border/transnational crime. The ECOWAS border corridor is neither secure nor effectively manned, thus con-stituting a teething problem for countries in the West African sub-region and especially for Nigeria, the regional power. Most critical among the challenges of border security for most countries in the region is the lack of adequate technology for surveilling the movement of people and goods (Addo, 2006). Other challenges identified in 2004 by the UN Secretary-General (2004) include youth unemployment, mass refugee movement and forced displace-ment, the weakening of the state security sectors, social exclusion, weak national institutions and civil society structures, the uncoordinated response of various state security agencies in the region, a lack of security hardware and equipment, and weak judicial and legal frameworks. These challenges are spread across different categories of cross-border criminal activity: trafficking in small arms and light weapons, trafficking in drugs and narcotics, smuggling of contraband goods, people trafficking, money laundering, and cross-border robbery.

Blum (2014) uses the Benin–Nigeria border corridor to highlight the gravity of this border security situation. He cites some transnational criminal incidents, including the 2003 international bank robbery led by the notorious Hamani Tijani. The incident was so serious that Nigeria had to close its border with Benin after the robbery. In 2008 there were multiple bank robberies at the Dantokpa Market in Cotonou by a Nigerian crime syndicate that made its way into Benin from the Lagos Lagoon. Not only did the gang get away with

Table 3.1 Tabular representation of cross-border/transnational crimes by countries and key actors

Dominant Border Crimes	Country/Border zones of activity	Group/Actors involved	Transit states	Recipient states
Narcotics/ Drugs	Cape Verde, Ghana, Nigeria, Togo.	Drug dealers.	Ghana, Togo, Benin, Nigeria.	Spain, US, Portugal.
Advance fee fraud/Money laundering	Nigeria, Ghana, Côte d'Ivoire, Sierra Leone.	Advance fee fraud syndicates, business tycoons, government officials.	Syndicates operate from the West to East Africa.	Nigeria and other countries harbouring advance fee fraudsters.
Human trafficking	Prevalent throughout West Africa, but most common in Nigeria, Burkina Faso, and Benin.	Traffickers serving as middlemen, trade and business partners.	Ghana, Sierra Leone.	West African countries, North America, Europe, the Middle East.
Fire arms trafficking	Ghana, Togo, Benin, Liberia, Senegal.	Rebels, local fire arms manufacturers, middlemen.	Benin, Gambia, Guinea.	Liberia, Sierra Leone, Nigeria

huge sums of money, they also left many casualties in their wake. This situation is not exclusive to the Nigeria–Benin corridor. According to the United Nations Office on Drugs and Crime in West Africa, similar criminal activities take place in Guinea-Bissau, where international criminal elements operate on the tiny islands in the country's national waters.

Table 3.1 shows a tabular representation of cross-border/transnational crimes by countries and key actors. Data source: UNODC document on transnational organised crime in West Africa, New York, 2005, and research on cross-border crime by Addo (2006).

The issues

The extensive geographical coverage, including the effects of border security problems, depicted by the table above should be noted. Indeed, this situation only confirms the structural and professional deficiencies of national governments in West Africa in combatting the menace of transnational crime. According to Addo (2006) it was in recognition of the weaknesses of West Africa's respective national governments and the security of the sub-region as a whole that the European Union and the United Nations agreed to a tripartite response involving ECOWAS. Their central objective was to engage a unified and coordinated approach to addressing the border security challenges that had gone beyond proximate borders to become more transnational in nature, extending to the Americas and Europe. However, the sad reality is that even this initiative by the international community failed to stop the plague of border security problems, not only in the West African sub-region but in the entire continent, mostly in its western, eastern, and northern regions.

Flynn (1997) adopts a different approach to Addo (2006) and the UN, blaming the existence of cross-border crime on primordial social factors. In Flynn's view, all efforts to address cross-border crime must take cognisance of the important role borderlands play. As defined by Chan and Womack (2016), borderlands are geographical entities demarcated and defined by state-designed boundaries. Characteristically, borderlands, in the view of Chan and Womack (2016), exist on the margins of more than one state. Administratively, more than one system of governance and development usually operate in a territory. Communities and individuals living in the borderlands are usually closer to a foreign power than they are to their own government. The most distinctive feature of what happens in the borderlands is that besides being used by different government regimes, communities living in the borderlands are proficient in more than one language and are accustomed to conducting their business and daily exchanges with more than one currency. This language is largely derived from some of these border communities sharing a common ancestry with ethnic groups from the mainland and the daily trade between both sides. While these features may explain why borderlands are critical objects of interest to the theme under study, their relevance to border security remains unknown: why are borderlands crucial to border security management?

Blum (2014) explains that borderlands are essential to all efforts aimed at combatting cross-border crime. This is due to their geographical and strategic importance, and in the case of Africa their cultural and historical relevance. Borderlands are "... melting pots and security hot spots ... [T]hey are an arena for cross-border crime and represent a dynamic place of historically fostered cultural and socio-economic exchange ..." (Blum, 2014). In addition to their strategic importance, borderlands serve transactional purposes (formal and informal trade activities) for commodities legally and illegally exchanged, and they are occasional sanctuaries or hideouts for criminals operating between both countries, as in the case of the Benin–Nigeria borderland.

Trade is no less a factor driving cross-border crime than borderlands. Different types of trade occur at the border – formal and informal, legal and illicit, micro and macro. The existence of markets at the border brings first an awareness that anything can be exchanged or traded, legally in most cases, illegally in some others. However, it is on illicit trade, aided by proximate borders, that cross-border crime thrives. The Benin–Nigeria border is one of the most important corridors in the West-African region because of the major extent of the economic and sometimes illicit activities occurring there (Bassey and Oshita, 2010). Naturally, where there are trade interests, the threat of cross-border crime follows, often driven by porous borders.

Illicit trade between Nigeria and her proximate neighbours, Benin and Niger, is usually a by-product of two factors: Firstly, poor sales and a market economy in which items and products legally traded in markets no longer fetch enough profits for traders. In such situations many begin to venture into trading in illegal products like cannabis and contraband goods to make up for their market losses. Secondly, there is the porous nature of the borders. Lazare Sossou-Agbo (2011) describes the porous border conditions between Nigeria and Benin in these terms:

> Along the entire border lies a labyrinth of little creeks and streams, which have never been forbidden and are unmonitored by the police and the border control. The lagoon linking Porto Novo to Lagos ... facilitates the transport of agricultural goods... [T]he absence of natural bound-aries are important contributing factors [sic] in making contrabandism an "institution" within the entire region.

Although exploring the aforementioned causes of illicit trade/cross-border crime remains critical to efforts seeking to address the challenge, a more balanced approach situates these factors in the context of structural inad-equacies like poverty, unemployment, and bad governance to obtain more holistic countermeasures. Besides borderlands and trade, no other contem-porary phenomenon accentuates the transnational nature of border crimes like globalisation. Globalisation is to transnationalism what borderlands and trade are to cross-border crime. It keeps evolving, challenging the exclusive rights of nation states to maintain and control their territories by the processes of de-territorialisation and re-territorialisation. Globalisation not only alters territories, it affects human migration. Goods, ideologies, and humans no longer have to cross physical borders to enter territories. The internet makes everything possible and easy today. The precedent of globalisation has set in motion a new era in border security management, in which threats have become even more sophisticated and difficult to handle. Evidently, Newman (2006) aligns with this in positing that the best proof regarding the impact or sign of globalisation is what happens at the technological level, specifically in the domain of cyberspace, which is constantly changing territorial fixation and border permeability throughout the world. It is within the cyberspace realm that more sophisticated forms of transnational and cross-border crimes like money laundering and transnational radicalisation are domiciled. At the touch of a button, individuals can transact huge sums of money to sponsor terrorism or download illicit and dangerous content that could jeopardise national security.

The discussion of the role of trade and borderlands in cross-border crime may have been exhausted in this section, but there remains a paucity of information linking this security situation with the peculiarity of African borderlands, and why it will be so difficult to address this problem within the unique borderland geographical entity. These and discussions around the sociocultural make-up not only of the African borderlands but of transnational crime syndicates operating in the region dominate the next part of this chapter.

The history of African borders and the rise of transnational organised crime

Although highly contested among scholars, most African states and communities remain more loyal to the continent's territorial architecture before the partitioning of 1884–1886 than to the current artificially imposed borders and notions of state independence. Ikome (2012) recalls that Europe's economic balkanisation of Africa between 1884 and 1886 achieved two key objectives: a) the forceful fusion of incompatible territories that had never belonged together; and b) the unnegotiated or forceful separation of entities that had belonged together. It is therefore no surprise that parts of Lagos and Ogun States in Nigeria share linguistic and cultural similarities with the Republic of Benin: before colonialism, both territories were one kingdom under the Dahomey Empire. The same is true of parts of northern Nigeria, where states like Borno, Sokoto, and Damaturu were parts of the great Kanem-Bornu and Songhai Empires, extending from North Africa to the sub-Saharan region.

Hartshorne's (1938) classification of borders superimposes Africa's natural borders. By definition, they are borders drawn after the development of a cultural landscape but without recourse to cultural boundaries. Most African borders were drawn by Europeans without regard for the sociocultural characteristics of the people they partitioned. This historical background facilitates the understanding of the kinship relations playing out among the borderland communities within the boundaries of most African countries. Given that most of the borderlands were integral parts of large kingdoms and empires before the colonial era, kinship relations are distorted in the course of policing the borders and preventing the existence of cross-border crime largely perpetuated by family units and relations.

In continuing to integrate the discourse on the kinship system into the theme of transnational organised crime, Addo (2006) and Blum (2014) believe that Africa's transnational crime syndicates mostly comprise family members or households whose bonds of loyalty are strong and largely blood-related. In addition to their membership, West Africa's crime syndicates' operations, unlike those in Europe, are largely short term, with family members coming together as required to carry out operations and then disperse immediately. The complexity of tackling cross-border crime in the region is therefore derived first from it being largely a family business whose members remain loyal to one another. Second, the short-term nature of most of the operations greatly complicates security operatives' maintenance of the surveillance of criminal gangs and tracking them down.

Transnational organised crime, like the history of African borders, also has a history. Based on the account of Addo (2006), cross-border crime in the West African region began as far back as the 1960s. Groups of traders and merchants migrating to and from the ECOWAS corridor were also involved in the smuggling of goods, while organised crime syndicates smuggled mostly narcotics, humans, and small arms. Such were the means of survival for traders. Criminal syndicates usually operated a very flexible lineage-based system, involving mostly family relatives, who came together at the invitation of lead persons to carry out short-term operations. These family units were involved in cross-border criminal activities like human trafficking for the purposes of sexual and domestic exploitation. However, with the 1989 Liberian Civil War, the recruitment of mercenaries and child soldiers was added to the list of cross-border crimes. In the 1990s, cross-border criminal activities became more sophisticated, going beyond cross-border to transnational criminal activities in distant regions. Today, money laundering and transnational radicalisation have been added to the list of transnational crime, but the continent's nightmare lies not in the existence of these sophisticated criminal activities but in national governments' incapacity to secure their territories. This problem does not arise from policy, as the second section confirms, but from the lack of political will and sometimes the resources to do what is required.

Need for improved security and intelligence

In recognition of the stratified and ubiquitous nature of the continent's border challenges, African policymakers have also devised responses at various regional levels that speak to the peculiarities of each region. The content of policy documents from the African Union Border Programme (AUBP) and the ECOWAS Common Approach constitute the discourse for this section. By exploring the submissions of these policy documents, this section attempts to situate African border security problems mostly at the level of implementation rather than policy formulation, because every initiative required to keep Africa's borders secure is already in place at different sub-regional levels.

The African Union Border Programme

Efforts to establish the African Union Border Programme (AUBP) began with the defunct Organisation of African Unity (OAU) in 1964. The artificially superimposed borders designed by the colonial powers before the independence of many African countries were beginning to create many problems, generally resulting in war. Ikome (2012) explains that these problems, especially those connected with many borders' porous nature, were caused by the inappropriate demarcation and delimitation of Africa's borders by Europe between 1884 and 1885. Other issues further catalysing Africa's border security problems include a poor economy, forced displacement and migration due to war and natural disasters, and massive unemployment, leading to human flight and a brain drain. Even the threat of intra-state conflict quickly deteriorated to increased conflict between states, courtesy of the ease with which hostilities in one location spilled over to another because of the porous borders.

In July 1964, in view of this continent-wide problem, the Assembly of the Heads of State under the OAU met, resolving that states should maintain their existing borders on attaining independence, because the contrary would result in total chaos for the entire region. The 1964 meeting was followed by an ordinary session of the Council of Ministers in 1986, which adopted the use of negotiated settlements for the resolution of border conflicts between states. This was the last occasion such a continental gathering was anchored by the OAU: the African Union (AU) was created from the OAU in 2002 when a meeting in South Africa of the African heads of state agreed that Africa's borders needed to be re-demarcated and re-delimited in the interest of the continent's security, peace, and development. Following a resolution endorsing the African Union Border Programme (AUBP) and its implementation at the end of the Conference of African Ministers in Charge of Border Issues on 7 June 2007, it was ratified by the eleventh ordinary session of the Executive Council of the African Union Commission, meeting between 25 and 29 June 2007 (Diarrah, 2013).

Diarrah (2013) further outlines the key objectives the AUBP set out to achieve:

- To undertake the delimitation and demarcation of African borders in areas where this had yet to take place.
- To foster and promote the spirit of integration among Regional Economic Countries (RECs).
- To encourage capacity building in border management through research and special education.
- To create and maintain regional funds committed to cross-border initiatives.
- To boost the number of member states involved in the demarcation and delimitation of African borders.

The AUBP's objectives, totalling eleven, were compressed into three action points:

- Demarcation and delimitation,
- Promoting cross-border cooperation, and most importantly for this chapter,
- Capacity building – featuring activities ranging from training exercises and the procurement of security infrastructure to involving specialised institutions in the border security management process and research.

As this chapter addresses the theme of information technology and intelligence gathering in relation to border security management, the successes of the AUBP in this area or areas closest to it since its inception in 2007 are noteworthy:

1. The establishment of the African Union Boundary Information System (AUBIS), capturing all the vital information about the continent's borders.
2. The provision of the AUBP's member countries with both financial and technical assistance by the EU and the UN to implement the programmes' capacity-building objective.
3. Partnerships with international organisations like the German Corporation for International Cooperation (*Deutsche Gesellschaft für Internationalen Zusammenarbeit, GIZ*) in supporting the continent's ongoing demarcation and delimitation exercises.
4. Advances in the area of research – conferences and publications intended to enlighten the public on events in the continent related to the region's border issues – demarcation and delimitation, dispute resolution for border conflicts, and capacity building.

There is no doubt that the AUBP has made some strides since its inception, many of them laudable. Nevertheless, these accomplishments do not diminish the gaps in the area of implementation. One such conspicuous lacuna reveals that the implementation of the action points has been uneven. For example, more attention seems to be paid to demarcation, delimitation, and cooperation than to capacity building in the training and acquisition of technology to secure the border. There has been substantial investment by international organisations like the EU, UN, and the Organisation of American States in the demarcation and delimitation of land and maritime boundaries – more than in any other objective outlined by the AUBP. Preventive measures seem to have given way to mitigation, damage control, and reactionary approaches: most countries, especially in the West African sub-region, are accustomed to this in border security issues. To illustrate this further, it was not until the Boko Haram insurgency in northern Nigeria was at its peak that the region conceived the idea of establishing the Multi-National Joint Task Force to secure the West African sub-region's borders. Even this countermeasure's security architecture was designed largely to capture or kill terrorists instead of incorporating the interception of smugglers or contraband goods. The unevenness of the implementation of AUBP objectives is further revealed by the fact that some African regions have thrived better than others concerning border security. Compared to Southern, East, and North Africa, West Africa has the highest incidence of smuggling in contraband goods, narcotics, arms, and people. Most disturbingly, West Africa's membership of the AUBP seems to make little difference, especially to the AUBP's funding and investment in the region to help it address its peculiar border security challenges. It is likely that it was in recognition of these lapses that West Africa established the ECOWAS Common Approach as a sub-regional initiative dedicated to West Africa's border security affairs. However, it may be asked if this organisation has fared any better in the area of border security management.

The ECOWAS Common Approach principle – PROTOCOL A/P.1/5/79

ECOWAS Protocol A/P.1/5/79 concerns the principle of the Free Movement of Persons, Right of Residence, and the Right of Establishment. Although conjoined with the AUBP in the area of restoring the cultural and economic identities distorted by colonialism's arbitrary imposition of borders, the ECOWAS approach remains distinct in pursuing this goal via migration. ECOWAS Protocol A/P.1/5/79 is more emphatic about issues relating to migration than the approach of the AUBP. It seeks regional integration through the advance of mobility across the West African sub-region.

According to Adepoju, Boulton, and Levin (2006) ECOWAS Protocol A/P.1/5/79 was enacted in May 1979, exactly four years after the establishment of ECOWAS on 28 May 1975. Based on the Protocol, the right of entry, residence, and establishment is to be achieved in a transition period of fifteen years and three phases, each phase lasting five years.

Phase 1 – Right to entry and the abolition of visas (5 years)

The Protocol stipulates that ECOWAS citizens are allowed to enter the territory of fellow ECOWAS states without visas. Besides regular migrants along the ECOWAS corridor, this extends to refugees, as long as they are citizens of the ECOWAS region.

Phase 2 – The right to residency (5 years)

Regardless of their status, ECOWAS citizens have the right to live and acquire residences in their host country. Even irregular migrants have rights under this category of persons protected and enshrined in Articles 5 and 7 of the 1985 Supplementary Protocol A/SP.1/7/85.

Phase 3 – The right to establishment (5 years)

The right to establishment allows migrants within the approved timeframe to conduct income-generating ventures. It includes the right to be employed, as long as they have a residence card or permit. The Protocol also prevails on ECOWAS member states to extend the same right to migrant workers who satisfy the aforementioned condition.

LIMITATIONS OF THE PROTOCOL

- Regardless of bestowing the right of entry and residence on ECOWAS citizens, Article 4 of the protocol recognises the right of a state to deny certain persons entry in accordance with its domestic law. However, protocol is silent concerning how states defend themselves against attacks by the people they are sheltering. An example is the protracted conflict between Fulani herdsmen and many countries in the West African sub-region – Ghana, Nigeria, Mali, Burkina Faso, and Côte d'Ivoire – which have come under deadly attack from the group. This remains a potent security situation that has caused the destruction of many lives and much property. While the nomadic herders have argued their right to enter any West African country and reside with their cattle, as enshrined in the Protocol, host countries seem at a loss concerning how they can legally defend themselves. This uncertainty has raised fears in many communities, which have resorted to vigilantism, a major threat to the security of the region should this become the norm.

- As a follow-up to the previous point, the situation is further complicated by the lack of political will on the part of African leaders to act in the worsening security situation. Some leaders have also been fearful of politicising the security problem or deliberately misinterpreting the situation to serve their ethnic, religious, or political interest. Many have paid dearly, some with their lives, because of this civic betrayal.

- The problem with the ECOWAS Protocol is as much about its implementation as it is about it being complete, especially in the security area. The Protocol basically situates the integration of the region in mobility alone, understating the role of cross-border trade with its potential for accomplishing the same integration – naturally, ignoring the strength of cross-border trading results in overlooking security measures for sustaining and promoting not only trade but the security of the region. This is lacking particularly in Phase 3 of the Protocol, which deals with the right of establishment.

- Adepoju, Boulton, and Levin (2006) add to the list of limitations, stating that Protocol A/P.1/5/79 has yet to be successfully implemented. Despite the existence of monitoring committees, many countries have failed in this respect. They further add that the challenge of implementation is accompanied by the absence of an accurate and central database containing information about migrants in the region. This problem cascades down to the national level. Access is no less a challenge. Most national security agencies cannot rely on the information from a central database, simply because it is either non-existent or inaccurate. According to Ba (2006) the International Labour Organization acknowledges that information on international labour migration is characterised by both paucity and unreliability.

Best practice in securing borders

Information technology and intelligence gathering: The new face of border security management

> It is the combination of physical barriers, advanced detection technology, and manned patrols that raises the stakes for intruders, increasing the time and effort it takes to set across and influencing their decisions. When the risks become great enough, fewer people will try to cross ... but it is the technology that makes that equation possible.
>
> David Aguilar
> Former US Deputy Commissioner of Customs
> and Border Protection (CBP)

As Chavez (2015) puts it, transnational crime is a phenomenon that will continue to evolve. This explains why Naegele (2018), in recognising this reality, clearly states that the presence of infrastructure like walls and fences does very little to deter cross-border or transnational crime. This is in sharp contrast with what can be achieved with state-of-the-art technology like motion sensors, lasers, satellites, chemical detectors, x-rays, and sensor-loaded unmanned vehicles. In the event of greater threats to the border, more sophisticated technology like aerial vehicles, aerostats, and biometrics is deployed (Military and Aerospace Electronics 2019). Information technology, and the convenience and ease it brings to border security management, is also interwoven with intelligence gathering by its data collection feature and capabilities in the area of situational analysis. One such piece of state-of-the-art equipment identified by Naegele (2018) is the Remote Video Surveillance System (RVSS). This technology is designed not only to secure the border but to protect the lives of border security agents. Merely having it in the arsenal of border security agencies is enough to keep criminal elements at bay (Naegele, 2018). Modern RVSS-es are equipped with day and night cameras, loudspeakers, and floodlights. Current plans of the United States Border Patrol Agency seek to further upgrade the RVSS by making it capable of day and night surveillance from both static and kinetic positions. Cameras will also be enhanced by event resolution.

For all its far-reaching and impressive benefits in the area of data collection and cross-border security, an effective, holistic, and strategic border security response must not feature technology alone. There must be an integration of three key components – human, infrastructure, and technology. Even Artificial Intelligence (AI) has its limitations. According to Steve McCraw, a former FBI agent, it is the combination of human personnel and technology that guarantees the invincibility of security measures at the border, transforming the security equation. Improvements in border security must involve the right mix. In the words of Ronald Colburn, former Deputy Chief, US Customs and Border Protection, "without the tactical infrastructure, [the border] is too weak. Without the right number of agents, it is too weak. Without the right mix of technology, it is too weak." America's border security measures have been so effective and formidable that it can withstand the activities of drug cartels from neighbouring Mexico, whose operations, Colburn admits, are far deadlier and more ruthless than those of ISIS. The advocacy for increased technology at the border is however caveated by McCraw, who advises that technology alone is not enough. The continued maintenance and upgrade of technology is required to keep pace with security threats.

Doubtless, as a security expert, McCraw believes in the infallibility of advanced technology in stopping or mitigating the activity of criminals or irregular migrants. Unfortunately, this is not as flawless as has been presented: heightened security is accompanied by more desperate measures, particularly by daredevil migrants more than willing to counter any security measure, however advanced. As the saying goes, the greater the risk, the greater the reward. Nothing illustrates this better than the risks taken by many Africans in travelling through Agadez in the Sahara and Libya to Europe. Almost on a daily basis news comes of large numbers of African migrants drowning on their way to the Italian island of Lampedusa. The dangers in no way deter migrants – rather, they reveal the resolve of many. If they are prepared to risk the dangerous elements, what will they not do to overcome advanced technology? The solution lies in targeting what strengthens the resolve of these people.

Chavez (2015) continues the discourse on contemporary border security management, focusing on intelligence-driven border security. She states that the best model in border security management is one that synthesises intelligence gathering with law enforcement. Sadly, it has been very difficult to achieve this standard because of some of the issues this section covers. What Chavez identifies as a problem for border security is not exclusive to the United States. The lack of synergy between intelligence gathering and operations in other countries and regions of the world has deprived policymakers of the critical information they require for decision-making.

In this study, intelligence is information that measures up to the stated or understood needs of policymakers. It is information that has been collected, processed, analysed, and narrowed to meet these needs. Intelligence is intended to provide stakeholders with a better understanding of their operating context or environment. While all intelligence is information, not all information is intelligence. One of the major problems Chavez (2015) identifies in modern border security intelligence gathering is the lack of synergy and cooperation between security agencies on the one hand and security agencies and locals on the other. The United States Office of Intelligence and Investigative Liaison (OIIL) has affirmed this is a challenge, and has begun to work towards building relationships and partnerships with both sister security agencies and local and tribal investigative agencies – a model replicable in West Africa's border security problem. The backbone of information sharing and intelligence gathering is in building connections and strong networks with people at different levels. This circle encompasses what Chavez (2015) refers to as Communities of Interest (COIs) consisting of individuals living and operating on the border. Chavez uses the term Friendly Force Network (FFN) to describe this group. The FFN comprises a framework of nodes (friendly force actors) and links (the communication channel and the relationship between different actors).

Effective intelligence gathering must understand the perspective of intelligence officers, work with their perceptions and views, and align with intelligence officers' various operational demands. It is also imperative to note that the peculiarities of contemporary border security management demand that the responsibility for information collection and dissemination does not remain the exclusive preserve of intelligence officers. Chavez (2015) starts with the basic requirement for more effort and resources to be committed to the training of border security personnel in areas such as intelligence methodologies and basic intelligence functions. A more radical approach seeks to train law enforcement officers in intelligence gathering and intelligence officers in law enforcement. This mirrors the current saying in American military parlance that "every soldier is a censor". According to the United States Army's 2008 Posture Statement, "the routine observation and reporting of patterns and changes in the operating environment through interaction with the local populace are ES2 tasks now incorporated in Army doctrine".

Intelligence gathering involves data identification, collection, storage, processing, analysis, and dissemination at the strategic, operational, and tactical levels. For the optimal performance of the intelligence community, especially in the dissemination of information, the dangers of operating in a bureaucratic setting need to be understood. Luikart (2002) avers that bureaucracy can impede the operations of intelligence operators. He cautions against this, stating that the more distant the intelligence officer is from the policymaker, the less seriously his information will be taken. Faced with bureaucratic bottlenecks, the efficacy of early warning and response weakens. In addition to allowing intelligence officers unhindered and easy access to decision-makers, it is imperative that intelligence gathering is objective in the collection, processing, and analysis of data, especially as it relates to issues of border security.

Although the intelligence-gathering model and information technology discussed in this study centre mostly on US border security measures and crime at the US's northern and southern borders, many of their recommendations for best practice in the sector are applicable and replicable at various regional, sub-regional, and national levels in African border security circles. Only the political will and resources to adopt and implement contemporary best practice in information technology and intelligence gathering as they relate to policing West Africa's borders and preventing cross-border and transnational crime are lacking.

Conclusion

The discourse about West Africa's border security management is one that may linger for a while. The challenge is not the deficiency of knowledge concerning how to solve this problem confronting both Africa and Europe, nor does it concern the resources and expertise required to do what is necessary. There is already an avalanche of important stakeholder meetings discussing these themes, and donors, especially from Europe, have contributed significantly to the realising of the numerous action points raised in these sub-continental gatherings. The lack of enhanced border security management in West Africa, especially in the areas of intelligence gathering and information technology, is rooted in the region's respective governments' poor prioritisation over time.

There is no doubt that if the various governments in the region become committed to building an invincible West African border security architecture, this can be achieved in record time. However, interests at different levels continue to stall any reasonable progress that could have been made in this area. In extreme cases, some countries are actually thankful for the existence of porous borders, because it has enabled them to continue their predatory activities towards their neighbours' economies. These divergent national interests are also attended by the threats presented by structural problems such as poor economic growth, unemployment, and poverty – the catalysts and direct causes of cross-border criminal activity. The various national governments in West Africa can therefore either decide to spend minimally on preventive proactive border security measures by reducing the cases of forced and irregular migration that usually stem from poor economic growth, poverty, unemployment, and violent conflict, or spend heavily on the procurement of state-of-the-art facilities in the areas of information technology and intelligence gathering. If what this chapter sees as inevitable is the option, appropriate steps must be taken to ensure that it is done correctly and in line with the chapter's recommendations. As long as human beings need to migrate, such a phenomenon is not without its risks, which must be contained by technology and intelligence gathering.

As Africa's partners in migration and border security management, European countries have played and continue to play genuine roles in ensuring the best outcomes from cross-border migration between Europe and Africa. Their roles have included providing funds and technical assistance for development projects. It is expected that in providing aid or donating funds for development, European countries should hold African leaders to account by ensuring that these funds are strictly applied to the purposes for which they were provided. When every partner understands that there are grave consequences for the mismanagement of such funds, there is every likelihood that African leaders will adopt a more responsible approach to strategic planning and development. African countries' historic ties with Europe mean there is no doubt that the latter's global power and influence can have a positive effect on the former. European leaders can ensure that oppressive African governments that force their citizens to flee are held to account and, where necessary, punished by sanctions and isolationist policies. Europe is thus expected to remain an active and dependable partner of Africa in the migration continuum.

References

Addo, P. (2006) Cross-border criminal activities in West Africa: Options for effective responses. *KAIPTC*, Paper No. 12.

Adepoju, A., Boulton, A., and Levin, M. (2006) *Promoting Integration through Mobility*. Free Movement under ECOWAS commissioned by the UNHCR.

Ba, H. (2006) *Labour Migration Statistics in West Africa. ILO International Migration Papers No. 79E*. Geneve: International Labour Office.

Bassey, C. and Oshita, O. (2010) *Governance and Border Security in Africa*. Lagos: Malthouse Press.

Blum, C. (2014) *Cross-border Flows between Nigeria and Benin: What are the Challenges for (Human) Security?* Abuja: Friedrich-Ebert-Stiftung.

Chan, W.Y. and Womack, B. (2016) Not merely a border: Borderland, governance, development, and trans-border relations in Asia. *Asian Anthropology,* 15(2), pp. 95–103.

Chavez, G. (2015) *Intelligence-driven Border Security: A Promethean View of U.S. Border Patrol Intelligence Operations*. Masters dissertation, Naval Postgraduate School, Monterey.

Diarrah, A. (2013) *An Overview of the African Union Border Programme*. Commission of the African Union Department of Peace & Security (African Union Border Programme).

Flynn, D. (1997) "We are the border": Identity, exchange, and the State along the Benin–Nigeria border. *American Ethnologist*, 24(2), pp. 311–30.

Hartshorne, R. (1938) A survey of the boundary problems of Europe. In: C.C. Colby, ed., *Geographic Aspects of International Relations*. Chicago: University of Chicago Press Chicago, pp. 163–213.

Ikome, F. (2012) Africa's international borders as potential sources of conflict and future threats to peace and security. *Institute for Security Studies,* Paper No. 233.

Lamine, C. (2006) *ECOWAS and the Daily Events: The Present Realities of the Integration Process within the Sub-Region in Agenda 2006*. Accra: Ghana Journalist Association and Friedrich Ebert Stiftung.

Lazare Sossou-Agbo, A. (2011) *Territorial dynamics at the Beninese Nigerian border: The role of the Southeast markets*. A Paper presented at Mobile Frontiers Conference, 11th BRIT Network Meetings, and Geneva.

Luikart, K. (2002) Homeland security: Intelligence indications and warning. *Strategic Insights*, 1, 3.

Military and Aerospace Electronics (2018) The role of technology in securing the nation's borders. (online) Available at www.militaryaerospace.com/unmanned/article/16707261/the-role-of-technology-in-securing-the-nations-borders (Accessed 2 Feb. 2020).

Naegele, T. (2018) Technology is border patrol's 'Highest Need'. Retrieved from (online) Available at www.govtechworks.com-technology-is-border-patrols-highest-need. (Accessed 2 Feb. 2020).

Newman, D. (2006) The lines that continue to separate us: Borders in our "borderless" world. *Human Geography*, 30(2), pp. 1–19.

UN Secretary-General (2004), Report of the Secretary-General on ways to combat sub-regional and cross-border problems in West Africa, S/2004/200, UN Security Council, 12 March 2004.

4 Death as policy

The EU's criminalisation of solidarity with undocumented migrants

Rodrigo Bueno Lacy and Henk van Houtum

Introduction

"I didn't have the right to obey [...] They were asking me to take them back to Libya. From a legal standpoint, these were people fleeing a country at war [and] the law bars you from taking them back there". This is how Carola Rackete, the captain of the Sea-Watch 3 (a boat devoted to the rescue of drowning migrants in the Mediterranean), justified forcing her way into Lampedusa with forty migrants onboard after being arrested (Agence France-Presse, 2019). Before an Italian court ordered her release soon afterwards, she faced a three to ten-year prison sentence. Although hers has been one of the most headline-grabbing stories, the harassment that the Italian state has put her through is by no means an isolated incident. The case of Pia Klemp, another German captain facing up to twenty years in jail for saving 6,000 migrants from drowning in the Mediterranean, has stirred at least as much political furore (Klemp, 2019a). And yet, captains Rackete and Klemp are but the most well-known names in an expanding list of Europeans facing prison time as a consequence of the generosity that they showed to undocumented migrants.

Over the last five years, not only have a rising number of ship crews seen their rescue activities increasingly criminalised along the Mediterranean (Bulman, 2019), but a growing number of Europeans have been forced to endure ever more displays of harassment at the hands of EU member states, which have taken it upon themselves to expand the criminalisation of humanitarianism within the EU's internal borders (Fekete, 2018). Examples abound. Domenico Lucano, the mayor of Riace – a hamlet in southern Italy – was arrested for encouraging migrants to settle in his increasingly depopulated town (Musolino, 2018). Cédric Herrou, a French farmer, was facing up to five years in prison and a €30,000 fine for helping African migrants cross the Italian border – only recently, the Appeals Court of Lyon dropped all charges against him (New York Times 2017). Martine Landry, a seventy-three-year-old grandmother from a small town bordering Italy, was facing five years in prison and also a €30,000 fine for helping two Guinean teenagers seek asylum in France – after years of trials and appeals, she was acquitted in July 2020. (Amnesty International 2018). Spanish journalist Helena Maleno Garzón

DOI: 10.4324/9781003083726-5

was accused of colluding with human traffickers, even though she probably saved hundreds of lives by alerting the Spanish coastguard to the distress calls of migrants crossing the Mediterranean (Hernanz, 2018). In August of 2019, the criminalisation of solidarity by the EU reached a new low when it refused to share with NGOs distress signals picked up by the EU's surveillance aircraft hovering over the Mediterranean –in contravention of the Law of the Sea (De Standaard, 2019).

How did it come this far? How can we make sense of the EU's persistent criminalisation of its own citizens merely for upholding principles of non-discrimination and solidarity, while the human beings they are trying to rescue are left to drown at sea or are abandoned to agonise in the squalor of EU's migrant camps and externalised detention centres (Specia, 2019)? What to make of the cognitive dissonance that such criminalisation reveals about a political project founded to stand up collectively against extreme nationalism and violence and which still prides itself in "Drawing inspiration from the cultural, religious, and humanist inheritance of Europe, from which have developed the universal values of the inviolable and inalienable rights of the human person, freedom, democracy, equality and the rule of law..." (EU 2008)? How has the unthinkable become mundane?

In this chapter, we rely on Hannah Arendt's reflection on "the banality of evil" (1963) and Zygmunt Bauman's distrust for the deceivingly civilising ethos of modernity (1989) to explain how this recent turn in EU's policy has unfolded, why it is taking place and what its implications are for the larger project of post-war European integration. We contend that the criminalisation of life-saving NGOs along the Mediterranean is neither an anomaly nor an exception but merely the extreme manifestation of a chronic trend towards *thanatopolitics* (Agamben, 1995; 1998): the politics of death. The power to decide who lives and who dies is inherent to the deadly border architecture that the EU has put in place. It consists of a normalised, technical system of paper, iron, and camp borders that has now even lead to the criminalisation of solidarity with those who are violently and oftentimes mortally excluded by it. This, we argue, is the banality of evil of our time.

The banality of a deadly bureaucracy

As philosophers preoccupied with unravelling the self-righteous conviction in one's own civilisational superiority that – espoused by European totalitarian regimes – led to the Holocaust, both Arendt and Bauman shared the counter-intuitive suspicion that this European cataclysm was not as extraordinary an event as the incredulity of the post-war lamentations made it appear. The volatility of Arendt's view – which received a torrent of mixed criticism upon its publication – was summed up in the very phrasing of her scepticism. "The banality of evil" conceptualised the impression that Adolf Eichmann made upon her as he stood trial in Jerusalem, in 1960: he downplayed his crucial role in the genocide of the European Jewry as though it amounted to nothing more than a mere bureaucrat doing his job. The ordinariness with which

Eichmann described his part in the pitiless persecution, coldblooded transportation, and systematic German attempt to exterminate Europe's Jewish population lies at the core of Arendt's moral oxymoron. Her shrewdness was to realise that Eichmann's own account could be seen not only as a cynical defence but also as a darker yet unspoken explanation of the Shoah: not the peak of barbarism reached by a few empowered brutes that the mainstream post-war narrative had portrayed it to be but, rather, the culmination of a civilisational ideal in which German society had taken part with democratic consent and utmost enthusiasm (Langbehn and Salama, 2011).

Like Arendt, Bauman recognised in accounts such as Eichmann's more than a cowardly excuse: he saw a symptom of a chronic ailment that could not be extricated from the project of European modernity (Bauman, 1989). His critique of the Holocaust remains an indispensable complement to Arendt's astonishment about the lack of responsibility shown by people like Eichmann, who seemed able to perpetrate the worst crimes without being assaulted by their own conscience. Bauman's analysis constitutes a devastating indictment of modernity and, particularly, of its unquenchable thirst for progress. Hence, for Bauman, the Holocaust should not be comfortably disparaged as an act committed by blood-thirsty and irrational barbarians but rather as a conscious policy by a regime that prided itself in having reached a superior degree of civilisation, and for whom the Final Solution represented modern sophistication and rational progress predicated upon science – conspicuously, scientific racism and eugenics (e.g., Günther, 1934). The extermination of "lesser" people in the pursuit of a "perfect society" defined and produced according to the state-of-the-art scientific knowledge was thus not a deviation but rather a natural consequence of the Nazis' commitment to modernity – a project whose roots can be traced back to the biopolitics developed in Europe's colonial dominions and to the segregationist politics of the US (Olusoga and Erichsen, 2010; Whitman, 2017). Perhaps Bauman's critique of modernity could be encapsulated in a concise but evocative turn of phrase: *savagery with perfume*.

What amazed Arendt about the testimonies given at the trial in Jerusalem was the mundanity, civility, and normality with which such inhumanity as Eichmann's could be carried out without meeting much resistance from either those charged with executing such atrocities nor from the victims at the receiving end – Jews and non-Jews alike. Listening to Eichmann and Jewish survivors, the Holocaust seemed to her as though it had been a mere bureaucratic procedure where the Satan one imagined in charge of planning the efficient system of trains that took Jews to extermination camps was no one more diabolic than an unassuming German bureaucrat with an impeccable concern for efficiency; a man who calmed whatever moral qualms may have bothered his mind with the simple palliative thought that he was merely following orders and doing his job. On the other side of this banality were both a European Jewry and an entire European society who stood still while a succession of worsening omens descended upon them and waited patiently until six million Jews and eleven million other victims were taken to the slaughterhouse (Arendt, 1963, pp. 8–9).

Hannah Arendt's opposition to the post-war narrative of the Holocaust stirred much controversy because it seemed to downplay the evil of Nazism by characterising it as an act of "banality", a stance that gave the impression to demean the death of millions murdered in Nazi extermination camps. Bauman's scepticism about the virtues of modernity seems equally counterintuitive: how can modernity be responsible for our unparalleled technological comfort yet simultaneously the cause of humanity's most monstrous crimes? The answer, we believe, can only be found by acknowledging the uncanny complexity of humanity, which is precisely the humanist core of Arendt and Bauman's critique of modernity: by no means an exculpation of the Nazi horrors but certainly not not a demonisation either.

Arendt's and Bauman's warning regarding the singularisation of the Holocaust derives from a typical humanist preoccupation. By exoticising the Nazis and their atrocities as inimitably monstrous; their victims and their plights as uniquely misfortunate; and their experiences as a distressing but harmless past safely buried under the progress of our times, we may handicap our ability to come to terms with a gruesome but necessary realisation about our personal and collective existence: we have done this before and we might do it again, not in spite of modern technologies and cutting-edge ideologies but on the contrary – aided by them.

The paradox that Arendt and Bauman identified thus lies in the mirage of refinement that modernity conjures up through its baffling technological breakthroughs: their complexity might disguise increasingly sophisticated brutality under the cloak of progress, thus allowing savagery to pass for morality. This is the warning: evil is neither an unusual human disposition nor is it self-evidently curtailed by progress. Should we remain anesthetised by the comfortably deceiving allure of modernity's superficial sophistication and inexorable advancement, we may risk falling prey to the overpowering course of history and become such abysmal monsters or such hopeless victims as those we today believe confined to herky-jerky, black-and-white films of the past – without even noticing it.

EU's train wreck in slow motion

What do we see when we examine the deadly politics of the EU through the sharp lens that Arendt and Bauman crafted for us? In order to understand the EU's criminalisation of humanitarian aid we need to zoom out – just like Arendt and Bauman did – and focus on what made this extreme not only possible but "normal" (van Houtum and Bueno Lacy, 2017). What we take away from their perspective is an invaluable scepticism for an uncritical faith in one's own moral rectitude that is supported by an unfaltering trust in history's indomitable progress (Popper, 1966). Such faith contains a latent violence for the imagined misfits – those who, as a matter of choice or fortune, have been either unable or unwilling to seamlessly integrate into an imagined idealisation of modernity, progress, and prosperity; those whose unusual customs, phenotype, politics, or any other expression of uniqueness might challenge established archetypes of order, proper behaviour, cleanliness, and perfection. The rationalistic ethos that relies on the standardisation, homogenisation, and readability of space, population, and culture (Scott, 1998) is threatened by those who, by the very aesthetics of their cultural richness, countercultural idiosyncrasy, or political nonconformism might tarnish the sense of accomplishment of a society that has learned to see in such eccentricity a burden holding it back from the mirage of modern paradise.

We suggest that the EU's rationalisation and normalisation of the extreme – to criminalise solidarity with those that are dying because of its own policy – most manifestly began with the introduction of Schengen in 1985: particularly, with the asymmetrical rights it started to dish out among EUropeans and non-Europeans (van Houtum and Bueno Lacy, 2019, 2020). This distinction manifested itself as policy in 2001, when the common list of nationalities requiring a visa to enter Schengen was introduced. In the eyes of the EU, the establishment of this pre-border of paper was an almost logical necessity given the introduction of a common EUropean external border. However, it represents a watershed in the history of European integration: the EU collectively started to make a sharp distinction ("the Schengen list") between countries whose citizens require a visa to enter the EU (largely Muslim and less affluent countries) and those exempted from it (largely rich OECD members and a few exceptions in South America and Asia) (van Houtum, 2010; van Houtum and Bueno Lacy, 2020). This discrimination is based on a nativist principle otherwise expressly forbidden by fundamental rights laws in all EU member states and which runs against the EU's own Lisbon Treaty and accession (Copenhagen) criteria. The implication of this *paper border* – the most impenetrable of all – is enormous: it relies on border controls which have been outsourced to faraway embassies in third countries, which means that the EU has almost entirely closed off legal migration channels for most of the world (Bueno Lacy and van Houtum, 2013; van Houtum and Bueno Lacy, 2020). For the most part, citizens of these countries can only enter the EU irregularly – e.g., by overstaying their visas, through smugglers, or by crossing borders in other illicit ways. In other words, the criminalisation of solidarity is in fact already built into the very architecture of the Schengen list of 2001. Specifically, the rampant criminalisation of solidarity with migrants is even enshrined in an EU Facilitation Directive against "illegal immigration" that foresees no exception for humanitarian activities (Directive 2002/90/EC) – a legal blind spot that the EU Commission has stubbornly resisted to amend (Bayer, 2019; FRA, 2018).

Without a doubt, deadliness is the most shamefully visible consequence of this paper border architecture. According to the latest estimates, over 40,000 people have died trying to reach the EU since the Schengen area was established (McIntyre and Rice-Oxley, 2018; Laine, 2020; UNITED, 2020). This makes the EU the deadliest border on the planet. Of all the deaths at the world's borders, seventy-five percent of them occur along the borderlands of the EU. Alarmingly, the EU's comfort with the predictable production of death suggests a border governmentality that conforms to what Achille Mbembe called *necropolitics* (2003) and to what Giorgio Agamben termed *thanatopolitics* (1998): the politics to decide who lives and who dies as well as how and why.

The external paper b/ordering and othering by the EU, which we argue is the first EU border, has created a cat-and-mouse game between smugglers and border guards that has resulted in the fortification of a second – ever higher – *iron* border, by which we mean all the land fences, razor wire, and other physical hurdles intended to prevent undocumented border crossings at the territorial limits of the EU; as well as surveillance patrols along the EU's maritime borders aimed at stopping undocumented migrants from reaching the EU – whose ever more callous violence has been normalised over the last decades (van Houtum, 2010; van Houtum and Lucassen, 2016; Howden, Fotiadis, and Campbell, 2020; Edwards, 2020; van Houtum and Bueno Lacy, 2020). Over the past few years, the iron border has even been increasingly pushed away from the actual perimeters of the EU, into northern Africa and eastern Europe. The EU is willingly and consciously financing the efforts by authoritarian regimes beyond its borders, thus effectively hiring them as the EU's gatekeepers of undocumented migration to the EU. These "Pilate deals" – for they evoke Pontius Pilate's infamous hand-washing, which he used as a symbolic gesture to exculpate himself from yielding to a riotous mob's demand to crucify an innocent man (Matthew 27 in Coogan, 2010, p. 1787) – offshore the EU's responsibility for the well-being of asylum seekers to regimes that employ inhumane methods to deter their migration to the EU in exchange for money – e.g., Libya since 2003 and Turkey since 2016 (Bialasiewicz, 2012; Amnesty International 2017). As Turkey's prime minister's recent threat to "open the gates" – i.e., let migrants travel unimpeded to the EU unless it pays more money to Turkey – has made clear (Wesel, 2019), Pilate deals are a strategic liability, for they make the EU vulnerable to blackmail by erratic autocrats. Ultimately, the effect of outsourced border controls is thus, counterproductively, the surrender of responsibility for one's own jurisdiction, the jeopardy of one's own values, and thus, the sell-out of one's own sovereignty.

The third bordering strategy that the EU has been developing and normalising as part of its border architecture is its post-border that could be termed *camp border*: the collection of distant and isolating waiting chambers that the EU's cordoned societies have designed to "warehouse" surplus migrants who have managed to overcome its paper and iron borders (van Houtum and Bueno Lacy, 2020). According to Agamben (1998, p. 9), the camp is "the space that is opened when the state of exception begins to become the rule" – where the rule of law is replaced by unpredictable despotism. All across the EU, these spaces of exception have become the dominant policy to manage undocumented migrants, whose scarce political representation leaves them vulnerable to languish far away from the scrutiny of EU societies and thus prevents them from holding accountable those responsible for such abuses. The new camps of the EU have become the most gruesome confirmation of Étienne Balibar's posit about Europe's borders which – as he famously remarked – far from disappearing, are multiplying, yet becoming ever more detached from self-evident political borders (Balibar, 1998, p. 220).

In the archipelago of detention camps that EU member states have set up along the Mediterranean, the rights granted by their liberal democratic constitutions no longer apply to a diverse collection of Muslims, Middle Easterners, and Africans who EU member states have deemed unworthy of the rule of law's protection. The EU is taking no responsibility for contributing to the psychological and physical devastation of imprisoned migrants, which undermines its own legal commitment against "torture and inhuman or degrading treatment or punishment" (Article 4 of the EU Charter of Fundamental Rights, see: EU, 2000). There are reports of sweeping human rights violations in Greece, Chios, Samos, and Lesvos, the latter of which hosts the infamous Moria camp, which features a chamber of horrors so grim that it is astonishing as well as painfully revealing why the EU is not doing everything in its power to stop this border violence (Lucas, Ramsay, and Keen, 2019). As Bauman concluded in his critique of modernity, "Responsibility is silenced once proximity is eroded; it may eventually be replaced with resentment once the fellow human subject is transformed into an Other" (Bauman, 1989, p. 179). Solidarity – a concern for the Other based not on charity but on a sense of oneness – requires physical or spiritual proximity and is, in contrast to callousness, undermined by social distance. EU populations see neither the suffering nor the wars nor the economic ruin nor the climatic pressures that push migrants to the EU: they do not see their bodies and minds rotting away in prisons funded by their own taxes either.

What is striking about the banality of the EU's border evil is that, unlike border regimes that show no qualms about espousing outright racism as the rationale for their stringent migration policies (e.g., the US), the EU keeps championing its staunch defence of human dignity and life as the moral imperatives driving its increasingly merciless b/ordering and othering governmentality (van Houtum and van Naerssen, 2002). The EU makes as if its glaringly anti-humanitarian policies should in fact be seen as part of a higher civilisational ideal. Yet, by co-opting the language of humanitarianism and human rights to legitimise an increasingly coldblooded migration policy (Cuttitta, 2017), the EU has exposed the banality of its alleged humanist ethos. Against this backdrop, it is telling that one of the first decisions of Ursula von der Leyen – the recently appointed president of the EU Commission – has been to create the position of "vice-president for Protecting our European Way of Life". Many commentators have widely denounced this as a "shameful concession to the continent's far-right" (Plenel, 2019). Unsurprisingly, the position was celebrated as an ideological victory by French far-right politician Marine Le Pen (Euractiv, 2019; Stone, 2019).

Moreover, by hollowing out its own foundational principles, the EU is counterproductively feeding the authoritarian nationalism that it was established to keep at bay. Through the creation of a border system that forces non-EU migrants into destitution and violence as well as mental and bodily decay, the EU is fuelling the imaginations of anti-immigrant authoritarian parties across the EU, whose views on immigration are influenced by conspiracy theories such as the "white replacement theory", which postulates that primitive immigrants threaten Europe's way of life (Camus, 2012). Paradoxically, the normalisation, even glorification, of Europe's way of life – a floating and malleable signifier – is legitimising the banalisation of increasingly atrocious policies and discourse which do undermine the EU's way of life as stipulated in its foundational treaties and as conceived throughout its postwar experience. We would argue, therefore, that through its own bordering strategies and the ethno-exclusionary discourses that they promote, the EU is hollowing out the very solidarity which is needed to safeguard the rule of law and human rights that it prides itself to be founded upon. This is the auto-immunity of the EU's border policy which we have discussed elsewhere (van Houtum and Bueno Lacy, 2020).

We are living through momentous times: we are witnessing now what would have been unthinkable three decades ago, when the EU was established. Today, the EU's policies are helping smugglers line their pockets and laying fertile ground for the proliferation of human rights violations and death among the most vulnerable migrants. Incomprehensibly, these policies have simultaneously weakened the EU by making it vulnerable to geopolitical blackmail by countries like Turkey and Libya while reducing its overall control over its own borders. Insidiously, this border regime is breeding a political culture that teaches division and antagonism while glorifying the criminalisation of the most noble feelings as progress.

The criminalising hubris across the EU is the latest tweak to a border architecture that aspires to fence off the "European way of life" at all costs – even at the expense of the entire post-war project of European integration. It is hard to conceive how this criminalisation of solidarity could teach EU citizens anything other than an aversion for helping others in distress – a venerable sentiment that across the EU is becoming wrong, illegal, and punishable. The Orwellian connotations of this EU border governmentality are as unmistakeable as they are foreboding: SOLIDARITY IS CRIME. How close we are to an EU bureaucracy and political establishment that increasingly exculpates the inhumane and deadly border regime they have erected themselves by claiming that they are just fulfilling "the will of the people" or that they are merely "doing their job".

Conclusion

The EU, this once-most-promising and peaceful project of liberal democracy and solidarity, is experiencing an unprecedented authoritarian turn driven by the patchwork of increasingly illiberal migration policies that have been put in place to manage the arrival of higher numbers of migrants. However, rather than migrants – the all-purpose punching bags in contemporary EU political discourse – the pressure forcing this ever more careless border approach is being exerted by the EU's own inability to articulate a response that is able to host and distribute migrants in a fair way among its member states and in a manner that honours "the universal values of the inviolable and inalienable rights of the human person, freedom, democracy, equality, and the rule of law" enshrined in the Lisbon Treaty (EU, 2007). Given the proximity of the mass horrors inflicted by World War II as well as the unquestionable prosperity that the EU enjoys when compared to the rest of the world, one would believe that the EU's commitment to solidarity, humanism, and peace is unwavering. Yet, it has become increasingly harder to believe in the sincerity – or viability – of the project that the EU claims to embody when, under our very eyes, its leaders are willingly advocating a policy that punishes those who strive to rescue people in need along the ever more perilous borderlands of an EU that, inexplicably, simultaneously aspires to be perceived as a beacon of peace and lawfulness.

We have identified three borders and several border strategies that typify the growing despotism characterising the border policy the EU has developed since Schengen was established in 1985. This border regime makes it impossible, for a large part of the citizens of the world, to travel to the EU legally and safely, thus creating the legal figure of the "undocumented migrant" who in turn is shaped by the paper border, the iron border, and what we have termed the "camp border". The paper borders refer to the lack of legal channels – either inside the EU or beyond its borders – that prevent potential visitors, students, workers, and asylum seekers from fulfilling their ambition to migrate to the EU with the predictability and safety that only travel documents allow. The iron border refers to the actual material obstacles that attempt to passively or actively stop migrants from reaching the EU, i.e., (externalised) border controls, fences, barbed wire, an ever more militarised EU coast guard (i.e., Frontex), and the *purposefully* unsupervised waters of the Mediterranean. The EU's border camps along the Mediterranean constitute perhaps the most worrying biopolitical contraption since the second World War: a rational decision to cause the psychological impairment of undocumented migrants by housing them in spatially segregated camps sometimes so horrifying that migrants will either fall into a state of psychological disrepair so debilitating that they will either be persuaded to go back home "voluntarily" or simply dispose of themselves by committing suicide. Either way, their unenviable fates are intended as a warning to future undocumented migrants. Meanwhile, the location of these detention camps in remote Mediterranean islands keeps the agony of their unlawfully detained prisoners away from public view, thus securing unaccountability for the very possible violation of EU and public international law – with the additional advantage of staving off the outburst of political outrage against the EU.

This tripartite border architecture of pre-borders of paper, *in-situ* borders of iron, and a post-border consisting of camps that the EU has developed over time has become an inhuman system of deterrence that refuses to recognise its violence (van Houtum and Bueno Lacy, 2020). Yet, in spite of all the EU's efforts to deflect blame for its criminalisation of solidarity with refugees, its increasingly appalling treatment of them has grabbed so many headlines over the last few years that the EU's illiberal and authoritarian inclinations are now for everyone to see – particularly for member states' governments attempting to subvert the liberal, democratic, and universalist foundations of the EU (Zakaria, 1997). One could even argue that the lack of solidarity with migrants has created an autoimmune reaction: the solidarity that the EU has criminalised with refugees has also undermined solidarity among its member states, particularly by eroding the sanctity of the rule of law and the discourse and practice of open borders on which the EU rests (van Houtum and Bueno Lacy, 2020). It is worth remembering that, at the peak of the – miscalled – "refugee crisis" in the EU, asylum applications doubled from 430,000 in 2013 to over a million in 2015. Although this was an unusual event, it precipitated a trend that, only five years later, has changed the political landscape across the EU so dramatically that the end of the EU is, for the first time, conceivable. Not only do voters across the EU seem adamant to keep putting in power people who show an overt xenophobia towards the usual suspects of traditional European racism but Viktor Orbán has exploited the latest COVID-19 pandemic to turn Hungary into the first de facto dictatorship in the EU – and Poland seems poised to follow the same path (Berendt 2020). As if these authoritarian trends were not enough, there is a growing confidence noticeable across the EU's diverse political arenas to either resuscitate ideas from entirely discredited fields like scientific racism or to paraphrase fascist and national-socialist politicians from the 1930s (Besnier, 2018; Petrović, 2018). Against this backdrop, there is at least one invaluable lesson that we can take by heeding Arendt and Bauman's warning: it is urgent to rein in the carelessness of those who feel their safety guaranteed by a comfortable position outside of history – as if hardship and suffering were confined to images in sepia documentaries and otherworldly stories in dusty books.

Having said that, there seem to be sparks of hope. One of the most striking are the charges presented against the EU before the International Criminal Court (ICC) for crimes against humanity (Bowcott, 2019). This is both a shameful yet hopeful indictment of a political entity that, by its own admission, was built with the purpose of creating peace and prosperity in Europe through the cultivation of universal rights and freedoms. Although the EU's supranational and national bureaucracies have veered off into uncharted waters, hope is being kept alive by courageous displays of solidarity stemming from the European population. Fortunately, there are women like Carola Rackete, Pia Klemp, and many other European citizens willing to challenge the unconscionable laws that make it punishable to help undocumented migrants. These courageous Europeans are the spearhead of the moral revolt that will be needed to overpower the deadly return of history to which the EU's political elites seem to be sleepwalking us into: our conformity with the most contemptible cruelty has become so internalised that the inherent authoritarianism on which it is predicated and the apartheid it is factually normalising seem to go largely unnoticed. This banality of evil is perhaps epitomised by the opportunistic medals that EU leaders grant to those who assist the victims of their own border policies. Such is the case of the medal that Anne Hidalgo, the mayor of Paris, awarded to Pia Klemp: not only a gesture too small to honour the tragedy of preventable deaths that the German captain was trying to mitigate but also a token of utter hypocrisy coming from one of the states bearing much of the responsibility for this deadly border policy (Chevallereau, 2019). We bring this contribution to a closure drawing on the words of Klemp herself:

> Madame Hidalgo, you want to award me a medal for my solidarian action in the Mediterranean Sea, because our crews "work to rescue migrants from difficult conditions on a daily basis". At the same time your police is stealing blankets from people that you force to live on the streets, while you raid protests and criminalize people that are standing up for rights of migrants and asylum seekers. You want to give me a medal for actions that you fight in your own ramparts. I am sure you won't be surprised that I decline the medaille Grand Vermeil […] Paris, I'm not a humanitarian. I am not there to "aid". I stand with you in solidarity. We do not need medals. We do not need authorities deciding about who is a "hero" and who is "illegal". In fact they are in no position to make this call, because we are all equal […] What we need are freedom and rights. It is time we call out hypocrite honorings and fill the void with social justice. It is time we cast all medals into spearheads of revolution!
>
> (Klemp, 2019b)

References

Agamben, G. (1995) *Homo sacer*. Turin: Einaudi.

Agamben, G. (1998) *Quel che resta di Auschwitz*. Turin: Bollati Boringhieri.

Agence France-Presse. (2019) Captain defends her decision to force rescue boat into Italian port. *The Guardian*, 30 June 2019.

Amnesty International. (2017) Libya's dark web of collusion abuses against Europe-bound refugees and migrants (online). Available at: https://www.amnesty.org/download/Documents/MDE1975612017ENGLISH.PDF (Accessed 14 Feb 2020).

Amnesty International. (2018) France: Acquittal of pensioner for showing compassion to children shows solidarity is not a crime (online). Available at: www.amnesty.org/en/latest/news/2018/07/france-acquittal-of-pensioner-for-showing-compassion-to-children-shows-solidarity-is-not-a-crime/ (Accessed 12 Mar. 2020).

Arendt, H. (1963) *Eichmann in Jerusalem: A Report on the Banality of Evil*. London: Penguin Classics.

Balibar, E. (1998) The borders of Europe. In: P. Cheah and B. Robbins, eds., *Cosmopolitics: Thinking and Feeling beyond the Nation*. Minneapolis, MN: University of Minnesota Press, pp. 216–33.

Bauman, Z. (1989) *Modernity and the Holocaust*. Cambridge: Polity Press.

Bayer, L. (2019) Timmermans to Warsaw and Budapest: Rule of law fight isn't over. *Politico*, 16 Sep 2019.

Berendt, J. (2020). E.U. court rules poland must suspend disciplinary panel for judges. New York Times, 8 Apr 2020.

Besnier, L. (2018) *The Past in the Present: On the Role of Cultural Memory in the Rise of Radical Right Populist Parties in Germany and Italy* (master's thesis). Leiden: Leiden University.

Bialasiewicz, L. (2012) Off-shoring and out-sourcing the borders of EUrope: Libya and EU border work in the Mediterranean. *Geopolitics,* 17(4), pp. 843–66.

Bowcott, O. (2019. ICC submission calls for prosecution of EU over migrant deaths. *The Guardian*, 3 June 2019.

Bueno Lacy, R. and van Houtum, H. (2013) Europe's Border disorder. *E-International Relations*, 5 Dec 2013.

Bulman, M. (2019) Hundreds of Europeans including firefighters and priests arrested for "solidarity" with refugees, data shows. *The Independent*, 18 May 2019.

Camus, R. (2012) *Le Grand Remplacement*. Self-published.

Chevallereau, S. (2019) Pia Klemp, capitaine du bateau Sea Watch, refuse la médaille de la Ville de Paris. *Le Parisien*, 20 Aug 2019.

Coogan, M. D. (2010) *The New Oxford Annotated Bible*. Oxford: Oxford University Press.

Cuttitta, P. (2017) Delocalization, humanitarianism, and human rights: The Mediterranean border between exclusion and inclusion. *Antipode*, 50(3), pp. 783–803.

De Standaard. (2019) Europese Unie weigert nood–signalen te delen met ngo's. *De Standaard*, 7 Sep 2019.

Edwards, M. (2020) "A bloody method of control": the struggle to take down Europe's razor wire walls. *The Guardian*, 13 May 2020.

EU. (2000) Charter of Fundamental Rights of the European Union. European Parliament, 18 Dec 2000.

EU. (2007) Treaty of Lisbon. EUR-Lex, 7 Dec 2007.

EU. (2008). Consolidated version of the Treaty on European Union. *Official Journal*, 115, pp. 0013–004.

Euractiv. (2019) Le Pen hails EU "way of life" job as victory on path to Élysée. *Euractiv*, 16 Sep 2019.

Fekete, L. (2018) Migrants, borders and the criminalisation of solidarity in the EU. *Race & Class*, 59(4), pp. 65–83.

FRA. (2018) Fundamental rights considerations: NGO ships involved in search and rescue in the Mediterranean and criminal investigations – 2018. *FRA* (Oct).

Günther, H. F. K. (1934) *Die Nordische Rasse bei den Indogermanen Asiens*. München: JF Lehmanns.

Hernanz, C. (2018) When helping a refugee gets you threatened with a prison sentence. *VICE*, 8 June 2018.

Howden, D., Fotiadis, A., and Campbell, Z. (2020) Revealed: The great European refugee scandal. *The Guardian*, 12 Mar 2020.

Klemp, P. (2019a) Why I fight for solidarity. *TEDxBerlin*, 20 Aug (online) Available at: www.ted.com/talks/pia_klemp_why_i_fight_for_solidarity (Accessed 12 Feb 2020).

Klemp, P. (2019b) The city of Paris is awarding Pia Klemp the Medaille Grand Vermeil. *Facebook*. (online) Available at: www.facebook.com/GlocalRoots/posts/the-city-of-paris-is-awarding-pia-klemp-the-medaille-grand-vermeilthis-is-what-t/1421407694689066/ (Accessed 22 Mar 2020).

Laine, J. P. (2020) Ambiguous Bordering Practices at the EU's edges. In: A. Bissonnette and É. Vallet, eds., *Borders and border walls: In-security, symbolism, vulnerabilities*. London: Routledge, pp. 69–87.

Langbehn, V. and Salama, M., eds. (2011) *German Colonialism. Race, the Holocaust and Postwar Germany*. New York: Columbia University Press.

Lucas, A., Ramsay, P., and Keen, L. (2019) *No End in Sight: The Mistreatment of Asylum Seekers in Greece*. Refugee Rights Europe. (online) Available at: www.humanrights360.org/no-end-in-sight-the-mistreatment-of-asylum-seekers-in-greece/ (Accessed 2 Oct 2019).

Mbembe, A. (2003) Necropolitics. *Public Culture*, 15(1), pp.11–40.

McIntyre, N. and Rice-Oxley, M. (2018) It's 34,361 and rising: How the list tallies Europe's migrant body count. *The Guardian*, 20 June (online) Available at: www.theguardian.com/world/2018/jun/20/the-list-europe-migrant-bodycount (Accessed 21 June 2018).

Musolino, L. (2018) Mimmo Lucano, arrestato il sindaco di Riace che accoglie i migranti: "Favoriva l'immigrazione clandestina". *Il Fatto Quotidiano*, 2 Oct (online) Available at: tinyurl.com/y4y3go8d (Accessed 21 June 2018).

New York Times. (2017) French farmer who aided migrants is given suspended fine. New York Times, 10 Feb 2017.

Olusoga, D. and Erichsen, C. (2010) *The Kaiser's Holocaust*. London: Faber and Faber.

Petrović, N. (2018) Divided national memories and EU crises: how Eurosceptic parties mobilize historical narratives. *Innovation: The European Journal of Social Science Research*, 32(3), pp. 363–84.

Plenel, E. (2019) Cette Europe qui nous fait honte. *Mediapart*. (online) Available at: www.mediapart.fr/journal/international/120919/cette-europe-qui-nous-fait-honte (Accessed 2 Feb 2020).

Popper, K. (1966) *The Open Society and Its Enemies*. Princeton, NJ: Princeton University Press.

Scott, J. C. (1998) *Seeing Like a State*. New Haven, CT: Yale University Press.

Specia, M. (2019) Hundreds of migrants stranded in Mediterranean in standoff over aid ships. *The New York Times*, 12 Aug 2019.

Stone, J. (2019) EU accused of adopting "fascist rhetoric" with new Commissioner for Protecting Our European Way of Life to oversee immigration policy. *The Independent*, 11 Sep 2019.

UNITED. (2020) Death by Policy – Time for Change! [online] Available at: http://unitedagainstrefugeedeaths.eu/wp-content/uploads/2014/06/ListofDeathsActual.pdf [Accessed 1 Nov. 2020].

van Houtum, H. (2010) Human blacklisting: the global apartheid of the EU's external border regime. *Environment and Planning D: Society and Space*, 28(6), pp. 957–76.

van Houtum, H. and Bueno Lacy, R. (2017) The political extreme as the new normal: the cases of Brexit, the French state of emergency and Dutch Islamophobia. *Fennia*, 195(1), pp. 85–101.

van Houtum, H. and Bueno Lacy, R. (2020) The autoimmunity of the EU's deadly b/ordering regime; Overcoming its paradoxical paper, iron and camp borders. *Geopolitics*, 25(3), pp. 706–33.

van Houtum, H. and Lucassen, L. (2016) *Voorbij Fort Europa, een nieuwe visie op migratie*. Amsterdam: Atlas/Contact.

van Houtum, H. and Van Naerssen, T. (2002) Bordering, ordering and othering. *Tijdschrift voor economische en sociale geografie*, 93(2), pp. 125–36.

Wesel, B. (2019) Opinion: EU must react to pressure from Turkey. *Deutsche Welle*, 15 Sep 2019.

Whitman, J. Q. (2017) Hitler's American Model: The United States and the Making of Nazi Race Law. Princeton: Princeton University Press.

Zakaria, F. (1997) The rise of illiberal democracy. *Foreign Affairs*, 76(6), pp. 22–43.

5 The Euro–African frontier regime between humanitarian reason and the security imperative

Anna Casaglia

Introduction

Since it has been recognised that we are not witnessing the end of the state and the beginning of a borderless world, scholars in political geography have analysed how borders have become more subtly pervasive, dislocated, embodied, and even dangerous. Furthermore, outside the European academic context, borders have become a topic of debate, especially as a consequence of the apparent increase of migration fluxes in the "refugee crisis". The bordering space of the Mediterranean, simultaneously portrayed as fragile and impassable, has become a symbol of migration and walling, and of one of the main outposts of European security against Africa. It has been charged with discourses and politics regarding its control directed at avoiding illegal crossing and terrorism, as well as smuggling and the death of migrants at sea. The war against smuggling networks has especially permeated the security discourse, been invoked to legitimise the changes applied to the patrolling of the Mediterranean, and accompanied the humanitarian effort of various actors seeking to rescue people in distress at sea.

At the same time, the association of asylum and migration with security issues has become increasingly solidified. This has resulted in a shift in border management, in the composition of actors involved in control procedures, and in the practices and understandings of security. As was pointed out almost twenty years ago, immigration has been placed within "a continuum of threats and general unease" (Bigo, 2002, p. 63) that has resulted in a convergence of the meanings of international and domestic security. Although the security–migration nexus has been widely analysed and discussed in the academic literature, in-depth analyses of the local contexts in which the discursive connection between migration and security is made and acted on or challenged are still largely lacking. The literature discussing the securitisation of migration has grown with the phenomenon. It has focused on the performative and discursive character of this association. Representations of and narratives on migration, both in the media and in the political discourse, increasingly support an idea of international mobility that is connected with threats to national cultural, economic, and social security.

DOI: 10.4324/9781003083726-6

The definition of threat in relation to migration is central to the adoption of security answers that are shaped according to the kind of danger that is faced. There are certainly links between security and migration. For example, international migration can be a consequence of other security issues such as human rights violations, ethnic conflict, and civil war. It can be related to threats such as xenophobia and racial violence, not to mention the human security concerns regarding migrants' journeys and the risks they take when crossing undocumented. However, such risks tend to be seldom discussed outside scholars' critical work. The common arguments sustaining the migration–security nexus are often grounded in the smuggling industry, the number of people moving (implying discursive metaphors of natural disasters), difficulties in controlling and managing flows (pointing to the legitimation of violent measures and the development of sophisticated control practices), and the risks represented by migrants themselves, who are considered potential threats. This definition of the migration–security nexus also determines the idea we have of different migrant typologies because they are generally represented as belonging to a category of dangerous economic migrants or vulnerable refugees.

This contribution seeks to explore how the discursive connection between migration and security, which creates categories of migrants and migration, is also produced and reproduced by humanitarian border action. The concept of vulnerability is explored to unveil its performativity in creating a hierarchy among migrants based on their deserving of safe access to mobility and enhancing the biopolitical governmentality of migration. It is our contention that humanitarian action, by often working through a logic of deservingness, can sustain a securitising bordering model that categorises people along different grades of vulnerability that create a selective filter.

Starting from a critical understanding of the humanitarian border (Walters, 2011), this paper focuses on the Mediterranean frontier of the Euro–African border, presenting the case of humanitarian corridors established by Italian non-profit and religious organisations with the Italian government. Humanitarian corridors, with the explicit aim of deterring dangerous journeys and combating trafficking, grant legal entry to Italian territory with a humanitarian visa to people in "conditions of vulnerability". These projects have direct consequences for migrants, because they constitute a safe way of migrating but also imply a process of selectivity, and therefore of categorisation of people according to their "deservingness" to be part of the programme. This process also involves the risk of a patronising attitude on the part of the northern countries of the west that can also conceal migrants' political subjectivities by denying the understanding of mobility as a practice of resistance. Furthermore, "humanitarian reason" (Fassin, 2012) creates new hierarchies of rights based on different forms of vulnerability.

Despite the undeniable utility and importance of such a programme, the aim of this contribution is to relate this and other forms of humanitarianism to a specific discourse that is emerging around the question of "who deserves a good life". It uses the literature on humanitarianism and Butler's arguments on vulnerability (2012) to stress the problematics inherent in this discourse.

To this end, and based on research and interviews conducted in 2018 and 2019[1], I will critically analyse humanitarian corridors, showing their potential in challenging current border management and adding scrutiny of the performative character of the concept of vulnerability in relation to the biopolitical categorisation of people on the move. The chapter also exposes the entangled relationship between humanitarian actions and security, adding to the existing literature on military humanitarianism and the securitisation of aid.

Humanitarian action within a securitised space

This contribution is part of a more general attempt to propose an understanding of borders as technologies for the articulation of various controls and managements of flows, which are always in a tension between inclusion and exclusion. It is also important to focus on the increasing embodiment of borders as devices of control by those who cross or attempt to cross them, considering the body as "the most elementary space" (Balibar and De Genova, 2018, p. 752) where border technology applies.

The literature of border studies has long underlined the violence inherent in current border management, and the increasing risks associated with the attempt to cross a border undocumented from the global south to wealthier countries (Jones, 2016). Several studies have shown that this is reflected in everyday practices and procedures. They analyse the "paper" walls constituted by the hardening of visa systems, which results in major mobility inequalities (Bigo and Guild, 2005; Glouftsios, 2018; Laine, 2018). They denounce how the security complex implies a boosting of the smuggling business (Nadig, 2002), showing the unacceptable risks taken by migrants in "fatal journeys" (Topak, 2014; De León, 2015; Davies, Isakjee, and Dhesi, 2017; Heller and Pezzani, 2017). They also reason on the dangers of growing xenophobic and racist discourses advanced by right-wing populist leaders in Europe and other western countries (Casaglia et al., 2020).

Recent changes in the management of migration in the context of the European Union have created new sites for people's containment and forms of control. They have also created different ways and logics to contain migrants (Mitchell and Sparke, 2018; Tazzioli, 2020; Tazzioli and De Genova, 2020). Besides the externalisation of the control of external frontiers in neighbouring countries – defined as bio-political re-territorialisation (Vaughan-Williams, 2008) – the EU's countries of arrival have established places and practices related to search and rescue (SAR) operations in the Mediterranean, the welcoming and filtering of arriving migrants, their containment while awaiting recognition as refugees, or their detainment while awaiting deportation.

A consistent number of academic studies has examined the humanitarian effort that has responded to this exacerbation of border securitisation, showing the importance of different kinds of initiative taken by NGOs, activists, and other non-institutional actors to prevent the death of migrants, ease their journeys, and advance the quest for a universal right to mobility (Jones, 2019). At the same time, the problematisation of such efforts has shown their grievous paradoxical effects in relation to migration discourses and narratives. The critique of what has been defined as the humanitarian border regime has developed around the unexpected outcomes of humanitarian interventions related to the depoliticisation of border management (Walters, 2011) and governmental deresponsibilisation (Cuttitta, 2017).

This humanitarian response "crystallizes as a way of governing this new and alarming situation, and tries to compensate for the social violence embodied in the logic of controlling migration" (Walters, 2011, pp. 138–9), ultimately making it acceptable. The very idea of the humanitarian border and what this concept represents beyond the obvious usefulness of an intervention that has the aim of saving lives in danger can have the unforeseen effect of depoliticising the border itself and the migration question. Cuttitta (2017) explains how the depoliticisation process consists of the tendency of institutional actors to deny the purely political character of policies, presenting them as necessary and neutral processes.

By focusing on relief efforts, humanitarian intervention assumes that the border is a dangerous place where crossing can be fatal and acts within this framework, somehow accepting it. The political implications of the border are further overshadowed by the technical aspects concerning search and rescue methods, the definition of each country's territorial waters, the identification of safe ports, the reception quotas of the various countries, the Dublin protocol, and so on.

With respect to this debate it is certainly interesting to note that the depoliticisation of border management processes results in depriving the migrants who move across them of their political essence. One of the fundamental problems in examining migration undoubtedly concerns the representation in public, political, and media discourse, which presents migrants as either victims (of the conflicts from which they flee, smugglers, the sea, trafficking, etc.) or criminals – refugees entitled to seek asylum or dangerous economic migrants – and again as divided into categories according to their geographical origin, and therefore associated with conflicts and specific narratives and stereotypes. In each of these cases, the result is the categorisation of people and a process of distancing: no importance is given to the individualities, paths, motivations, and projects that impel migrants to leave and choose a destination. If the risk of depoliticisation adds to this process of homogenisation, the result is the total negation of migrants as political subjects and mobility as a practice of resistance.

In the Mediterranean space, the intertwining of securitisation aimed at combating smuggling and humanitarian aid aimed at saving lives is giving place to what has recently been defined as military humanitarianism (Garelli and Tazzioli, 2019). This original migration management logic is creating new geographies of containment because it pushes migrants' spatial containment further from Europe – that is, by bringing rescued people back to Libya – and it depoliticises border security by operating at sea and therefore making the border invisible (Chambers, 2019) to those living on the sea's northern shore.

On one hand, rescue becomes a way through which it is possible to contain migration because once people are saved, they are either brought back to African shores or transferred to hotspots in Europe. On the other, the space of action is distanced from the humanitarian border spectacle (Cuttitta, 2014) of the Mediterranean because operations are often conducted in the arguable Libyan SAR, and migration is increasingly deterred in transit countries.

This archipelago of control and detention (Mountz, 2011) implies issues of sovereignty and re-territorialisation, as well as biopolitical concerns about the control of migrant bodies whose "safety" is constantly interpreted, redefined, and ultimately related to smuggling, rather than to the possibility of safely accessing mobility. These new forms of containment and control are often hidden by technicalities and procedures, always depoliticised and normalised, and increasingly supported by hegemonic discourses.

Safe corridors for a right to mobility

The case study analysed in this contribution adds another important aspect related to the humanitarian response to the securitisation of the border regime: the problem of "deservingness" to migrate in relation to certain characteristics. The argument presented here concerns a specific humanitarian programme providing safe corridors for vulnerable migrants, which exemplifies the biopolitical feature of processes of selectivity among migrants who can or cannot access mobility in this legal and protected way.

Mediterranean Hope is an overarching project organised, financed, and conducted by the Federation of Evangelical Churches in Italy (FCEI). Different actions occur within this framework, all of them concerning the space of the Mediterranean and issues of mobility across it. Some projects, such as the Observatory on Migration in Lampedusa, are based in Italy, where personnel welcome migrants, provide mediators, and conduct research on the evolution of migratory processes through the island and the Mediterranean space. The welcoming centre in Scicli (the "home of cultures") in Sicily is another local endeavour. It is open to people who have undergone traumatic events during the migration journey. The centre hosts "vulnerable" migrants like minors, sole women, women with small children, and, in some cases, families. In Sicily, the project also involves the monitoring and assistance of the migrant day labourers exploited in farming industries. Within the framework of Mediterranean Hope, we can also find activities related to the support of non-governmental organisations (NGOs) conducting search and rescue

(SAR) activities at sea: the FCEI helps Proactiva Open Arms and Sea-Watch with funding and personnel and supports the work of Pilotes Volontaires[2].

Finally, the project includes the creation of humanitarian corridors (HCs) from Lebanon and Ethiopia mostly to Italy, but also to other countries involved in the activity, coordinated by the FCEI, the Waldensian Church, and the Sant'Egidio Community, a Catholic organisation. These safe passages are a way to give migrants the possibility to reach European soil without risking their life by boarding boats organised by smugglers. The research presented here specifically concerns the corridors opened in 2016 between Lebanon and Italy. The interviews were conducted among people from the FCEI engaged in this activity.

These corridors "are governed by a Memorandum of Understanding signed on 15 December 2015 by the sponsoring bodies and by the Foreign and Interior Ministries to allow, for a period of two years, 1,000 Syrian refugees who fled to Lebanon to reach Italy in a legal and safe manner with normally scheduled flight"[3]. After long negotiations, an agreement was reached between the Italian government and the network of churches and communities, according to which the government would provide a thousand humanitarian visas for two years, starting from January 2016. The agreement foresaw the possibility of renewal every second year, and another two-year period ended in December 2019[4].

The HC project is entirely funded by fundraising and through the "8x1000" money of the Italian Waldensian and Methodist Churches – that is, the annual collection of tax donations from Italian taxpayers. It therefore does not rely on state money, and it guarantees the continuity of funding to the project despite changes in the government's composition. The first corridor was opened in February 2016, and the entire activity finds its juridical base in the European regulation that allows Schengen countries to release humanitarian visas with territorial limitations. Once in Italy, the beneficiaries of this programme can apply for asylum, and, if it is granted, they can access a less exceptional visa status.

According to a dossier published by the Sant'Egidio Community (2019), updated in June 2019, 2,148 people arrived in Italy through HCs, which rises to a total of 2,669 if we also consider those who arrived in France (364), Belgium (150), and Andorra (7). Most arrivals in Italy were from Lebanon (1,626) and were Syrian refugees; about five hundred refugees (mostly Eritreans, Somalis, and South Sudanese) arrived from Ethiopia. In both cases, ninety percent were households.[5]

According to the official presentation of the HCs, their main aims are saving human lives and avoiding tragedies at sea, countering the business of smuggling and criminal organisations, allowing vulnerable people to legally reach Europe, and managing migrants' safe arrival in Italy.[6] Given the involvement of the Italian government, security standards are guaranteed, and the concept of "safety" in relation to entry includes migrants and Italian residents.

The identification of potential beneficiaries of the programme occurs in Lebanon, mostly through the work of local contacts such as NGOs, churches, associations, and the United Nations High Commissioner for Refugees (UNHCR). These diverse actors relate with locally based personnel from the FCEI, to whom they signal an average of twenty to thirty cases per week. "Cases" can be individuals or families in conditions of extreme difficulty, as we shall see.

These people then go through three rounds of interviews with the HC team where their situation is assessed in relation to their vulnerability, motivation, and personal resources. The first is the prerequisite to access the programme, and we will analyse it further; the latter is considered an asset for successful integration once in Italy. As one member of the team explained to me:

> We try to keep together the dimension of serious vulnerability with the dimension of the sustainability of the reception. The criterion considers both vulnerability and easy integration. We also try to balance the two in relation to our reception system, which cannot bear only serious health cases, for example. It is not easy, because we have to consider everyone, but if we brought only seriously ill people, it would be dramatically unsustainable.
>
> (F.P., Mediterranean Hope operator, my translation from Italian)

Similarly, another operator of the project insisted on the importance of achieving autonomy once in Italy:

> We evaluate the awareness of the migration project and the possibility of integration. For example, if there is an important medical case in a family unit, there must be a person who has resources and may be able to become independent, because independence is precisely the goal of this project. They have the opportunity to move, be welcomed, receive all the possible tools to integrate in the territory, but then the goal is that they can walk, so they must be people able to do this.
>
> (S.T., HC team operator, my translation from Italian)

After people who meet the criteria have been identified, the Italian embassy in Beirut conducts in-depth interviews and takes fingerprints. The Italian Ministry of the Interior then deals with the people's security checks. If they conclude that the selected people do not constitute a security risk, the Italian embassy can issue a humanitarian visa with limited territorial validity with which they can go to Italy, where they must remain until they obtain refugee status. Once the visa is obtained, those involved in the programme leave Lebanon. When they land at the airport in Italy, they formally express their wish to apply for asylum and then proceed with the legal procedures. According to the interviewees, most get refugee status. They are welcomed mainly in apartments, and more rarely in centres. Operators work with them on legal issues and on issues related to school, health, and work, ensuring their integration is facilitated. A follow-up in the next three years guarantees the continuity of the different possible paths undertaken by the individuals or families in their access to education, work, and everyday life.

Who deserves to cross?

The HC project for Syrian and other refugees has very strong potential in that it demonstrates the concrete possibility to access safe mobility. Its power lies in the creation of a space of refusal (Jones, 2012) in which and through which people escaping from violent situations of any kind can express the right to start a new life in a safer country and access the opportunity to fully develop their existences. The project also shows that a different kind of migration is possible, with the coordination of institutions and organisations that aim to provide the space for moving legally and without risks.

There is also strong awareness among most working in the programme of the political features of HCs and their role as an example of feasibility. In July 2019, the president of the FCEI presented to the Italian parliament the intention to open a corridor from the infamous Libyan camps to several European countries possibly involved in this venture.[7] This idea has been further advanced and discussed in different contexts with the precise plan of "evacuating" 50,000 refugees stuck in Libyan camps over two years. The declared aim of the FCEI in presenting this programme is to show that the model is feasible and replicable, as one of my interviewees stated clearly: "Human Humanitarian corridors are a political project, born as a response to death at sea. It's a model – we want to build an example that is replicable with regard to costs, security, and the involvement of civil society" (F.P., Mediterranean Hope operator, my translation from Italian).

This intention reveals an interesting aspect of HCs with regard to the risk of depoliticisation that is often entailed in humanitarian interventions, because it shows the will to constitute a precedent and to open a debate on mobility rights:

> There is an element that the corridors open and do not resolve: for the first time people who don't have a high status, who cannot pay for their visa, who cannot pay their travel, exercise a subjective right recognised by the states that allows them safe passage to seek international protection. This will open up a huge debate on the future terrain of who has this right.
>
> (F.P., Mediterranean Hope operator, my translation from Italian)

We can therefore see an attempt to create a space of refusal that can be tested in the field, and whose success could eventually make it the norm. The acceptance of the risks entailed in undocumented mobility due to the hardening of bordering procedures translates into the imagination and realisation of concrete opportunities, as well as challenges to this very system.

However, besides the powerful aspects of the programme, it is important to reflect on the very meaning of the humanitarian government of the border, which has been defined "as the administration of human collectivities in the name of a higher moral principle which sees the preservation of life and the alleviation of suffering as the highest value of action" (Fassin, 2007, p. 11). This definition underlines the orientation of humanitarian actions towards what Redfield calls "'minimalist' biopolitics: the temporary administration of survival within wider circumstances that do not favour it" (Redfield, 2008, p. 344). The action undertaken under the HC programme can indeed represent a challenge to and a good practice of mobility, but it also has limits that arise between particular bodies and the larger political regime of the humanitarian border (ibid.). The alternative created by the HCs is temporary and limited, and it can hardly encompass bordering practices and migration tout court, because to work it adopts a conditional logic that ultimately reinforces the "border and asylum politics in which some lives are seen as worthy of protection while others are rendered obsolete and disposable" (Holzberg, Kolbe, and Zaborowski, 2018, p. 535).

As we have seen, the criteria that guide the choice of people involved in the programme are based on two separate sets of individual and familiar characteristics, both ascribed and acquired: the first can be understood through the concepts of vulnerability and adaptability; the second relates to security standards. Together, they form the level of deservingness for a "case" to become an HC beneficiary.

Whichever evaluation of vulnerability is adopted, its main features are related to standardised ideas of weakness that correspond to being subject to possible forms of violence and the inability to protect oneself. Given the use of classifications, fragility is essentialised. This ultimately flattens the subjectivities of people on the move. Moreover, their vulnerability highlights an important aspect of the general discourse on migration and migrant subjects, which concerns the responsibility they have for their condition. "The western migration narrative operates a systematic reductionism by categorising migrants as either victims or criminals, and therefore as people who must either be saved or rejected" (Casaglia, 2020, p. 13), and this has consequences for the recognition of migrant subjects' agency and political subjectivity. Vulnerability is hardly compatible with the recognition of agency, especially when this also entails a risk of paternalism and a patronising attitude. The moral character of the decisions taken and the recognition of individual merits to access the programme is problematic if the aim is the creation of a feasible alternative to risky and illegal mobility.

In her discussion of what it means to lead a good life, Butler (2012, p. 15) conceptualises vulnerability as something that "can be projected and denied (psychological categories), but also exploited and manipulated (social and economic categories) in the course of producing and naturalizing forms of social inequality. This is what is meant by the unequal distribution of vulnerability". The biopolitical character of the moral definition of vulnerability brings to the fore the elements of power that organise life and dispose of lives, also through the definition of evaluation criteria (ibid., p. 10). This implies both the presupposition that some people have the right to judge other people's lives and the identification of the characteristics that make the latter deserving of a good life. The process through which deservingness is evaluated shapes power relations between "victims" and "saviours", creating hierarchies in which the victims are defined by deficiencies, dependency, and needs (Perkowski, 2016).

We must not forget that this act also entails that some other people are denied the possibility to safely access a better life, which clarifies Butler's argument about the connection between vulnerability and inequality. The discourse of deservingness is a founding element of the humanitarian securitisation of borders (Vaughan-Williams, 2015), and it brings us to the connection between protecting and securing, which are two sides of the same coin – actions derived from the same narrative. "Humanitarian efforts do not necessarily impede but often go hand in hand with securitizing logics, with the consequence being that the protection of some lives remains contingent on the deterrence of others" (Holzberg, Kolbe, and Zaborowski, 2018, p. 536).

Indeed, as we have seen, the second set of characteristics that makes a "case" for deserving to be included in the HC programme concerns security standards. People who have already been classified as vulnerable go through a security check conducted by the Italian authorities. This passage is obvious, given that HCs can only work through institutional channels, which is part of their political force but also limits their ability to challenge border securitisation. Authorities at the Italian embassy conduct interviews with the "cases" in Lebanon, and Italian Ministry of the Interior personnel check people's criminal records and origins and collect biometric data with the aim of comparing their traceable history with their stories.

In the words of one of HCs' team workers, one of the main issues concerns the possible connection with the Islamic State in their place of origin (which in most cases is Syria), because the target of extensive investigations is,

> for example, families from villages controlled for a period by the Islamic State. [...] People who have directly dealt with such a reality or who have been forced to take indoctrination courses, which often happens, are investigated more. Then also on the basis of fingerprints and names ...
>
> (S.T., HC team operator, my translation from Italian)

Another aspect that results in further investigations is related to the coincidence of the personal story told to the embassy authorities with previous accounts – collected, for example, by the UNHCR on arrival in the Lebanese refugee camps – and the information gathered by security officers. The involvement of the UNHCR in the collection of information on people again shows the inevitable entanglement of humanitarianism and securitisation in the definition of bordering processes.

Finally, the team involved in the HC programme is never told the reason for a rejection of a humanitarian visa application, an aspect revealing the non-accountability of the control process.

> Recently, [it] has happened almost every time. We present people in groups, maybe sixty people, and almost every time one or two cases are blocked. [...] Some are left on standby as doubtful cases for further controls, others are rejected, and unfortunately, we aren't given the reasons. They only tell us there are "security reasons".
>
> (S.T., HC team operator, my translation from Italian)

The political transformations in the composition of the Italian government have obvious consequences for the process, because every HC operator told me that controls had become much more restrictive in recent years, which coincided with the rise of populist right-wing parties and the brief, though detrimental, coalition led by the Five Star Movement and the Lega. During their mandate, a security decree was issued concerning aspects such as the cancellation of humanitarian reasons as a sufficient reason motivation to be granted asylum. This created obvious problems for a project based on the concession of humanitarian visas and resulted in more rejections, always with no explanation given to the team.

At the same time, anti-immigration political leaders have been instrumentalising the HCs by using their legality and procedural aspects to show that any other way of reaching Europe is wrong and unacceptable. In May 2019, commenting on the recent arrival in Italy through HCs of a group of refugees selected by the UNHCR in Libya, the former Italian Minister of the Interior Matteo Salvini stated that there were:

> one hundred and fifty certified men and women on the plane from Libya. They are fleeing the war through a humanitarian corridor organised by the Ministry of the Interior because this is how you get to Italy, not with boats or barges or human traffickers. It is proof that the doors of Italy are wide open for women, children, and young people who are genuinely fleeing war and who are welcomed with a full blessing.[8]

In affirming that HCs were the only correct way to migrate, Salvini also used them to strengthen the idea of good versus bad migrants, of a category of people deserving a good life – people "genuinely" fleeing war – and another that did not. This means the political discourse considers economic migrants, people escaping from the consequences of the climate crisis, those who suffer discrimination for political, sexual, or other reasons, and many more cannot be considered worthy of asylum, accessing safe mobility, and living a good life.

Conclusions

The conditional logic of humanitarianism in the case analysed here leads to the emergence of an idea of deservingness based on categories that can change over time and that is related to both ascribed characteristics and socio-political conditions. People's vulnerability can be traced through their nationality in relation to the political situation in their countries of origin, their physical characteristics, gender, age, and so on. A logic of deservingness based on vulnerability is subject to changes in the definition of the latter, and consequently to changes in the definition of migrants' diverse typologies.

Moreover, the idea of vulnerability is strictly connected with the identification of security risks and threats. These are almost always recognised in the smuggling industry, which places migrants at risk and endangers their lives. There is generally no mention of the securitising evolution of bordering practices that has made the border a dangerous and often lethal space in the first place. Such a recognition implies that the safety of migrants is first and foremost related to bordering processes, and that the entire smuggling industry depends on the hardening of security measures and border control.

Throughout this chapter, we have seen that the flexible and ambiguous definition of safety has two main consequences – one connected to discursive aspects of the migration issue, the other related to processes of diversification and the selection of people deserving of safe mobility. HCs have the merit of showing that it is possible to offer just conditions to migrate to a safer life, whatever that means. Whereas this safety is related to the avoidance of "illegal" forms of border crossing for the Italian government, for migrants themselves it can signify very different issues and represent the only alternative to suffering, poverty, and death.

This contribution has offered an illustration of how the conditionality underlying border humanitarian actions can reinforce discourses dividing migrants between good and bad, vulnerable and dangerous, acceptable and unacceptable, and can end up strengthening the migration–security nexus. More generally, asylum and mobility cannot be tied to ideas of deservingness and to criteria that are chosen and altered in accordance with specific and volatile conceptualisations of security. This in itself constitutes a bordering practice in every respect, which works through the biopolitical governmentality of people's bodies, framing them along binary classifications and contributing to hiding the actual roots and causes of global migration.

Humanitarian responses to deaths at sea along the Euro-African frontier have the potential to repoliticise borders, offer alternative representations of the mobile bodies, and also reconnect the two sides of the Mediterranean in a joint effort to give migration a different meaning. However, as long as the borders of the EU remain impervious to the crossing of "undeserving" migrants, relations between the northern and southern shores of the basin will continue to represent global asymmetries, injustice, and neo-colonial practices.

Notes

1 The research entailed the collection of informative material of different kinds (documents, data, documentaries, brochures), attending events related to the humanitarian corridor project, and the conduction of five in-depth interviews with operators involved in the project.
2 Information was gained through interviews and taken from the website of the Mediterranean Hope project: www.mediterraneanhope.com.
3 www.mediterraneanhope.com/corridoi-umanitari/ (my translation).
4 A new protocol was signed in May 2018 with biennial validity (2019 and 2020) that renews the agreement on the corridor from Ethiopia and extends it to Jordan and Niger. Among the signatories of the agreement are the Ministries of the Interior and Foreign Affairs, the Sant'Egidio Community, and the Italian Episcopal Conference.
5 www.santegidio.org/downloads/Dossier-Corridoi-Umanitari-20190627-web. pdf#page=9.
6 www.mediterraneanhope.com/corridoi-umanitari/.
7 riforma.it/it/articolo/2019/07/09/libia-ora-i-corridoi-umanitari.
8 www.ilsole24ore.com/art/migranti-salvini-e-trenta-distanti-porti-chiusi-ma-vicini-corridoi-umanitari–AC6BFMB (my translation).

References

Balibar, E. and De Genova, N. (2018) Mediterranean struggles for movement and the european government of bodies: An interview with Étienne Balibar and Nicholas De Genova. *Antipode*, 50(3), pp. 748–62.

Bigo, D. (2002) Security and immigration: Toward a critique of the governmentality of unease. *Alternatives: Global, Local, Political*, 27, pp. 63–92.

Bigo, D. and Guild, E. (2005) Policing at a distance: Schengen visa policies. In: D. Bigo and E. Guild, eds, *Controlling Frontiers. Free Movement into and within Europe*. London: Ashgate, pp. 233–63.

Butler, J. (2012) Can one lead a good life in a bad life? Radical philosophy, [online]. Available at: www.radicalphilosophy.com/article/can-one-lead-a-good-life-in-a-bad-life. [Accessed 14 April 2020].

Casaglia A. (2020) Pornography at the border: Ethnosexual borderscapes, gendered violence, embodied control, *Geopolitics*, Article first published online: 27 April 2020.

Casaglia, A., Coletti, R., Lizotte, C., Agnew, J., Mamadouh, V., and Minca, C. (2020) Interventions on European nationalist populism and bordering in time of emergencies. *Political Geography*, 82: doi: 10.1016/j.polgeo.2020.102238.

Chambers, P. (2019) Walling through seas: The Indian Ocean, Australian border security, and the political present. In: A. M. Brighenti and M. Karrholm, eds, *Urban Walls. Political and Cultural Meanings of Vertical Structures and Surfaces*. New York: Routledge, pp. 59–78.

Cuttitta, P. (2014) "Borderizing" the island. Setting and narratives of the Lampedusa border play. *ACME*, 13(2), pp. 196–219.

Cuttitta, P. (2017) Repoliticization through search and rescue? Humanitarian NGOs and migration management in the Central Mediterranean. *Geopolitics*, 23(3), pp. 632–60.

Davies, T., Isakjee, A., and Dhesi, S. (2017) Violent inaction: The necropolitical experience of refugees in Europe. *Antipode*, 49(5), pp. 1263–84.

De León, J. (2015) *The Land of Open Graves: Living and Dying on the Migrant Trail.* Oakland: University of California Press.

Fassin, D. (2007) Humanitarianism: A nongovernmental government. In: M. Feher, ed., *Nongovernmental Politics*. New York: Zone Books, pp. 149–60.

Fassin, D. (2012) *Humanitarian Reason. A Moral History of the Present*. Los Angeles: University of California Press.

Garelli, G. and Tazzioli, M. (2019) Military-humanitarianism. In: K. Mitchell, R. Jones, and J. L. Fluri, eds, *Handbook on Critical Geographies of Migration*. Cheltenham & Northampton: Edward Elgar, pp. 182–92.

Glouftsios, G. (2018) Governing circulation through technology within EU border security practice-networks. *Mobilities*, 13(2), pp. 185–99.

Heller, C. and Pezzani, L. (2017) Liquid traces: Investigating the deaths of migrants at the EU's maritime frontier. In: N. De Genova, ed., *The Borders of "Europe": Autonomy of Migration, Tactics of Bordering*. Durham, NC: Duke University Press, pp. 95–119.

Holzberg, B., Kolbe, K., and Zaborowski, R. (2018) Figures of crisis: The delineation of (un)deserving refugees in the German media. *Sociology*, 52(3), pp. 534–50.

Jones, R. (2012) Spaces of refusal: Rethinking sovereign power and resistance at the border. *Annals of the American Geographers*, 102(3), pp. 685–99.

Jones, R. (2016) *Violent Borders: Refugees and the Right to Move*. London: Verso.

Jones, R., ed. (2019) *Open Borders: In Defence of Free Movement*. New York: Verso.

Laine, J. P. (2018) The ethics of bordering: A critical reading of the refugee "crisis". In: G. Besier and K. Stoklosa, eds., *How to Deal with Refugees? Europe as a Continent of Dreams*. Berlin: LIT Verlag, pp. 278–301.

Mitchell, K. and Sparke, M. (2018) Hotspot geopolitics versus geosocial solidarity: Contending constructions of safe space for migrants in Europe. *Environment and Planning D: Society and Space*, Article first published online: 21 August 2018.

Mountz, A. (2011) The enforcement archipelago: Detention, haunting, and asylum on islands. *Political Geography*, 30(3), pp. 118–28.

Nadig, A. (2002) Human smuggling, national security, and refugee protection. *Journal of Refugee Studies*, 15(1), pp. 1–25.

Perkowski, N. (2016) Deaths, interventions, humanitarianism and human rights in the Mediterranean "migration crisis". *Mediterranean Politics*, 21(2), pp. 331–5.

Redfield, P. (2008) Doctors, borders and life in crisis. *Cultural Anthropology*, 20(3), pp. 328–61.

Sant'Egidio.org (2019) Corridoi Umanitari in Europa [online]. Available at: www.santegidio.org/pageID/34176/langID/en/Humanitarian-corridors-in-Europe.html. (Accessed 6 May 2020).

Tazzioli, M. (2020) Governing migrant mobility through mobility: Containment and dispersal at the internal frontiers of Europe. *Environment and Planning C: Politics and Space*, 38(1), pp. 3–19.

Tazzioli, M. and De Genova, N. (2020) Kidnapping migrants as a tactic of border enforcement. *Environment and Planning D: Society and Space*, article first published online: 22 May 2020.

Topak, Ö. E. (2014) The biopolitical border in practice: Surveillance and death at the Greece–Turkey borderzones. *Environment and Planning D: Society and Space*, 32(5), pp. 815–33.

Vaughan-Williams, N. (2008) *Border Politics: The Limits of Sovereign Power*. Edinburgh University Press.

Vaughan-Williams, N. (2015) *Europe's Border Crisis: Biopolitical Security and Beyond*. Oxford: Oxford University Press.

Walters, W. (2011) Foucault and frontiers: Notes on the birth of the humanitarian border. In: U. Bröckling, S. Krasmann and T. Lemke, eds, *Governmentality: Current Issues and Future Challenges*. New York: Routledge, pp. 138–64.

Part II

Political transnationalism and policy impact

6 African and European legal regimes for intra-continental migration

Towards an Afro-European integration scheme

Tomasz Milej

Introduction

Many international legal instruments regulate the intra-continental cross-border movement of persons. In Africa, the intra-continental cross-border movement of persons is mostly considered an element of a Common Market, which the various African Regional Economic Communities (RECs) intend to achieve. In Europe, free movement is considered a fundamental EU freedom. It is provided for in the EU's founding treaties and secondary law. Conversely, there is hardly any comprehensive legal framework establishing a migration regime between Europe and Africa. Such migration has, however, been thematised in various policy declarations, and it certainly plays a prominent political role. It is also part of the ongoing post-Cotonou negotiations, which will be explored in the present chapter.

The decision to leave one's home country and take up residence in another is not an easy one (UNECA, 2017, p. 5; Nita, 2013, p. 10). If the relocation is not for a limited period (e.g. for study), several factors will militate against it: separation from the familiar, including friends and family, the relinquishing of a job or home, and so on. In the new host country, a potential migrant might have initial difficulties in dealing with the authorities, different cultural habits, navigating the job market, or language. There will also be important questions to answer. Can I work there legally? How long will it take to regularise my stay? Do foreigners suffer discrimination? Do they have the same job security? What about professional qualifications? Will they be recognised? What about the family? Can they come too? Can the kids attend school? Are there fees? Can I join a medical scheme? What happens to the social security contributions I've already paid? The law and the reality of its implementation should provide answers to these questions. If the answers are unsatisfactory, those considering migration may decide against it. Given the multitude of reasons for staying in one's place of origin, the answers must help to overcome the doubts, fears, and concerns that the existential decision to migrate necessarily entails. Therefore, if the law is to promote free movement – and this is the assumption of most regional integration schemes in Africa and

DOI: 10.4324/9781003083726-7

Europe – its function is not merely to facilitate it but to provide tangible incentives to migrate.

This is not to say that the law is the only driver of migration. Obviously, numerous migrants decide to move to another country despite the prevailing hostile environment and oppressive labour and immigration laws. An empirical study of Africa suggests that, while migrants from poorer, landlocked countries migrate to nearby African countries, the processes of development and social transformation increase not only young Africans' capabilities and aspirations to migrate but also the geographical extent of migration (Flahaux and de Haas, 2016, p. 23). However, as much as the level of socioeconomic development plays a significant role, state policies also matter, too (ibid., p. 22).

The present chapter compares the framework of the intra-European and intra-African cross-border movement of persons, focusing on four areas. First, it examines the legal instruments used to regulate cross-border movement. Second, it briefly captures the actual content of the right of free movement. Third, it discusses the historical evolution of both legal frameworks. Fourth, it compares the efficiency of implementation mechanisms. This comparison serves as a basis for some lessons for the ongoing post-Cotonou negotiations, which are to shape the relationship between the ACP (Africa, Caribbean, Pacific) group of states and the European Union. Finally, the chapter outlines how racist narratives of European and African identity underpin the oppressive regulations governing the migration of Africans to the EU, and how the EU's negotiating mandate fails to challenge them. This forms the basis of some modest recommendations concerning an Afro-European integration scheme that will be more adequate in an international legal order based on good faith and cooperation.

Legal instruments

In both Europe and Africa, the legal instruments regulating cross-border movement are embedded in larger integration projects. Consequently, they reflect the approach to regional integration. The approaches to regional integration were famously conceptualised by Ernst Haas. Accordingly, the "minimum common denominator approach" is characterised by negotiations between equal bargaining partners – states – and the outcome does not go beyond what the least cooperative state is willing to accept. At the other end of the scale, there is the "upgrading of the common interest approach", whereby the decision-making procedures are approximated to legislative procedures in a political community. These procedures are handled by agencies and institutions which promote converging interests and give voice to interest groups. Those voices may differ from what the carefully instructed government negotiators are willing to agree to, generating new expectations and policies (Haas, 1961, p. 373).

To provide incentives to migrate, the laws of the migrant's home country and the target country must have some degree of harmonisation. Examining the questions asked in the introduction, the recognition of qualifications will require some equivalence of degrees and approximation of curricula. Transferability of social benefits will require that social security systems are compatible. Furthermore, migrant family's access to healthcare and education must not be discriminatory. This is where legal guarantees become important.

The approaches to regional integration translate into approaches to legal harmonisation. Their choice affects the speed of harmonisation and its results. Accordingly, the "minimum common denominator approach" means harmonisation based on international treaties negotiated between participating states or even non-binding agreements (soft law), referred to as the contractual approach (in its hard or soft version). Conversely, the "upgrading of the common interest approach" produces a regulatory approach to harmonisation characterised by the enactment of uniform legislation by supranational institutions – that is, institutions which are empowered to create law that is directly effective within the territories of the states under their jurisdiction (Devuyst, 1999, p. 116; Milej, 2018, p. 142).

The European Union stands for the latter approach. The EU has two founding treaties of equal legal rank – the Treaty on European Union (TEU) and the Treaty on the Functioning of the European Union (TFEU) – as well as a body of secondary law enacted in the procedure they lay down. This procedure includes majority voting, parliamentary participation, and a *de facto* monopoly to initiate legislation held by a strong European bureaucracy in charge of promoting the EU's common interest (the European Commission). Concerning the right of free movement, this approach has produced various pieces of harmonising legislation. The 1968 Regulation on the free movement of workers, which was in force until 2011, is one of the first examples. Since 2004, free movement rights are provided for comprehensively in the directive on the right of citizens of the Union and their family members to move and reside freely within the territory of the Member States. In 2005 the EU organs also came up with a systemic solution for recognising qualifications, adopting the recognition of a professional qualifications directive.

However, the history of the common regulation of qualifications is quite long. Various pieces of legislation have been adopted by European organs over the years, dating back to the 1960s (Kortese, 2016, p. 46). The current recognition of professional qualifications directive is based on Article 53 of the TFEU, which authorises the European Parliament and the Council (both EU organs) to act "in accordance with the ordinary legislative procedure, issue directives for the mutual recognition of diplomas, certificates and other evidence of formal qualifications and for the coordination of the provisions laid down by law, regulation, or administrative action in Member States concerning the taking-up and pursuit of activities as self-employed persons".

Regional integration in Africa is based on a script provided for in the Treaty for the Establishment of the African Economic Community (the Abuja Treaty) of 1991, adopted following the 1980 Lagos Plan of Action (Organisation of African Unity, 1980). According to the Abuja Treaty, a strong consolidated common market is to be achieved in six stages and take effect in 2028; the common market will, by definition, involve the free movement of people. The first stage of the plan's realisation was a formation of the Regional Economic Communities (RECs), which will be gradually merged into one Pan-African organisation – the African Economic Community (AEC). Currently, eight RECs are recognised as building blocks of the AEC, and each has more or less articulate regulations on the free movement of people within it. It was only in 2018 that the Protocol to the Treaty Establishing the African Economic Community Relating to the Free Movement of Persons, Right of Residence and Right of Establishment (AU Free Movement Protocol) was adopted. This is technically a protocol to the 1992 Abuja Treaty.

Contractual approaches to harmonisation of laws in the African system prevail. Unlike in the EU, there is no division of powers between the member states of an REC and the REC itself; no regulatory powers are conferred on the latter. If an REC is authorised to make regulations, their enactment is conditional on the unanimity of the member states' governments. For example, according to Article 63 of the EAC-Treaty, an "Act of the Community" requires the assent of all heads of state, who can grant or withhold it at their discretion without any recourse for interest groups which may have legitimately pushed for the adoption of the given Act.

Following the contractual approach, the free movement of persons is to be achieved through the implementation of treaties by concluding further treaties. The treaty establishing the given REC provides for a broad integration framework. Its specific areas of cooperation – the movement of persons is one – are operationalised by protocols. Those protocols are technically also treaties, concluded by the same state parties that concluded the founding treaties. However, the protocols' scope of application is reduced to a specific aspect of integration, for example, the free movement of persons.

In line with the scheme, the 1999 Treaty Establishing the East African Community (EAC-Treaty), which is one of the eight African RECs, provides for the operationalisation of an EAC Common Market through a Common Market Protocol. This was indeed concluded in 2009. However, the protocol does not unconditionally open the labour markets of the EAC partner states to the citizens of the other EAC partner states. It retains work permit regimes and does not comprehensively regulate many important aspects of free movement, such as the recognition of qualifications or portability of social security benefits, limiting itself to general harmonisation commitments. Most importantly, the protocol's personal scope of application is restricted to highly skilled professionals, who make up only a small percentage of the labour force.

The Common Market Protocol is complemented by annexes and schedules, in which each EAC partner state specifies the professional groups for whom it commits itself to opening its labour market. Accordingly, Kenya's commitments encompass the largest group of professions, while Burundi agreed to open its labour market to a much smaller group. This regulation is an expression of the principle of asymmetry, mitigating one of the major flaws of the "minimum common denominator approach", which agrees only on commitments to which the least cooperative partner is ready to agree. According to the principle of asymmetry, the least cooperative partner state may simply take on fewer commitments than those who are more cooperative while remaining in the agreement rather than blocking the integration process. A similar device is the principle of variable geometry, which enables some states to push ahead with the integration agenda, while allowing others to join later. A good example in the area of free movement is the authorisation to cross the border with an ID card, which is limited to Kenya, Rwanda, and Uganda. Of course, these devices come at a price, which is above all the fragmentation of the common market. Those states which take on more obligations will also be reluctant to implement them for nationals of those states which take on fewer.

Compared to the other RECs, the EAC model may be regarded as advanced. For example, according to the SADC Protocol from 2005, the member states agreed only to "develop policies aimed at the progressive elimination of obstacles to free movement". Tellingly, this protocol is not even in force.

Finally, no REC has a central authority of a composition and powers comparable to the European Commission, capable of overseeing the enforcement of obligations, proposing, or even enacting regulations. There is thus no international institution within the RECs and in Africa which has the effective power to make free movement guarantees work on the ground. It is up to the states to implement those guarantees by gradually amending their national laws. This is exemplified by a network of Mutual Recognition Agreements (not necessarily agreed by the states or even national bodies) limited to certain professional groups. The 2018 continental Free Movement Protocol largely replicates the regulatory approaches of the RECs.

Content of the Free Movement Directive

Article 21 of the TFEU accords to every citizen of the Union the right to move and reside freely within the territory of the member states, subject to the limitations and conditions laid down in the treaties and the measures adopted to give them effect, in particular the 2004 Free Movement Directive mentioned earlier. As a matter of principle, EU law provides for a comprehensive right to move "without being subject to any conditions and any formalities", as the 2004 directive underscores in its preamble. This most notably means the prohibition of discrimination and abolition of work permit requirements. However, the guarantee goes even further. Its origin lies in the union's citizenship provisions, which, according to the Court of Justice of the European Union (CJEU) case law, determine the fundamental status of EU member states' nationals (Rudy

Grzelczyk vs Centre public d'aide sociale d'Ottignies-Louvain-la-Neuve [2001]). Consequently, the right to move freely across borders is detached from the economic activity of the citizen, and the CJEU has taken a tough stance on policing national rules that are liable to hamper or render this right less attractive. The Court is quite keen on scrutinising all national policy choices from the perspective of smoothing cross-border movement.

The 1998 CJEU's judgement in the *Martinez Sala* case demonstrates the "humanisation" of free movement right. In declaring that it is contrary to EU law to deny the child benefit available to German nationals to a Spanish national lawfully residing in Germany, the court considered the EU citizen's life concerns, which went beyond their economic activity (María Martínez Sala vs Freistaat Bayern [1998]). Hence, people are clearly no longer regarded as factors of production alone (see also Gerardo Ruiz Zambrano vs Office national de l'emploi [2011]).

The balance between free movement rights on one hand and legitimate national policy concerns on the other is still assured. However, it is achieved not by the national laws that place obstacles to the influx of foreign nationals, but on the supranational (EU) level, most notably by the 2004 movement directive, one of whose main objectives is to ensure that "persons exercising their right of residence [do not] become an unreasonable burden on the social assistance system of the host Member State during an initial period of residence".

This conception is not one that was adopted in Africa, despite the Pan-Africanist roots of the regional integration process. The language of the free movement provisions across the African RECs is very cautious. In many instances it falls short of establishing the individual's right to move, while only creating a broad obligation on the part of the state to gradually eliminate obstacles to cross-border movement. Even if individual rights are established, as is arguably the case with the EAC, their exercise depends on professional skills. Thus, it can be concluded that the migrant is regarded only as an economic resource (a factor of production) and will be accepted only if he or she makes a contribution to the economy of the target state. This attitude exaggerates the short-term market needs of each state while frustrating the long-term gains (addressed further below) the enhanced migration might generate for the community – in this case the EAC – as a whole. This is a consequence of the contractual approach to the harmonisation of laws, which allows too little space for the "upgrading of common interests". As a result, intra-African migration is hampered by work permit regimes, red tape, and high work permit fees (Milej, 2019, p. 964, African Centre for Migration and Society, 2018).

The historical evolution

The historical evolution of the labour migration regimes in Africa and in Europe was shaped by an interplay between the political visions and economic necessities. It was the need for an efficient allocation of resources, in this case the labour factor, which made free movement appear economically necessary.

Current studies posit that both higher-skilled and lower-skilled labour movement increase welfare. While the EU framework does not distinguish between higher-skilled and lower-skilled migrants, African frameworks do, reducing migration's positive potential. According to the 2018 United Nations Conference on Trade and Development (UNCTAD) Report on Migration in the destination states, "lower-skilled migrants fill occupations neglected by citizens, allowing the latter to move to higher-skilled jobs" (UNCTAD 2018, p.29), while home states benefit from remittances. The latter positively affects development in terms of investment, transfer of skills, expertise, or increased trade opportunities because of the contacts created by the diaspora (UNCTAD 2018, p. 144). Despite the existing barriers to migration, the inflow of remittances is one of the key factors contributing to the economy of African states. For example, remittances in Ethiopia constituted fifty-one per cent of all capital inflows in 2016 (UNCTAD 2018, p. 136; Basnett, 2013, p. 134).

In Africa, the early Pan-Africanist projects associated with Kwame Nkrumah, the Casablanca Group, and the United States of Africa project, of which the Ghana–Guinea–Mali Union was to be a nucleus, were much more political visions than pragmatic answers to the needs of the economy; a political union was to come first (Nkrumah, 1963, p. 149; Dirar, 2014, p. 130). Consequently, little attention was paid to migration at the time. The post-colonial infrastructure, with most of its communication routes pointing outwards, did not encourage conceptualisations of intra-African migration. However, the realisation of the more ambitious political union projects would certainly produce a kind of common market, in which the free movement of people would play a role. Ultimately, however, those projects did not materialise (Adi, 2018, p. 151).

The second wave of regional integration was based on the 1980 Lagos Plan of Action, which took a functionalist approach and was intended to address Africa's economic issues (D'Sa, 1983, p. 5). In the plan, free movement was regarded as an economic factor in the context of resource allocation, and certainly not as an individual right or as a nucleus of political integration. Accordingly, African states were urged to develop employment policies which would facilitate the absorption of "surplus trained manpower" in one country by other countries (Organisation of African Unity, 1980, p. 111). The current policy documents are more outspoken, acknowledging the economic benefits of free movement and linking them to broader political projects. For example, a 2017 AU Peace and Security Council resolution acknowledged that the benefits of free movement "far outweighed" the risks. In 2016, the AU Summit of African heads of state launched the African passport as a "symbolic Act of Pan-Africanism". The EAC Vision 2050 also envisages the East African Community's political federation, enshrined in the EAC Treaty as a final stage of integration, a borderless region in which people can move freely.

Europeans were first allowed to move freely as factors of production. The citizenship dimension of free movement came later, when the concept of EU citizenship was introduced by the 1992 Treaty of Maastricht. However, this is not to say there was no political vision. Winston Churchill's idea of the United States of Europe going back to political projects of the nineteenth century comes to mind (Bülck, 1981, p. 809). Yet there were also more practical ideas, like the common European passport, on which the Council of Europe started working as early as 1949 (Turack, 1966–67, p. 782). Those visions suffered a setback in view of the political disputes around the post-war European order in the 1940s and 1950s (Dedman, 1996, p. 89). It was at that time that European governments started thinking more in economic terms of the integration of markets rather than in terms of political visions (Dedman, 1996, p. 91; Ward, 2009, p. 11). But the visionary dimension of the European integration project did not disappear, as evidenced by the Declaration on the European Identity adopted by the European Summit in Copenhagen in 1973, which spoke of a "dynamic construction of a United Europe". As early as the 1970s, the free movement of workers was referred to as the nucleus of a European citizenship (Magiera, 1987, p. 221).

Implementation of free movement regulatory frameworks

Much has been said about the unsatisfactory record of African regional integration schemes' failure (Dirar, 2014, p. 152; Milej, 2015, p. 615; Oppong, 2018, p. 137), and the commitments to facilitate free movement are no exception. Both substantive commitments and implementation strategies based on the gradual abolition of restrictions to free movement and "appropriate actions" are to be taken by national authorities, eventually subjecting free movement rights to the latter's good will.

As a consequence of the lack of self-executing effect and the establishment of individual rights mentioned earlier, these obligations are very rarely justiciable. This means that cases in which an individual establishes a violation of a right to move and take up employment in another African country in court are extremely rare. Even if the scope of the obligations is clear, which is rarely the case, there is insufficient clarity regarding the powers of local courts with regard to the obligations arising from regional integration treaties (Milej, 2015, p. 596). Are the courts allowed to disapply domestic laws if they are not in compliance with the treaties?

As there is no crystallised body of case law on free movement, there is also no judicial guidance on how free movement obligations are to be implemented and enforced. Eventually, the progress of intra-African labour migration is impeded by the vagueness of free movement commitments, their limitation to higher-skilled workers, and weak implementation mechanisms.

The situation is very different in Europe. European integration is as a matter of principle integration through law, whose efficiency is ensured by the proximity of the judge to the individuals (Milej, 2018, p. 147). Accordingly, every national judge is considered to be an EU judge at the same time. The principles of the direct effect and supremacy of EU law give him or her efficient instruments to ensure that EU law is followed. Should the judge conclude that a national regulation is not in conformity with the European one, he or she is under the obligation not to apply it (Amministrazione delle Finanze dello Stato v Simmenthal SpA. [1978]). The right – or in some cases obligation – to refer questions of law to the Court of Justice of the European Union in a preliminary reference procedure has contributed to the emergence of comprehensive case law providing important orientation points for national legislators and policymakers (Milej, 2018, p. 152). A radical empowerment of regional and national court has been suggested as one means to improve the implementation record of the African integration agendas (Oppong, 2018, p. 131).

Post-Cotonou negotiations: Lessons learned?

The Cotonou Agreement (a partnership agreement between the members of the African, Caribbean, and Pacific Group of States and the European Community and its member states) was concluded in 2000 for a twenty-year period. On its expiry in 2020, the parties entered into negotiations on a treaty framework aimed at governing their relationship beyond this date – the post-Cotonou negotiations. The treaty relationship dates back to the Yaoundé and Lomé Conventions concerning preferential trade regimes and development assistance, which were concluded in the 1960s and 1970s between the European Economic Community, first with the former French colonies, and after the establishment of the African, Caribbean, and Pacific Group of States (ACP group) in 1975 with all ACP States. It is important to note that not all African states are members of the ACP group; this is especially true of states in North Africa such as Morocco, Algeria, and Egypt, which play a significant role in migration between Africa and Europe.

The current Cotonou agreement has a three-pillar structure: development assistance, trade, and the political dimension. Interestingly, Article 13 on migration is in the chapter on the political dimension. Hence, being systematically separated from the trade dimension, the question of movement of people does not constitute part of a larger common market project, unlike in the African RECs and the EU. Article 13 is also very far from opening the doors to migration. It involves only two unequivocal legal obligations. One concerns the duty of ACP states to "accept the return of and readmission of any of its nationals who are illegally present on the territory of a Member State of the European Union, at that Member State's request and without further formalities" with the corresponding commitment of the EU member states to accept returns and readmissions of their nationals from ACP states.

The other legal obligation is the prohibition of discrimination against migrants who have already acquired a right of residence. Otherwise, the language of the provision resembles the open-ended declarations typical of

African RECs, yet with no hint of a commitment to open the borders, even to a limited extent. The cited provision explicitly concerns "migration", not "free movement", and migration is portrayed as an issue, not an opportunity. This is exemplified by the provision of Article 13 (4), whereby "the Parties consider that strategies aiming at reducing poverty, improving living and working conditions, creating employment, and developing training contribute in the long term to normalising migratory flows". Similarly, Article 13 (5) speaks of prevention strategies with regard to illegal migration.

In addition to the Cotonou agreement, the principles for Africa-Europe cooperation were outlined in the Joint Africa-EU Declaration on Migration and Development from 2006 (Tripoli Declaration) and the Joint Africa-EU Strategy (JAES), a declaration adopted by African and EU heads of state and government in 2007. Even if those documents are not legally binding, they establish dialogue formats and set some standards against which the quality of the treaty relationship can be measured. These documents make two important statements: first, that migration is a positive phenomenon, which, if well managed, makes a positive contribution to development in the countries of origin and destination; second, that migration should be looked at in the context of the wider EU–Africa development partnership. These statements correspond with the regulatory approach to migration both within Africa and Europe.

The ACP negotiating mandate for the post-Cotonou negotiations converges with an emphasis on the benefits of migration, as it postulates that "more focus be placed on this in the successor agreement, creating the conditions to promote legal migration and the right of movement of persons, sharing skills and experiences which could be portrayed as the positive side of migration" (ACP, 2018, p. 38). Regrettably, the mandate document does not seek to link migration to trade in goods. Yet given the focus on free movement as an efficient allocation of resources, it is the least it could have done.

The EU's mandate is very different. It stresses the need to stem illegal migration, the duty to unconditionally readmit migrants "irregularly present on the territory of another Party", and effective border management (Council of the European Union, 2018: 42). Although the mandate also sets the objective "to harness the benefits of regular migration", it offers little to facilitate it. The only commitments the EU is ready to enter are enhanced "mobility schemes for students, researchers, and professionals" and facilitation of "visits for business and investment purposes".

By virtue of this mandate, the EU seems to allow at the very most only what the most reluctant African mobility frameworks are ready to allow: the movement of highly-skilled professionals and researchers. Implicitly, however, the mandate also acknowledges the benefits of the migration of lower-skilled migrants. It does so by pledging a reduction in the transaction cost of remittances to less than three percent (Council of the European Union, 2018: 43). Nevertheless, borders for lower-skilled migrants are apparently to remain closed. The institutional and enforcement framework for the enhanced mobility schemes, especially that for "professionals", is weak; the mandate scarcely goes beyond political consultations. There is also no roadmap for how and when these schemes are to be rolled out (Council of the European Union, 2018: 85).

In short, the EU's negotiating mandate replicates all the weaknesses of the African mobility schemes while offering none of their visions. It shows no signs that the efficient intra-EU free movement mechanism will be used to facilitate migration from African countries into the EU. Worse still, the EU's policy paradigm is to keep Africans out of the EU, as huge – and still increasing – investments in the border management infrastructure demonstrate (Laine, 2020). The mandate reinforces the securitised discourse about migration, which African schemes seek to overcome. By delinking migration from trade, neither the Cotonou agreement currently in force nor the negotiating mandates take into account the existing experience of regional integration in both African and Europe, where the free movement of people forms part of larger integration schemes. The contribution that enhanced migration would make to increased investment, trade volumes, and development in general (UNCTAD 2018: 149) is not duly acknowledged.

Conclusion

What lessons can be learned from the experience with free movement schemes in Africa and Europe for the migration between the two continents? Any solution must consider the effectiveness and workability of the "upgrading common interest approach", placing migration within a broader integration scheme and having a political vision which the potential Afro-European integration project with a built-in increased cross-border movement component will serve.

Europe used to have bold visions throughout the integration process and at its inception, but those visions seem to be fading. What remains unshaken are the rules and bureaucratic efficiency. Given the recent uncoordinated response to the COVID-19 pandemic, there is rather more efficiency in day-to-day administration than there is in the imaginative tackling of new and complex challenges. Africa's integration schemes may be much weaker on efficiency, but they are strong on visions. One of the reasons those visions are so hard to accomplish may be that they are not internalised and ratified in democratic debate. A debate is crucial for both – visions and the efficiency. At least in East Africa, there is hardly any debate on migration. Voices are heard saying Tanzanians steal jobs from Kenyans in Kenya, and that Kenyans steal jobs from Tanzanians in Tanzania (African Centre for Migration and Society, 2018, p. 17). The lack of a broad debate to underpin a common vision makes it attractive for populists to create and exaggerate anxiety about strangers and offer protection against perceived threats. Such identity politics is very much present in Europe with regard to migrants from Africa. Sometimes it also applies to migrants within the EU. Immigration from new member states was one of the Brexit proponents' crucial arguments. According to Theresa May it was one of the key issues. "Free movement will end" was therefore one of her key messages in negotiating the post-Brexit settlement with the EU (Adam and Booth, 2018).

Yet the rejection of African migrants by the EU has much deeper roots. Over decades, if not centuries, European identity has been constructed to a large extent in opposition to outsiders, and more specifically to Africans. European philosophers, anthropologists, missionaries, and, more recently, media outlets have been keen to construct African "otherness" as a contrast to the idea of a European self (Gathii, 1998, p. 195; Janz, 2007, p. 691). The "western" type of rational mentality was opposed to the African type, allegedly "prelogical, depending on the law of mystical participation" (Mudimbe, 1988, p. 149). European anthropologists such as Lucien Levy-Bruhl reduced Africans to objects of science, depicting them as "primitives" who must evolve from a frozen state to catch up with western civilisation (Mudimbe, 1988, pp. 85–8; Janz, 2007, p. 696). In similar vein, a contemporary analysis of the main-stream media discourse reveals that "Africa is frequently presented as the object of Western gaze, and this gaze objectifies, exoticizes, and lingers on traits that are different, noteworthy, and 'other', by contrast to safety, pros-perity, and enlightenment of a Western 'home'" (Bunce, 2015: 42). It is this nefarious discourse which helps to portray migrants as a threat to European culture, identity, values, and conventional way of life (Laine, 2020). It is also a discourse which was deployed to justify the colonisation of Africa and legit-imise European domination (Gathii, 1998, pp. 194–8).

An Afro-European integration project that includes a free movement scheme offers an opportunity to limit the impact of the current power imbal-ance that reproduces itself in migration policies. EU member states are still free to operate unilateral immigration schemes that aim to attract only high-skilled professionals. Such approaches may be favourable for the European but not necessarily for the African economies. A multilateral approach to migration would allow all partners to capitalise on the benefits of migration. However, it may not take the form of the EU using its bargaining power to translate longstanding European obsessions into binding norms of international law, as the current EU mandate suggests. This would go against the very idea of international law based on cooperation, which challenges sectarian interests and embraces the idea of pursuing common interests (Koskenniemi, 2007, p. 20). Such an integration project is also a way of initiating and sustaining a debate that is not limited to populists and specialists, and which may be helpful to overcome historically entrenched, shameful, and racist European narratives about European and African identities. In the long run it may also change the paradigm in Africa–EU relations.

The free movement scheme may be limited by quotas, it may make use of the variable geometry and asymmetry principles applied in Africa, and it may have transitional periods, but it must be universal, based on strong institutions, open to both higher-skilled and lower-skilled migrants, and quite importantly, it must work. Even if it does not provide incentives to migrate, which an efficient migration scheme should do, it should at least eliminate the stumbling blocks and cater for the human and labour rights of migrants. The prohibition of discrimination in Article 13 of the Cotonou Agreement is a good step.

The Afro-European integration project must spell out its vision, but its foundational treaty must not be framed in a language of broad political declarations and left at the mercy of politicians' discretion. It must upgrade and upscale the dialogue formats of the 2006 Tripoli Declaration and the JAES. To this end, directly effective individual free-movement rights must be enforceable through a proper mechanism offering effective remedies, ideally by a court with judges. This should be concluded between the AU and the EU to leverage the bargaining power of African states and to allow for a fine-tuning with intra-African integration schemes. A success story thus created may have potential to shift the securitised paradigm towards migration, addressing it not only through the prism of security risks but through the opportunities that are created, and perhaps even more importantly, as an element of the individual's freedom to move.

References

African, Caribbean and Pacific Group of States (ACP). (2018). ACP negotiating mandate for a post–Cotonou partnership agreement with the European Union. ACP/00/011/18 FINAL Lomé, 30 May 2018 PAHD Dept: DWS/cko.

Adam, K. and Booth, W. (2018) Immigration worries drove the Brexit vote. Then attitudes changed. *The Washington Post*. (online) Available at: www.washingtonpost.com/world/europe/immigration-worries-drove-the-brexit-vote-then-attitudes-changed/2018/11/16/c216b6a2-bcdb-11e8-8243-f3ae9c99658a_story.html (Accessed 30 Apr. 2020).

Adi, H. (2018) *Pan-Africanism. A History*. London: Bloomsbury Academic.

African Centre for Migration and Society, University of Witwatersrand (2018) *Free and Safe Movement in East Africa. Research to Promote People's Safe and Unencumbered Movement Across International Borders*. Nairobi: Open Society Foundations.

African Union Peace and Security Council (2017) *Communique SC/PR/COMM.1 (DCLXI)*.

Basnett, Y. (2013) Labour mobility in East Africa: An analysis of the East African community's common market and the free movement of workers. *Development Policy Review*, 31, pp. 131–48.

Bülck, H. (1981) Der Europabürger. In: I. von Münch, ed., *Staatsrecht-Völkerrecht-Europarecht. Festschrift für Hans-Jürgen Schlochauer zum 75. Geburtstag*. Berlin-New York: De Gruyter, pp. 777–811.

Bunce, M. (2015) International news and the image of Africa: New storytellers, new narratives? In: J. Gallagher and V. Mudimbe, ed., *Images of Africa. Creation, negotiation and subversion*. Manchester: Manchester University Press, pp. 42–62.

Council of the European Union. (2018) Negotiating directives for a partnership agreement between the European Union and its member states of the one part, and with countries of the African, Caribbean and Pacific group of states, of the other part. 8094/18 ADD 1 LIMITE.

D'Sa, R. (1983) The Lagos plan of action – Legal mechanisms for co-operation between the Organisation of African Unity and the United Nations Economic Commission for Africa. *Journal of African Law*, 27(1), pp. 4–21.

Dedman, M. (1996) *The Origins and Development of the European Union 1945–1995*. Hoboken: Taylor and Francis.

Devuyst, Y. (1999) The community-method after Amsterdam. *Journal of Common Market Studies*, 37(1), pp. 109–20.

Dirar, L. (2014) Rethinking and theorizing regional integration in Southern Africa. *Emory International Law Review*, 28, pp. 123–65.

Directive 2004/38/EC of the European Parliament and of the Council of 29 April 2004 on the right of citizens of the Union and their family members to move and reside freely within the territory of the Member States.

Directive 2005/36/EC of the European Parliament and of the Council of 7 September 2005 on the recognition of professional qualifications.

East African Community (EAC) Heads of State Summit (2016) *East African Community, Vision 2050*.

EU–Africa Summit in Lisbon (2007) *The Africa-EU Strategic Partnership. A Joint Africa-EU Strategy*.

EU–African Union meeting (2006) *Joint Africa-EU Declaration on Migration and Development*.

European Union, Heads of State or Government (1973) *Declaration on European Identity*.

Flahaux, M. and de Haas, H. (2016) African migration: Trends, patterns, drivers. *Comparative Migration Studies*, 4(1), pp. 1–25.

Gathii, J. (1998) International law and Eurocentricity. *European Journal of International Law*, 9(1), pp. 184–211.

Gerardo Ruiz Zambrano v Office national de l'emploi (2011) 2011-I (CJEU), p. 01177.

Haas, E. (1961) International integration: The European and the universal process. *International Organization*, 15, pp. 366–92.

Janz, B. (2007) African philosophy. In: C. Boundas, ed., *The Edinburgh Companion to Twentieth-Century Philosophies*. Edinburgh: Edinburgh University Press, pp. 689–701.

Kortese, L. (2016) Exploring professional recognition in the EU: A legal perspective. *Journal of international Mobility*, 1(4), pp. 43–58.

Koskenniemi, M. (2007) International law: Constitutionalism, managerialism and the ethos of legal education. *European Journal of Legal Studies*, 1(1), pp. 8–24.

Laine, J. P. (2020) Ambiguous bordering practices at the EU's edges. In: A. Bissonnette and É. Vallet, eds., *Borders and Border Walls: In-Security, Symbolism, Vulnerabilities*. London: Routledge, pp. 69–87.

Magiera, S. (1987) Die Europäische Gemeinschaft auf dem Wege zu einem Europa der Bürger. *Die Öffentliche Verwaltung*, 40(6), pp. 221–31.

María Martínez Sala v Freistaat Bayern. (1998) CJEU 1998-I, p. 02691.

Milej, T. (2015) What is wrong about supranational laws? The sources of East African community law in light of the EU's experience. *Heidelberg Journal of International Law*, 75(4), pp. 579–617.

Milej, T. (2018) Legal harmonisation in regional economic communities – The case of the European Union. In: J. Döveling, H. Majamba, R. Oppong and U. Wanitzek, ed., *Harmonisation of Laws in the East African Community. The State of Affairs with Comparative Insights from the European Union and other Regional Economic Communities*. Nairobi: LawAfrica, pp. 139–53.

Milej, T. (2019) Legal framework for free movement of people within Africa – a view from the East African Community (EAC). *Heidelberg Journal of International Law*, 79(4), pp. 935–70.

Mudimbe, V. (1988) *The Invention of Africa: Gnosis, Philosophy and The Foundation of Knowledge*. Bloomington: Indiana University Press.

Nita, S. (2013) Regional free movement of people: The case of African Regional Economic Communities. *Regions and Cohesion*, 3(3), pp. 8–29.

Nkrumah, K. (1963) *Africa Must Unite*. London: Heinemann.

Oppong, R. (2018) Legal harmonisation in African regional economic communities: Progress, inertia or regress. In: J. Döveling, H. Majamba, R. Oppong and U. Wanitzek, ed., *Harmonisation of Laws in the East African Community. The State of Affairs with Comparative Insights from the European Union and other Regional Economic Communities*. Nairobi: LawAfrica, pp. 113–38.

Organisation of African Unity. (1980) *Lagos Plan of Action for The Economic Development of Africa 1980–2000*.

Protocol on the Establishment of the East African Community Common Market (2009).

Protocol to the Treaty Establishing the African Economic Community Relating to Free Movement of Persons, Right of Residence and Right of Establishment (2018).

Regulation (EEC) No 1612/68 of the Council of 15 October 1968 on freedom of movement for workers within the Community.

Rudy Grzelczyk v Centre public d'aide sociale d'Ottignies-Louvain-la-Neuve. (2001) 2001-I (CJEU), p. 06193.

Simmenthal SpA v Amministrazione delle finanze. (1978) 1978-I (CJEU), p. 01453.

Southern African Community Protocol on the Free Movement of Persons (2005).

Treaty Establishing the African Economic Community – Abuja Treaty (1991).

Treaty for the Establishment of the East African Community (1999).

Turack, D. (1966–67) Freedom of movement in Western Europe: The contribution of the Council of Europe. *The American Journal of Comparative Law*, 15(4), pp. 781–97.

United Nations Conference on Trade and Development (UNCTAD). (2018) *Economic Development in Africa Report 2018: Migration for Structural Transformation*. New York and Geneva, United Nations.

United Nations Economic Commission for Africa (UNECA). (2017) *African Migration. Drivers for Migration in Africa*.

Ward, I. (2009) *A Critical Introduction to European Law*. Cambridge: Cambridge University Press.

7 "*Solidarité en mouvement*" against homeland authoritarianism

Political transnationalism of Europe-based Central African migrants

Leon Mwamba Tshimpaka

Introduction

Over the last decade, little attention has been paid to the transnational political activities of Europe-based Central African migrants[1] in solidarity against homeland authoritarianism. Traditionally, studies on migrant political transnationalism emphasise migrants and refugees' solidarity in demanding the fundamental rights attached to their integration and socioeconomic well-being in receiving sites, but to a lesser extent their solidarity, which is promoted by both lived experiences during their mobility and their having survived similar homeland authoritarian practices. These imply that migrants' solidarity can also be nurtured by social bonds from shared experiences during their mobility which foster the later creation of horizontal networks to collectively fight against homeland authoritarianism from their receiving sites. As they traverse foreign terrains to either Europe or North America and Southern Africa, migrants are collectively exposed to smuggling tragedies which affect them equally, despite their age, race, gender, or nationality (Motlagh, 2016; BBC, 2019). Harrowing journeys across the Mediterranean, the Darién Gap, and the Amazon jungle, for example, are all consummative examples (Press, 2017). Through them, migrants develop social relational proximity when the travel distance and transit points increase, and the density of homeland personal ties decrease (Zhang, Sanchez, and Achilli, 2018). Furthermore, social relational proximity during mobility jogs migrants' memory of repressive political regimes at home, which nurtures another political bond within mobilising structures to collectively contest homeland state power from the receiving sites.

In this study, Europe-based Central African migrants initially entered into solidarity, nurtured by shared smuggling tragedies during their perilous mobility from various smuggling routes to Europe. On arrival in Europe they create social networks as mobilising structures to exercise intercontinental citizenship in public protests and demonstrations, brutal attacks on homeland politicians and allies during their visits abroad – colloquially known as *mutakalisation,* and the prohibition of homeland artists performing in

DOI: 10.4324/9781003083726-8

Europe to demand homeland democratic change. Apart from their individually exercised transnational political activities, Europe-based Central African migrants strengthen their exercised citizenship by entering into solidarity to contest homeland authoritarian regimes that unite them abroad. This study seeks to identify the integrated transnational political activities of Europe-based migrants from Central African countries in a form of networks with the aim of fighting against homeland authoritarianism, which unites them in Europe. The chapter expands on the notion of migrants' solidarity mobility, homeland authoritarianism, and political transnationalism for its conceptual and theoretical considerations. Methodological considerations are briefly discussed, followed by a brief discussion of how intercontinental citizenship networks are created by Europe-based Central African migrants in solidarity against homeland authoritarianism.

Conceptual and theoretical considerations

Homeland authoritarianism

This study understands authoritarianism as a top-down political regime, associated with monarchical absolutism, traditional dictatorships, and most forms of military rule (Heywood, 2013; Glasius, 2018; Linz, 2000). It highlights the understanding of façade regimes, or cosmetic democracy, established in Central African countries such as the DRC, Congo-Brazzaville, Rwanda, and Burundi (Bertelsmann Transformation Index (BTI) 2018, Mo Ibrahim Foundation 2018, EIU, 2018). That is, homeland authoritarianism entails political rule, typically established by pervasive ideological manipulation and open terror, which is associated with monarchical absolutism, traditional dictatorships, electoral authoritarianism, and most forms of military rule. It seeks to exclude most ordinary citizens from politics rather than abolish the public sphere at the national or local level of migrants' country of origin (Dahl, 1998; Fukuyama, 2011; Schedler, 2013). In sharing the same experiences of authoritarian practices from their respective countries, migrants from Central Africa stand in solidarity during their mobility and abroad.

Solidarité en mouvement

"Solidarité en mouvement" means solidarity in motion or solidarity mobility in French. This study is concerned with mechanical solidarity, based on similarities featuring, in particular, African migrants from Central Africa: shared tragic experiences during their mobility, the same receiving site, European territory, and homeland authoritarian practices as shared common push factors (Durkheim, 1947[1893]; Habermas, 1989; Laitinen and Pessi, 2015). The tragedies encountered during migrants' mobility have nurtured collective consciousness for a change in homeland governance. Here, the solidarity

triggered by crises is emphasised to foster political transformation. According to May (1996), solidarity consists of: i) conscious identification with groups; ii) bonds of sentiment; iii) a common interest in the group's well-being; iv) shared values and beliefs; and v) readiness to show moral support.

These elements are very important in this study, because they highlight how solidarity among Europe-based Central African migrants is nurtured by their collective identification as a group of migrants, the shared sentiment of striving to reach their final destination at all costs, the showing of mutual support during tragedies, shared values and beliefs in change and a better future, and readiness to strengthen each other through transnational citizenship against homeland political regimes. Solidarity is formed on the move, because perceived homeland authoritarian practices and tragedies at transit sites nurture social bonds among migrants that later trigger collective mobilisation around a common goal to contest homeland state powers from Europe.

Understanding "solidarité en mouvement" through the political transnationalism lens

This study uses political transnationalism as a suitable core theoretical lens through which to understand transnational political practices exercised by Europe-based Central African migrants in solidarity against homeland authoritarianism beyond nation state borders. This enables them to preserve ties with their countries of origin. Transnationalism merely focuses on migrants' networks and activities that involve them in politics associated with their country of origin (Bauböck, 2006). It covers a broad spectrum of border-crossing activities; as Østergaard-Nielsen coined it, "direct cross-border participation in the politics of their country of origin by both migrants and refugees [...] as well as their indirect participation via the political institutions of the host country" (Østergaard-Nielsen, 2003, p. 762). Here, it concerns understanding transnational political activities of migrants exercised in solidarity within networks.

The study emphasises transnationalism as political participation and a site of political engagement, enabling the researcher to understand intercontinental citizenship exercised by Europe-based Central African migrants from the Democratic Republic of the Congo (the DRC), Congo-Brazzaville, Rwanda, and Burundi within social networks in solidarity during their mobility and in the receiving country to collaborate against homeland authoritarian practices (Bauböck and Faist, 2010). The internet revolution has facilitated these social networks and bonds stemming from shared tragic experiences during migrants' perilous journeys and experiences from common homeland governance systems (Vertovec, 2009). This has not only changed how ordinary citizens relate with other in their home country, but also with other diasporic migrants (Lima, 2010).

To retain their ties with their country of origin, migrants create social fields as part of their engagement in transnational activities in receiving countries for their socioeconomic well-being and political change. These transnational social fields may be presented in a form of interconnected and overlapping political, economic, and sociocultural activities undertaken in receiving countries but extending to countries of origin (Lima, 2010). They may be simultaneously formal and self-organised, ranging from a retained membership in country-based political parties to the transfer or dissemination of political ideas, norms, blog writing, political websites, or lobbying both host and local people for political change at home (Lima, 2010). These transnational political activities depend on a context of exit and political opportunity that can either foster and/or grant or deny the rights to migrants to be included or excluded, and allow or inhibit them from embarking on any form of political activities within the host countries' borders (Guarnizo, Portes, and Haller, 2003; Lima, 2010). For example, given the established European democratic political structure of freedom of assembly and speech, migrants from African countries categorised by the BTI (2018) and the Mo Ibrahim Foundation (2018) as authoritarian like the DRC, Burundi, Congo-Brazzaville, and Rwanda are tempted to form political associations demanding democratic change in their respective countries of origin. Similarly, apart from the acculturation preferences (Guarnizo et al., 2003; Portes, 2001; Erdal and Oeppen, 2013; Stürmer and Simon, 2004), transnational political involvement and transnational political behaviour respectively shape political transnationalism (Green, Sarrasin, and Maggi, 2014; Al-Ali, Black, and Koser, 2001).

Intercontinental citizenship exercised by one group of African migrants from the DRC, for example, can motivate other groups of African migrants from Congo-Brazzaville to emulate the same transnational practices devised by the migrant group from the DRC to demand democratic change in their country of origin. Transnational political behaviour involves electoral participation through membership of a political party or as a financial contributor, or non-electoral participation as a member of civil society or as a sponsor of civic associations (Bloch, 2008; Faist, 2008; Green et al., 2014). In this context, some Europe-based Central African migrants unite in solidarity against homeland authoritarianism and identify themselves with opposition political parties from their countries of origin while abroad. These may include members or partisans from opposition political parties such as the Union for Democracy and Social Progress (UDPS) from the DRC, the FDU-Inkingi (*Forces Democratiques Unifiées*), and Dalfa Umurunzi (Development and Liberty for all) from Rwanda, the National Congress for Freedom (NCF) from Burundi, the Congolese Movement for Democracy and Integral Development (CMDID) from Congo-Brazzaville, among others (LaLibre, 2009; Refworld, 2015 and 2018; RFI, 2019; HRW, 2019). However, the study is not limited to Europe-based African migrants who are partisans of opposition political formations at home. It is also concerned with African migrants who are non-partisan members of opposition political parties. All these Europe-based Central African migrants entered into solidarity through networks and associations within the African migrant community in Europe to exercise transnational citizenship against homeland authoritarianism. Migrants' transnational political activities are undertaken thanks to social nodes such as tragic experiences during asylum-seeking processes and similarities between repressive political regimes at home, which constitute social network elements which bind migrants abroad as well as to the politics of their homeland (May, 1996). This entails migrants internalising and reproducing practices that occur in their networks at a given time.

Methodology

In addition to engaging with the existing secondary data, this study utilises the Democracy Index from the Economist Intelligence Unit (EIU, 2018) to explore the level of democratic governance in both the sending and receiving countries of Europe-based Central African migrants. The BTI (2018) and Ibrahim Index on African Governance (Mo Ibrahim Foundation, 2018) are also used to triangulate the democracy trend in the DRC, Rwanda, Congo-Brazzaville, and Burundi. These countries were used as migrant sending sites between 1990 and 2018 based on the following:

i.   they were rated authoritarian (BTI 2018, Mo Ibrahim Foundation 2018, and EIU, 2018);
ii. they each simultaneously experienced democratic transition and democratic deficit and/or politics of uncertainty (Schedler, 2013); and
iii. they all belong to Francophone Central Africa and share borders and culture, with the DRC at the centre.

The qualitative content analysis is used to enable the author to deeply analyse YouTube videos featuring male and female Europe-based Central African migrants exercising transnational political activities to contest homeland authoritarianism (Holsti, 1969; Merriam, 2009). The study uses the solidarity analytical framework for migrants by Agustín and Jørgensen (2019) as a core analytical tool to demonstrate how Europe-based Central African migrants practise, organise, and articulate solidarity against perceived homeland authoritarianism within political transnationalism.

Cosmetic democracy and harrowing treks

The context in which citizens exit their homeland is frequently complex and varies between socioeconomic, environmental, and political reasons such as violent conflict, recession, persecution, and disaster (IOM, 2019). In this context, three decades after the end of colonial rule in Africa and following the call for democratisation in the 1990s, post-independent African states such as the DRC, Congo-Brazzaville, Burundi, and Rwanda were all criticised for failing to democratically transform their political dynamics. Instead, they simply established a cosmetic democratic transition by allowing multiple political parties to exist without real political power and control. These glimpses of democracy later evaporated in fraudulent elections legalised by tailored constitutions (Versteeg et al., 2019). An array of reports from the EIU (EIU, 2018), the BTI (2018), and the Mo Ibrahim Foundation (2018) has rated these countries' political regimes as authoritarian. However, with the successful nation state reconstruction after the Rwandan genocide, some observers contend that these rating institutions are western-driven, undermining African political contexts. To others, these African political regimes undermine democratic principles despite the holding of elections and inflammation of recurring political turmoil, threatening fragile state institutions and forcing ordinary citizens into exile.

Political turmoil in Central Africa has been epitomised by tragedy and violent conflict that has claimed many lives. These have included recurring civil wars in the eastern part of the DRC since 1997 (Montague, 2002; Kisangani, 2012); the Rwandan genocide in 1994 (Thompson, 2007; Waldorf, 2009); recurring coups and political conflicts in Burundi (Des Forges, 1994; Ndikumana, 2005); recurring civil wars in Congo-Brazzaville, with opposing militia groups led respectively by then-President Lissouba, Bernard Kolélas, and Denis Sassou Nguesso, disrupting a fragile democracy in the 1990s, to name a few (Bazenguissa-Ganga, 1999; Englebert and Ron, 2004). Moreover, confiscation of political power tempering constitutional presidential term limits was perceived by citizens as a regional political mantra. The political elites then forcefully embarked on alterations of the country's constitution to secure either a third term or presidency for life (Versteeg et al., 2019). For example, in 2015, the Congo-Brazzaville government embarked on a constitutional amendment decried by the opposition coalition, which accused the seventy-one-year-old President Sassou Nguesso of seeking to get around age and term limits to run again in elections in 2016 (Reuters, 2015, Constitution of the Republic of Congo, 2015).

In Rwanda, a constitutional amendment allowed President Paul Kagame a third term in office from 2017 or to stand for a further term until 2034. It was criticized by the Democratic Green Party as tailor-made for one person and a blank cheque for a presidency for life (BBC News, 2016; Constitution of the Republic of Rwanda 2003 amended through, 2015; Pruitt, 2018). Burundi followed suit. The 2018 constitutional amendment gives President Nkurunziza the right to stand for re-election despite having already served three terms (Vandeginste, 2017; Al Jazeera, 2018, Burundi Constitution 2018). The DRC deviated from the above scenarios: the constitutional number of years in office was expanded in place of constitutional amendments after a complicated process that led to the delay of the 2016 elections (Trefon, 2013; Versteeg et al., 2019). These constitutional amendments were decried by many as inflaming existing violent conflicts, which displaced many citizens of these countries to seek protection elsewhere. In the quest for protection, African asylum seekers embarked on harrowing treks, experiencing tragedy and danger in horrific transit sites in Libya, Morocco, and Turkey (Bruey, 2018).

Some perished in the smuggling process, but others succeeded in reaching their European destination. Central African migrants found themselves at the crossroads between cosmetic democracy and harrowing treks, nurturing social bonds to collectively exert pressure on homeland political elites within horizontal networks to demand democratic change at home when they had reached Europe.

Contesting homeland authoritarianism from Europe

The 2011 Arab Spring initially demonstrated that migrants' cross-border political practices were capable of shaping and/or countering homeland political regimes from abroad. Most observers believe that citizens' political mobilisation beyond their territorial boundaries can foster political change in their country of origin (Betts and Jones, 2016). Migrants exploit their transboundary operation as actors simultaneously inside and outside their countries, and use the available political resources and structures in their receiving countries to demand democratic change in their countries of origin (Shain and Barth, 2003).

Against this backdrop African migrants exploit established democratic governance in Europe to collectively exercise intercontinental citizenship against their respective homeland political elites while in Europe (Roberts, 2010, EIU, 2018). The European political opportunity structure offers guaranteed freedom of association and assembly to many in Europe (BTI 2018, EIU, 2018). For example, an African migrant in Europe reports: "I got the idea it was easy to go to Europe, the land of tolerance. They will give you your rights" (Press, 2017, p. 3). For this study, African migrants from the DRC, Congo-Brazzaville, Burundi, and Rwanda based in European countries stand in solidarity within horizontal counter-networks and undertake transnational political activities demanding political transformation at home (Kimbalanga, 2012; Garbin and Godin, 2013). Most of these combatants are members and/ or partisans of the main opposition parties and resistance movements like the Union for Democracy and Social Progress (UDPS) from the DRC, the FDU-Inkingi – *Forces Democratiques Unifiées*- and Dalfa Umurunzi – Development and Liberty for All from Rwanda, the National Congress for Freedom (NCF) from Burundi, and the Congolese Movement for Democracy and Integral Development (CMDID) from Congo-Brazzaville.

It has been found that in the harrowing quest for a better life, migrants from East, Central, and West Africa are bound by their experience of tragedy between their transit and destination sites. For example, when being smuggled across the Mediterranean and Sahara through Morocco or Libya, some Central African migrants have faced the desertion of their smugglers, lost their loved ones when crafts or boats have capsized, been stranded and exposed to human rights abuse, experienced shortages of food and medical supplies, been illegally detained at transit sites in Libya and Morocco, and been deprived of human dignity and sold into slavery (Weber and Pickering,

2011). According to the UNODC (2011) nearly 55,000 African migrants from East, North, and West Africa are smuggled into Europe every year. Between 1990 and 2018, more than 20,750 migrants died attempting to reach Europe (Laine, 2020). Many observers believe more African migrants die at sea than is recorded (Weber and Pickering, 2011). These collective tragic experiences in transiting to Europe nurture social bonds that see migrants unite in solidarity on arrival at their destinations.

However, in addition to the above, migrants share other tragic political experiences: the recurring authoritarian practices of the rulers of their homelands who have forced them into exile. The political atrocities they have encountered lead Europe-based African migrants to develop collective political opposition to the political elites of their homelands. The latter are blamed for both the oppression they experienced at home and the misfortune they experienced in transit sites. These African *"combattants"*[2] within intercontinental citizenship networks demand democratic change in their homelands through different transnational strategies. They stand in solidarity to undertake intercontinental citizenship within (in)visible transnational networks of African migrants from the DRC, Congo-Brazzaville, Burundi, and Rwanda. These include collectively assisting fellow migrants during their public protests and demonstrations, collaborating during the *mutakalisation* of homeland government elites, and prohibiting homeland artists performing in Europe.

Mutual assistance during transnational public protests and demonstrations

Europe-based Central African migrants often join forces during public demonstrations initiated by a migrant combatant movement from a country that forms part of a large migrant network. On the streets of countries like the Netherlands, Belgium, France, and Switzerland, this migrant group denounces the persistence of authoritarian practices perpetrated at home by those they perceive as authoritarian rulers (Garbin and Godin, 2013; Demart, 2013). Apart from the *Place de la Republique* in France and *Matonge* in Belgium, African migrants' public demonstrations take place at the European Parliament in Brussels, the United Nations Human Rights Commission and World Trade Organisation in Geneva, and the International Criminal Court in the Netherlands (Reuters, 2011; Kimbalanga, 2012). These migrant combatants usually unite within a network sharing similar modus operandi to exert pressure on the international community and raise transnational awareness of pressing political issues in their respective countries of origin. They strategise together and assist each other in different ways, especially in covering their legal costs after their arrest as a result of their transnational citizenship. For example, the contested 2011 presidential elections and the delay to the 2016 general elections in the DRC both sparked a plethora of transnational public protests against President Kabila that were joined by other migrants hostile to political regimes in Congo-Brazzaville, Rwanda, and Burundi (Carter Center, 2011; Reid, 2013; Bensimon, 2015). As the Collectif

Sauvons le Congo[3] coordinator said when interviewed: *"Nous sommes un même peuple, nous avons les mêmes problèmes. Nous y arriverons en agissant ensemble et non pas chacun de son côté"* (TV5Monde, 2017)[4].

These migrant demonstrators thus believe they are one people separated by artificial and colonial borders. Their shared opposition to the authoritarian regimes of their homelands give them the opportunity to stand in solidarity to raise transnational awareness of the political unrest at home. At the 2011 UNESCO Conference in Paris, Rwandan migrant demonstrators from "Jambo ASBL"[5] were supported by their fellow migrants from the DRC in protesting against the attendance of President Paul Kagame, accusing him of being a dictator and of campaigning to amend the constitution to allow him to serve as president for life. One Congolese demonstrator from the DRC lamented in French that "[w]e are against his [President Kagame's] attendance. After all, atrocities are perpetrated in the DRC in complicity with his ally Joseph Kabila – that's why as the opposition Congolese resistance in Paris, we're part of this demonstration" (TV5Monde, 2011).

Some local and international organisations have criticised the Rwandan government for its involvement in inflaming violent conflict in the eastern part of the DRC (BBC, 2012; HRW, 2012). Based on these claims, Europe-based Congolese migrants often accuse President Kagame of being the mastermind of political turmoil at home. They therefore network with other Europe-based Rwandan combatants to oppose Kagame's regime from Europe (TV5Monde, 2011). *Le Potentiel*[6] (2012) reiterates that "200 to 300 rebels were recruited in Rwanda to be infiltrated into the DRC. They underwent brief military training before being deployed against the armed forces of the DRC". However, Kagame has repeatedly rebutted these allegations as unfounded and baseless. On Wednesday 7 June 2017, while attending the European Development Days 2017, President Kagame received both boos and acclaim in Brussels. Jambo ASBL led the Europe-based Rwandan migrants' *"Hashtag KagameGetOut"* protest, assisted by other migrants from Central Africa (Jambo Asbl, 2017).

Collaborating during mutakalisation *of homeland government elites*

Mutakalisation is a colloquial Congolese colloquial word used to describe brutal attacks on homeland politicians and allies during their visits abroad. It is also the violent stripping naked of someone, followed by humiliation on social media platforms (Inaka, 2017). Bonded by similar homeland political unrest, Europe-based African migrant combatants stand in solidarity to aggressively humiliate homeland politicians and their family members, including embassy staff. Combatants mobilise themselves from all over Europe to express their discontent by violently attacking anyone connected with politicians or institutions at home. *Mutakalisation* is viewed by other observers as belonging to the undemocratic and authoritarian strategies used by migrants abroad (Adamson, 2020). It seeks to display African migrants' discontent by exerting pressure on homeland politicians to abandon their authoritarian practices. Yet it also seeks to raise transnational awareness to demand the establishment of democratic governance at home. *Mutakalisation* is exercised at airports, railway stations, restaurants, shopping centres, and in the vicinity of public event venues. Homeland politicians and their representatives are often brutally attacked during official or private visits to Europe. Family members based in Europe are victimised when opposition leaders are assassinated or imprisoned at home. Embassy staff in Europe are also targeted. For example, on 31 December 2011, during a private visit to France, the then president of the Congolese Senate, Leon Kengo, was brutally attacked by a group of Europe-based Congolese migrants supported by migrants from Congo-Brazzaville. They reproached him for being an ally of former President Kabila and a cosmetic opposition figure (Boisbouvier, 2012). Apart from repeatedly setting their embassy on fire in June 2016 and November 2018 in Paris, migrant combatants, *"les indignés du 242"*[7], from Congo-Brazzaville, assisted by some from the DRC, also brutally attacked embassy officials and publicised the incident on social media (Mbena, 2018; Monama, 2018).

Networking during disruption of homeland artists' performance in Europe

Reproached as an opiate that distracts the general citizenry and diaspora from politics while aiming to advance authoritarian rulers in their homeland, African musicians, especially from the DRC and Congo-Brazzaville, have suffered attacks and/or disruption of their European performances by Central African migrants. Teddy Minar, a Europe-based Congolese migrant rapper and activist from the DRC, laments in French: *"On ne va pas faire la fête pendant que la mère patrie est en train de souffrir. Les artistes se maintiennent dans un silence assourdissant face aux violences"*.[8]

No one can underestimate the power of music's persuasion to manipulate public opinion (Teitelbaum, 2017; Ansari, 2018). It encapsulates and promotes political attitudes and positions (Bleiker, 2005; Manuel, 2017). Although informal, these African combatants have succeeded in stopping or disrupting performances by artists from their countries of origin. Musical artists from the DRC and Congo-Brazzaville like to entertain their fans in major European cities like Paris, Brussels, Dublin, and London. For example, when a concert is announced, combatants mobilise within a network to destroy advertising materials, threaten the producer and artists, and agitate with the host municipality authorities to cancel the event. On the concert day, they threaten fans who refuse to buy into their grievances with *mutakalisation*. If the concert is authorised by the Parisian city municipality, discontented combatants network to raise transnational awareness by smashing shop and car windows, throwing projectiles, tipping dustbins over, and barricading public roads to cause traffic jams in the venue's vicinity (Radio Okapi, 2012).

In May 2018, on the eve of a concert by Mr Roga Roga, a famous artist from Congo-Brazzaville, the entrance of the Palais du Congrès Paris Est Montreuil was set alight, cars were burnt, and their windows smashed by a coalition of Central African migrants. They came in numbers to disrupt the concert under heavy police surveillance (Afrique Replay TV, 2018; TV5Monde, 2018). Donald Ngouma, a leader of the combatants, lamented: "We don't need this concert here. We didn't leave our countries to be here and allow these artists to sing to the praise of our dictators to us [...] pretending everything is going well at home. No..." (TV5Monde, 2018).

Other artists from the DRC such as Werrason, J-B Mpiana, Fally Ipupa, Koffi Olomidé, Felix Wazekwa, and Ferre Gola have experienced the same fate from the same groups of combatants (Radio Okapi, 2012; Bazzara, 2017). They have therefore been obliged to perform at home and in neighbouring African countries. The artists complain that concerts at home yield less income than concerts in Europe.

Towards the solidarity against homeland authoritarianism

In this study, political transnationalism has served as a theoretical lens to understand the transnational field of Central African migrants' political activities in connection with their countries of origin, the DRC, Congo-Brazzaville, Burundi, and Rwanda (Bauböck, 2006). This theoretical lens simultaneously highlights how these migrants also collaboratively enter into alliances to exhibit cross-border political practices that they deem relevant to collectively challenging their homeland rulers to abandon their authoritarianism.

To achieve this, the study used the relational and spatial dimensions of the solidarity analytical framework of Agustín and Jørgensen (2019) to assess how political transnationalism solidarity was practised, organised, and articulated by the Europe-based Central African migrants against perceived homeland authoritarianism. It was found that these combatants' political transnationalism was exercised through relational and spatial solidarities. The relational and spatial dimensions of solidarity served as analytical tools. First, according to Agustín and Jørgensen (2019), "relational solidarity enhances relations between different actors and generates political subjectivities and collective identities". In this respect, social bonds nurtured between female and male Congolese, Rwandan, Burundian, and DRC migrants engender both scepticism of their homelands' perceived authoritarian politics and the collective identity of survivors of tragic mobility experiences and repressive politics at home. As indicated in the preceding section, the political turmoil in the Central African region and the tragedies encountered in transit sites like Libya and Morocco have united Central African migrants in Europe. Between 1990 and 2018 Central African political elites from the DRC, Congo-Brazzaville, Rwanda, and Burundi were all criticised for their use of repression to cement their claim to leadership, putting democracy under pressure (BTI 2018, Mo Ibrahim Foundation 2018). These perceived authoritarian practices were deemed not only to be among the many key push factors in the massive exodus of ordinary citizens but as a recipe for the unity of survivors within European social structures. These migrant combatants are also united by the shared aspiration for political transformation.

Second, concerning spatial migrant solidarity, "alliances are built and imaginaries invented and multi-scalar relations can be developed by connecting different spaces" (Agustín and Jørgensen 2019). During their mobility, these Central Africans build invisible spaces for survivors of tragic experiences at transit sites. On arrival at their host sites, they build other (in)visible spaces, grouping migrants from one country in networks like *"les indignés du 242"*[9], "Jambo ASBL", and *"Combattants"*, and thereafter they enter into alliances with other associations of African migrants to form a wide horizontal mutual collaboration network between Congolese, Burundian, Rwandan, and DRC migrants in Europe. It was observed that other factors such as geographical location and shared cultural identity have combined to nurture relational and spatial solidarity among Europe-based Central African migrants. The DRC shares borders with Rwanda, Burundi, and Congo-Brazzaville. Citizens of these countries share common local languages that connect them abroad. The DRC and Congo-Brazzaville share near-identical names and similar cultures. People from these countries communicate in Lingala and Kikongo. In addition, South Kivu citizens from the DRC use Swahili, as do Rwandans and Burundians. French is the common official language in the region. In this respect Congolese migrants develop social relational proximity with every migrant network from Congo-Brazzaville, Rwanda, and Burundi. Consequently, they shape and/or influence the political transnationalism of Europe-based Central African migrants, promoting the same modus operandi during the exercise of intercontinental citizenship (Kimbalanga, 2012). The above factors amplify solidarity among these African migrants. May (1996) points out that solidarity consists of conscious identification with groups, bonds of sentiment, a common interest in the group's well-being, shared values and beliefs, and readiness to show moral support. Figure 7.1 summarises the above analysis.

Briefly, these combatants practise solidarity in the form of mutual assistance during transnational public protests and demonstrations, collaborate in the *mutakalisation* of homeland government elites, and network to disrupt homeland artists' performances in Europe. Although they demand democratic change in their homelands, the combatants are criticised by many for employing undemocratic and authoritarian strategies as part of their overall political transnationalism (Adamson, 2020). As survivors and/or resisters of perceived homeland authoritarian practices, Europe-based Central African migrants employ aggressive strategies deemed appropriate to counter the regimes of their homelands.

Conclusion

This study constitutes an empirical African perspective that should be considered in dealing with the current migration issue, which threatens

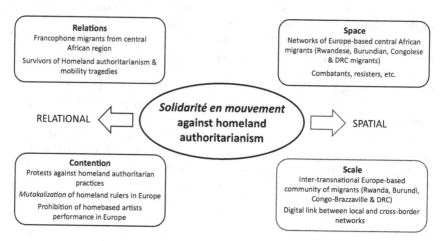

Figure 7.1 Political transnationalism solidarity of Europe-based Central African migrants against homeland authoritarianism.

By author, adapted from Agustin and Jørgensen (2019).

African-European common intercontinental migration policies. Given the misleading narrative on African migration to Europe and the fact that African voices are still seldom heard, Europe-based combatants from Central Africa unite to create alternative avenues to combat the perceived authoritarian regimes of their homelands. That is, these Europe-based Central African migrants from Congo-Brazzaville, Burundi, the DRC, and Rwanda collaborate while exiting their respective countries of origin. Once in Europe, they strategise within horizontal networks during their political activities. These strategies include mutual assistance during transnational public protests and demonstrations, collaborating during the *mutakalisation* of the government elites of their homelands, and networking during the disruption of homeland-based artists' European performances. Thus, "*solidarité en mouvement*" has triggered intercontinental citizenship networks of Europe-based African migrants and transnational public awareness that may be a recipe for democratic change at home. There is a need to rethink the relations between Africa and Europe around migration, and the African situation should not continue to be poorly understood.

Notes

1 Europe-based Central African migrants include both intercontinental migrants and refugees and asylum seekers from Burundi, the Democratic Republic of Congo, Congo-Brazzaville, and Rwanda staying in Europe. They are also referred to as resisters, combatants, etc.
2 From French, meaning "Resisters" to homeland political regimes.

3 Save the Congo Consortium.
4 "We are one people and we share common problems. Together we shall win but not in isolation".
5 "Hello" in Swahili. It is an association of Rwandan migrants in Europe.
6 A local newspaper in the DRC.
7 In French, the "outraged of Congo-Brazzaville".
8 "We cannot celebrate here while the nation is sick. Artists have shockingly turned a blind eye to the violence in Congo" (Bazzara, 2017).
9 Ibid. 5.

References

Adamson, F. B. (2020) Non-state authoritarianism and diaspora politics. *Global Networks*, 20(1), 150–69.

Afrique Replay TV. (2018) Concert de Roga Roga Les combattants en colère brulent le palais des congrès de Paris Est Montreuil. (online) Available at: youtu.be/L1-BpckLSDc Accessed 12/11/2019 (Accessed 9 Mar. 2019).

Al-Ali, N., Black, R. and Koser, K. (2001) The limits to "transnationalism": Bosnian and Eritrean refugees in Europe as emerging transnational communities. *Ethnic and Racial Studies*, 24(4), pp. 578–600.

Al Jazeera. (2018) Burundi backs new constitution extending presidential term limits, 22 May. (online) Available at: www.aljazeera.com/news/africa/2018/05/burundi-backs-constitution-extending-presidential-term-limits-180521134736408.html (Accessed 11 Nov. 2019).

Ansari, E. A. (2018) *The Sound of a Superpower: Musical Americanism and the Cold War*. Oxford: Oxford University Press.

Bauböck, R. and Faist, T., eds. (2010) *Diaspora and Transnationalism: Concepts, Theories and Methods*. Amsterdam: Amsterdam University Press.

Agustín, Ó. G. and Jørgensen, M. B. (2019) Solidarity cities and cosmopolitanism from Below: Barcelona as a refugee city. Social Inclusion, 7(2), pp. 198–207.

Bauböck, R. (2006) *Migration and Citizenship: Legal Status, Rights And Political Participation*. Amsterdam: Amsterdam University Press.

Bazenguissa-Ganga, R. (1999) The spread of political violence in Congo-Brazzaville. *African Affairs*, 98(390), pp. 37–54.

Bazzara, A. (2017) Qui sont « les combattants », ces opposants radicaux qui empêchent les concerts d'artistes congolais? (online) Available at: www.20minutes.fr/culture/2108915-20170724-video-combattants-opposants-radicaux-empechent-concerts-artistes-congolais. (Accessed 14 Dec. 2019).

BBC. (2012) Rwanda supporting DR Congo mutineers. BBC News Africa, 28 May 2012. (online) Available at: www.bbc.co.uk/news/world-africa-18231128 (Accessed 17 Dec. 2019).

BBC. (2016) Rwanda's Paul Kagame to run for third presidential term. (online) Available at: www.bbc.com/news/world-africa-35209186 (Accessed 17 Dec. 2019).

BBC. (2019) Migrant crisis: UN says six die every day in Mediterranean crossings. BBC News 30 January 2019. (online) Available at: www.bbc.com/news/world-europe-47055619. Accessed. (Accessed 10 Feb. 2020).

Bensimon, C. (2015) Les Congolais crient à leur tour «Kabila dégage». Le Temps jeudi 22 janvier 2015. (online) Available at: www.letemps.ch/monde/congolais-crient-tour-kabila-degage. (Accessed 10 May. 2019).

Bertelsmann Transformation Index (BTI). (2018) Transformation Index BTI 2018: Governance in International Comparison. Gütersloh: Bertelsmann Stiftung.

Betts, A. and Jones, W. (2016) *Mobilising the Diaspora.* Cambridge: Cambridge University Press.

Bleiker, R. (2005) Of things we hear but cannot see: Musical explorations of international politics. In: M. I. Franklin, ed., *Resounding International Relations: On Music, Culture, and Politics.* New York: Palgrave Macmillan, pp. 179–98.

Bloch, A. (2008) Zimbabweans in Britain: Transnational activities and capabilities. *Journal of Ethnic and Migration Studies,* 34(2), pp. 287–305.

Boisbouvier, C. (2012) RDC: quand les « combattants » s'en mêlent 20 janvier 2012 à 12h20. (online) www.jeuneafrique.com/207585/politique/rdc-quand-les-combattants-s-en-m-lent/. (Accessed 12 Dec. 2019).

Bruey, V. F. (2018) Fatal journeys of displaced African migrants crossing the Mediterranean. *Journal of Internal Displacement,* 8(1), 45–82.

Carter Center. (2011) DRC Presidential election results lack credibility, 10 December. (online) Available at: www.cartercenter.org/news/pr/drc-121011.html (Accessed 11 Jun. 2019).

Constitution of the Republic of Congo. (2015) (online) Available at: www. constituteproject.org/constitution/Congo_2015.pdf?lang=en (Accessed 11 Nov. 2019).

Constitution of the Republic of Rwanda 2003 amended through. (2015) (online) Available at: www.constituteproject.org/constitution/Rwanda_2015.pdf?lang=en. (Accessed 11 Nov. 2019).

Constitution of the Republic of Burundi. (2018) (online) Available at: www.assemblee. bi/IMG/pdf/constitution.pdf. (Accessed 11 Nov. 2019).

Dahl, R. A. (1998) *On Democracy.* New Haven: Yale University Press

Demart, S. (2013) Riots in Matonge and … the indifference of public authority? *Brussels Studies* 68. (online) Available at: journals.openedition.org/brussels/1168. (Accessed 11 Nov. 2019).

Des Forges, A. (1994) Burundi: Failed coup or creeping coup? *Current History,* 93(583), pp. 203–07.

Durkheim, E. (1947[1893]) *The Division of Labour in Society,* transl. D. Simpson. Glencoe IL: Free Press.

Erdal, M. B. and Oeppen, C. (2013) Migrant balancing acts: Understanding the interactions between integration and transnationalism. *Journal of Ethnic and Migration Studies,* 39(6), pp. 867–84.

Economic Index Unit (EIU). (2018) Democracy Index 2018: Me too? Political participation, protest and democracy. (online) Available at: 275rzy1ul4252pt1hv2dqyuf-wpengine.netdna-ssl.com/wp-content/uploads/2019/01/Democracy_Index_2018. pdf. (Accessed 14 Jan. 2020).

Englebert, P. and Ron, J. (2004) Primary commodities and war: Congo-Brazzaville's ambivalent resource curse. *Comparative Politics,* 37(1), pp. 61–81.

Faist, T. (2008) Migrants as transnational development agents: An inquiry into the newest round of the migration–development nexus. *Population, space and place,* 14(1), pp. 21–42.

Fukuyama, F. (2011) *The Origins of Political Order: From Prehuman Times to the French Revolution.* New York: Farrar, Straus and Giroux.

Glasius, M. (2018) What authoritarianism is … and is not: A practice perspective. *International Affairs,* 94(3), pp. 515–33.

Garbin, D. and Godin, M. (2013) "Saving the Congo": Transnational social fields and politics of home in the Congolese diaspora. *African and Black Diaspora: An International Journal*, 6(2), pp. 113–30.

Green, E. G., Sarrasin, O., and Maggi, J. (2014) Understanding transnational political involvement among Senegalese migrants: The role of acculturation preferences and perceived discrimination. *International Journal of Intercultural Relations*, 41, pp. 91–101.

Guarnizo, L. E., Portes, A., and Haller, W. (2003) Assimilation and transnationalism: Determinants of transnational political action among contemporary migrants. *American journal of sociology*, 108(6), pp. 1211–48.

Habermas, J. (1989) *The Structural Transformation of the Public Sphere*, trans. T. Burger. Cambridge: MIT Press.

Heywood, A. (2013) *Politics*. Basingstoke: Palgrave Macmillan

Holsti, O. R. (1969) *Content Analysis for the Social Sciences and Humanities*. Reading, MA: Addison-Wesley.

HRW. (2012) Human Rights Watch DR Congo: Rwanda should stop aiding war crimes suspect Congolese Renegade General Bosco Ntaganda receives recruits and weapons from Rwanda. (online) Available at: www.hrw.org/news/2012/06/03/dr-congo-rwanda-should-stop-aiding-war-crimes-suspect (Accessed 17 Jan. 2020).

HRW. (2019) Human Rights Watch Burundi: Rampant abuses against Opposition, 12 June 2019. (online) Available at: www.hrw.org/news/2019/06/12/burundi-rampant-abuses-against-opposition. (Accessed 20 Feb. 2020).

Inaka, S. J. (2017) Congolese middle class migrants labour market incorporation in Pretoria. In C. C. Nshimbi and I. Moyo, eds., *Migration, Cross-Border Trade and Development in Africa*. Cham: Palgrave Macmillan, pp. 63–97.

Mo Ibrahim Foundation (2018) Ibrahim index of African governance Report. (online) Available at: mo-s3.ibrahim.foundation/u/2018/11/27173840/2018-Index-Report. pdf. (Accessed 17 Feb. 2020).

International Organisation of Migration (IOM). (2019) World Migration Report 2020. (online) Available at: publications.iom.int/system/files/pdf/wmr_2020.pdf (Accessed 5 Feb. 2020).

Jambo Asbl. (2017) #KagameGetOut: Large protest against Paul Kagame in Brussels. (online) Available at: youtu.be/tS4tVppOTvM Accessed 12/2/2020. (Accessed 5 Feb. 2020).

Kisangani, E. F. (2012) *Civil Wars in the Democratic Republic of Congo, 1960–2010*. Boulder, CO: Lynne Rienner.

Kimbalanga, H. (2012) Les Combattants Congolais d'Europe, seul mouvement de pression africain qui fait peur à sa dictature. (online) Available at: ensemble.nous. pouvons.changer.over-blog.com/ (Accessed 11 Dec. 2019).

Laine, J. P. (2020) Ambiguous bordering practices at the EU's edges. In: A. Bissonnette and É. Vallet, eds., *Borders and border walls: in-security, symbolism, vulnerabilities*. London: Routledge, pp. 69–87.

LaLibre. (2009) La descente aux enfers de l'UDPS. LaLibre.be Marie-France Cros.

Le Potentiel. (2012) Face à l'indéniable implication du Rwanda dans la guerre au Kivu, les Etats-Unis, la Grande-Bretagne, l'UE… mis devant leurs responsabilités!, Kinshasa, 20 Dec. 2019.

Lima, A. (2010) *Transnationalism: A New Mode of Immigrant Integration*. Boston: University of Massachusetts.

Linz, J. J. (2000) *Totalitarian and Authoritarian Regimes*. Boulder, Co.: Lynne Rienner Publishers.

Manuel, P. (2017) World music and activism since the end of history [sic]. *Music and Politics*, XI(1), DOI: dx.doi.org/10.3998/mp.9460447.0011.101

May, L. (1996) *The Socially Responsive Self*. Chicago: The University of Chicago Press.

Mbena, O. (2018) Grave incendie à l'ambassade du Congo en France. *AfrikMag* of 27 November 2018. (online) Available at: www.afrikmag.com/grave-incendie-lambassade-congo-brazzaville/ (Accessed 7 Jan. 2019).

Merriam, S. B. (2009) *Qualitative Research: A Guide to Design and Implementation*. New York: John Wiley and Sons.

Monama, F. (2018) L'ambassade du Congo a Paris de nouveau brûlé. (online) Available at: youtu.be/5ih_h9hBdaw (Accessed 7 Jan. 2019).

Montague, D. (2002) Stolen goods: Coltan and conflict in the Democratic Republic of Congo. *Sais Review*, 22(1), pp. 103–18.

Motlagh J. (2016) A terrifying journey through the world's most dangerous jungle. Outside, 19 July 2016. (online) Available at: www.outsideonline.com/2098801/skull-stake-darien-gap (Accessed 7 Jan. 2019).

Ndikumana, L. (2005) Distributional conflict, the state and peace building in Burundi. *The Round Table*, 94(381), pp. 413–27.

Laitinen, A. and Pessi, A. B., eds. (2015) *Solidarity: Theory and Practice*. London: Lexington.

Radio Okapi. (2012) La musique Congolaise confrontée à la violence politique des Congolais de la diaspora, 22 June 2012. (online) Available at: radiookapi.net/societe/2012/06/21/la-musiqu... (Accessed 17 Dec. 2019).

Refworld. (2015) Republic of the Congo: The Congolese Movement for Democracy and Integral Development (January 2015-November 2015). (online) Available at: www.refworld.org/docid/575526114.html (Accessed 14 Dec. 2019).

Refworld. (2018) Democratic Republic of Congo: The Union for Democracy and Social Progress. (online) Available at: www.refworld.org/cgibin/texis/vtx/rwmain?page=printdoc&docid=5b9b61824. (Accessed 14 Dec. 2019).

Reid, T. B. (2013) Congolese elections 2011: Mostly a problem of global governance and negative "soft power", not resources. *Journal of African Elections*, 12(1), pp. 34–64.

Reuters. (2011) Brussels police arrest 200 over Congo vote violence, 10 Dec. 2011. (online) Available at: www.reuters.com/article/us-congo-belgium-riots/brussels-police-arrest-200-over-congo-vote-violence-idUSTRE7B909J20111210 (Accessed 9 Dec. 2019).

Reuters. (2015) Congo votes by landslide to allow third presidential term. Philon Bondenga 27 Oct. 2015. (online) Available at: www.reuters.com/article/us-congo-politics/congo-votes-by-landslide-to-allow-third-presidential-term-idUSKCN0SL0JW20151027 (Accessed 18 Nov. 2019).

RFI. (2019) Rwanda: l'opposante Victoire Ingabire lance un nouveau parti. Radio France Internationale 10 Nov. 2019. (online) Available at: www.rfi.fr/fr/afrique/20191110-rwanda-opposante-victoire-ingabire-lance-nouveau-parti. (Accessed 9 Feb. 2020).

Roberts, A. (2010) *The Quality of Democracy in Eastern Europe. Public Preferences and Policy Reforms*. Cambridge: Cambridge University Press.

Østergaard-Nielsen, E., ed. (2003) *International Migration and Sending Countries: Perceptions, Policies and Transnational Relations*. Basingstoke: Palgrave Macmillan.

Portes, A. (2001) Introduction: The debates and significance of immigrant trans-nationalism. *Global Networks*, 1(3), pp. 181–94.

Press, R. (2017) Dangerous crossings: Voices from the African Migration to Italy/Europe. *Africa Today*, 64(1), pp. 3–27.

Pruitt, W. R. (2018) Why Kagame should not seek another term. *African Journal of Criminology & Justice Studies*, 11(1), pp. 55–70.

Schedler, A. (2013) *The Politics of Uncertainty: Sustaining and Subverting Electoral Authoritarianism*. Oxford: Oxford University Press.

Shain, Y. and Barth, A. (2003) Diasporas and international relations theory. *International Organization*, 57(3), pp. 449–79.

Stürmer, S. and Simon, B. (2004) Collective action: Towards a dual-pathway model. *European Review of Social Psychology*, 15(1), pp. 59–99.

Teitelbaum, B. R. (2017) *Lions of the North: Sounds of the New Nordic Radical Nationalism*. Oxford: Oxford University Press.

Thompson, A. (2007) *Media and the Rwanda Genocide*. Ottawa: IDRC.

Trefon, T. (2013) Uncertainty and powerlessness in Congo 2012. *Review of African Political Economy*, 40(135), pp. 141–51.

TV5Monde. (2018) A Montreuil, les "combattants Congolais" manifestent. (online) Available at: youtu.be/SPAkhGj5A2k (Accessed 12 Nov. 2019).

TV5Monde. (2011) Paul Kagame en visite à Paris, ses partisans et opposants défilent dans la capitale. (online) Available at: www.youtube.com/watch?v=yp_0vc3ojkk (Accessed 12 Nov. 2019).

TV5Monde. (2017) RDC: qui sont ces "combattants" qui s'opposent au Président Kabila? (online) Available at: information.tv5monde.com/afrique/rdc-qui-sont-ces-combattants-qui-s-opposent-au-president-kabila-181189 (Accessed 12 Nov. 2019).

UNODC. (2011) Issue Paper: Smuggling of Migrants by Sea. (online) Available at: www.unodc.org/documents/human-trafficking/Migrant-Smuggling/Issue-Papers/Issue_Paper_Smuggling_of_Migrants_by_Sea.pdf (Accessed 22 Nov. 2019).

Vandeginste, S. (2017) *Burundi's Constitutional Amendment: What Do We Know So Far?* Antwerp: University of Antwerp.

Versteeg, M., Horley, T., Meng, A., Guim, M., and Guirguis, M. (2019) the law and politics of presidential term limit evasion. *Columbia Law Review, 2020; Virginia Public Law and Legal Theory Research Paper* No. 2019-14.

Vertovec, S. (2009) *Transnationalism: Key Ideas*. London: Routledge.

Waldorf, L. (2009) Revisiting Hotel Rwanda: Genocide ideology, reconciliation, and rescuers. *Journal of Genocide Research*, 11(1), 101–25.

Weber, L. and Pickering, S. (2011) *Globalization and Borders: Death at the Global Frontier*. Dordrecht: Springer.

Zhang, S. X., Sanchez, G. E., and Achilli, L. (2018) Crimes of solidarity in mobility: Alternative views on migrant smuggling. *The ANNALS of the American Academy of Political and Social Science*, 676(1), pp. 6–15.

8 Staying because of all odds

Lived experiences of African student migrants in Finland

Quivine Ndomo

Changing mobilities and changing spaces

The political, social, and economic importance of migrants for contemporary societies cannot be overstated in this epoch of demographic crisis and the knowledge economy. In the last five decades, human mobility across national borders has changed significantly, influenced mainly by globalisation and its practices, climate change, and war and conflict. Contemporary migrant geographies therefore differ starkly from those of five decades ago. These changes to human mobility processes occur within societies that are also transforming politically and economically – for example, regional de-bordering in the EU, the rise of nationalist and populist ideologies, and the terrorism and securitisation turn – as well as socially – for example, labour market precarisation and diminishing social security (Laine, 2018; Yuval-Davis, 2011).

The convergence of persistent dynamic human flows across national borders and global transformation processes in turn produces an uneasy union, rife with political and socioeconomic dilemmas, perhaps most concretely portrayed in the sociopolitically constructed post-2014 "migration crisis" in Europe (Laine, 2018, p. 231; Anderson, 2013). These dilemmas influence individual nation states' interpretation of migratory acts and the consequent migration management approaches pursued, setting the stage for perversely regulated, mediated, and contested migration experiences. Moreover, contemporary state borders are no longer at the periphery of society but have moved into daily experience within nation state territories (Somers, 2008; Balibar, 2004). Thus, the new migrant flows into Europe and a changing globalised Europe produce migratory processes characterised by stringent regulation within nation state territories – a feature I call pervasive internal bordering.

The contemporary border can be conceived as a processual phenomenon that constitutes administrative procedures for excluding non-citizens to regulate their presence and access within a community of value (Balibar, 2004). This chapter adopts a multidisciplinary and constructivist understanding of borders based on scholarship on the processes, institutions, and structures that regulate migrants' activities within host countries (see e.g. Mezzadra and Neilson, 2013; Yuval-Davis, 2011; Lyon, 2005; Balibar, 2004). A border is

DOI: 10.4324/9781003083726-9

therefore any regulatory institution and its corresponding practices, which function through differentiation to produce a hierarchy with a clear distinction between citizens and non-citizens in society.

Such borders are also "expansionist", extending their reach into transborder phenomena, particularly by mandating social state and private social structures such as healthcare facilities, banks, schools, housing offices, and employers to function as the internal border's administrative personnel (Zureik and Salter, 2013; Yuval-Davis, 2011). Together, personalised bordering and administrative bordering are used to highlight the extent to which bordering permeates migrants' lives. Administrative bordering includes all the bureaucratic gatekeeping activities implemented by institutions like hospitals, banks, and schools, while personalised bordering refers to and implies activities of differentiation that migrants learn to exert on themselves due to "*chronic*" exclusion (Könönen, 2018). Bordering is therefore a technology of flexibility, determining who is in and who is out of specific aspects of society.

Contemporary Africa–Europe migration: the Finnish case

The universal Nordic welfare states offer a rich country context for investigating the impact of emerging trends in migration control and regulation in the global west. With the fresh fears of welfare burden, crime, and other distasteful cultural norms sparked by the migration crisis, the universal Nordic welfare states come to mind because of their generous residence-based welfare arrangements. Moreover, the welfare magnet rhetoric (Tervonen, Pellander, and Yuval-Davis, 2018) has prompted potentially tighter formal migration control in these countries, albeit of varying national degrees. However, in light of binding international law and its practices, such as de-bordering in the EU, these states are also turning to pervasive internal bordering techniques to manage migrants within their borders. Such techniques include gatekeeping, differentiation and sorting, regulation, surveillance, and precarisation (Zureik and Salter, 2013; Lyon, 2005).

Net migration to Finland only materialised in the 1990s. However, international migrants are crucial for the Finnish economy and society today. The demographic crisis is a pressing reality for Finland, with various sectors of the economy experiencing labour shortages, and the dependency ratio rapidly weakening (Ministry of the Interior, 2018).

Finland has therefore adopted migration as a strategy to address its socioeconomic challenges with strategies like *The Future of Migration 2020* and legislation like the *Act on the Promotion of Immigrant Integration (1386/ 2010)* to attract and retain international skills, students, and labour. However, Finnish employers maintain a limited geographical purview of desirable migrants, minimising the labour market integration potential of peripheral migrant groups such as African and Middle Eastern migrants (European Migration Network (EMN), 2018, pp. 6–7). Student migrants are the second

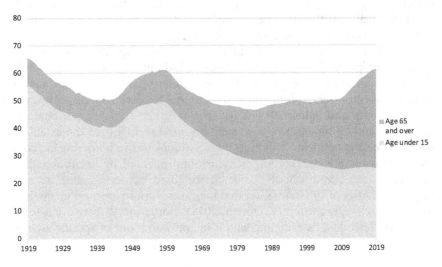

Figure 8.1 Finland's demographic dependency ratio, 1919–2019. Number of children and elderly per 100 persons of working age.

Data source: Statistics Finland.

largest migrant group in Finland. In 2016 seventy-six percent of student migrants originated from outside the EU/EEA, of whom eighty percent were from Asia, while students from Africa, the Americas, and Oceania contributed about twenty per cent (Centre for International Mobility (CIMO), 2016). The number of applications by African students to Finland declined significantly in 2017, largely because of a change in legislation that introduced fees for non-EU/EEA students, rose in 2018, and dipped slightly in 2019 (Migri, 2020).

However, concerning return migration rates, a survey of post-graduation mobility in Finland reported a stay rate of eighty-five percent for African graduates, eighteen percentage points above the general stay rate for all foreign graduates in Finland (Shumilova and Cai, 2015). A previous empirical study of return migration in Denmark outlined relatable findings, indicating that migrants from less developed countries produce the lowest return rates (Jensen and Pedersen, 2007). African student migrants' tendency to settle means they constitute a significant proportion of the Finnish international migrant stock and an especially interesting integration study group in post-2014 migrant crisis Europe, especially given their *"unwanted brand"*. Disappointingly, previous studies, for example, Maury (2017), and participant stories collected in this study portray a group of African student migrants staying in Finland who are forced to contend with pervasive disabling internal bordering in the legal-administrative, social, and economic spheres on a daily basis.

The purpose of this chapter is to explore the daily lived experiences of a group of African migrants staying in Finland to understand the practices of migrants' bordering within European nation state territories in the context of the post-2014 migration crisis. Further, the study investigates the adverse socioeconomic consequences of such practices for both migrants and host societies, offering an alternative perspective on migrant decision-making behaviour and especially the decision to settle in a host country. The chapter aims to contribute to the discussion about rethinking EU–Africa relations from a migration perspective. The rest of the chapter proceeds as follows. The next section addresses the study's methodology. It is followed by an extensive analysis section. A section summarising the study's findings follows. Finally, some concluding remarks call for an ideological reconstruction of migration practices.

Mode of inquiry

The chapter is based on an analysis of data collected in twenty-three in-depth one-on-one narrative interviews with African student migrants from Gambia, Ghana, Kenya, Nigeria, and Zambia who have remained in Finland. Remaining refers to the choice to continue living in Finland on completion of studies. Nigeria, Ghana, and Kenya are the biggest senders of African student migrants to Finland; Gambia and Zambia were chosen on a convenience snowball-sampling basis. Data collection and analysis followed the procedures of the narrative approach to qualitative research (Creswell and Poth, 2018). Interviews were conducted in English between January and April 2018, and in January 2020 in Helsinki, the capital, and Jyväskylä, a university town, with a theoretically sampled group (Corbin and Strauss, 2008). Interview questions sought a holistic biographical narrative, including stories from the period before the decision to migrate, the decision, journey, and the process of settling in Finland.

Data analysis focused on the elements of participant stories – interaction, continuity, and situation – through a data-driven thematic analysis (Riessman, 2008). I followed a four-step procedure adapted from the stepwise procedures of Creswell and Poth (2018) and Corbin and Strauss (2008, pp. 159–274) for qualitative data analysis. My analysis and interpretation uphold the constructivist ideal that the world can only be known through representation, which explains the focus on told narratives and their attached meanings. Thus, in analysing the data I interacted with it in an attempt to make sense of the material, guided by my understanding of migration processes, informed by existing literature, as well as my own experiences as an African migrant living in Finland (Denzin, 2011).

Unpacking the practices of exclusion

In this section of the chapter, I present a narrative of the systematic, extensive, and institutionally executed exclusion of a group of African migrants from various spaces of the society in which they live, study, and work. The premise and core of the narrative is the status and "replace" of belonging, which emerged as a central theme in the migrant stories during data analysis. Yuval-Davis (2011) describes belonging as a natural, organic, and emotive attachment to a place, and feeling "at home" thus becomes part of people's everyday lives. These arguments are supported by the migrant stories collected in this study, in which belonging is centrally situated in informants' daily experiences. Belonging derives from full inclusion through membership of a targeted collective with a boundary, thus enabling access to the legal, social, and economic opportunities and resources necessary for forging a life perceived as worth living (see e.g. Yuval-Davis, 2011; Somers, 2008; Marshall and Bottomore, 1992). Finally, informed by informants' elaboration, I define belonging as the struggle for the status of valid existence in the communities and society in which one lives, and to which one contributes through duties and obligations.

Anthias (2008) explains that belonging is fundamental to migrants' socioeconomic integration in host societies. Finland is a notably homogenous country, and as interview data indicates, the status of belonging is a significant socioeconomic resource for successful integration in Finnish society. However, the same data shows that a variety of structures obstruct migrants' access to this resource by excluding them from Finnish society and its privileges. Nevertheless, informants retain the quest to belong as a key milestone towards their objective of attaining a valid presence in Finland. The informants' quest to belong therefore marks the beginning of an evolutionary process of coming face-to-face with and responding to exclusion, and rationalising the decision to stay in Finland in terms of migration experiences. Data analysis highlights a positive correlation between time and human resource investment in migration processes and settlement. Indeed, most migration laws reinforce this (Anderson, 2013, p. 103). Participant accounts demonstrate that gaining substantial acceptance in Finnish society legally, socially, and economically is extremely challenging, especially for individuals perceived as culturally distant.

> I don't feel I belong, no. So many things are different here – the culture, the people... and there are issues that nobody wants to speak of here like racism, which still exists. Immigrants can only get certain kinds of improper jobs regardless of their qualifications, which shows that the system is problematic.
>
> (Participant 7)

The remaining discussion of migrants' quest to belong continues in three sub-sections in themed discussions of the informant group's narrated experiences with the legal, social, and economic spaces of Finnish society. Each thematic discussion begins by identifying instances of internal bordering and is followed by an illustration of migrants' reaction to such bordering activities.

The Finnish residence regime and the legal other

This thematic discussion illustrates migrants' dilemma in securing a formal presence in Finland through the residence permit and the national identity card (Finnish ID) – instruments that aid bordering through sorting, regulation, and precarisation. All twenty-three participants are legal residents of Finland, and all entered Finland as international student migrants on a fixed term "B" resident study permit. At the time of the interviews, the participants had various residential statuses, ranging from naturalised citizens to fixed-term "B" residents, underscoring that bordering activities are generalising in nature and not limited to irregular immigrants. In this chapter, I argue that the Finnish residence permit is a legal structural bordering instrument used to manage the presence of migrants and migrants' access to various rights and opportunities in Finland, while outlining implicit duties and responsibilities for migrants. The residence permit provides a concrete tool for sorting, classifying, and ultimately "othering" migrants via national legislation. For example, third-country student migrants receive an annually renewable one-year temporary residence permit, which sets them apart from student migrants from the EU.

First, not all residence permits in Finland function as official identity cards, which means the informants each obtained a national identity card, a document very seldom held by Finns, to access several basic services in Finland. The Finnish ID for a migrant is also temporary, and the authority making the decision arbitrarily decides on validity. De facto, the ID is an identification tool via differentiation, thus acting as a sorting tool. It extends the national boundary into the nation, into spaces such as online banking sites, university portals, or nightclubs, where the ID regulates a migrant's access to services. Moreover, the real reason for the insufficiency of the residence permit as an identification document is fuzzy – and certainly unknown to migrants – but can be theorised as regulative. Second, the Finnish residence permit is renewed for €190 in a process that demands migrants prove their capacity to cover their living costs in Finland with an income statement of at least €6,700 per year (Migri, 2020). These two legal status demands play a significant role in determining the social and economic activities on which informants embark on arrival in the host country, an instrumental element of bordering in the labour market.

Third, various Finnish institutions use the residence permit to classify and categorise migrants in a hierarchy that determines inclusion or exclusion from rights and responsibilities. For example, a "B" permit completely excludes the holder from all the services of the Social Insurance Institution in Finland (Kela), which are exclusively available for holders of a continuous "A" permit. The minimum requirement for a continuous "A" permit is full-time employment. This means that many international students who work part-time in Finland have no access to public healthcare, a basic social necessity for workers, especially those in risky secondary sector work like construction. Meanwhile, various institutions effortlessly sort migrants into classes by their legal status, a process that engenders the act of othering, which in turn reinforces the practice of personalised bordering by migrants themselves. Moreover, migrants' legal belonging, defined by the residence permit, serves to reinforce other versions of bordering in social and economic spaces in Finland.

Participant stories highlight a variety of reactions to the exclusionary tendencies of the Finnish residence regime. However, the most notable of these concern joining the labour market immediately after arriving in Finland and rushing into a marriage of convenience.

> I took up three jobs during the summer: newspaper delivery, cleaning, and home nursing. I did newspaper delivery from 12.20 a.m. to 6 a.m., slept for two hours, did cleaning from 10 a.m. to 3 p.m., and home nursing from 4 p.m. to 9 p.m., slept for another two hours every day to make the €6,000 to renew my permit.
>
> (Participant 17)

The initial response to the residence permit's limitations was to acquire a Finnish ID. However, this was done out of necessity and did not register as an act of resistance, adaptation, or manoeuvring. Second, in anticipation of the financial burden of renewing the first residence permit, participants took up paid work. The need to secure their legal status at the end of their first year in Finland drove nineteen of the twenty-three participants to join the labour market in their first year in Finland. Two participants sought social or romantic relationships with Finnish nationals with the goal of cohabitation and obtaining a physical address, as well as acquiring the necessary human capital for seeking and obtaining either a permanent residence permit or Finnish citizenship. These responses to the limiting nature of the Finnish residence regime have profound implications for the development of informants' migration trajectories. More important is the link between migrants' experiences of the legal (political) space of the host country and migrants' socioeconomic performance, especially because this informant group without exception sought migration to Finland to improve their opportunities to forge a better life. This is explored further in the following sub-sections.

Courting the Finnish community of value

Belonging as membership follows full acceptance into a desired social and political collective. As a naturalised, emotive act of attachment and identification, belonging is multi-layered, because individuals can belong to another individual, community, nation, job, union, etc. (Yuval-Davis, 2011). Social, cultural, economic, and political belonging are very often explicitly addressed in discourses of belonging and citizenship (see e.g. Yuval-Davis, 2011; Somers, 2008). In this section social belonging refers to inclusive membership of the state and its recognition of migrants, and consequently of various societal collectives, which in turn enables members to overcome embodied markers of legal status, race, gender, and class that otherwise serve the default role of othering and enabling exclusion. The link between citizenship and belonging is evident (see e.g. Anderson, 2013; Yuval-Davis, 2011; Somers, 2008). Belonging follows acceptance, which ensures admission via full membership into a collective, which endows recognition based on equality between humans. However, historically, such recognition is tied to belonging to a nation state by blood, effectively excluding migrants from belonging in their host countries. Nonetheless, the crucial role played by such membership for economic and political engagement and the social well-being that such activities engender remains. Social inclusion is a crucial starting point for migrants in the quest to belong, yet informants' stories indicate that gaining meaningful acceptance in Finnish society – and thus validation – is nearly impossible for most.

Participant stories describe Finnish society – the social collective of relations, recognition, and acceptance – as homogenous and closed to certain migrant groups. Widely acknowledged stereotypes about culture and tradition, language deficiency, and differences based on culture or ethnicity regulate migrants' access to Finnish social circles. When employed in decision-making, these perceptions result in unfavourable sorting, and systematic institutional regulatory practices of exclusion follow. Failure to integrate into or gain Finnish social networks materialises in varying degrees of severity, from difficulties in securing basic rights such as a place to live and getting a job to admission in a desired university course. Four participants explained the difficult process they endured when looking for rental apartments in Helsinki, in which applicants were sorted by embodied traits through a face-to-face interview before admission or rejection.

> We waited outside in a long queue for the interview. After we were seen, for reasons we can only assume were related to our looks, it was impossible to see the apartment at that time. We walked out, and soon afterwards the agent went to show the apartment to another person, this time a white person.
>
> (Participant 7)

International student migrants also faced exclusion from opportunities such as degree programmes. Participant 5 explained that courses with the potential to improve his standing in the Finnish labour market were inaccessible to him and other migrants like him. He was excluded because of language deficiency, which also ensures that migrant students do not even realise that they are excluded from their rightful privileges as international students who are legally accepted for university studies. Language is a rationalised tool for bordering and excluding migrants from various social locations and positions in Finnish society, while administrative decision-makers take on the role of border guard. Moreover, statistical and taste-based discrimination are almost normative in Finland. However, according to Ahmad (2019), this largely stereotypical prejudiced behaviour has been used to keep migrants out of desirable jobs while masking institutional and structural discriminatory prejudice. Furthermore, in taste-based discrimination, the populace becomes the border guard, because it is its taste preferences that determine the limits of migrants' inclusion and access. Participant stories also highlighted instances of social bordering on public transport, in parks, and in the workplace.

> I never had the urge to go for Finnish citizenship, but at some point I just decided to go for a Finnish passport to avoid the many instances I had to explain to my Finnish children why we had to join separate queues at airports.
>
> (Participant 12)

To demonstrate sufficiently the impact of the pervasive social bordering patterns on the decisions made by the informant group, I introduce the concepts of precariousness, adaptation, compromise, identity management, and learning. Precariousness captures the crucial impact of endless social exclusion; the other concepts elaborate the various ways in which participants responded to social exclusion. This discussion delves into participants' experiences of vulnerability because they fail to fit into the host society as full and valid members, as well as into their dilemmas in maintaining and adjusting their career goals, self-perception, identity, and absolute or relative confidence vis-à-vis citizens.

Participants' reaction to social bordering was significantly elaborate and predicted their migration trajectory in the host country. Several migrant stories indicated feelings of invalidity and inconsequentiality arising from multiple failed attempts to integrate meaningfully in Finland through relations and networking with nationals, through work and colleagues, and through social and cultural engagement. Their acquired precarious social standing cemented their perception of exclusion and instrumentally led to acts of "*self-bordering*". Those who experienced the most instances of exclusion from social spaces in Finland accepted the rhetoric of "*cultural distance*" and personalised their own bordering, beginning to blame their cultural and ethnic traits for their exclusion from the host society. The reaction that followed was to retreat from the host society into ethnic migrant communities and networks, in which social activities mimicked the origin country's norms. The multi-layered ethnic community networks identified – continental, national, and intimate group-based – were organised around the value of solidarity and a collective approach to addressing immigration challenges. Networks equipped members with a unique "*African migrant in Finland culture*". Moreover, since the networks tended to spring up around seasoned migrants, they enculturated the norm of settling, rather than return and/or on-migration.

However, apart from self-bordering, the chapter identifies four different ways in which participants expanded their Finland-embedded social capital, or leveraged such capital to advance their social belonging in Finland. The first was marriage to or cohabiting with a Finn. Six interview participants with Finnish spouses/partners explained that their Finnish family was instrumental in their quest to belong in Finland, because it improved their social standing (location) and especially their visibility in society. The second was having a Finnish child (not necessarily with an ethnic Finn). Ten participants had children in Finland whose well-being they sought through the opportunities afforded by advanced education and security among other opportunities under the universal social welfare regime. Parenting a Finnish child or bearing a child in Finland helped to validate their presence in Finland by socially embedding interactions. For example, school-going children expanded a parent's network to include teachers and fellow parents, who sometimes became acquaintances or friends; parenting also involved unavoidable and validating engagement with various national institutions, such as schools, churches, and health centres, which embedded parents to a defining extent in the host society. It also scaled down the conscious burden of proving one's validity through the single route of full membership in society.

The third was building a Finnish network. Participant stories underscored the importance of Finnish networks in "*surviving*" in Finland, from getting a house to getting a job. Differentiation of citizens from non-citizens, especially culturally distant groups like African migrants, is central in the regulation of access in Finnish society. The in-group does not trust the out-group, and this manifests in exclusion from several substantive and instrumental social opportunities and activities. Migrants therefore use Finnish networks to compensate for their cultural deficit. Indeed, Participant 12 acknowledged that she had an easier experience compared to her friends because she had a Finnish family network from the beginning. The fourth was embedding the self in Finland by self-identifying as a Finn.

Collectives (and membership of them) develop around shared culture, beliefs, professions, values, religion, etc., generating a link between belonging and identity. Furthermore, holistic belonging in a nation state is based on identity. Migrants' reverting to identity politics to improve their social standing in the host society is therefore not unusual. As Yuval-Davis (2011) argues – and as reflected in this study – identity stories include narratives that refer to migrants' pasts, which help to problematise the current situation and project a desired future trajectory. Participant 8 explained that he adopted a fluid identity to optimise his experiences in Finland.

> I become whatever the other person wants me to be. I exist in context. So, when a drunk person in a bar asks me why I came to Finland, I say I came to drink!
>
> (Participant 8)

The four techniques described above, as well as the initial reaction of retreating to an ethnic enclave, are migrants' constructions of belonging, which serve a performative role (Butler 1990, cited in Yuval-Davis, 2011). Such a performance can be resistance, as in retreating to an ethnic enclave; resilience, as in identity reformulation and projecting perceived Finnish identities; or manoeuvring, as in marriage and cohabitation with a native Finn.

Alternative belonging: economic citizenship and valid workers

This final thematic discussion illustrates internal bordering as experienced by the informant group in the Finnish labour market. Administrative bordering is especially rampant in the Finnish labour market, which is a dual segmented market with a clear division of primary and secondary sectors, as well as labour. Accompanying the sectoral distinction is a criterion for worker distribution based on differential embodied characteristics such us nationality, race, ethnicity, or gender (Piore, 1979). Migrants thus face ad-hoc sorting, differentiating, regulating, and discriminatory acts from employers, contracting agencies, and those controlling job vacancies and recruitment processes in the Finnish labour market (Ahmad, 2019).

The first and overarching border imposed by a bifurcated labour market is the institutionalised obstruction of mobility between sectors (Piore, 1979). All twenty-three informants were active participants in the Finnish labour market, with nineteen working in the secondary labour market. The nineteen participants expressed dissatisfaction with their unskilled manual work, which they described as demeaning, deskilling, and dehumanising, thus sharing their ambition for primary sector work even as they acknowledged its unlikelihood.

> I'm not working in my area of expertise now, simply because I'm a foreigner, and in a country like this not all institutions are so accepting of people like me, especially in white-collar jobs, apart from in a few fields like IT. And even there, you have to prove yourself first, and how do you do that when you won't get a first chance?
>
> (Participant 3)

> ... Without a Finnish surname it's not easy to get a job in most fields in Finland, even when you speak Finnish. Speaking Finnish isn't everything.
>
> (Participant 10)

The second is discrimination. Valtonen (2001) explains that the Finnish labour market operates under two discriminatory premises, statistical and taste-based discrimination, which regulate and streamline migrants' access to the labour market. Recent studies concur and further identify discrimination based on cultural and ethnic traits, which becomes a key challenge in the Finnish labour market for culturally distant groups like my participant group (OECD, 2017). Although they had received tertiary education in Finland, nineteen participants were unable to find jobs in their areas of expertise. Moreover, past work experience was unrecognised and therefore worthless in seeking employment. Participant 5 explained that even internationally recognised and lucrative certifications such as Project Management Professional (PMP) and Certified Information Systems Auditor (CISA) were unrecognised and therefore useless in Finland. The failure to recognise foreign academic qualifications and accumulated professional experience keeps migrants in Finland in jobs with the lowest status.

> In Finland, "we" only do these "shoddy jobs". Before I came here I was a teacher, you know. I've travelled and I'm well educated, but now I clean and wash dishes…
>
> (Participant 8)

Third are the cumulative barriers in legal and social spaces such as the temporary residence regime, language deficiency, underdeveloped or inaccessible Finnish networks, and negative stereotypes which aggravate migrants' bordering in the labour market by cementing their status of precariousness. After completing his master's degree, Participant 7, who held the fixed term "B" permit, could not access municipal employment services that should have improved his chances of getting meaningful work in Finland. Indeed, all the participants had missed a job or promotional opportunity because of language deficiency. Moreover, a foregrounded discourse of trust in worker recruitment practices in Finland excluded participants from consideration for several work opportunities for which they were qualified, simply because they were perceived as lacking the trustworthiness associated with an endorsement from a Finn. The residence permit, trust, and language were therefore tools used by employers and recruiters to bar participants from accessing the Finnish labour market on an equal footing with nationals. Thus, human agency could not measure up to the systematic and embedded nature of these bordering tools.

The participants' reaction to bordering in the labour market took the form of acceptance, diversion, and compromise. Participants' inability to employ manoeuvring tactics in this space was fundamental, contributing significantly to the emerging migrant trajectory of their extended stay in Finland. Participants accepted their fate in the Finnish labour market, understanding that their kind mostly performed manual and unskilled work, and that was just how it was. Indeed, some understood Finland's decision to exclude them, although this was limited to exclusion from the labour market.

> As a human being, I might not be okay with my fate as a jobseeker here, but I also understand that there are laws that prioritise the Finn and the European over me.
>
> (Participant 8)

Diversion and compromise worked together to provide participants with alternative validation. Participants identified and reified other aspects of their work experience such as wages and salaries that were higher than in their home country, as well as facilities at work like coffee rooms, which compensated for the unpleasant nature of the work itself. A key technique of diversion was alternative membership based on labour market participation. Labour market membership, or "*economic citizenship*" (based on work), validates participants' stay in Finland with work as migrants' core purpose in Finland. Membership through tax obligations broadens participants' validity beyond the labour market to society through tax utility value when used for national socioeconomic development.

Finally, class membership obtained through wages, income, and lifestyle validates migrants as equal beings with nationals of similar social classes. However, the most significant reaction to bordering in this sector is the decision to stay in Finland as workers, albeit in unskilled, deskilling, and dehumanising jobs. Indeed, this chapter argues that the bordering role of these jobs is crucial in altering migrants' trajectories towards a settling tendency by enforcing temporariness and precariousness, which slows down every migration process and decision.

Outcomes of pervasive internal bordering

I have analysed the extent of bordering as it is materialised in the daily life experiences of a group of African migrants in Finland. The encountered borders were both administrative and personalised. The analysis also highlights the various techniques and behaviour patterns adopted by migrants in reaction to such bordering, individually and in ethnic networks. In general, migrants resolve to either adapt or manoeuvre around exclusionary activities through a personalised protracted struggle between the processes of defining the migration trajectory and overcoming the processes of exclusion in daily encounters. Thus, my analysis underscores the link between the pervasive internal bordering of migrants and the prevailing migration trajectory, which in this case is the change from a trajectory of remaining temporarily to settling in the host country. Migrant stories indicate that pervasive bordering reinforced an extended stay in Finland by delaying migrants' acquisition of a status of belonging and validity through perverse exclusion from social and economic spaces in Finland. Moreover, experiences of pervasive bordering reinforced the desire to belong, which took on additional value as an avenue for inclusion, as well as a status reward for the social and economic resources invested during the stay in the host country. My analysis of the interviews with migrants shows that participants adopt the migration "culture" – strategies, knowledge, and coping mechanisms – of the African migrant living in Finland.

The findings of the chapter can be summarised in three phases through which internal bordering shapes participants' migration trajectory. First, the residence regime triggers bordering in which participants pursue a permanent residence permit and citizenship status early in their immigration. Second, the attempt to advance legal status initiates a quest for social belonging, sought through marrying a national, having a Finnish child, joining an ethnic enclave, and reconstructing identity. Third, failures related to the participants' attempts to gain meaningful inclusion in Finnish society produce precarious individuals whose experiences in the Finnish labour market are marred by discrimination and social exclusion. The socioeconomic failure experienced by these participants amounts to a loss not only to the migrants but to a brain drain for both the origin countries and Finland, which fails to optimise its human resource pool.

Concluding remarks

The pervasive internal bordering of African student migrants in Finland incentivises their longer and even permanent stays in their new host country. Increased internal bordering thus reinforces a settling tendency in migration. However, as I have illustrated, the nature of migration enforced by such bordering is arduous, unsystematic, and time consuming. It often results in a socioeconomic loss for both migrants and host societies. In short, internal bordering reinforces inefficient and ineffective migration processes.

Increased internal bordering is not unique to Finland. Migrants categorised as culturally distant from a host population commonly experience migrant exclusion through language barriers, statistical discrimination, and the mismatch between migrant labour demand and supply. Yet these challenges are critical and should be addressed, because they undermine both the well-being of migrants and the socioeconomic life of host societies. Since 2009, the Finnish government has incrementally implemented migration programmes – for example, Talent Boost – that aim to increase and improve economic migration activities in the country with a focus on competitiveness, attraction, and retention. However, though positive, programmes like Talent Boost focus narrowly on migrant groups in the country and strategically on economic inclusion alone.

Based on the outcomes of this study, I recommend the following for a socially inclusive integration regime. First, the focus of integration should emphasise migrants' well-being as much as the host country's economic gain. A first step towards this might be better matching between international course programmes at universities and the host country's labour market needs. Second, integration programmes should be targeted, acknowledging the different needs of migrant groups in the country to better reduce discretionary space for exclusion. Third, integration programmes should be designed with an understanding that overlooks stereotypical claims and definitions that further the exclusion of African migrants in host society communities.

References

Ahmad, A. (2019) When the name matters: an experimental investigation of ethnic discrimination in the Finnish labour market. *Sociological Inquiry*, 1–29. DOI: 10.1111/soin.12276.

Anderson, B. (2013) *Us and Them*. Oxford: Oxford University Press.

Anthias, F. (2008) Thinking through the lens of translocational positionality: an intersectionality frame for understanding identity and belonging. *Translocations: Migration and Social Change*, 4(1), pp. 5–20.

Balibar, E. (2004) *We, The People of Europe?: Reflections on Transnational Citizenship*. Princeton, N.J.: Princeton University Press.

Corbin, J. and Strauss, A. (2008) *Basics of Qualitative Research: Techniques and Procedures for developing grounded theory*. 3rd ed. Los Angeles, CA: Sage.

Centre for International Mobility (CIMO). (2016). *Tutkinto-opiskelu Suomesta ja Suomeen 2006-2016: Korkeakoulut* (online). Available at: www.cimo.fi/instancedata/prime_product_julkaisu/cimo/embeds/cimo wwwstructure/163728_Tutkinto-opiskelu_Suomesta_ja_Suomeen_2006- 2016_korkeakoulut.pdf (Accessed 17 Nov. 2019).

Creswell, J. and Poth, C. (2016) *Qualitative Inquiry and Research Design: Choosing among Five Approaches*. 4th ed. Los Angeles: Sage.

Denzin, N. (2011) Assumptions of the method. In: N. Denzin, and Y. Lincoln eds., *The Sage Handbook of Qualitative Research*. 4th ed. Thousand Oaks: Sage.

European Migration Network (EMN). (2018) *Annual Report on Migration and Asylum FINLAND*. Helsinki: Finnish Immigration Service.

Jensen, P. & Pedersen, P. J. (2007) To stay or not to stay? Out-migration of immigrants from Denmark. *International Migration*, 45(5), pp. 87–113.

Könönen, J. (2018) Differential inclusion of non-citizens in a universalistic welfare state. *Citizenship Studies*, 22(1), pp. 53–69.

Laine, J. P. (2018) Conditional welcome and the ambivalent self – commentary to Gill. *Fennia*, 196 (2), pp. 230–35.

Lyon, D. (2005) The border is everywhere: ID cards, surveillance and the other. In: E. Zureik and M. Salter, eds, *Global Surveillance and Policing: Borders, Security and Identity*. Devon: Willan, pp. 78–94.

Maury, O. (2017) Student-migrant-workers. *Nordic Journal of Migration Research*, 7(4), 224–32.

Marshall, T. and Bottomore, T. (1992) *Citizenship and Social Class*. London: Pluto.

Mezzadra, S. and Neilson, B. (2013) *Border as Method, or, the Multiplication of Labor*. Durham, NC.: Duke University Press.

Migri. (2020) *Residence Permit*. Finnish Immigration Service. (online) Available at: migri.fi/en/residence-permit-application-for-studies (Accessed 14 Mar. 2020).

Ministry of the Interior. (2018) *Work in Finland*. Helsinki: Ministry of the Interior.

OECD. (2017) Finding the way: a discussion of the Finnish Migrant Integration System. (online). Available at: www.oecd.org/migration/mig/Finding-the-Way-Finland.pdf (Accessed 14 Mar. 2020).

Piore, M. (1979) *Birds of Passage: Migrant Labor and Industrial Societies*. Cambridge: Cambridge University Press.

Riessman, C. (2008) *Narrative Methods for the Human Sciences*. Thousand Oaks: Sage.

Shumilova, Y. and Cai, Y. (2015) Factors affecting the employability of international graduates. *International Scientific Journal of Universities and Leadership*, 1(1), pp. 24–30.

Simone, B., Montgomery, T., and Calo F. (2020) *Social Partners Barriers and Enablers*. SIRIUS: D5.2. (Online) Available at: www.sirius-project.eu/sites/default/files/attachments/Social%20Partners%20Enablers%20and%20Barriers%20-%20D5.2.pdf (Accessed 8 Apr. 2020).

Somers, M. (2008) *Genealogies of Citizenship: Markets, Statelessness, and the Right to Have Rights*. Cambridge: Cambridge University Press.

Tervonen, M., Pellander, S., and Yuval-Davis, N. (2018) Everyday bordering in the Nordic countries. *Nordic Journal of Migration Research*, 8(3), pp. 139–42.

Valtonen, K. (2001) Cracking monopoly: immigrants and employment in Finland. *Journal of Ethnic and Migration studies*. 27(3), pp. 421–38.

Yuval-Davis, N. (2011) *The Politics of Belonging: Intersectional Contestations*. Thousand Oaks: Sage.

Zureik, E and Salter, M. B. eds. (2013) *Global Surveillance and Policing: Borders, Security, Identity*. Cullompton, UK: Willan Publishing.

9 Untying the migration knot through trade

A case study of Nigeria

Omotomilola Ikotun and Juliet Ogbodo

Introduction

Globalisation has opened up the borders of countries, with migration forming an integral part of the phenomenon. Migration has been in existence as long as humans have existed on the face of the earth. Migration has birthed the societies that exist today and has been instrumental in the exchange of ideas, innovation and the rebuilding of war-torn societies. Migration has also occured along the pre-existing relationship lines with former colonial masters, which has created inordinate destination-dependence ideations in the youth of formerly colonised countries. This prior relationship created a knot which still ties pre-colonised countries to their colonial masters, a knot which attracts the youth looking for opportunities for a better life.

There is a palpable tension brewing amongst the 670-million-strong youth population of Africa. It is a buzzing that has become more intense in the face of the current depressing economic outlooks and increasing unemployment levels, which have kept youths unable to access avenues for making things better for themselves. Nigeria's teeming thirty-three million–plus youth population, for example, have become increasingly vulnerable to tribalistic, secessionist ideations, both in the south-eastern and the north-eastern regions of Nigeria. These agitations have heightened the lure to flee rural areas for the urban areas and the shores of the country.

There is, therefore, a need to repossess the imagination of the youth using joint and innovative projects centred around agriculture and agro-processing and trade purposes. It has become imperative for the government of Nigeria to harness the collective identity of the youth, using the Sustainability Development Goals (SDGs) of "No Poverty", "Zero Hunger", and "Industry, Innovation and Infrastructure" as focal points in order to develop innovative, trade export–focused, value-added agricultural businesses. These projects would be instrumental in untying the dependence on Europe as the "promised land" for economic opportunities and ensuring retaining the vibrancy of youth in the sectors most needed to help break Nigeria and other African countries out of the "one commodity" economy. Given the volatility of the one product economy that Nigeria currently showcases and the recent crash

DOI: 10.4324/9781003083726-10

in prices of crude oil (Nigeria's chief foreign exchange earner), it has become imperative to diversify the economy of the country by using the potential the country possesses in its natural resources and human capital.

This chapter will, therefore, focus on the position that agribusiness and trade are crucial for the untying of the migration knot between the EU and Africa. It will show how the return to agribusiness and trade-related activities for agricultural products will create employment for the youth, harness their creative and innovative abilities, and put an end to the lure of leaving the shores of the country.

Background

Before crude oil was discovered in Oloibiri, Bayelsa State in 1958, Nigeria was an agrarian nation which boasted of the groundnut pyramids in the north, the palm-oil plantations of the south-east, and the cocoa plantations of the south-west. In the 1950s and 1960s, agriculture and agriculture-related activities accounted for 60–70 percent of total exports and foreign exchange earnings (Daramola et al., 2007). Government revenues depended heavily on agricultural export taxes, and both the current account and fiscal balances depended to some extent on agriculture. This sector, therefore, had become the most important economic sector because of its contribution to the GDP of the country. According to African Development Fund report, compiled by the African Development Bank (2002), agriculture contributed 41 percent of the country's GDP, employed about 65 percent of the overall populace and was directly responsible for the employment of close to 80 percent of the rural population. With the oil boom of the 1970s, revenue from oil sales contributed more than 98 percent of the country's total export value and 73 percent of GDP. The focus on crude oil ushered in the era of the negligent execution of agricultural policies and programmes, and the eventual abandonment of established agricultural projects by succeeding military regimes.

Nigeria's population has snowballed from some thirty million at the time of regaining its independence in 1960 to approximately 200 million people in 2019 – and it is expected to grow by another 200 million by 2050 (United Nations, 2019), which will make it the world's fourth most populous country. Nigeria is one of Africa's fastest-growing economies and remains the largest economy; ironically, Nigeria also possesses the largest population of poor people in the world. The youth population is especially hard hit by poverty and other underlying issues such as unemployment and a lack of opportunities. The Nigeria Bureau of Statistics (NBS) states that as much as 55 percent of young Nigerians (between the age of fifteen and thirty-five) are unemployed (NBS Q4 2017-Q3 2018). Accordingly, it can be asserted that much of the violence and the insurgency crises that plague Nigeria and parts of the West African sub-region are the consequence of high unemployment rates as many young, unemployed people have resorted to violence in order to occupy their

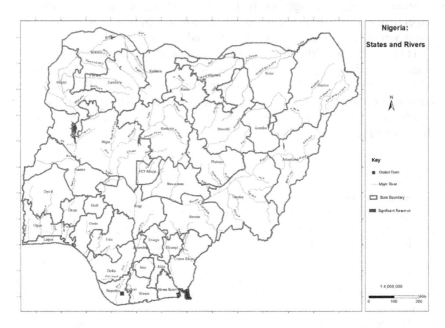

Map 9.1 A map of Nigeria showing the thirty-six states and the Federal Capital
Territory.
Map by: Usman Yahaya Balarabe.

time, demonstrate their discontentment with their governments, and, perhaps
most importantly, earn a living. While many young people have resorted to
violence, others have opted to seek greener pastures beyond the borders of
Nigeria and, indeed, of entire Africa.

Dialogues centred around migration from the African continent have been
represented as a pedestrian pattern of movement of people from the continent
towards Europe and other destinations. Researchers have, however, been able
to prove and continue to show that African migration is not as homogenous
as it is often depicted and that migration flows are not only directed towards
Europe; many more Africans are moving within the continent than there are
attempting to move out of it (Flahaux and De Haas, 2016; Laine, 2020). In
the West African sub-region alone, as many as 8.4 million people are reported
to be migrating within the region; this represents the most extensive stock
of migrants and also the highest number of intra-regional migrants on the
continent (IOM, 2020). It must be stated, though, that of the population of
migrants moving within and out of Africa, a large percentage has reported
that migration was a voluntary decision, although war, famine, and other
disasters played roles; they were moving precisely in search of better opportunities (Mo Ibrahim Foundation, 2019).

The impact of this mass exodus on sending communities includes population loss, especially of young people, and increased dependence on remittances, both of which promote underdevelopment and undermine the social viability of communities (Mberu, 2005). Thus, these migration figures present an insurmountable loss for the countries of origin of the migrants; for the receiving countries, migration tends to create an economical and structural transformation which can lead to potential increase in output and productivity where unnecessary restrictions are not established.

Beyond international migration, internal migration within nations also leaves in its wake a dearth of skills and workforce. Rural–urban migration, for instance, is particularly selective for young people, of both genders, who are also educated and are innovative. Once this population leaves rural areas, those left behind are often a mix of the very young, the too old to engage in farming activities or those who have just retired from active service in urban areas and returned to the rural areas, and the uneducated. As a result of such migration trends, rural populations, particularly in sub-Saharan Africa, are often characterised by high gender and dependency ratios and low social, educational, and economic status (Mberu, 2005). Still, the young and educated, driven by the scarcity of opportunities for commensurate paying work, coupled with the glaring lack of basic amenities, are migrating in droves to large cities from rural areas.

These mass rural–urban migration patterns have had profound impacts on agricultural production as a result of the loss in human resources that are critical for agricultural production and development. The deterioration of rural areas in Nigeria is partly explainable by the outward migration of able-bodied youths in search of "easier" white-collar jobs in the cities in comparison with the supposedly "back-breaking" and thankless job that agriculture has come to be identified with (Iruonagbe, 2009). The incidence of migration is highest among the most productive age group (those fifteen to thirty-five years old); this is the same demographic that is caught by the lure of escaping to Europe (Nwalatu, 2016). This demographic is made up of the most educated age group in the villages. This educated group is needed to achieve the active participation of a sizable, informed, healthy, and economically and socially motivated population in the renewal of the agriculture sector in Nigeria.

The discourse on such migratory trends and the consequent impact on rural development and agriculture is made up of convoluted dimensions that are knotty to untie. It is however imperative to understand that at the root of the rural–urban migration – and the eventual outward migration to Europe – is the chronically persistent inequality in the allocation of social and economic infrastructure in rural and urban communities. The push factors propelling young people out of rural areas is related to the pull factor, which attracts them to urban areas and consequently leads to some moving out of the country. This is the phenomenon that has to be addressed through the use of carefully developed agriculture programmes and through well-planned and adequately negotiated trade agreements.

The migration knot and dependency theory

The system of development which advocates for continuous aid from the global north to the global south has faced many criticisms over the years. Prominent among these criticisms is dependency theory, yet there have been intellectual disagreements about its intricacies. In short, the theory interprets the world to be divided into the centre / the industrialised countries and the periphery / the underdeveloped countries (Agbebi and Virtanen, 2017). This system asserts that trade between the more-developed states and the less-developed states is often characterised by an unequal exchange which has reinforced the underdevelopment of the latter. As Agbebi and Virtanen (2017) couched it, underdevelopment in third world countries can be directly linked to the expansion of the world capitalist system. Invariably, this leads to a complicated knot of dependence on the developed nations, by the underdeveloped ones, and migration from the latter to the former.

The dependency theory is one of several attempts to explain the present underdeveloped state of many countries across the world. It has successfully done so by examining the patterns of interactions among nations and by arguing that inequality among nations is an intrinsic part of those interactions (Ferraro, 2008). In charting a new path towards growth and development, one that reduces the dependence of less-developed states on their more-developed counterparts, it is necessary to abandon the notion of "aid", which in this context inherently fosters inequality by the underlying assumption that countries in the global south are worse off than countries in the global North and require rescuing by them. This would go a long way towards curbing unwanted patterns, such as poverty-driven migration among other development issues, in countries like Nigeria.

It is also important to note that the dependency theory does not only apply to the global north and global south divide. The theory also applies to the internal structuring of countries. An example is the development of cities into metropolises to the detriment of the rural areas. The under-developed state of rural areas has more often than not led to the youths in rural areas migrating to cities. How can this persistent dependence on urban areas be contained?

Firstly, there is a need to understand what fuels unwanted patterns. As discussed above, socio-economic factors are the primary reason for migration. Therefore, to curtail "unwanted" migration, diversifying and increasing income flows to developing countries is essential. While international trade holds no monopoly in achieving this objective, it plays an important role.

The second step is to examine the trade agreements between developing countries – in this case, the agreements Nigeria has with developed countries such as those in the EU. The content of trade agreements should include genuine development objectives such as agreeing on commodity-specific developments and the training of youth in "farmer-preneur" skills, amongst other objectives. Doing so would ensure that rather than merely purchasing goods and raw materials, adequate attention is given to the growth and development of various sectors in developing countries. As such, trade agreements could be designed to include strategies aimed at addressing key development challenges in Nigeria, for instance, thus making them measurable and achievable. This approach to development is preferable and more sustainable in the long term than merely "throwing" money in the form of aid which can hardly be measurable and which maintains the system of dependency that is already in place. A third step is to focus on the development of rural areas and bettering the lives of the citizens who live there.

Why trade?

There is an undeniable correlation between migration and trade. Much theoretical and empirical research over recent decades has pointed towards one-directional trade and migration being interlinked in more ways than one (Carbaugh, 2007; Hatzigeorgiou, 2010; Schmieg, 2019). There are three main paths along which trade and migration have a positive correlation. The first path is trading as a facilitator for migration. Trade can facilitate migration by strengthening the relationship between trading partners and increasing the available information about the partner country. The availability of information reduces the cost of migration and can generate more migration flow between those partners. The chances of migrating to a country that holds a trading relationship with one's country of origin are higher than the chances of migrating to a country without any historical or trade ties with one's country of origin (Barslund, Backhaus, and Di Salvo, 2019). Other factors, such as historical linkages (such as colonisation), also increase the choice of migration destination (Gatsios, Hatzipanayotou, and Michael, 1999). For example, an African migrant from an anglophone country will most likely prefer to migrate to the United Kingdom because of the language, which presents a certain level of familiarity born from history, language, the style of education, and available information. Trade can also facilitate migration through the increase of per capita GDP, thus providing more financial capability and options for those who are lured to migrate. However, this usually leads to "organised" migration within the context of the World Trade Organisation's General Agreement on Trade and Services (GATS) Mode IV on facilitating the short-term movement of a natural person to the territory of another member state to supply services (GATS, Art. XXIX [2]).

The second path is where migration can facilitate and can increase prospects for bilateral trade. Empirical studies show that the presence of migrants increases exports from their country of origin and generally has a positive impact on maintaining and enabling access to new markets (Faini, De Mello, and Zimmermann, 1999). The impact of this trade relationship is higher on imports, driven by the preferences of immigrants for nostalgia goods. Migration also has a significant positive impact on the receiving country. Specifically, migration contributes to the labour force of the host country, which is a significant factor for production. An increased workforce means higher potential to produce more.

Migrants also bridge the cultural divide and build or depend on established networks from their countries of origin in order to enable trade partnerships. They can break communication barriers as well as supply their host country with production- or sector-specific knowledge of their home country, which not only drives up targeted exports, it also reduces the cost of distribution and marketing (Hatzigeorgiou, 2010). These positive inputs occur when receiving countries acknowledge and tap into the potential of migrants, a situation not currently appreciated in the EU where migration is deemed as a crisis that requires aggressive management (UN Report 2018; Laine, 2020; Okafor, 2020). However, where immigration is unplanned or irregular, these positive impacts might be reduced due to unfavourable conditions for migrants such as hostile migration policies in receiving countries.

Finally, on the last path, trade can serve as a substitute for migration. This posits that an increase in trade will, eventually, lead to a decrease in migration. Inspired by the Ricardian theory on comparative advantage (Ricardo, 1821) and the Heckscher-Ohlin theory on factor endowments (Heckscher and Ohlin, 1991), free trade encourages efficiency in the production of a commodity (or service), which is driven by the natural capital and production factors that a country has in abundance.

Consequently, this gives the producing country a comparative advantage on the production and exportation of that product (or service) in the international global chain. The logic behind this position is that if a country increases production efficiency in a particular sector or commodity, it triggers a production cycle that would continuously require labour factor input, thereby creating job opportunities. In trading the product (or service) with countries with scarce natural capital in the production of that product (or service), the exporting country generates more income, increasing its per capita GDP, subsequently reducing unemployment and the appetite to migrate. Furthermore, by increasing trade and eliminating trade barriers, the wage gap that exists between countries, especially between the developing and developed countries, is minimised. As aptly summarised by Bruder (2004), "trade leads to a convergence of goods prices which implies price equalization. From this, it follows that the incentives for factor movements are reduced".

Although trade holds the potential to disincentivise migration, there are some caveats. The first caveat is that trade does not provide a short-term, immediate solution; contrarily, it is a medium- and long-term sustainable solution to the migration crisis. This is because the impact of trade on the economy is not felt in the short term; it requires time, efficiency, and consistency. Another caveat is that while trade agreements, bilateral or unilateral, are good policies for encouraging free trade, the agreements in themselves are not sufficient to generate the needed outcomes. For trade reforms to be useful as a substitute for migration, other factors – such as the efficient administration and management of natural and human capital, adequate infrastructure, and effective trade policies – are essential. Conversely, the mismanagement of these factors can lead to the opposite outcome: instability, unemployment, underdevelopment, and, subsequently, a stronger motive to migrate.

Harnessing agribusiness for trade and development

Agribusiness as a concept was developed in the late fifties by two Harvard scholars: John Davis and Ray Goldberg. Their work in the then-budding field of agribusiness provided a new perspective for understanding agricultural activities as a viable sector of the economy. Davis, Rust, and Goldberg (1957) defined agribusiness as "the sum of all operations involved in manufacture and distribution of farm supplies, production operations on the farm, and the storage, processing, and distribution of farm commodities". Their work in agribusiness was pivotal in the field and is the foundation for the evolution of the agribusiness system (Zylbersztajn, 2016). The result is the systematic study of how agro-based food systems and agriculture can be used to expand economies and promote growth and development.

For developing countries, and especially for Nigeria, there is much to be gleaned from agribusiness. It is not just as a field of academic study, it is a viable means of boosting the economy and tackling the socio-economic challenges which have plagued the nation. Agribusiness offers all players in the agricultural sector the opportunity to be part of a business system without necessarily belonging to large agricultural companies. The practice of agribusiness has evolved and expanded since it was first studied. Technological changes and advancements have meant that ideas, concepts, and practical solutions which were not thought of fifty-to-sixty years ago are now being considered part of agribusiness. What this means is that there are now tremendous opportunities in the agribusiness sector that did not previously exist.

To drive home our understanding of agribusiness and the diverse opportunities it holds for trade and development, a theoretical framework is suggested here. This framework highlights the various opportunities which exist in a sound agribusiness environment while stressing that the agribusiness sector depends on various services, some of which might not necessarily be in the agricultural sector. It is crucial to think of agribusiness in terms of more than just farming; in that way, it can be viewed with all the potential it holds for economic growth and development. It is a system that encompasses farming and all the other industries and services that constitute the supply chain from the farm, covering processing, wholesaling, retailing, and the consumer (Babu and Shaw, 2015). An estimate by the World Bank (2013) showed that the agriculture and agribusiness sectors could contribute nearly one trillion dollars to the African regional economy by 2030. What this shows is that there are many opportunities to take advantage of in the agribusiness sector and doing so should be on the agendas of Nigerian leaders in order to realise the economic transformation and development of Nigeria, both in the public and private sectors.

In the West African sub-region, food agriculture is already the largest employer of labour, accounting for about 78 percent of all employment in the agricultural sector (Allen, Heinrigs, and Heoii, 2018). Even with significant differences across countries, at least two-thirds of total food economy employment in all West African countries is found in agriculture. This high share of employment in the sector has been linked with the existing farming systems and production techniques. Allen et al. (2018) argued that agriculture in the West African region is characterised by a high share of family farms and small-holders who employ the use of labour-intensive production techniques on their small farms. This points to the availability of labour and essential skills that could be employed in a developed agribusiness sector.

Nigeria and other African countries are in a position to take advantage of the opportunities in the agribusiness sector, not only because of an abundance of labour but also as a result of the increased global interconnectedness of food markets. A specialised and developed agribusiness sector not only creates employment for the teeming youth population, but it also possesses the potential to position Nigeria to become a competitive player in the regional and international food markets (Babu and Shaw, 2015). Additionally, rapid urbanisation is seen to coincide with the demand for high-value food products, thus creating an opportunity within Nigeria for the production and exportation of these goods. This can transform the activities of small farmers from subsistence-based farming to more entrepreneurial-based farming and thereby expand their activities and create additional opportunities across the other nodes of the agribusiness value chain.

With such a high potential for economic growth and development, the agribusiness sector presents a viable opportunity for young Nigerians who are seeking greener pastures. Perhaps the most crucial aspect of this opportunity is that young Nigerians do not need to embark on a long journey outside of Nigeria to tap into such prospects. For policymakers in Nigeria and those in crucial migrant-receiving countries, the agribusiness sector presents a viable solution for keeping the migrating population within Nigeria and engaging them within this profitable sector.

Beyond curbing international migration, the development of the agribusiness sector in Nigeria also presents an opportunity to tackle the rapid rural–urban migration, which, as stated earlier, is depriving rural areas of a rather important demographic. Growing the agribusiness sector in Nigeria would keep young people in rural areas gainfully employed and would, in turn, reduce the rate of rural–urban migration, which has been linked to high rates of urban poverty and increased insecurity. To achieve this, Nigeria and its trade partners need to invest time and resources into creating an enabling environment for the agribusiness sector to thrive. An enabling environment can only be forged by a collective approach and endeavour, which includes traditional, broader, macro-level forces, including the political, social, and economic forces which are relevant to other sectors of an economy (Konig, da Silva, and Mhlanga, 2013).

EU–Africa trade agreements: Why have they failed?

Trade liberalisation is crucial in fostering international trade, especially in this globalised era. Utilising trade agreements as a solution to the migration crisis is not unknown to industrialised nations. The EU has used trade agreements to manage trade flows from its poorer neighbours and, by extension, to former colonies (Barslund et al., 2019). Similarly, the North American Free Trade Agreement (NAFTA) between the USA, Canada, and Mexico was designed to minimise the migration influx from Mexico (Martin, 1993). However, these agreements have failed in this objective; on the contrary, they have achieved the opposite and made the developed country partners attractive migration destinations. The problem, however, lies not in free trade or reaching trade agreements; instead, the challenge lies with the content and implementation of these agreements, which highlights the asymmetrical negotiating powers of the industrialised and developing partners.

In the case of the EU, several trade agreements have been in place with former African colonies since 1963, with the first of the Yaoundé Conventions. Since then, other multiple trade agreements have followed, including the Lomé Conventions, the Cotonou Agreements, and now the Economic Partnership Agreements which are yet to be concluded. The primary purpose of these agreements was to guarantee the continuous access of the EU to raw materials from former colonies (Banthia, 2007). These agreements were supposedly designed to support sustainable development in African countries. Precisely, these agreements follow the similar development wording pattern: to continue joint efforts for the economic, social, and cultural progress of Africa.[1] However, it can be argued that these agreements have achieved little of their ambitious agendas as African countries are still majorly underdeveloped as 70 percent of the world's poorest, least-developed countries are in Africa (UN-OHRLLS, 2020). Furthermore, only four African countries account for over half of EU imports from Africa, namely South Africa, Algeria, Nigeria, and Morocco. The EU mostly imports raw materials from these countries and exports manufactured and processed goods (Schmieg, 2019), further accentuating the asymmetry in the negotiating power of both regions as trading partners.

These trade agreements failed for one primary reason. They all failed to take cognisance the peculiar governance and structure of the African countries: most African countries have different circumstances, have different needs, and are at different stages of development. For example, Nigeria's development needs and priorities differ from those of her neighbours. In comparison with its neighbours, Nigeria has a substantial youth population. Therefore, any trade agreement that does consider this "elephant-in-the-room" factor and harness its potential is not likely to yield sustainable results.

Additionally, the trade agreements so far have not been very specific about the development measures that they agree to undertake in order to achieve the sustainable development that is stated as a goal in the preambles, other than the inclusion of the Economic Developmental Fund (EDF). The EDF was available to African countries upon meeting certain conditionalities, including human rights and the rule of law, and political conditionalities such as good governance (Del Biondo, 2011). In many cases, these conditionalities were unattainable, considering that most of these countries were newly independent. This, however, did not deter the EU from threatening violating countries and, in some cases, suspending them from access the EDF, highlighting the asymmetrical negotiating powers of the EU and the African countries in the drafting of these agreements (Banthia, 2007).

Thus, aid in the context it has been used in trade agreements so far has not provided sustainable outcomes. To achieve far-reaching impacts, a different approach to trade negotiations is, therefore, pivotal in breaking the aid dependency on the EU and providing stability in the migrant-sending countries. One path towards achieving this is by incorporating specific, measurable, achievable, realistic, and timely (SMART) development objectives into future trade agreements between the EU and Africa, for example, the Economic Partnership Agreements.

A SMART development objective: developing the agribusiness sector in Nigeria

A practical way of incorporating and implementing SMART development objectives in the EU's trade agreements with developing countries is through sector-specific development. This approach would remedy the one-size-fits-all approach that the EU has so far used in its dealings with African countries. It would also ensure that countries are developing the production sector in which they have a comparative advantage, thus increasing their standing in global value chains and subsequently achieving sustained economic growth and development. For Nigeria, one of the EU's major trading partners, developing the agribusiness sector is a developmental need and priority for many reasons.

Firstly, agriculture plays a vital role in the Nigerian economy; it is a significant employer, employing approximately 38 percent of the labour force (ILO, 2016). Additionally, over 76 percent of the Nigerian population is below the age of thirty-five (NPC, NBS, 2017). Unemployment rates are estimated at 23 percent, which sends worrying signals unless job opportunities are created to absorb the youth who are already unemployed and those joining the workforce (NBS, 2019). Most importantly, current global realities, including the record low fall in oil prices (Lockett and McCormick, 2020), have elicited the importance of diversifying Nigeria's economy. Nigeria's exports are still heavily reliant on crude oil, with approximately 76 percent being exported in the last quarter of 2019 (NBS, 2019). Additionally, global crises, such as the COVID-19 pandemic outbreak, place agriculture at the epicentre of survival, both in terms of feeding the population and also supporting economies towards recovery.

Improving agricultural processes can create new employment opportunities both in on- and off-farm sectors. Thus, agribusiness goes beyond farming, which Nigerian youths in rural areas shun as they consider farming to be low-paying and hard labour (FAO, 2019). Consequently, youth are pulled to cities and out of Nigeria in the search for well-paying jobs. Interestingly, agribusiness is the sector that holds the most potential to absorb a large portion of the youths in parts of the agribusiness value chain where their skills can be harnessed and utilised. It is therefore pivotal to target, capture, and engage the Nigerian youths in the agribusiness value chain, especially considering that they are the demographic most probable to migrate.

Agribusiness in Nigeria can be developed either through increased and improved efficiency in the agricultural value chain or through commodity-specific development, which can be promoted in future trade agreements. The PricewaterhouseCoopers, in its 2017 and 2019 reports on the agricultural export potential of Nigeria, identified crucial value chains in which increased production would intensify Nigeria's export potential.[2] Thus, investing in the value chain holds the potential for youth engagement and employment while providing an excellent opportunity to diversify Nigeria's economy, as has been its development priority in recent years (African Development Fund, 2013). Developing the agribusiness value chain also ensures the effective utilisation of Nigeria's natural capital, which includes over eighty-four million hectares of arable land and a youthful labour force (FMARD, 2016).

It has become imperative that efficiency in production along the agriculture value chains is improved in order to prepare Nigeria for a smoother transition into contributing to the global value chains. Specifically, some measures required to develop agribusiness value chains through youth engagement include knowledge and technology transfer from the EU regarding modernised farming and the best practices of agribusiness value chains, to the extent that they are compatible with Nigerian realities and take cognisance of the existing traditional knowledge on agricultural processes. Equally important is improving infrastructure (transportation and road networks) or providing further incentives for these to be developed by the private sector. These measures would maximise profits for youth-owned businesses and increase the appetite of young people to engage with agribusiness (Figure. 9.1).

Capacity building is also vital for young people to succeed in agribusiness. It is essential to train young people in rural and urban areas on utilising modern farming techniques to improve efficiency and maximise production outcomes. It is critical to empower them to learn how to utilise information,

Figure 9.1 The agricultural value chain.

communication, and technology in order to access relevant data (such as commodity prices, weather, pest control advice) and provide access to additive manufacturing to aid in innovation in the agricultural sector.

Conclusion

Untying the EU–Africa migration knot requires a new approach that moves away from the usual aid and conditionality approach that the EU has used in previous years. Instead, mutual respect and a more precise understanding of the varied African circumstances and realities are essential. This chapter argues that trade is a solution to migration, especially considering the established linkages between migration and trade. However, this solution is medium and long term and depends on other factors, such as provisions in trade agreements and efficiency in the production value chain. This solution necessitates the review of current trade agreements between the EU and Africa; they should include genuine development objectives that are SMART.

The development of the agribusiness sector in Nigeria provides an illustrative case study on how SMART development can achieve sustainable results. Within this context, engaging the Nigerian youth – who are a target demographic, prone to rural–urban and cross-border migration – developing their skills, and absorbing them into gainful employment within the agribusiness value chain would boost Nigeria's agricultural production and economic growth. Achieving this economic growth would contribute to stability and would reduce the appetite for migration of a significant proportion of youths. Although the results of this solution would not be immediately felt, the impact would be sustainable and, given the projected rise in the African population over the next three decades, considering this approach is highly recommended. Therefore, the EU-allocated funds for migration can be best utilised if invested in sector-specific value chains.

Notes

1 The original text refers to Africa since the initial agreement was between the EU and the African, Caribbean, and Pacific group of states.
2 The PWC identified crucial value chains in sesame seeds, cashew nuts, fermented cocoa beans, superior quality cocoa beans, and frozen shrimps and prawns.

References

African Development Bank. (2002) *African Development Report 2002: Rural Development and Poverty Reduction in Africa.* Oxford: Oxford University Press.
African Development Fund. (2013) Agricultural Transformation Agenda Support Program – Phase 1 (ATASP-1) Nigeria. (online) Available at www.afdb.org/en/ documents/ (Accessed 10 May 2020).

Agbebi, M. and Virtanen, P. (2017) Dependency Theory – A Conceptual Lens to Understand China's Presence in Africa? *Forum for Development Studies*, 44(3), pp. 429–51.

Allen, T. A., Heinrigs, P., and Heoii, I. (2018) Agriculture, Food and Jobs in West Africa. *West African Papers*, 14, DOI: 10.1787/dc152bc0-en.

Babu, S. C. and Shaw, C. (2015) Role of Agribusiness and Opportunities for Young Africans. *Africa Times*. (online) Available at: africatimes.com/2015/09/24/role-of-agribusiness-and-opportunities-for-young-africans/ (Accessed 20 April 2020).

Banthia, A. (2007) Success or Failure? An Evaluation of Fifty Years (1957–2007) of the European Union Development Policy in Africa, the Caribbean and the Pacific. *Political Perspectives EPRU*, 2(1).

Barslund, M., Backhaus A., and Di Salvo, M. (2019) *Rethinking EU Migration and Asylum Policies: Managing Immigration Jointly with Countries of Origin and Transit*. Brussels: Mercator Dialogue on Asylum and Migration.

Bruder, J. (2004) Are Trade and Migration Substitutes or Complements? The Case of Germany, 1970–1998. (online) Available at: www.researchgate.net/publication/228796068_Are_Trade_and_Migration_Substitutes_or_Complements_-_The_Case_of_Germany_1970-1998 (Accessed 9 April 2020).

Carbaugh, R. (2007) Is International Trade a Substitute for Migration? *Global Economy Journal*, 7(3), 1–15.

Davis, J. Rust, I., and Goldberg, R. (1957) A Concept of Agribusiness, John H. Davis and Ray A. Goldberg. Boston: Division of Research, Graduate School of Business Administration, Harvard University. *American Journal of Agricultural Economics*, 39(4), 1042–5.

Daramola, A., Ehui, S., Ukeje, E., and McIntire, J. (2007) *Agricultural Export Potential in Nigeria*. (online) Available at: www.csae.ox.ac.uk/books/epopn/Agriculturalexpo rtpotentialinNigeria.pdf (Accessed 13 April 2020).

Del Biondo, K. (2011) EU Aid Conditionality in ACP Countries: Explaining Inconsistency in EU Sanctions Practice. Journal of Contemporary European Research, 7(3), 380–95.

Faini, R., De Melo, J., and Zimmermann, K. F. (1999) Trade and Migration: An Introduction. In: R. Faini, J. De Melo and K. F. Zimmermann, eds., *Migration: The Controversies and the Evidence*. 1st ed. Cambridge: Cambridge University Press, pp. 1–20.

Federal Ministry of Agriculture and Rural Development (FMARD). (2016) *The Agriculture Promotion Policy 2016, 2020: Building on the Successes of the ATA, Closing Key Gaps*. Abuja: FMARD.

Ferraro, V. (2008) Dependency Theory: An Introduction. In: G. Secondi, eds., *The Development Economics Reader*. London: Taylor & Francis US, pp. 58–64.

Flahaux, M. and De Haas, H. (2016) African Migration: Trends, Patterns, Drivers. *Comparative Migration Studies* 4(1), DOI: 10.1186/s40878-015-0015-6.

Food and Agriculture Organisation of the United Nations (FAO). (2019) Empowering Youth to Engage in Responsible Investment in Agriculture and Food Systems: Challenges, Opportunities and Lessons Learned from Six African Countries. Rome: FAO. (online) Available at: www.fao.org/3/ca2877en/ca2877en.pdf (Accessed 18 March 2020).

Gatsios, K., Hatzipanayotou, P., and Michael, M. S. (1999) Trade Liberalization and Public-Good Provision: Migration-Promoting or Migration-Deterring? In: R.

Faini, J. De Melo and K. F. Zimmermann, eds, *Migration: The Controversies and the Evidence*. Cambridge: Cambridge University Press, pp. 94–115.

Heckscher, E. F. and Ohlin, B. (1991) *Heckscher-Ohlin Trade Theory*, transl. P. A. Samuelson. Cambridge: MIT Press.

Hatzigeorgiou, A. (2010). Migration as Trade Facilitation: Assessing the Links between International Trade and Migration. The B.E. Journal of Economic Analysis & Policy, 10(1), 1–35.

International Labour Organisation (ILO). (2016) *ILOSTAT: The Country Profile, Nigeria*. (online) Available at: ilostat.ilo.org/data/country-profiles/ (Accessed 20 March 2020).

International Organisation for Migration (IOM). (2020) *World Migration Report 2020*. Geneva: IOM. (online) Available at: publications.iom.int/system/files/pdf/wmr_2020.pdf Accessed 29 April 2020.

Iruonagbe, T. C. (2009) Rural-Urban Migration and Agricultural Development in Nigeria. *Arts and Social Sciences International Research Journal*, 1(3), 28–49.

Konig, G., da Silva, C. A., and Mhlanga, N. (2013) *Enabling Environments for Agribusiness and Agroindustries Development, Regional and Country Perspectives*. Rome: Food and Agriculture Organization.

Laine, J. (2020) Reframing African migration to Europe: An Alternative Narrative. In: I. Moyo, C. C. Nshimbi and J. P. Laine, eds, *Migration Conundrums, Regional Integration and Development: Africa–Europe Relations in a Changing Global Order*. London: Palgrave Macmillan, pp. 93–116.

Lockett, H. and McCormick, M. (2020) International Oil Prices Fall to More Than Two-Decade Low. *Financial Times*. (online) Available at: www.ft.com/content/f878ae96-0b20-49fb-a997-30cb13b4bb77 (Accessed 21 April 2020).

Martin, P. (1993) Trade and Migration: The Case of NAFTA. *Asian and Pacific Migration Journal*, 2(3), 329–67.

Mberu, B. U. (2005) Who Moves and Who Stays? Rural Out-Migration in Nigeria. *Journal of Population Research*, *22*(2), 141–61.

Mo Ibrahim Foundation (2019) *Africa's Youth: Jobs or Migration? Demography, Economic Prospects, and Mobility*. (online) Available at: mo.ibrahim.foundation/sites/default/files/2019-10/2019%20Forum%20Report.pdf (Accessed 20 April 2020).

National Population Commission and National Bureau of Statistics, Nigeria (NPC, NBS). (2017) *National Population Estimates*.

Nigeria Bureau for Statistics (NBS). (2019) *Labor Force Statistics – Volume I: Unemployment and Underemployment Report* (Q4 2017-Q3, 2018). National Bureau of Statistics. Labour Force Statistics-Volume 2, Unemployment and Underemployment by State, Q3 2018.

Nwalatu, M. (2016) *From Africa to Europe, Youth and Transnational Migration: Examining the Lived Experiences of Nigerian Migrant Youth in Malta*. Toronto: University of Toronto.

Okafor, O. C . (2020) The Future of International Solidarity in Global Refugee Protection. *Hum Rights Review* (online). Available at doi.org/10.1007/s12142-020-00587-w (Accessed 20 April).

PricewaterhouseCoopers Limited. (2017) *Transforming Nigeria's Agricultural Value Chain: A Case Study of the Cocoa and Dairy Industries*. Lagos: PricewaterhouseCoopers Limited.

PricewaterhouseCoopers Limited. (2019) *Unlocking Nigeria's Agricultural Exports.* (online). Available at: www.pwc.com/ng/en/assets/pdf/unlocking-ngr-agric-export. pdf (Accessed 18 March 2020).

Ricardo, D. (1821[1817]) *The Principles of Political Economy and* Taxation, 3rd ed. London: John Murray.

Schmieg, E. (2019) *Connections between Trade Policy and Migration: A Sphere of Action for the EU.* German Institute for International and Security Affairs (SWP), Research paper 15, Berlin. (online) Available at www.swp-berlin.org/10.18449/ 2019RP15/ (Accessed 20 April 2020).

United Nations, General Assembly. (2018) *Human Rights and International Solidarity: Report of the Independent Expert* A/73/206.

United Nations, Department of Economic and Social Affairs, Population Division. (2019) *World Population Prospects 2019: Highlights.* (online) Available at: popu-lation.un.org/wpp/Publications/Files/WPP2019_Highlights.pdf (Accessed 20 April 2020).

United Nations Office of the High Representative for the Least Developed Countries, Landlocked Developing Countries and Small Island Developing States (UN-OHRLLS). (online) Available at unohrlls.org/about-ldcs/ (Accessed 14 April 2020).

World Bank. (2013) *Growing Africa, Unlocking the Potential of Agribusiness. Washington: World Bank.* (online) Available at: openknowledge.worldbank.org/ handle/10986/26082 (Accessed 20 April 2020).

Zylbersztajn, D. (2017) Agribusiness Systems Analysis: Origin, Evolution and Research Perspectives. *Revista de Administração, 52*(1), 114–17.

10 Transnationalising business and innovation ecosystems shaping EU-Africa relations

A case study of Finland and Namibia

Mika Raunio and Disney Andreas

Introduction

African development has serious consequences – not only on the continent itself, but globally, and especially for Europe in terms of future migration flows and economic co-operation opportunities. Pressure for human migration to Europe will grow substantially due to fast population growth, the lack of economic opportunities, and climate change. Based on estimations, these flows might reach beyond the political, social, and economic absorptive capacity of Europe (Migration Data Portal, 2020). Simultaneously, decades-long brain drain hinders the development potential in countries of origin, especially in sub-Saharan Africa (Gonzalez-Garcia et al., 2016).

Paradoxically, many African economies are the fastest growing in the world, with strong prospects that create significant economic opportunities for European economies and businesses. The continent with the youngest population may also provide a much-needed labour migration to greying Europe. The governance of EU-Africa relations, including migration and development processes, may either be harmful or beneficial to both Europe and Africa.

In this chapter, we will discuss a specific governance approach that aims to build mutually beneficial relations between Europe and Africa, as well as connect their economies and businesses. Contemporary business-oriented development policies foster the emergence of transnational business and innovation ecosystems with strong local anchors in Africa. We will explore these policy measures between Finland and southern Africa by asking: What are the practices and challenges in development of mutually beneficial innovation and business ecosystems between the EU and southern Africa?

This specific case focuses on Finnish-Namibian relations, initiated in the nineteenth century by Finnish missionaries. Two contemporary development policy programmes, the Development Markets Platform and the Southern Africa Innovation Support (SAIS) programme, illustrate the business with impact policy design. A more detailed micro-level empirical case focuses on local anchoring actor, Dololo Operations (Pty) Ltd, a young Windhoek-based

DOI: 10.4324/9781003083726-11

privately owned company that aims to work as catalyst and enhance the growth of the Namibian entrepreneurship ecosystem. The empirical data was gathered in this context via participatory action research by the authors.

Our contribution to the academic discussion emerges from linking the contemporary development policy approach to challenges of migration by analysing the economic learning processes in transnational ecosystems with a proximity approach (e.g. Boschma, 2005). With a proximity approach of knowledge-based regional development studies, we aim to better understand the development of learning capabilities within these ecosystems. The main outcome for policy suggests that the ecosystem approach is a feasible way to develop mutually beneficial and sustainable socio-economic relations between the two continents, but both the ecosystem policy and platform management require specific capabilities. To systematically apply the ecosystem approach, these capabilities should be developed at all levels – from local entrepreneurs to international agencies. The transnational ecosystems with strong local anchors offer approaches to engage EU-African partners to co-creation processes when solving grand global challenges in Africa and beyond.

Ecosystems for economic learning

Policy fostering the ecosystems and platforms

In regional economic development-related literature, the concept of an "ecosystem" has recently emerged to describe relations among economic actors. This concept is used to replace or complement some more established concepts like innovation systems, networks, or value chains. While the concept is vague in academic terms, in policy and business, it is widely used. In the academic literature, the common denominator is that actors of the ecosystem are interdependent and benefit from the success of the other members of the ecosystem. Because the notion is also increasingly used in the development policy context, we provide some clarification on how concepts are used in this context. The prefix related to the concept usually refers to the different compositions and aims of the ecosystem.

- *Business ecosystems* refer to networks in mature lines of business, or even to extended value chains of one key company with existing business activities and provisions of products and/or services. Especially in software development, an ecosystem may organise itself around one "focal offer" rather than the sector (e.g. Apple iPhone), while members bring their complementary assets to be part of the offering for customers (Moore, 1993; Kapoor, 2018).
- *Innovation ecosystems* often refer to the strong role of research organisations and universities in which the aim of the ecosystem is to innovate and develop new products and services. In regional economic

development literature, the concept very often overlaps with a more established innovation system concept (Cooke, Uranga, Etxebarria, 1998; Lundvall, 1992; Oh et al., 2016).

• *Entrepreneurial ecosystems* of growth companies (start-ups) focus on entrepreneurs themselves rather than all small and medium-sized enterprises (SMEs) and aim to enhance the growth mindset and start-up activities among the ecosystem (Stam and Van de Ven, 2019; Brown and Mawson, 2019).

Intermediating agencies have played an important role in knowledge- and innovation-based economic development (Lundvall et al., 2009; World Bank, 2010). Intermediaries provide information and connect actors who might mutually benefit from each other's knowledge or resources and may, through mutual learning processes, create something new (e.g. technology transfer offices, development companies). Intermediaries typically enable and foster various modes of interactions among universities or research institutions (who produce knowledge) with firms (who turn knowledge into products and services) and other stakeholders who support or define the process (e.g. users, financers).

Recently, various innovation hubs, labs, and centres have been established for this task by policymakers, companies, universities, and other stakeholders. Hub and lab models often refer to more open, start-up and innovation-oriented activities than earlier intermediaries, as well as broader engagement of stakeholders, frequently including users and citizens.

We label these intermediaries that foster interactions according to a more open (innovation) model as platforms. Here, platform is a mode of interaction that is facilitated by the third party to provide mutually beneficial interactions among the users of the platform within the ecosystem. Of course, the platform owner may be one of the beneficiaries.

The notion of a platform has a strong technical connotation that is related to various entities based on internet and related technological solutions (e.g. Apple iPhone, Facebook) that clearly have changed the interaction models of various parties and provided new paths for business and value creating (Gawer and Cusumano, 2002; Raunio et al., 2018). However, it should be noted that platforms, as modes of operation, are not new or based on technology. Platforms aim to add the governance model to networks to seek, create, and share value for different members of networks, through organised interaction models. The success of a platform is based on its capability to facilitate interactions that are beneficial for all its users. That is, the capability to create value for all user parties from interactions. Therefore, we consider the broadly understood platform model that is frequently – but not necessarily – powered by technology as a relevant conceptual tool to describe the characteristics of contemporary intermediaries of ecosystems fostering the economic learning and socio-technical changes.

Proximities enabling economic learning on platforms

We analyse economic learning through five different proximities based on a Schumpeterian innovation-driven view to economic development (Nooteboom, 2009). At regional level, innovation and business may be a process of "collective economic learning" among individuals and organisations. If successful, learning will improve the (collective) economic performance of the actors and, thus, the economic development of the region. The proximity approach assumes that physical proximity is beneficial, but not compulsory for learning. However, it is crucial that other forms of proximities – cognitive, social, institutional, or organisational – are sufficient for learning (Balland, Boschma, and Frenken, 2014).

To foster development among a diverse group of actors, not only meeting but learning sites that help actors to communicate, understand, and trust each other are needed. This enhances opportunities for innovation and economic learning among the actors and makes the ecosystem dynamic. A short description of the key dimensions provides us with tools to analyse the role of platform practices in the development of innovation and business ecosystems. Boschma (2005) introduced five dimensions of proximity, while Balland et al. (2015) further added dynamic processes to explain the knowledge generation and use in the spatial context. Proximity includes the idea that there are capabilities that enhance the search of "optimal distance" for learning (e.g. absorptive capacity, reshaping of practices).

- **Cognitive proximity** makes the use of knowledge and mutual learning possible, however, too much similarity makes knowledge bases worthless to each other if they both have the same knowledge. Without any overlap in knowledge bases, meaningful interaction is impossible. Cognitive distance "has a positive effect on learning by interaction because it yields opportunities for novel combinations of complementary resources. When cognitive distance becomes too wide to preclude adequate mutual understanding, it loses its usefulness". Therefore, cognitive distance should be wide enough to bring about something new, but not too distant, as mutual understanding may become very vague (Nooteboom, 2007). Through interactive learning, actors reduce cognitive distance and converge mental models during the knowledge exchange. With a high absorptive capacity (Cohen and Levinthal, 1990), the actor can collaborate in an efficient and innovative way with different partners on the field.
- **Social proximity** is a dynamic process because it refers to the embeddedness of knowledge relationships in an evolving social context (Balland, Boschma, and Frenken, 2014). Relations need to contain trust and are personal, micro-level phenomena. A degree of social proximity is measured by the personal acquaintance between two actors. Analysis focuses on relations between individuals belonging to different

organisations and to "decoupling", which means independent personal relations and their origins (e.g. former colleagues remain acquainted after others leave the organisation). Excessive social proximity may lead to over-embeddedness, lack of diversity, and blocking of newcomers.

• **Institutional proximity** comes close to the concept of habitus (Bourdieu, 1985) and refers to a code of conduct constructed through the socialisation process of individuals and organisations that provides rules and values for behaviour. Repeated interactions contribute to the creation of common practices, values, rules, ethics, and, finally, institutional structures. The constant reshaping and redefinition of practices and rules has been an important success factor for innovation activities.

• **Organisational proximity** refers to collaboration, subsidiaries, departments, and other organisational structures that provide proximity among the actors in knowledge creation and use, even over long distances. In many interpretations, organisational proximity includes or overlaps strongly with cognitive proximity. Integration with other organisations may, for example, be an important tool to control certain strategic knowledge.

• **Geographical or physical proximity** refers to the vicinity of actors in the same region, but does not ensure interaction and mutual learning. However, the inertia of geographical proximity due to limited mobility of individuals and organisations may increase the development of agglomeration around the specific knowledge base and further increase the attractiveness of the location. The benefits of immobility can make the spatial dimension less dynamic than the others (Balland et al., 2015; Boschma, 2005).

The proximity approach adds spatial and dynamic dimensions to learning and interaction processes. All proximities are dynamic, but not equally dynamic, because changes in proximity do not imply the same economic costs. Cognitive proximity is the most dynamic because knowledge changes all the time. Social proximity is a little less dynamic, because changing social relations often requires loosening some other networks and because actors can maintain only a certain number of networks.

While institutional structures are constantly adjusted, changes in institutional proximity require significant investments when new societal structures are created and destroyed. The least dynamic is geographical proximity, as the change from one location to another is more common than working in multiple locations, and that requires the abandonment of all links one had in the previous location (Balland et al., 2015). Other proximities may thus be seen as "substitutes" for physical proximity (i.e. migration) in the case of economic learning.

The development of an ecosystem via an innovation platform may thus be analysed through stylised proximities; the platform facilitates the emergence of proximities locally and globally, knitting together the ecosystem and its innovative capabilities. Platforms may provide tools to cross cognitive, social, and cultural, as well as physical borders.

Data and method: "Approach in identifying a platform in an ecosystem"

It should be noted that we aim to understand and analyse the dynamics and processes or ecosystem-building approach in each theoretical and economic context. As a basic methodological approach, we deployed participatory action research (PAR). PAR emphasises participation and action and intends to make sense of the world through collective efforts to change it. Research is conducted *with* people instead of "on" or "for" people, in a collaborative manner, especially when the object of the study is co-creation processes and how to promote them. According to Greenwood and Levin (2007), a typical team encompasses (a) the researcher(s) and the stakeholder(s) who are members of an organisation, community, or network with the aim to improve the stakeholders' situation. Thus, broad participation and the improved situation of stakeholders are characteristics of action research. The problem is defined and examined together and thus action research democratises the relationship between the researcher and the other members of the research process.

Empirical data for this chapter has been gathered mostly by Andreas, in her capacity as the co-founder and communications manager of Dololo Namibia. Dozens of meetings, interviews, and other activities as well as memos and documents are used in an eclectic manner to develop the interpretation presented in this chapter.

The data is reflected in the theory and the experiences of both authors for a three-year period based on work on "SmartCom", a BEAM project (see Oksman, Raunio, and Andreas, 2018) from 2015 to 2018 in Namibia and Finland (University of Tampere, Finland, and Finnish technical research centre, VTT). The aim is to provide insight into content and the potential of the relations based on ecosystems building between Africa and the EU rather than highly generic scientific results about the impact of the policy model, the latter being a highly "place sensitive" matter.

Building ecosystems between Finland and Namibia

Innovation hubs and start-ups for development

Innovation, entrepreneurs, technology, ecosystems, or global value chains have been on the development policy agenda of many actors (World Bank, 2010; 2020). Furthermore, various innovation hubs and labs have been on the agenda in Africa for some time already, often with support from multinational corporations (MNC) or international development agencies. For example, technology companies like the Nokia Group built several entrepreneurship-enhancing "Mlabs" in Africa in cooperation with the World Bank (infoDev programme) and local actors during the 2010s. Microsoft Innovation Centres have been established in over a hundred locations, mostly in developing countries and emerging economies, in cooperation with local universities or economic development agencies during the 2000s (many of them closed over time). In these cases, the advancement of digitalized technologies (e.g. mobile) was frequently the motivation for the activities. Thus, the logic may be found from the business models of MNCs, not only from the blueprints of policymakers.

Parallel policy measures, often with international partner(s), have been on the rise, both globally and in Namibia. These include Demola Namibia, for example. Based on the format of a Finnish company, Demola Global, it provides the possibility to run a demo project to gather understanding and testing experiences from the local environment with local students from universities in Namibia. This initiative's activities started in 2016 and completed two cycles. A Windhoek start-up festival was initiated by local start-up ecosystem builders, who joined forces to launch the first festival of its kind in Namibia in 2017. In 2018, it included various events, speakers and networking opportunities, including links to the Slush event in Helsinki, Finland. FABlab[1] Namibia is an "advanced manufacturing, prototyping and design lab and the largest FABlab currently within Africa". It is part of the Namibian University of Science and Technology (NUST) and emerged bottom-up as result of two local entrepreneurs. The model was franchised from USA-based FabLab. Namibian universities, for example the Namibia Business Innovation Institute (NBII) through NUST, provide access to various innovation competitions, like the Southern African Start-Up Awards (SASA) and services for businesses. Thus, there is a phenomenon with strong global advocates, universities, and transplanted models from abroad.

Finnish business with impact policy in southern Africa

Our specific case focuses on relations between two small countries, Finland (5.5 million inhabitants) and Namibia (2.2 million inhabitants). These countries share a long history reaching back to the nineteenth century, before independence of either nation. From the well-received missionaries in northern Namibia all the way to the 1990s and reconciliation process with support of then forthcoming Finnish president Martti Ahtisaari as well as development projects building support systems for entrepreneurship in Namibia fostered by Finnish development actors, relations between the two nations have been strong and positive, and never colonial by nature. Thus, proximities have been developed over a very long time between the nations and their people. Two contemporary development programmes continue this work with a strong emphasis on innovation and business ecosystems: The *Developing Markets Platform* and *SAIS*. Both programmes emphasise business as a means to make development sustainable over time, and both have activities in Namibia. Bluntly, they provide organizational and, to some extent, institutional proximities among the actors and thus enable the further development of other forms of proximities for more efficient economic learning.

With the Developing Markets Platform, the Finnish innovation and business investment agency, Business Finland, the Ministry for Foreign Affairs, the development project funding agency Finnpartnership and the recent United Nations Technology and Innovation Lab (UNTIL) of Finland as well as other key partners in business-based development policy and service provision have collaborated.

Previously, the programme was called Business with Impact (BEAM), and it supported Finnish SMES and their research or business partners in "developing sustainable businesses" in developing markets and to globalise and grow. Business relevance lies in the view that markets in many parts of Africa and Asia grow much faster than any other location globally and institutions like the United Nations (UN) and development banks place substantial investments to foster sustainable and scalable solutions at these locations. Furthermore, Finnish companies and research institutions have technology and knowledge that may help to provide such solutions that are compatible with the UN Sustainable Development Goals (SDGs). In short, the programme helps Finnish SMEs to launch innovative projects for developing markets in collaboration with local partners (Business Finland, 2020).

Experiences from the BEAM programme suggest that combining business and development objectives is challenging, but also a rewarding approach. According to funded project managers, projects achieved the planned object-ives and even more, but at least 30 percent confronted some unexpected challenges, especially due to cultural differences and the slow progress of projects. Most project funding lasts only two to three years. Despite some successful projects, there is not yet evaluation-based evidence on substantial sustainable business or development impacts (BEAM Evaluation Report, 2019). Funding for receiving country partners was an important aspect to resolve, and there has been some progress in this matter.

More critical voices claim that SMEs do not do enough to distinguish between the outcome of their projects and wider societal impacts. Also, employment impact frequently focuses on educated people rather than the less advantaged, and local business partners are found but not really engaged in business and co-creation processes. Further critique, based on interviews of representatives of BEAM projects, has been motivated by the paradigm shift in development policy that cuts off substantial amounts of funding from non-governmental organisations and civil society organisations – who have traditionally been actors in the development field – and channelled it to SMEs (United Nations Children's Fund, 2017).

The SAIS programme for the period of 2017 to 2021, known as SAIS 2 is a follow-up for a previous programme (SAIS 1), which suggests that the model was considered to be successful. It supports "the growth of new businesses through strengthening innovation ecosystems and the promotion of cross-border collaboration between innovation players in southern Africa" (SAIS2,

2020). The Finnish Ministry for Foreign Affairs (MFA) works in partnership with African ministries that are responsible for science, technology, and innovation in Botswana, Namibia, South Africa, Tanzania, and Zambia, and with the Southern African Development Community (SADC) Secretariat.

This programme aims to strengthen early-stage enterprises and young entrepreneurs, connect innovation ecosystems, and promote innovations serving socially or economically challenged populations. The objective to "enhance regional innovation cooperation and national innovation systems contributing to inclusive business and development" refers mostly to local capability building. Strengthening the practices and connectivity of local and southern African innovation ecosystems, SAIS 2 offers support for innovation funding, capacity building, and networking with a specific focus on the capability of early-stage firms or start-ups. It offers "connected hub" status for innovation hubs in the region to increase their mutual interaction and learning. In 2020, there were nineteen connected hubs (SAIS 2, 2020).

Moreover, the programme links entrepreneurial ecosystems between Finland and Namibia. They, for instance, organised a Slush side event called "Investing and Partnering with African Innovators" and brought together impact start-ups, investors, and other ecosystem players from the Finnish and African ecosystem. The event included a "fireside" chat on how to invest in African start-ups and included guest speakers from South Africa and Finland. This event also included the final pitch competition, which consisted of start-ups from southern Africa, West Africa and Europe. In short, like the Developing Markets Platform programme, SAIS 2 builds linkages between the ecosystems from Finland to Africa, but SAIS 2 especially builds capacity in southern Africa. In sum, they provide organizational and institutional proximities among the actors of different ecosystems.

Local innovation platform rooting for the transnational ecosystem

To analyse the micro-level anchoring activities in ecosystem development and economic learning in the local context, we focus on Dololo Namibia, defined as one of the innovation platforms in southern Africa in this study. Both SAIS and BEAM have utilised its services or networks to anchor their activities locally. We put forward three issues that are likely to anchor the development supported by transnational ecosystems to the local economy.

Local bottom-up development of the entrepreneurial community provides strong roots. Dololo Namibia has local founders and a team of five people facilitates its activities and community. Two of the founders are also representatives of local businesses. Dololo Namibia is a privately owned company that was established in 2017 in Windhoek, but it is also a community of entrepreneurs, start-ups, and "people who aim to make a change", according to its own definition. It should be noted that in local slang, "dololo" means "nothing", and it is aimed at moving from nothing to something. Dololo Namibia works closely with national and international partners to enable organisations and leaders to connect with "the next generation of change-makers". For firms, they provide risk assessments, access to innovation processes, business incubation, co-working spaces, and support to entrepreneurs including basic tools, training, and networking opportunities to develop their ideas into businesses. The bottom-up approach and local ownership is relevant for long-term impact.

Mission orientation and links to local institutions strengthen the development view. Dololo Namibia is also committed to use internationally sourced solutions to help address the unemployment crisis in Namibia (50% of people under the age of thirty-five are unemployed). In fact, a large part of its activities relates to non-profit projects and generating a positive impact in the entrepreneurship ecosystem in Namibia. Here, they work with actors that support and develop the entrepreneurial ecosystem in Namibia, including the Ministry of Industrialisation, Trade and SME Development, the National Commission on Research Science and Technology, and local universities and international organisations. Thus, many of the topics at Dololo Namibia are not only business- but development-oriented. Business-oriented solutions to societal challenges seem to fit very well to platform and ecosystem-building. Dololo Namibia represents the view that technology has the power to excel Namibia and bring its younger generation to a brighter future. It supports a young generation of growth-minded individuals to remove the conventional constraints of their geographical location, political constraints, income disparity, and other bottlenecks that might otherwise stand in the way of them reaching their full potential.

The facilitation of proximity development for economic learning processes is crucial. We analyse the development of five modes of proximity fostering innovation and economic learning and their role in the ecosystem-building activities of *Dololo Namibia.* We introduce practical experiences and practices building "sufficient proximities" and highlight some lessons for further policy development and academic discussion.

In increasing **organisational proximity**, we place specific attention on increasing convergence and linkages of southern African and Finnish organisational structures that foster mutually beneficial interactions among individuals and organisations. The Connected Hubs co-operation model, which is initiated and coordinated by SAIS 2, is a network that currently connects nineteen innovation support organisations in the SADC, based on a joint cause. The main goal is to build a regional community and facilitate knowledge exchange by sharing best practices in innovation support and further building a networked community of innovation actors in the SADC region.

Dololo Namibia is a Connected Hub member and they have facilitated start-up activities through an initiative called BOOST UP. It is a three-part series of start-up events that targets early-stage start-ups who want to solve societal problems using technology and are looking for skills that could help them articulate their business ideas. The BOOST UP series comprises an online incubation programme and an in-person boot camp with SAIS

2 knowledge partners in Finland. The activities thus reach beyond SADC countries and connect start-ups and platforms with Finland's innovation ecosystem. Dololo Namibia is used especially as a platform to identify these start-ups and further facilitate, in collaboration with SAIS 2, to help start-up teams arrive in Finland to expose their business ideas to potential funders and partners at Slush, marketed as "the world's leading start-up and tech event" in Helsinki, Finland. For example, a start-up from Tanzania made it to the highly competitive "Slush 100" and pitched their company to a live audience of people from all over the world and a panel of judges consisting of founders of successful companies. This was an important learning experience for the BOOST UP start-up delegation and for the members of Dololo Namibia.

Institutional proximity, in terms of "sufficiently shared" rules, cultures, and other framing codes of conducts of behaviour, emerged through start-up culture. The business culture of MNCs, the academic culture of universities, and the tech culture of software developers have efficiently structured international interaction and learning cultures for decades. They also provide a base for the culture prevailing in most "start-up ecosystems", which also have a strong local dimension. Searching for new innovative solutions or business models takes place in start-up culture with many globally shared practices, values, and elements, as well as the visual set-up of offices and venues.

Dololo Namibia has clearly acquired this culture, and global start-up culture provides a framework for most interactions that take place on the platform. However, it has a strong local aspect and aims to engage local entrepreneurs in global ecosystem structures. This is a learning process for local actors. One of the cultural learning experiences was introduced above, in the case of African start-ups going to the international investor event Slush in Finland, but there are also many local events where a cultural framework, based on global "start-up culture" with a mix of science and business culture, eases mutual interactions and provides a code of conduct for participants. Dololo Namibia is not alone when it comes to creating this culture and proximity, but it is part of it. Of course, for international partners, they provide knowledge about local rules and conditions, so learning is mutual, although characterised by start-up culture.

In *cognitive proximity*, technological and business intelligence may be the key elements that should be sufficiently developed to start meaningful business relations between parties. An illustrative example is the Dololearn project, which was a part of BEAM and was initiated by Finnish companies. In this project, both pedagogical methods and class environments based on Finnish expertise have been co-created in two schools in Windhoek, one private in a better-off area and one public in a less-advantaged area. During the process, a group of teachers from Windhoek schools visited Finland and familiarised themselves with the educational system and practices. This especially creates better mutual professional understanding among various actors – cognitive proximity – that enables further discussion about goals and solutions. Of course, professionals in education already have some cognitive proximity due to their training, but in the case of more complex systemic innovations, the understanding of systemic differences is important.

Social proximity, relations that last after the individuals cease working together or in the same organisation, are also highly important for the economic learning process. As it is frequently a challenge to find suitable local partners for business development, it is even more challenging to find a partner for serious innovation and development collaboration. Connecting with interested start-up founders and teams and getting support from the public has brought great meaning to Dololo Namibia as a hub manager and the entrepreneurial ecosystem reaching from Namibia to southern Africa to Europe. Furthermore, Dololo Namibia hosts, for example, breakfast meetings with various "ecosystem players" in entrepreneurship development in Namibia. Here, various local stakeholders discuss their projects, find common ground, and identify new ways to cooperate to reach shared objectives more effectively. These events have hosted over forty people meeting related to topics like women empowerment, social entrepreneurship, and professionalising women-owned businesses, amongst many others. Social networks are built around topics, bringing individuals together.

These are very practical examples on how to build proximities among actors to make an ecosystem more capable to learn and to innovate. Proximities, as a conceptual tool, help to evaluate and distinguish different key processes of economic learning. These dimensions are helpful when evaluating and designing policies and policy measures to renew ecosystem-based relations between the EU and Africa.

Ecosystems, development, and changing migration dynamics

The new Africa strategy is among the priorities of the EU. New relations between the EU and African nations should foster the search for solutions to grand global challenges like climate change, the digital divide, or migration, in Africa and beyond. Consequently, the lessons learnt from business- and innovation-oriented development policies offer tested tools for this purpose. Platforms, ecosystems, and innovation processes provide concepts and practices for economically efficient interaction, co-creation, and facilitation of mutually beneficial learning processes to come up with feasible solutions and businesses. The major challenge is to transfer these value-creating models in a systemic way to orchestrate the relations between the EU and Africa among entrepreneurs, companies, the public sector, and other stakeholders in a way that will support long-term sustainable development. Mechanisms themselves are crucial, but not sufficient conditions for inclusive and sustainable development. While ecosystems and platforms seem to provide a feasible framework for mutually beneficial economic learning, at least three of the following observations should be carefully considered.

Firstly, new capabilities for ecosystem-building and platform management are needed. Ecosystems and platforms provide promising tools to create mutually beneficial environments for entrepreneurship and innovation, but their governance and facilitation require specific skills. Innovation ecosystem policies are in use in various countries with supportive platform and hub activities, but it is not a magic formula for success. The capabilities to provide entrepreneurial ecosystem policies are still scattered and at very different stages of maturity in most EU and North American regions (Brown and Mason, 2017). Efficient platform management is also only just emerging and is frequently explained with an abstract, or even vague, set of competences (Choudary, 2014; Raunio et al., 2018). To support EU-African relations, these emerging capabilities need to be systematically developed for this specific purpose. Many transplanted, even globally successful and MNC-related models have failed in Africa and other places while others have succeeded with the same or close to the same mode of operation (World Bank, 2014; World Bank, 2017). Frequently, the facilitators' or project managers' competences to work and execute diverse activities in very uncertain conditions comes up as an important factor for successful processes. This is a challenge in terms of policy design.

Secondly, integration of activities to broader knowledge infrastructure is important. Ecosystems, especially start-up ecosystems, often focus on actors, individuals, entrepreneurs, or start-ups. However, even in cases of policy fostering start-up ecosystems, we should not forget the system level. In fact, it is important to make a distinction between the *system-based* policy and the *actor-based* policy. While ecosystems and platforms clearly serve start-ups, entrepreneurs, and projects, actors and the institutional improvements in (higher) education, as well as business and research infrastructure serve the system. Technology and business development programmes in locations where the lack of education and technological capabilities hinders the capability to absorb and develop a new knowledge (absorptive capacity) are referred in literature as "cathedrals in a desert" (Isaksen, Tödtling, and Trippl, 2018). Development of new knowledge and capabilities is not efficient if local actors are not able to acquire and deploy the new knowledge and opportunities sufficiently, and vice versa. Thus, it is crucial to develop educational and research systems of regions to provide more technology-savvy and knowledge-oriented businesses.

The roles of research and education are crucial for the implementation of many systemic innovations that widely impact society. Competence building and research should remain a priority in tandem with business development orientation. For example, during the Dololearn project, but apart from it, a group of Namibian teachers were studying at the Finnish university. It was well acknowledged that this education would provide professional knowledge that would importantly support systemic changes in pedagogical practices and environments that were planned in the project, in case they would take place in Namibia more broadly. Education and existing knowledge bases increase the absorptive capacity of systems to receive and deploy more knowledge and innovation. In other words, they create cognitive proximity with potential collaborators or customers to join technologically advanced and global business efforts.

Thirdly, the business and innovation-oriented development policy with emerging transnational ecosystems offers a new approach for both development and mobility, although the idea of development as a substitute for migration is not new (de Haas, 2010). From developing African economies, the focus shifts to mutually beneficial business relations that are powered by locally rooted innovation platforms and mission-oriented communities which will solve global challenges. This framework provides a different scope for development and suggests providing a more sustainable impact. Importantly, the innovation capacity of ecosystems should be targeted at those challenges that may be found to have an impact on migration dynamics. It should be noted that recent research in sub-Saharan Africa suggests that moderate development enhances emigration, rather than making people stay. The emerging trend in migration in Africa is increasingly caused by societal transformation and development that provides people with sufficient capabilities to move, rather than poverty as such (Flahaux and de Haas, 2016). Therefore, it is important to root the development and prospects to local environments if the aim of the development is to hinder the migration flows and brain drain from these progressing African regions.

The observation that the most mobile are young and educated people (Afrobarometer, 2019) makes this goal even more important to avoid accelerating the brain drain from the regions that move a few steps ahead. This is compatible with the idea of innovation and start-up ecosystems that aim to bottom-up development and increase individuals' self-esteem and business opportunities. Start-up activities and entrepreneurial ecosystems are strongly connected to positive future vision and prospects, and link especially young people to the movement at grassroots level. Also, the sustainability agenda supports the goal when, for example, local challenges related to climate change or food production are partially solved by business communities with mission. These developments may lower the estimated numbers of "climate refugees" in the forthcoming decades. Moreover, the mode of mobility that ecosystems create reflects more virtual and short-term business travelling type of visits and meetings than long-term or permanent out-bound mobility in search of a better life. In fact, through positive development, the aim should be attracting newcomers to join developmental efforts, not just retaining those who are already there. While development is clearly linked to the dynamics of migration flows, better measures and analysis of this connection and causalities should be developed.

Finally, cognitive and social proximities in transnational ecosystems may lower the need to migrate in order to learn new skills and build individual competences. Cross-border learning offers potential alternatives to the migration in search of more rewarding environments for one's intellectual capacity to develop or to be deployed. Thus, in terms of migration management, these policy measures are part of the toolbox when the aim is to offer the carrot to people instead of more commonly used sticks (e.g. in the form of various visa requirements within Africa).

Conclusions

In conclusion, the main lessons from the Finland-Namibia experiences suggest that the sustainable and mutually beneficial business-oriented ecosystem development between the continents of Africa and Europe is a feasible approach to governance of relations. It also provides some insight to more development- and business-related migration management. While many practices have been tested over the years, the more systematic approach is still in its infancy. Capability development for platform management and ecosystem policy design is needed, along with parallel development of educational and research infrastructures in the EU-African context.

Two Finnish development policy programmes and Dololo Namibia, as a platform facilitating the ecosystem development, provided examples of the bottom-up approach in practice. Not just practice, but also supportive mindset, prospects, skills, and networks were important for the activation of entrepreneurial individuals in the region. Platforms and ecosystems increased the social, cultural, and cognitive proximities, i.e. the capability to work and innovate together. This, again, improves the economic learning and innovation capabilities of the region.

While widespread creation of wealth and opportunities in the short-term is not likely to happen, more local development and participation to community-building practices may create the expectation and the role models that better engage people towards future developments. It creates a better vision of what people will achieve over time and with whom. This, again with access to transnational networks and resources, has impact on migration dynamics as well.

To halt the brain drain – both intra- and inter-continental – this improves prospects for some locations with positive development. However, the main linkage between the development and migration is on the engagement of these transnational ecosystems to solve global problems, such as climate change, poverty, or a lack of opportunities, with practical, local solutions and with local entrepreneurs. The locally rooted innovation capabilities should be empowered to solve those societal challenges with sustainable solutions.

These questions concern self-initiated, highly skilled migrants as well as refugees and migrants in general. Migration flows have spurred major political and economic concerns in the EU and globally during the last decade, with tremendous societal impacts. The "Fortress" of Europe desperately needs an alternative model, which the practices and developments discussed in this chapter can perhaps foster by enhancing the local knowledge development and innovative activities. Supporting local development in sending countries is not a new idea in migration management, but now it is better equipped than before. It is important to keep seeking the linkages between micro-level real-life practices and the global policies and phenomena discussed above, to develop feasible policy measures to be a part of the solution, rather than the problem.

Note

1 See fablab.nust.na.

References

Afrobarometer. (2019) (online) Available at: www.afrobarometer.org (Accessed 19 Mar. 2020).

BEAM Evaluation Report. (2019) *Developmental Evaluation of Business with Impact (BEAM) Programme.* Evaluation on Finland's Development Policy and Cooperation 2019/4. Ministry of Foreign Affairs of Finland.

Balland, P., Boschma, R., and Frenken, K. (2014) Proximity and Innovation: From Statics to Dynamics. *Regional Studies*, 49(6), pp. 1–14.

Boschma, R. (2005) Proximity and Innovation: A Critical Assessment. *Regional Studies,* 39(1), pp. 61–74.

Bourdieu, P. (1985) The Social Space and the Genesis of Groups. *Social Science Information,* 24(2), pp. 195–220.

Brown, R. and Mason. C. (2017) Looking Inside the Spiky Bits: A Critical Review and Conceptualisation of Entrepreneurial Ecosystems. *Small Business Economics,* 49, pp. 11–30.

Brown, R. and Mawson, S. (2019) Entrepreneurial Ecosystems and Public Policy in Action: A Critique of the Latest Industrial Policy Blockbuster. *Cambridge Journal of Regions Economy and Society,* 12(3), pp. 327–45.

Business Finland. (2020) Development Market Platform, www.businessfinland.fi.

Choudary, S. P. (2014) *Platform Scale: How an Emerging Business Model Helps Startups Build Large Empires with Minimum Investment.* Singapore: Platform Thinking Lab ltd.

Cohen, W. and Levinthal, D. (1990) Absorptive Capacity A New Perspective on Learning and Innovation. *Administrative Science Quarterly*, 35, pp. 128–52.

Cooke, P., Uranga, M. G., and Etxebarria, G. (1998) Regional Systems of Innovation: An Evolutionary Perspective. *Environment and Planning A. Economy and Society*, 30(9), pp. 1563–84.

de Haas, H. (2010) Migration and Development: A Theoretical Perspective. *International Migration Review,* 44(1), pp. 227–64.

Flahaux, M-L. and de Haas, H. (2016) African Migration: Trends, Patterns, Drivers. *Comparative Migration Studies,* 4(1).

Gawer, A. and Cusumano, M. A. (2002) *Platform Leadership. How Intel, Microsoft, and Cisco Drive Industry Innovation.* Boston: Harvard Business School Publishing.

Gonzalez-Garcia, J. Hitaj, E., Mlachila, M., Viseth, A., and Yenice, M. (2016). *Sub-Saharan African Migration. Patterns and Spillovers.* Washington: International Monetary Fund.

Greenwood, D.J. and Levin, M. (2007) Introduction to *A*ction *R*esearch: Social Research for Social Change. Thousand Oaks: Sage.

Isaksen, A, Tödtling, F., and Trippl, M. (2018) Innovation Policies for Regional Structural Change: Combining Actor-Based and System-Based Strategies, In A. Isaksen, M. Trippl, and R. Martin, eds., *New Avenues for Regional Innovation Systems – Theoretical Advances, Empirical Cases and Policy Lessons*. Cham: Springer, pp. 221–38.

Kapoor, R. (2018) Ecosystems: Broadening the Locus of Value Creation. *Journal of Organization Design*, 7(12), pp. 1–16.

Lundvall, B-Å., ed. (1992) *National Systems of Innovation: Towards a Theory of Innovation and Interactive Learning*, London: Pinter Publishers.

Lundvall, B-Å., Chaminade, C., Joseph, K. J., and Vang, J. (2009) *Handbook of Innovation Systems and Developing Countries. Building Domestic Capabilities in a Global Setting*. London: Routledge.

Migration Data Portal. (2020) (online) Available at: migrationdataportal.org/themes/environmental_migration (Accessed 2 May 2020).

Moore, J. F. (1993) Predators and Prey: A New Ecology *of Competition. Harvard Business Review*, 71, pp. 75–86.

Nooteboom, B. (2009) *A Cognitive Theory of the Firm. Learning, Governance and Dynamic Capabilities*. Cornwall: Edward Elgar.

Nooteboom, B. (2007) Elements of Cognitive Theory of the Firm. In E. Krecke, C. Krecke, and R. G. Koppl, Eds., *Cognition and Economics. Advances in Austrian Economics vol. 9*. Amsterdam: Elsevier, pp. 145–76.

Oh, D-S, Phillips, F., Park, S., and Lee, E. (2016) Innovation Ecosystems: A Critical Examination. *Technovation*, 54, pp. 1–6.

Oksman, V., Raunio, M., and Andreas. D. (2018) Reframing Smart City in Sub-Saharan Africa: Inclusive Engagement Approach and Co-Design Tools for a Developing Economy. *International Journal on Advances in Intelligent Systems*, 11(3/4), pp. 245–56.

Raunio, M., Nordling, N., Kautonen, M., and Räsänen, P. (2018) Open Innovation Platforms as a Knowledge Triangle Policy Tool–Evidence from Finland. *Foresight and STI Governance*.

SAIS2. (2020) (online) Available at: www.saisprogramme.org/ (Accessed 17 May 2020).

Stam, E. and van de Ven, A. (2019) Entrepreneurial Ecosystem Elements. *Small Business Economics*, doi.org/10.1007/s11187-019-00270-6.

United Nations Children's Fund. (2017) *Private Sector and Development: Finnish SMEs as Actors Contributing to Development*. UniResearch 1/2017.

World Bank. (2010) *Innovation Policy. A Guide for Developing Countries*. Washington D.C.: The World Bank.

World Bank. (2014) *Do mLabs Make a Difference? An Assessment*, InfoDev. Innovation and Entrepreneurship.

World Bank. (2017) *Do mLabs Still Make a Difference? A Second Assessment*, InfoDev. Innovation and Entrepreneurship.

World Bank. (2020) *World Development Report 2020. Trading for Development in the Age of Global Value Chains*. Washington: The World Bank.

Part III
Alternative framings for Europe-Africa relations

11 Contemporary representations of migration in African writing

Lena Englund

Literature as a reflection and representation of society has always had a political dimension that has taken issue with ongoing societal shifts and events. This is also highlighted in the present chapter, which examines how migration is represented in three contemporary texts by African writers. The focus is on the categorisation of migrants and how they are often seen as either victims of oppression and injustice or as opportunists hoping to ensure a better life elsewhere. Both views are problematic, as the present study aims to show. Literary texts offer a possibility to investigate representations of migration from a variety of perspectives. The use of such writing is significant from a societal perspective, because they participate in "making meaning of events and experiences through our tellings and retellings of stories for different purposes in various contexts" (Lyons, 2012, p. 6), and because they can be argued to "mark the widespread recognition of how 'we story the world'" (ibid.). Telling stories of migration has been a recurring feature of much contemporary African writing published in the last few decades, and the preoccupation with the topic also emerges with current societal debates (see for example the 2019 novel *Travellers* by Helon Habila, which provides a commentary on the refugee crisis of 2015).

The categorisation and labelling of migrants has been discussed in a number of recent studies (cf. Sajjad, 2018; Yarris and Castañeda, 2015; Persian, 2012) and continues to cause controversy. The dilemma is neatly summarised by Vicki Squire (2017, p. 255):

> The challenge then is how to develop analysis that fosters full understanding of the dynamics of unauthorised migration, yet in a way that can shift the terms of a debate which has become worryingly polarised. More precisely, how to do so in a way that does not perpetuate broader assumptions about people on the move as being victims of circumstance and/or culpable for their situation?

The three works at the centre of this chapter all address the issue of migrant categorisation and the question raised by Squire. They focus on illegality and have also received a great deal of scholarly attention. The texts in question are

DOI: 10.4324/9781003083726-12

Harare North (2009; henceforth *Harare*) by Brian Chikwava, *On Black Sisters' Street* (2009; henceforth *Sisters*) by Chika Unigwe, and *We Need New Names* (2013; henceforth *Names*) by NoViolet Bulawayo. It would be justified to ask why these novels have been so widely examined from a variety of migration perspectives, and one of the hypotheses is that researchers have detected a specific migrant aesthetic that might even be seen as a master narrative or blueprint for contemporary migration stories in these works – one which is concerned with representations of economic migration and victimhood from a dystopian perspective. Outlining this aesthetic is the chapter's starting point. However, as Huggan (2008, p. 43) asserts, too broad a generalisation of migration experiences is not ideal, as there are "conspicuously hierarchical attitudes towards different migrant groups". The aim here is therefore to be mindful of these hierarchies and disparate migration experiences, as well as to examine the extent to which the novels share a common aesthetic in relation to a few themes and recurring tropes. Rethinking the representation of migration in celebrated novels such as these is necessary to enable new perspectives on migration itself and the multifaceted experiences that emerge from it.

Migration and aesthetics

The concept of migrant or migratory aesthetics in relation to art and literature has been developed most notably by Mieke Bal (2007, p. 23), who explains the following: "The modifier 'migratory' does not refer to migrants or actual migration of people" but instead informs "possibilities for art to be politically effective". Bal further explains that "migratory" encompasses the idea "that migrants [...] and migration [...] are part of any society today", and the particular aesthetics connected with this notion are grounded in seeing "the mobility of people as given, as central, and as at the heart of what matters in the contemporary, that is 'globalized' world" (Bal 2007, pp. 23–4). Sam Durrant (2007, p. 145), for his part, makes an important observation in arguing that migration "threatens the destruction of aesthetics" if we are to define aesthetics as the "beautiful", or as Françoise Král (2009, pp. 20–1) writes about the meaning of aesthetics in her work on diasporic identities in Anglophone fiction, asserting that it implies a conception of art for art's sake. Durrant and Lord (2007, p. 15) offer a worthwhile perspective on aesthetics in this context, explaining that it can be seen in terms of "how we experience the everyday [...] taking the measure of cultures in transition, registering the impact of the migratory across different human environments and differently empowered subjects-in-process". Thus, aesthetics also comes to mean the concrete and tangible ways in which migration is represented.

These notions are reinforced in later research such as the work *The Culture of Migration* (2015). Moslund, Petersen, and Schramm (2015, pp. 3–5) take issue with the variety of concepts that have previously defined the migration debate in relation to cultural expressions of mobility. They mention terms such as hybridity and diaspora, arguing that they are all exclusive to some extent (ibid, p. 4). However, "aesthetic practices produce images, beliefs, and affects that can influence and change perceptions of migration" (ibid, p. 12). This statement forms the starting point for the analysis in the present chapter, which attempts to provide a new reading of three novels, *Sisters*, *Harare*, and *Names*, which offer three very different experiences of migration from somewhat comparable perspectives. *Sisters* focuses on four women who are trafficked into prostitution in Belgium; *Harare* explores the reality of an unnamed Zimbabwean asylum seeker in London who has fled his home after killing a member of the opposition party; *Names* tells the story of Darling, a young girl who lives in a Zimbabwean slum and later relocates to the USA, where she becomes an undocumented immigrant after overstaying her visa.

The literary aesthetic detected in these three novels has, according to previous research, largely focused on questions concerning victimhood versus being active, empowered agents, and these two aspects also divide scholars. Elisabeth Bekers (2015, p. 27), for example, writes that the women in *Sisters* "have all fallen victim to an unscrupulous Nigerian trafficker". Sarah De Mul (2014, p. 20), on the other hand, explains the following: "The four women are indeed not victims, as the novel conveys, but agents in a transnational world making choices, strategic choices that are restricted by circumstance". Dina Ligaga (2019) focuses her entire article on the "ambiguous agency" in the novel. The discussion of *Harare* reflects similar concerns. Pucherová (2015, p. 162) writes in her article that the novel "problematizes [...] the binary pair of victim/oppressor" and that the characters in the novel "are not portrayed as victims of the Mugabe regime or British immigration policy but instead as active agents who are participants in the very same oppressive regimes". Here, Pucherová is referring to the rent the inhabitants of the apartment pay to one of the people living there, even though they are all squatting.

Names, for its part, has been analysed in terms of displacement and dispossession, and Cobo-Piñero (2018, p. 22) argues that Bulawayo creates a story where "precarity and vulnerability are the connecting threads capable of weaving together diasporic identities". Moji (2015, p. 182) argues that the novel "depicts a cycle of displacements and ruptured kinships". Thus, the novels have been analysed from similar perspectives that raise questions about how migration is represented. Bearing Bal's words in mind is also imperative: migratory aesthetics is not explicitly about people's actual migration and their concrete experiences, but a way for art and literature to become politically involved. Chika Unigwe herself says the following in a round table discussion: "All narrative has a propagandist element, hidden or not. Every writing is political, whether we are aware of it or not. Stories choose us or we choose stories; the very act of choosing is politics" (Women Writer's Round Table, 2008, p. 116). It can therefore be argued that all three novels address social and political concerns related to migration, and have an aim and scope beyond purely literary issues, but also that scholars have emphasised certain aspects of the novels that reinforce this particular aesthetic and the polarisation mentioned by Squire (2017) in the introduction.

The analysis builds on these earlier studies and seeks to go beyond the previous notions of victimhood in the novels. Seeing the migrant as a victim has been called a trope (Petersen, 2015, p. 218), and Cohen and Sirkeci (2011, p. 19), for their part, argue that it is necessary to "move away from caricatures of migrants as lonely individuals without homes, dangerous rogues out to take jobs from unsuspecting citizens, and poor people avoiding responsibility and seeking employment and financial enrichment". These caricatures exist to some extent in the three novels examined here, and the unnamed main character in *Harare* could even be called a "dangerous rogue" due to his background as a member of a youth militia in Zimbabwe supporting the politics of the Mugabe regime. *Sisters* includes at least one character who could be deemed a lonely individual without a home, and most if not all of the characters in all three novels seek employment and "financial enrichment".

The following three sections focus on different aspects of the migration experience which can be said to be tropes, exemplifying a particular image of the migrant and creating a specific kind of aesthetic with dystopian undertones in doing so. As Francoise Král explains, the "canonization of the migrant as an emblematic figure of the twenty-first century" (Král, 2009, p. 2) has been somewhat problematic, and she also argues that immigration has been romanticised. In the analysed novels, immigration is not romanticised at all; on the contrary, it even contributes to what Helon Habila terms "poverty porn" in *We Need New Names*. This chapter thus proceeds to examine the three novels from the following perspectives: the trope of the undeserving migrant, as outlined by Cohen and Sirkeci; the trope of the victim of poverty and exploitation; and the complex agency (or "ambiguous agency" as Ligaga, 2019 calls it) portrayed as a counterpart to victimhood. The analysis also briefly addresses the return, which Knudsen and Rahbek (2017) have deemed a trope in diasporic African fiction.

The (undeserving) economic migrant

As researchers have concluded, there are differences in how migrants from various backgrounds are treated. For example, this issue is highlighted by Römhild (2017, p. 71), who explains that she does not intend to "sing the praises of seemingly cosmopolitan diversity without social boundaries". She also emphasises the different treatment of migrants depending on the location from which they arrive, calling it a "double standard" (ibid, p. 72). Andreouli and Dashtipour (2014) encountered a variety of conflicting attitudes to migrants from a citizenship perspective in their study in a British context, which confirms these notions. They assert the following:

> In these highly ambiguous accounts, the migrant shifts positions between "the person in need" and "the opportunist", while Britain's position alters between the "saviour/benefactor" and the "victim" of benefit abuse.

Although removing agency from migrants, especially asylum seekers, is fundamental for constructions of British humanitarianism, this agency has to be re-invoked to construct them as abusers of welfare benefits. As shown earlier, in addition to economic contribution, migrants were also seen as having the moral duty to be proud of becoming British citizens.

(Andreouli and Dashtipour, 2014, 107)

These results are relevant for the literature examined here, as they highlight a discrepancy and to some extent hypocrisy in attitudes to migrants. The term agency resurfaces here and will be discussed in more detail in the next section of the paper.

In terms of the refugee, Bishupal Limbu (2018, p. 80) talks about the "proper refugee" in his article on narratives and human rights, arguing that this implies being threatened with "politically motivated physical violence and terrible suffering" (Limbu, 2018, p. 81). This is particularly interesting and relevant in relation to *Harare North*. The story is told from the perspective of an unnamed narrator and main character, a former member of the Green Bombers youth militia, who left Zimbabwe after killing a member of the opposition party. The main character applies for asylum on arrival in London and proceeds to live in a squat with other Zimbabweans. From the very beginning, Chikwava thus introduces a conflicting and conflicted character who definitely does not easily fit into any kind of category of "person in need".

Furthermore, as Manase (2014, p. 72) accurately writes, the main character could also be described as "an uninspiring manipulative character and perhaps an anti-hero". His actions in Zimbabwe represent exactly the kind of violence and personal persecution that would force people to leave their homes and apply for asylum elsewhere. The paradox is thus introduced from the outset of the novel, with the asylum seeker cast as perpetrator. Noxolo (2014, p. 300) also emphasises the unreliability of the main character and connects this with the "constantly questioned credibility of the asylum seeker". This ties in with what Andreouli and Dashtipour concluded above about conflicting views of migrants who are often seen as exploiting western, or in this case British, hospitality and humanitarianism.

Furthermore, the main character's role as perpetrator has also been debated. Pucherová (2015, p. 162) argues that the novel does not follow any easy distinctions between victims and perpetrators, but the same cannot be said to the same degree about *Sisters* and *Names*, which are more explicit about their characters' victim status. However, all three novels display the economic migrant from a variety of perspectives, making it a common denominator of the three stories: "I just want to get myself good graft very quick, work like animal and save heap of money and then bang, me I am on my way back home" (Chikwava, 2009, p. 6). The novel also alludes to the hierarchy among economic migrants, highlighting what Römhild states about the importance of remembering the different approaches to migrants, depending on who they are and from where they come. The main character hears about the possibility of getting work for those who have a toolbox: "We don't have no toolboxes to pose with on this street, so we don't go there. Also there is now too many Polish builders to compete with there, someone say. And they all have toolboxes" (ibid, p. 50).

No such hierarchy is to be found in *Names*, which also pays considerable attention to the lives of economic migrants, particularly those without papers; a group to which Darling herself and the relatives with whom she lives also belong. The demeaning jobs and bad working conditions migrants without visas or residence permits must endure are made explicit:

> We worked with dangerous machines, holding our breath like crocodiles underwater, our minds on the money and never on our lives. [...] We cut ourselves working on meat; we got skin diseases. We inhaled bad smells until our lungs thundered.
>
> (Bulawayo, 2013, p. 244)

The inhuman and unsafe conditions highlight the plight of undocumented migrants in the US, but Bulawayo (2013, p. 243) does not connect these experiences with any specific nationality or ethnicity. Instead, her focus is on any and all migrants as the perpetual other.

The characters in *On Black Sisters' Street* all more or less belong to the category of "opportunists", but the fact that they have been trafficked blurs the boundaries. The novel also problematises the discrepancy between the women knowing for the most part what work they were going to do in Belgium (with the exception of Alek, or Joyce, as she is renamed in Antwerp) and going there willingly, or at least voluntarily. The girls are asked to apply for asylum on arrival in Antwerp by the Madam who runs the brothel where they work. Sisi's application process is revealed in detail, as well as the story Madam gives her, and which she is to tell the officials documenting her application. The fiction she is fed includes originally coming from Liberia, having narrowly escaped being brutally killed with the rest of her family (Unigwe, 2009, p. 120). The sad irony in the made-up background story is that Alek's actual experiences resemble them to a significant degree. Her family was brutally murdered while she hid in a cupboard with her brother. Eventually, she was raped by the intruders (ibid, pp. 190–1). Sisi's untruthful asylum application harrowingly converges with Alek's real-life experiences, simultaneously contradicting and confirming the asylum seeker as a person in need versus the immigrant as an opportunist.

The paradoxes portrayed, especially in *Harare North* and *On Black Sisters Street*, provide multifaceted perspectives on marginalisation, such as asylum seeking in which applications are made for practical reasons. *We Need New Names*, for its part, is more straightforward in its dystopian portrayal of undocumented migrants and their limited prospects. As the following section will show, the novels also offer different perspectives on questions relating to agency and to dreams and hopes for the future. The role of economic migrancy in post-migrant society remains unclear, because the novels do not offer any explicit solutions or ways forward, merely focusing on the degrading circumstances in which the characters are forced to live and the exploitation of undocumented workers. Illegality remains a central thread in all three novels, undermining the existence of any true agency or empowerment.

Victimhood and complex agency

As outlined in the previous section, the three novels offer many examples of various forms of exploitation and personal hardship. A brief discussion of Afropolitanism is needed to examine victimhood explicitly, as all the novels have been connected with this concept. Achille Mbembe (2007, p. 29) outlines in his essay on Afropolitanism that it rejects "any form of victim identity". He also says in an interview with Sarah Balakrishnan (2016: 29) that Afropolitanism can be defined as "a critical reflection on the many ways in which [...] there is no world without Africa and there is no Africa that is not part of it". These notions are positive, suggesting an empowered perspective of migration and transnational individuals occupying different spaces and moving across borders. However, the concept has also been criticised.

According to Chielozona Eze (2014, pp. 239–40), Afropolitan "is an African way of being cosmopolitan", suggesting both "exclusivity and elitism". Concerning the novels, Dustin Crowley (2018, p. 140), for his part, argues the following: "Where Afropolitanism posits being 'at home' in multiple places, *We Need New Names* explores a global diaspora where those without agency struggle to maintain any sense of home at all". Thus, he suggests that the novel cannot really be called Afropolitan. Mwesigire (2018, p. 109) likewise claims that neither *We Need New Names* nor *Harare North* can be termed Afropolitan, although he maintains that they are transnational. This highlights the difficulty of accurately categorising these novels, but it also reveals the influence of different concepts on the theorisation of migration narratives. The question of the extent to which migration shapes these concepts, and the extent to which the concepts shape perceptions of migration, remains.

Sisters has also been connected with the term Afropolitan, and researchers have debated the extent to which the women are Afropolitan. Interestingly, Patricia Bastida-Rodriguez (2017, p. 135) argues that the novel's characters cannot be said to be Afropolitan due to their lack of personal freedom and the work they do. She also mentions that they are "living in the diaspora" (ibid, p. 135). Such an unclear use of the term diaspora only serves to reinforce the lack of clarity surrounding the concept. Urama and Nwachukwu (2017, p. 124), for their part, assert that the women leave their countries of origin or residence "because they are marginalized", and that they accept the trafficker Dele's job offer "rather than dying in hardship". Such hardship includes sexual exploitation and abuse before travelling to Belgium: Alek is gang-raped as already mentioned; Ama is repeatedly raped by her stepfather in childhood

(Unigwe, 2009, p. 132); and Efe is exploited as a teenager by a much older man who gets her pregnant (Unigwe, 2009, p. 71) and leaves her. However, when she meets Dele, Efe is working as a cleaner to support her son (ibid, pp. 77–8), and Ama leaves her abusive home and is working at her aunt's restaurant (ibid, p. 162). They both at least to some extent manage to find ways to support themselves and move away from abusive relationships.

Thus, the three novels to a degree offer different perspectives on economic migrancy, aspirations, and the desire to move upward, forward, and onward with one's life. Researchers have walked a fine line between the sexual traumas and feminist interventions in *Sisters*, the unreliable and unsympathetic asylum seeker with a sharp eye for social hierarchies in *Harare*, and the desperate and degrading lives of migrants in *Names* who forever remain the other, living lives on the margins without basic human rights such as access to healthcare. Researchers also seem to have read *Names* as a thoroughly dystopian novel in which displacement, dispossession, personal struggle, and shortcomings remain central. At one point in the novel Darling sees a Lamborghini while out with her friends, and she is told by one of them that the car costs almost two million dollars (Bulawayo, 2013, pp. 224–5). This makes Darling ponder what it makes her if she can never afford such a car: "[D]oes that mean I'm poor, and if so, what is America for, then?" (ibid, p. 225). Masterson (2018, p. 7) even asserts that the passage in the novel ruins her "diaspirant dreams".

However, owning a two-million-dollar car is an impossible dream for most Americans, too, even if they have regular jobs and salaries. The car merely comes to symbolise migrants' utopian dreams, which, participate in creating a dystopian aesthetic of lost hope and failed dreams. A connection can be made here with the unrealistic demands and claims made by those who remain at home, which Darling also experiences during a phone call home. "Can you send me a Lady Gaga shirt and an iPod? I hear Sbho shout in the background" (Bulawayo, 2013, p. 208). These demands are also referred to in *Harare*: the main character opens letters to Shingi, his friend who lent him his ID, in which an uncle asks for a Land Rover Defender, and another whose writer wants £5,000 for gold-panning (Chikwava, 2009, pp. 197–9). Exploitation is thus multidirectional in these stories, and it is not always the receiving country alone that exploits the migrant. The novels' dystopian elements are also reinforced by the characters' unattainable dreams.

Of the three novels this paper scrutinises, the one which appears to have provoked the most debate about agency or its lack is *On Black Sisters' Street*. As outlined earlier in the paper, Elisabeth Bekers (2015, p. 27) and Sarah De Mul (2014, p. 20) disagree concerning the extent to which the women trafficked into prostitution can actually be deemed victims, and to which they possess agency concerning their own lives, choices, and decisions. However, Crowley (2018, p. 143) writes about Darling's situation in *Names* from a perspective that suggests there is little or no agency. He acknowledges her relatively easy access to the USA due to her aunt Fostalina living there but argues that "her restricted status means that she exists on the margins of legal migration and thus on the margins of society". Further, he explains that Darling is forced into a demeaning existence working in low-status jobs as an undocumented migrant, having "no way to go back to Zimbabwe freely without giving up any return access to the US" (Crowley, 2018, p. 143). Crowley calls the lack of agency in the novel the "subjectivity of subjugation" (ibid.) and "conditions of marginality" (ibid, p. 144). What seems to be at the core of Crowley's discussion of the novel (2018, p. 145) is a demand for "alternative spaces and processes of transnational agency and exchange", but the exact nature of these spaces and processes remains vague. In all three novels a lack of solutions and ways to overcome conditions of marginality is evident. It may even be argued that the novels suggest that migrating may not always be the desired or optimal solution in the first place. This is a notion which has not been discussed to any significant degree in previous research and which will require further examination.

The lack of solutions can also be related to the return which occurs in different contexts in the novels. In *Harare North*, the main character plans to return once he has earned enough money, $5,000, to pay the bribes needed to clear his name of the crime he committed in Zimbabwe:

> US$1,000 for my uncle because that's what I owe him for my plane ticket here, and US$4,000 to sweet that pack of them hyenas that chase me around Zimbabwe wanting to catch me until I have run away here because I don't have the money they want so they can make my troubles go away.
> (Chikwava, 2009, p. 20)

It is also clear from the start that the main character has no unrealistic ideas about life in London or elsewhere in the diasporas:

> Harare township is full of them stories about the misfortunes that people meet; they carry bags full of things and heads that is full of wonders of new life [...] only to have they dreams thrown back into they faces.
> (Chikwava, 2009, p. 5)

In this respect the unreliable and unsympathetic narrator of *Harare North* is actually the most pragmatic of all the characters in the three novels and harbours no unrealistic hopes or dreams.

Sisters, however, is all about hopes and dreams. When Efe agrees to go to Belgium and work for Dele, she "had dreamed up the riches she would amass and had calculated that she would be able to afford a Mercedes by the time she had spent a year working" (Unigwe, 2009, p. 84). The connection with Darling's Lamborghini is obvious. Even the flight to Belgium is a disappointment as "[s]he had always imagined that being on a plane [...] would feel a bit like flying with your own wings" (ibid, p. 88). Sisi has similar dreams: "She would set up a business or two. She could go into the business of importing second-hand cars into Nigeria" (ibid, pp. 44–5). Her parents seem to understand what her work will entail but do not interfere (ibid.), perhaps because they do not know how, or because they are aware that Sisi has few prospects in Nigeria. Ama also dreams of building a "business empire" and believes that travelling to Antwerp to work will make her dreams come true (ibid, p. 169).

Here, *Names* offers another disillusioned perspective on those that leave and actually return. Darling's father left for South Africa a long time ago, but then he "comes home after many years of forgetting us, of not sending us money, of not loving us, not visiting us, not anything us" (Bulawayo, 2013, p. 89). He too leaves in search of better fortunes elsewhere but never sends anything home to his family (ibid, p. 93). Instead, he returns terminally ill with AIDS (ibid, p. 100). Darling also wishes to return home for a few weeks when she has been in Michigan for a while, and her aunt explains to her that it is not possible because of her expired visa, meaning that she would not be able to return if she left (ibid, p. 189). This ties in with what Okolocha (2016, p. 146) says about the host country becoming "a place of transit". All three novels portray migration itself as a place of transit and the characters lack permanence and continuity in their lives, unable to move forward or go back. This is at the core of the aesthetic they convey and researchers have emphasised this. The novels also offer representations of the underprivileged migrant caught in the throes of globalisation, itself a well-worn trope.

Conclusion

The failed economic aspirations depicted in the three texts all speak to the tragedy not only of leaving home but of never getting wherever the characters in question are headed. It can be argued that this is a central dilemma of migration in general: what happens to people when the travels they undertake in search of better prospects elsewhere have no end date or final destination? Paradoxically, a migrant can be both perpetually on the move yet irrevocably stuck and no longer allowed further forward mobility and movement. *Harare*, *Sisters*, and *Names* all exemplify this condition. As examples of a dystopian migrant aesthetic, the novels reinforce stereotypes or caricatures of migrants as desperate, poor, exploited, unreliable, and inevitably doomed to hardship and failure due to their aspirations which may or may not be realistic. Crowley (2018, p. 143) goes so far as to argue that *Names*, through its main character Darling, "more closely mirrors the current refugee crisis on the continent, characterized less by ideals of transnationalism than by a sense of displacement and desperation". The question of agency thus seems easily answered in the negative.

However, the novels also indicate that agency may be an entirely irrelevant matter. The novels can definitely also be seen as a backlash against the romanticisation of immigration (Král, 2009). Instead of emphasising the empowerment of transnational individuals, the novels show the underbelly of migration in all its filth and gore. The characters remain lost in transit, where staying or returning become insurmountable challenges. Existing and surviving in such a void goes beyond any discourses of nostalgia or belonging. This is at the centre of the aesthetic examined here. As the novels outline, even survival is precarious, because the characters are largely left in limbo. Perhaps that is the true essence of a dystopian migrant aesthetic: it promises no future while holding the past and present hostage, making movement in any direction impossible.

The novels thus inspire new views of migration that do not focus on departure, arrival or return, homesickness, assimilation, and culture clash but on movement and the need to stay mobile. Paradoxically, arrival in the new location implies mobility, as it allows individuals to carry on with their lives and move forward. Arriving means moving on. The real tragedy of the novels is that such forward movement is denied, stripped away. The discrepancy between expectations and reality can also be discussed in terms of movement, as hopes and dreams propel people forward, and harsh realities force them to become immobile, physically, psychologically, socially, and economically. Even the return is connected with social upward mobility, although the novels portray the difficulties in such movement, too. This, at least to some extent, provides an answer to Squire's (2017) question in the introduction: instead of looking at levels of agency and the culpability of migrants, examining their different mobilities in terms of place, time, and personal prospects offers a way forward that goes beyond categorisation and instead sees the lives of migrants as equally complex and varied as the lives of those who stay put.

Such rethinking of the way in which migration is categorised and analysed also goes beyond literary texts and other cultural representations, and can offer new perspectives for migration's role and place in society at large. All three works examined in this study imagine realities that cannot be dismissed as mere fiction, but which reveal the complexities of migration not only for migrants themselves but for both sending and receiving societies. Addressing migration from a perspective of movement not only enables an examination of agency and victimhood, but also opens up new avenues of research through which creative solutions may be found that no longer focus solely on questions of culpability, deservingness, and righteousness. This is the central message of *Harare North*, *On Black Sisters' Street*, and *We Need New Names*.

References

Andreouli, E. and Dashtipour, P. (2014) British Citizenship and the "Other": An Analysis of the Earned Citizenship Discourse. *Journal of Community & Applied Social Psychology*, 24, pp. 100–10.

Bal, M. (2007) Lost in Space, Lost in the Library. In: S. Durrant and C. M. Lord, eds., *Essays in Migratory Aesthetics: Cultural Practices Between Migration and Art-Making*. Amsterdam: Rodopi, pp. 23–36.

Bastida-Rodriguez, P. (2017) Afropolitan in Their Own Way? Writing and Self-Identification in Aminatta Forna and Chika Unigwe. *European Journal of English Studies*, 21(2), pp. 129–43.

Bekers, E. (2015) Writing African in Belgium, Europe: A Conversation with Chika Unigwe. *Research in African Literatures*, 46(4), pp. 26–34.

Bulawayo, N. (2013) *We Need New Names*. London: Vintage.

Chikwava, B. (2009) *Harare North*. London: Vintage.

Cobo-Piñero, M. R. (2018) From Africa to America: Precarious Belongings in NoViolet Bulawayo's We Need New Names. *ATLANTIS Journal of the Spanish Association of Anglo-American Studies*, 40(2), pp. 11–25.

Cohen, J. H. and Sirkeci, I. (2011) *Cultures of Migration: The Global Nature of Contemporary Mobility*. Austin: University of Texas Press.

Crowley, D. (2018) How Did They Come to This? Afropolitanism, Migration, and Displacement. *Research in African Literatures*, 49(2), pp. 125–46.

De Mul, S. (2014) Becoming Black in Belgium: The Social Construction of Blackness in Chika Unigwe's Authorial Self-Representation and *On Black Sisters' Street*. *The Journal of Commonwealth Literature*, 49(1), pp. 11–27.

Durrant, S. (2007) Storytellers, Novelists, and Postcolonial Melancholia: Displaced Aesthetics in Chinua Achebe's Things Fall Apart. In: S. Durrant and C. M. Lord, eds., *Essays in Migratory Aesthetics: Cultural Practices Between Migration and Art-Making*. Amsterdam: Rodopi, pp. 145–59.

Durrant, S. and Lord, C. M. (2007) Introduction: Essays in Migratory Aesthetics: Cultural Practices Between Migration and Art-making. In: S. Durrant and C. M. Lord, eds., *Essays in Migratory Aesthetics: Cultural Practices Between Migration and Art-Making*. Amsterdam: Rodopi, pp. 11–19.

Eze, C, (2014) Rethinking African Culture and Identity: The Afropolitan Model. *Journal of African Cultural Studies*, 26(2), pp. 234–47.

Huggan, G. (2008) *Interdisciplinary Measures: Literature and the Future of Postcolonial Studies*. Liverpool: Liverpool University Press.

Knudsen, E. R. and Rahbek, U. (2017) An Afropolitan Literary Aesthetics? Afropolitan Style and Tropes in Recent Diasporic African Fiction. *European Journal of English Studies*, 21(2), pp. 115–28.

Král, F. (2009) *Critical Identities in Contemporary Anglophone Diasporic Literature*. New York: Palgrave Macmillan.

Ligaga, D. (2019) Ambiguous Agency in the Vulnerable Trafficked Body: Reading Sanusi's *Eyo* and Unigwe's *On Black Sisters' Street*. *Tydskrif vir Letterkunde*, 56(1), pp. 74–88.

Limbu, B. (2018) The Permissible Narratives of Human Rights; Or, How to Be a Refugee. *Criticism*, 60(1), pp. 75–98.

Lyons, N. (2012) Narrative Inquiry: What Possible Future Influence on Policy and Practice? In: D. J. Clandinin, ed., *Handbook of Narrative Inquiry: Mapping a Methodology*. Thousand Oaks: Sage, pp. 600–31.

Manase, I. (2014) Representations of the Post-2000 Zimbabwean Economic Migrancy in Petina Gappah's *An Elegy for Easterly* and Brian Chikwava's *Harare North*. *Journal of Black Studies*, 45(1), pp. 59–76.

Masterson, J. (2018) "DestroyedMichygen": Rerouting the Postnational in Contemporary Diaspirant Fiction. *Research in African Literatures*, 49(1), pp. 1–21.

Mbembe, A. and Balakrishnan, S. (2016) Pan-African Legacies, Afropolitan Futures. *Transition*, 120, pp. 28–37.

Mbembe, A. (2007) Afropolitanism. Translated by Laurent Chauvet. In Njami, Simon (ed.), *Africa Remix: Contemporary Art of a Continent*. Johannesburg: Johannesburg Art Gallery, 26–9.

Moji, P. B. (2015) New Names, Translational Subjectivities: (Dis)location and (Re) naming in NoViolet Bulawayo's *We Need New Names*. *Journal of African Cultural Studies*, 27(2), pp. 181–90.

Moslund, S. P., Petersen, A. R. and Schramm, M. (2015) Introduction. In: S. P. Moslund, A. R. Petersen and M. Schramm, eds. *The Culture of Migration: Politics, Aesthetics and Histories*. London: I.B. Tauris, p. 1–23.

Mwesigire, B. (2018) Beyond the Afropolitan Postnation: The Contemporaneity of Jennifer Makumbi's *Kintu*. *Research in African Literatures*, 49(1), pp. 103–16.

Noxolo, P. (2014) Towards and Embodies Securityscape: Brian Chikwava's *Harare North* and the Asylum Seeking Body as Site of Articulation. *Social & Cultural Geography*, 15(3), pp. 291–312.

Okolocha, H. O. (2016) Negotiating Race, Identity & Homecoming in Chimamanda Ngozi Adichie's *Americanah* & Pede Hollist's *So the Path Does Not Die*. In: H. Cousins and P. Dodgson-Katiyo, eds., *Diaspora & Returns in Fiction – African Literature Today 34*. Woodbridge: James Currey, pp. 143–63.

Persian, J. (2012) Displaced Persons and the Politics of International Categorisation(s). *Australian Journal of Politics and History*, 58(4), pp. 481–96.

Petersen, A. R. (2015) Migratory Aesthetics and the Politics of Irregular Migration: A Case Study of Isaac Julien's *Western Union: Small Boats*. In: S. P. Moslund, A. R. Petersen and M. Schramm, eds., *The Culture of Migration: Politics, Aesthetics and Histories*. London: I. B. Tauris, pp. 205–22.

Pucherová, D. (2015) Forms of Resistance Against the African Postcolony in Brian Chikwava's *Harare North*. *Brno Studies in English*, 41(1), pp. 157–73.

Römhild, R. (2017) Beyond the Bounds of the Ethnic: For Postmigrant Cultural and Social Research. *Journals of Aesthetics & Culture*, 9(2), pp. 69–75.

Sajjad, T. (2018) What's in a Name? "Refugees", "Migrants" and the Politics of Labelling. *Race & Class*, 60(2), pp. 40–62.

Squire, V. (2017) Unauthorised Migration Beyond Structure/Agency? Acts, Interventions, Effects. *Politics*, 37(3), pp. 254–72.

Unigwe, C. (2009) *On Black Sisters' Street*. London: Vintage.

Urama, E. N. and Nwachukwu, C. O. (2017) Human Trafficking: Commercial Sexual Exploitation and Forced Domestic Labour in African Literature. *Journal of Language and Cultural Education*, 5(2), pp. 123–37.

Women Writer's Round Table. (2008) Of Phase and Faces: Unoma Azuah Engages Sefi Atta and Chika Unigwe. *Research in African Literatures*, 38(2), pp. 108–16.

Yarris, K. and Castañeda, H. (2015) Special Issue – Discourses of Displacement and Deservingness: Interrogating Distinctions between "Economic" and "Forced" Migration. *International Migration*, 53(3), pp. 64–9.

12 Re-imagining the "Area of Freedom, Security and Justice"

Europe's security measures experienced by African migrants

Laura Sumari

Introduction

Migration continues to be one of the major topics that dictate the relations between Europe and Africa. In recent years, it has also been one of the most heated topics in the public discussion in Europe and, according to various polls and surveys, one of the biggest security concerns of European Union (EU) citizens (European Commission, 2018; Laine, 2020a). While new Africa strategies are being drafted and published in the EU and its member states, and there is an increased interest in forging stronger partnerships with Africa, finding solutions and EU-level consensus in issues related to managing migration seems like an impossible task. Although Africa hosts most of its own refugees, and far more people migrate inside Africa than from Africa towards Europe, the EU and its member states are concerned about this issue to the extent that most of the legal pathways to enter the Schengen-zone, especially from the formerly colonized countries in the "Global South", have been blocked (De Genova, 2018; FitzGerald, 2020). On one hand, this has led to asylum-seeking often being the only option for people hoping to move to Europe, regardless of their motivations and eligibility for international protection (UNDP, 2019, p. 4). On the other, the lack of legal ways to migrate encourages irregular movement and expensive and dangerous human smuggling and trafficking.

This chapter investigates the controversial securities of migration from sub-Saharan Africa towards Europe. Building on multi-sited ethnographic fieldwork in eastern Africa as well as southern and northern Europe, it reflects on the EU's and the Schengen countries' migration related "security measures" from the perspective of sub-Saharan African refugees and migrants. By these security measures, I refer to the constellation of policies, treaties, laws, and practices, which on the EU level are gathered under the umbrella of "Area of Freedom, Security and Justice" (AFSJ). Among other things, the AFSJ covers the management of the EU's external borders, visas, as well as asylum and migration policies (Walker, 2004, p. 6). Instead of analysing the AFSJ as a set of political tools and instruments as such, this chapter contributes towards

DOI: 10.4324/9781003083726-13

building a deeper understanding of the effects of these security measures on the "everyday securities" of the people towards whom they are targeted.

Deterring "unwanted" migration is performed through various methods that are designed to make irregular entries less attractive, for instance through restraining territorial access; reducing access to social welfare, other public services, and the labour market; detention during the asylum process, as well as expedited returns of rejected asylum applicants (Kent, Norman, and Tennis, 2019). In this chapter, I will focus specifically on how these aspects of the migration management apparatus are experienced by sub-Saharan African refugees, asylum seekers, returnees, and deportees from Schengen countries. I understand the concept of experience firstly in relation to thoughts, feelings, and perceptions, which are formed throughout our lives and affected by the various environments, interactions, events, actions, and lessons that we encounter. Secondly, I understand experiences as things that happen – passing events and situations that give meaning and construct our lives and the world around us (Sumari, 2016, p. 12).

This chapter draws on research material I have gathered by conducting multi-sited ethnographic fieldwork in Kenya, Ethiopia, Cyprus, Italy, and Finland between 2018–2020. Addressing the research problem required choosing fieldwork locations in Europe and in Africa that are positioned in variable ways in relation to Europe's migration management. In order to acknowledge the superficial distinction between refugees and so called "economic migrants", and to go beyond the over-studied European and northern African "hotspots" to better capture the variety of aspects, I interviewed people with experiences of "irregularity" from a multitude of countries and backgrounds: 1) *en route* to Europe, 2) in Europe, and 3) after leaving Europe. Map 12.1 represents the points of departure of the research participants, the interview locations, as well the migratory journeys to the extent that they have been shared with me. The chart included gives a more specific overview of the fieldwork locations and supporting organizations, as well as the number and legal-administrative categories of the interviewees. In addition to the thirty-two semi-structured, narrative interviews, the material consists of four interviews with people working with migrants, along with field notes and informal conversations with people "in the field".

The local contexts of the fieldwork environments varied greatly, as did the legal, social, and economic situations and life histories of the research participants. All of these factors, along with my own positionality as a young, blonde, and in many ways privileged European woman undoubtedly influenced the encounters with the research participants in various ways. Yet, as most of the interviewees were young, highly educated people like myself, it was easy to find shared thoughts and ideas and to build trust. Many of the interviewees also expressed that it was important for them to get to share their experiences so that things could change. I stay in contact with around half of them.

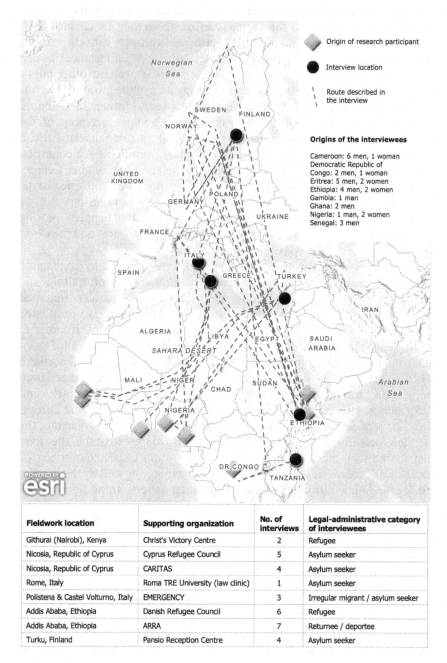

Origin of research participant

Interview location

Route described in the interview

Origins of the interviewees

Cameroon: 6 men, 1 woman
Democratic Republic of
Congo: 2 men, 1 woman
Eritrea: 5 men, 2 women
Ethiopia: 4 men, 2 women
Gambia: 1 man
Ghana: 2 men
Nigeria: 1 man, 2 women
Senegal: 3 men

Fieldwork location	Supporting organization	No. of interviews	Legal-administrative category of interviewees
Githurai (Nairobi), Kenya	Christ's Victory Centre	2	Refugee
Nicosia, Republic of Cyprus	Cyprus Refugee Council	5	Asylum seeker
Nicosia, Republic of Cyprus	CARITAS	4	Asylum seeker
Rome, Italy	Roma TRE University (law clinic)	1	Asylum seeker
Polistena & Castel Volturno, Italy	EMERGENCY	3	Irregular migrant / asylum seeker
Addis Ababa, Ethiopia	Danish Refugee Council	6	Refugee
Addis Ababa, Ethiopia	ARRA	7	Returnee / deportee
Turku, Finland	Pansio Reception Centre	4	Asylum seeker

Map 12.1 Fieldwork locations, information on the interviewees, and supporting organizations.

Created by the author on Esri "Topographic" [basemap]. Scale Not Given. "World Topographic Map". May 15, 2020. www.arcgis.com/home/item.html?id=30e5fe3149c 34df1ba922e6f5bbf808f. (May 15, 2020).

Securitizing migration – bordering Europe

During recent decades, migration has become almost self-evidently interpreted as a security issue. On one hand, this is related to a conceptual change in how security is understood and talked about: instead of perceiving security and threats as something objective and absolute, security theory today depicts it as a social construction, giving multiple meanings to security depending on the context (see e.g. Fierke, 2007; Huysmans, 2002; Spiro, 2009). Securitization theory (e.g. Wæver, 1993, 1995) explains the securitization of migration through rhetorical and discursive practices – speech acts – which frame migration, representing it as something dangerous, an existential threat. Once this construction is accepted, a variety of security measures and practices to contain the "threat" by dividing the "insiders" from the "outsiders" and the "welcome" from the "unwelcome" come to be justified (Walters, 2010). This can seem to provide ontological security – a feeling and experience of order and reliance on the continuity of the social and material living environment – for those feeling threatened (Giddens, 1991 pp. 92, 243; Laine, 2020a/b).

The securitizing methods to govern migratory flows become bordering practices, which occur through filtering and sorting of people attempting to migrate. They can be understood as "biopolitical architectures" that regulate circulation of people in the aim of controlling undesired movement (Pallister-Wilkins, 2016; Laine, 2020b). Bordering practices are manifested through the work of the border regime, for instance in the ways fences are erected, security checkpoints multiplied, detention centres built offshore, fingerprint and passport databases created, along with "borderwork" (Rumford, 2008; 2012), which happens far beyond actual state borders and is not undertaken only by state officials. Through these bordering practices, borders come to be understood not only as sites of control but also as social and political frames for setting agendas (Laine, 2020a). Thus, through reinforcing the assumption of existing danger, the security measures actually re-construct the threat they aim at overcoming.

Securitization studies have centred their attention on security discourses and techniques: how something becomes framed as a security concern and for what purposes (Wæver, 1995; Bigo, 2002). In these outputs, experiences of security governance "on the ground" have often gained less attention (Crawford and Hutchinson, 2015; Stevens and Vaughan-Williams, 2016, p. 2). The notion of "everyday security" responds to this lack, empirically investigating the "relationship(s) between security projects and extant social practices and relationships" by tying the everyday struggles of people to macro-structural processes (Crawford and Hutchinson, 2015, p. 1190). Asking people about their lived experiences of security measures and how they are felt and lived through offers keys towards understanding security governance and processes on a wider scale (ibid.). Paying attention to the perceptual and socially embedded nature of security enables examining the security experiences of those who are feeling threatened by migration, but also those who are being securitized (Laine, 2020a).

The various security measures and related bordering practices of the EU and Schengen countries have an enormous effect on the lives of people who are seeking or hope to seek protection in Europe – and for many others "on the move". The mere fact that these policies and security measures make getting into Europe life-threateningly difficult and practically impossible for most migrants and refugees speaks for the life-changing significance of how migration is managed. But how do migrants themselves think and feel about Europe's ways to manage migration? To answer this question, I start the analysis by discussing how African refugees in Africa experience the restrictions on movement and lack of legal channels to migrate to Europe.

Experiencing Europe's bordering practices in Africa

In the interviews and discussions with Congolese refugees in Kenya and Eritrean refugees in Ethiopia, one of the first things that became apparent was that not all refugees in Africa want to go to Europe. On the contrary, many wish to move to neighbouring countries or mention other preferable places such as South Africa, Canada, the United States, and Australia. Accordingly, thirty-seven percent of the forty-five thousand respondents to the Afrobarometer of 2019 were considering emigrating but more people preferred staying on the continent (36 percent) than moving to Europe (27 percent) (Appia-Nyamekye Sanny, Rocca, and Schultes, 2019). This challenges the misleading portrayal on which justifications for curtailing migration to Europe are often based: that most Africans think of Europe as a "dream destination" and hope to penetrate its borders by whichever means possible (Laine, 2020b).

Instead of dreaming about "something fancy" or living on government support, most of the research participants were looking for a place to live freely and without fear – a place where it would be possible to have a "normal life" and to be able to support one's family. For instance, the security situation of the Eritrean refugees interviewed in the Mebrat Hail Condominium housing scheme in Addis Ababa had improved significantly compared to their situation back in Eritrea, but many "building blocks" of having a normal life, like having a job or a means of living that would satisfy their basic needs, were still missing. This made them think about ways of getting to some place "better". Instead of planning to take the irregular route through Libya to Europe, they were weighing different options of getting not to Europe but to any Western or "more developed" places through family reunification, resettlement, student visa, or marriage. In addition to refugees, also many students, employees of NGOs working with refugee-related issues, and people I met on the streets of Addis Ababa seemed more than ready to move out of Ethiopia to work or to study, given the chance. All of this had proven to be difficult.

In addition to walls and fences, the EU's security measures and politics of bordering are concretized through what FitzGerald (2020) characterizes as a remote control system of cages, buffers, domes, moats, and barbicans that reflect global power dynamics and prevent irregular movement far from the actual borders. Often "paper walls" – visa regimes and passport hierarchies – are more powerful in filtering and preventing unwanted movement than concrete walls and barbed wire fences that aim to secure state borders. Although a number of African countries require visas also from Europeans, for many Africans, claiming a passport and a travel visa to Europe is a challenge. This is getting even more difficult with European fears of people overstaying the visa, disappearing from the officials, or seeking asylum. The practices of remote control are felt in Africa in various ways by people hoping to move through legal channels.

Partly for this reason, the Eritreans in Ethiopia told me that although jumping into a rubber boat in Libya was not seen as a particularly attractive option for them, they could understand the people who took the route towards Europe with no guarantees of getting there alive. According to an Eritrean refugee in his late twenties, who had escaped Eritrea with the assistance of smugglers a year before I interviewed him in Addis Ababa, neither the dangers and obstacles on the way nor the possible challenges in the receiving country stop young people in particular from leaving as long as there is nothing to make them stay:

> They take the risk. Because, if I am here doing nothing, it's better to do that route, whatever the outcome, they tell you. Here also if I'm doing nothing, I'm dying. So this is the mentality of the youngsters. They cannot stay here. Just go to college, or university, do something, just progress yourself. If you tell them this, they will not accept you. So many people are already in Europe: their friends, their families, their relatives.

Unwillingness to accept a certain destiny and the belief in a better tomorrow make people take a leap of faith and reach further. This confirms the idea of borders as unnatural and porous, and presents the border crossing simultaneously as a means for survival and a conscious or subconscious form of resistance towards migration management. When staying is experienced as "dying", taking the risk represents itself as an individual security strategy, albeit one that also includes the possibility of dying.

Unfortunately, thousands of people do die taking that risk. This became apparent in the interviews, as some of the research participants spoke about people they had known who had died on the way to Europe. The risk of border-crossing death is disproportionately high on the Central Mediterranean route from Libya to Italy, which is mostly taken by migrants and refugees from sub-Saharan Africa. The conditions for the possibility of these deaths are generated by the European border regime's restrictions on movement, which push people into irregularity and into taking bigger risks (De Genova, 2018; Laine, 2020b; Squire, 2017). Equally, some of the respondents, such as a Cameroonian woman interviewed in Cyprus after being released from three months in detention, felt that by making crossings more difficult, the EU and member states are causing deaths of people, or "killing them".

Encountering the border and the image of Europe

Few interviewees spontaneously start talking about their actual border crossing from Africa to the EU area. Some distinctly avoided talking about it, which might be related to the traumatic experience itself, to questions of trust between the researcher and the researched, or to the fact that "everyone asks that question" and the European asylum determination procedure in some cases encourages lying in order to secure one's safety (Beneduce, 2015; Bohmer and Shuman, 2018, p. 10). At least one of the deported Ethiopians had been encouraged by his lawyer to circumvent the truth in order to build a stronger case for himself. The asylum system and encountering the border at the border and beyond affect not only the personal experiences and feelings of asylum seekers but also their perception of Europe and the EU. This is reflected in the following passage. A Cameroonian man, whom I interviewed three months after his arrival to Cyprus, described an unpleasant incident with the immigration police:

> When I first arrived, some experience with the immigration police reminds me of the past. I believe they were doing their job. When I got to the investigation unit, they took my bag and they empty it and shake everything out of it to try to scare me, so I told them immediately, this is exactly what we see in our country. They said if I have a problem, I can lodge a complaint on the other side. So that gives me some uncertainty. Especially when you are running from your life not being stable. You are taking each day as it comes, that maybe I can die today or tomorrow. And you manage to free yourself from that scenario. And then when you arrive, you experience a similar scenario.

Ill-treatment from officials had made him feel suspicious toward "Europe" because he had been treated in the EU in a way that he could have expected to happen more likely "back home". This pattern was repeated in other interviews as well. In particular, those who had already arrived in Europe reflected the EU's and its member states' actions and policies, comparing them to those of their countries and places of origin. When asked about the EU's policies towards restricting migration, their attention turned towards the security measures of their own national contexts: how the governments of their countries had made them insecure through forced confiscation, arbitrary arrests, violence from authorities, and different forms of structural violence and persecution that are meant to keep people afraid of questioning their governments. Controls of borders were also often more violent in African contexts, evidenced for example by the shoot-to-kill policy on the Eritrean-Ethiopian border mentioned by one of the Eritrean refugees. The EU's migration policies were, in this way, put into a wider perspective, which takes into account the political and cultural contexts in the places of origin of the respondents. Yet, when expectations of a "fair" European system based on the rule of law were not met, the understanding of Europe of the participants was shaken.

The EU's security measures and restricting movement from Africa also made the research participants consider European-African relations and the EU's role in the global world order. Some of the respondents felt that the EU and the international community were "turning a blind eye" to conflicts and human rights atrocities in Africa, and were even fuelling conflict towards their own ends. Others thought of Europe as a value leader who should intervene and advocate for peace and democracy in Africa instead of closing borders. In some interviews, the EU was also spoken of together with the UN, which elaborates the political and soft power given to the EU in the perceptions of the research participants. However, by publicly supporting humanitarian and development goals and at the same time building walls and criminalising movement, the EU's contradictory narratives and actions erode this soft power and hollow out the values the EU claims to stand for (Laine, 2020b). The EU's controversial actions in relation to its values were reflected also in the interviews.

The EU was described as "sly" or as a "hypocrite" for portraying itself as a protector of human rights, while simultaneously closing borders and continuing colonial endeavours in Africa and elsewhere. It was retained in some of the interviews that as long as Europe continues to be "a part of the problem", migration from Africa would not end. A man from Senegal who was now living in Cyprus as an asylum seeker described the relationship of migration and the colonial echoes in the current relations between Africa and Europe, namely France:

> France and EU have to leave Africa and let Africa make its own decisions. As long as it is like this, you cannot stop the migrants. This is the problem. France makes people corrupted and takes our money. In Senegal we have many natural resources, but France takes all the riches, billions and billions put in Swiss banks. The only truth is that Europe knows it would be in trouble without Africa, that's why they do not leave, but then migration will not end either.

In the passages above, the current and historical relationships between Europe and Africa are being problematized, given meaning, and used to make sense of the interviewees' own situation, as well as the global power asymmetries shaping it. The postcolonial mindset, which challenges Europe's actions in Africa, also reflects the interviewees frustration towards Europe's way of responding to migration. If the political, economic, and historical drivers for migration are to a certain extent created by forms of domination of the "Global North" towards the "Global South", taking this into consideration in the response to migration seems like an understandable request, especially when non-Western regions have been carrying the heaviest burden in hosting refugees with lesser resources (World Bank, 2020).

Security measures in the everyday

Security measures and related bordering practices do not end once a person has crossed a state border. On the contrary, these technologies of filtering and division extend far beyond physical borders and are experienced by migrants in their everyday lives, making it hard for them to build new lives in Europe and elsewhere (Laine, 2016; Nail, 2016, p. 4). Power dynamics are largely forged and reproduced through these kinds of policies of everyday life (Crawford and Hutchinson, 2015). In fact, security procedures deterring "unwanted" migration happen largely through practices of bordering that do not attract much attention, far from the governmental authorities and formal power, hidden and invisible to the eye of an "average citizen".

Although undocumented migrants are the least protected group in the EU (Kmak, 2020), in many countries asylum seekers' rights and freedoms related to working, studying, and access to services are limited in various ways. These restrictions have impacts on their emotions and opportunities in different arenas of daily life. The policies and practices vary on a country level and some countries have stricter limitations than others. Yet, these measures invade and disrupt the lives of asylum seekers, affecting their everyday experiences of security. When it comes to physical security and bodily integrity, most of the people interviewed in Europe considered Europe to be quite safe compared to the circumstances in their home countries. However, straight after stating that Europe is safe, many of them claimed that for an asylum seeker, Europe is not safe in the same way as for others living in Europe. The border regime and the asylum system produce insecurities and inequalities between the "deserving" and "undeserving" migrants, and often asylum seekers seem to be regarded as undeserving. This was pointed out by a man from the Anglophone part of Cameroon, who had come to Finland as a professional football player but ended up seeking asylum after the circumstances in Cameroon had deteriorated and he could no longer consider going back. He described how life in Finland was completely different as an asylum seeker and as a professional athlete. Among many other interviewees, an Ethiopian woman who had chosen voluntary repatriation after a negative asylum decision was disappointed by Europe and advised no one to go irregularly:

> So as Ethiopian, I don't advice anyone to go to Europe. From my experience, I never thought that Europe is like this. Because if you get the paper it's ok, but to get the papers, it's very hard so I don't advice anyone to go. Legally, for education or family, if you can get paper, it's ok. But crossing the sea and sacrifice your life going to Europe is nonsense for me.

Her experience elaborates on how she felt some migrants are more welcome than others. She emphasizes being Ethiopian, because, according to her, being from Eritrea would have made a difference in the asylum process. Other returned Ethiopians interviewed in Addis Ababa also mentioned this. Their perception was that Eritrean nationality would have made them eligible for protection, which was felt to be unfair, because firstly, although the situation in Eritrea is bad, some Ethiopians also have severe problems; and secondly, Eritrean refugees in Ethiopia are sometimes "better off" than Ethiopians in Ethiopia due to receiving remittances, which offer them a relatively good living standard.

Most concerns and worries that the migrants I interviewed in Cyprus and Italy expressed concerning policies that affect their everyday lives were related to limitations to working, finding a place to stay, and studying, as well as securing access to various services. As these restrictions to their freedom were related to the status of an asylum seeker, being recognized as a refugee was seen as a solution. This was put into words by a Senegalese man interviewed in Cyprus:

> Before you are accepted as refugee, you cannot go to school, you cannot work, you have no chance showing your experience. I have studied and worked my whole life. Now imagine my situation. It hurts me, I have experience and I am educated, it hurts me that I cannot use my skills and they do not let me work.

This passage brings forth how many of the migrants who had a higher education felt like they were, in a way, "losing more" because they could not use the skills they had acquired. They felt that all the money and effort that had been put into their education and the years of training had been wasted. When asked about how the system should be changed, practically all the people I interviewed in Europe expressed a wish that asylum seekers could work without limitations.

The restrictions and limitations related to being an asylum seeker in Europe make the life of some asylum seekers so unbearable that they consider ever having gone to Europe to be a mistake. Many also stressed how much they loved Africa and how they would have never come if they would have known the reality in Europe. About a year after I met him in Cyprus on his second day there, a Cameroonian man expressed the regrets of his fellow asylum seekers for coming to Europe in a WhatsApp message in the following way:

> Most of us regret ever embarking on this journey to Cyprus because we don't even know what is going on. They don't give us documents, no jobs. Even monthly benefits from the government have become a problem, as it is no longer regular but house rents and bills are increasing on daily basis. This frustrates us, the asylum seekers.

As there were very few reception centres in Cyprus at the time, most asylum seekers had to find apartments for themselves. This requires money, connections, and resourcefulness, and apartment owners are often reluctant to make contracts with asylum seekers and demand guarantees. Consequently, many were sleeping in the parks or were temporarily accommodated by churches or charitable organizations. Those who had managed to get rental contracts got into trouble due to helping other asylum seekers by letting them sleep in their apartments.

A large part of the everyday processes of bordering are felt and "managed" by individuals through mundane activities and day-to-day routines and practices people engage in to "foster security for themselves and for others while striving to live with insecurity" (Crawford and Hutchinson, 2015, p. 1188). To cope with the everyday insecurities related to the life of an asylum seeker, support from other people was essential to the research participants. Many of them talked about the relevance of fellow migrants, especially other Africans. Encountering the various levels of insecurity produced by the migration policies that restrict the lives of asylum seekers was easier together than alone. Making friends and connections helps in a situation where a person is unaware of the future and the duration one has to wait for a decision from the immigration authorities. Such an uncertainty, a "slow torture" (Könönen, 2014, p. 13), holds one's life back and nurtures frustration, shame, fear, and insecurity (Khosravi, 2011, pp. 93–7). In addition to social connections and helping and supporting each other, many interviewees emphasized the significance of spirituality and religion in not giving up hope and dealing with insecurity. Some were also volunteering in NGOs helping migrants and trying to keep themselves busy in other ways, such as getting involved in solidarity initiatives or doing sports.

Detention and deportation as forms of violent migration management

Detention and deportation are some of the most violent forms of the EU's migration management. Although they are examples of security measures, which deprive people of their basic liberties, they have become naturalised as almost self-evident consequences of "violating" the law. Securitizing discourses on migration justify detention as a legitimate measure to control the EU's external borders, but the increased use of detention actually manifests the EU's failure to control entries. Additionally, the increased "deportability" of migrants in the past couple of decades has led to detention being an ever-expanding feature of migration management, although there is no evidence that it would discourage people from migrating or seeking asylum (De Genova, 2019; Del Gaudio and Phillips, 2018). Migrants can be captured at the border at the point of entrance and taken to detention merely for crossing the border "illegally", while others are taken into custody for over-staying their visa or after a rejected asylum application to wait for voluntary return or expulsion (Könönen, 2014, p. 76; Del Gaudio and Phillips, 2018). One of the research participants in Cyprus, as well as six out of the seven Ethiopians who had been in Europe and were now back in Ethiopia after voluntary return or forced removal, talked about their experiences of being held in detention centres or prisons, which was the word that they mostly used to refer to them. The way they talked about their experience differed, for instance, based on how long had been spent in detention in relation to the whole time spent in Europe. For those who had been in Europe for years undocumented and had made a mistake and thus been noticed by the police, or had been stopped by the police without a specific reason, detention had been more of an experience they could already have anticipated, and thus they seemed mentally more prepared for it. As for those who had been taken into jail or a detention centre directly from the border or soon after arrival, all the money and effort that had been put into the attempt to migrate to Europe was lost, which created emotions of regret and deep frustration.

An Ethiopian woman and a mother of two, who I interviewed at ARRA's office in Addis Ababa, had spent most of her time in Europe in detention. After her arrival to Norway, she had travelled to France and Belgium, where she was captured and held for five months before being sent back to Norway to wait for an asylum decision, which was denied soon after with a decision of forced removal back to Ethiopia. She recalled that in detention she had not been given access to healthcare while being sick, she had only been given food once a day, and she had encountered acts of racism and aggressive behaviour from the authorities in Belgium and Norway. The detention and deportation characterize her whole experience of Europe, and that experience was, in her words, "very bad". Answering my question about her expectations of Europe, she described her experience in the following way:

> I expected better chances for education, for work, everything. More human rights and freedom. That was my expectation before exile. All Europe, they don't have even human rights. If you are not willing to go back to your country, they force you, they give you injection, inject you and you wake up in your country. I have friends who have been to Belgium and they forced them, took their hands and covered their eyes and sent them by force. And the police beats people. They tied their legs with a rope and they covered their eyes and after they arrived in Ethiopia.

What had happened to her had made her, in her own words, "hate Europe". If this is the aim of the security measures of the EU and Schengen countries, the price to pay in individual suffering and trauma is very high. Although her characterization of the behaviour of Norwegian and Belgian authorities was the most violent of the detention and deportation-related experiences shared with me in the interviews, others had also encountered different forms of "bullying" and trying to scare the detainees on purpose, for instance by banging on doors and barging into rooms unexpectedly, making loud noises.

This kind of behaviour kept the detainees on their toes and made it difficult for them to sleep and handle the already intensely stressful situation.

De Genova characterizes the susceptibility to deportation as "a virtually universal feature" of the non-citizen status of migrants: they "always remain more or less deportable" (De Genova, 2019, p. 93). However, research on experiences of deportation remains scarce. Deportation is a process far more complex than relocation of a person back to the country of citizenship. Involving various institutions and people, it stretches over several geographical locations and spans over long periods of time (Khosravi, 2018, p. 2), as was the case for many of the research participants. Being sent back was the biggest fear and mentioned most often when I asked about the fears of the interviewees, especially for those who had been living in Europe undocumented. For six people who I interviewed at ARRA's Returnees' Reintegration Project in Addis Ababa, including the woman mentioned in the passage above, this fear had concretized through forced return to Ethiopia. They had been sent back against their will from three Schengen countries, in this case Sweden, Norway, and Switzerland, but some had been attempting to seek asylum in various countries, namely Denmark, Germany, France, and Belgium, and had been sent back to the first country of entrance to the Schengen area according to the EU law. Their time spent in Europe varied from a couple of months to more than ten years.

The deportees attach multiple feelings and thoughts to the deportation depending on various intersecting cultural categories, as well as their own situation in Ethiopia and in Europe. They also have various methods to deal with the experience of having to come back involuntarily. For those who had family members or some attachments in Ethiopia, the return had been easier, although one of the deportees had been abandoned by his wife and children after returning penniless after ten years in Europe. The experience of a deportee can be that of a "double abandonment", being "expelled from one country and outcast in another" (Khosravi, 2018, p. 2). The effects of forced return are often negative, both for the deportees as well as for the receiving communities, which commonly struggle with unemployment, political instability, and social insecurity. The post-deportation condition is, in many cases, characterized by the same emotions of fear, anxiety, and insecurity as the condition before the return (ibid, pp. 2–4). Although some of the deportees had found jobs after the return, and as a part of the returnee programme funded by the EU they had received some form of support, all of them were struggling in one form or another with re-starting a life in Ethiopia, and some were hoping to go back to Europe. They also had trouble accepting the cause for the return, or felt that their rights had not been respected in the way the return had been executed in practice. For instance, a woman had not been allowed to collect her belongings from the place she had been staying, although she waited for two months in detention before the forced removal. Upon arrival, she had been left at the Addis Ababa airport without anything, although she had been promised two nights in a hotel. Another man had been celebrating the new year with his friends when he had been captured, and had not had time to prepare for leaving after years spent in Sweden.

Concluding remarks

Securitizing discourses and related bordering practices that see migration as a security threat overshadow the multiple benefits of migration. They also polarize societies, which creates ontological insecurity in the migrant receiving communities and makes it more difficult to solve migration-related challenges inside, as well as between, continents. (Laine, 2020a/b). This obstructs alternative imaginations that would make it possible to overcome the dualistic binaries like "us" and "them", or "national" and "foreigner" (Walters, 2010). Experiences of bordering and securitizing create new knowledge. Migrants are an important but underused resource of knowledge and information when it comes to European-African relations and finding solutions to the issues linked to migration.

As has been elaborated in this chapter, Europe's security measures produce multiple forms of suffering, fear, hate, uncertainty, and insecurity in the people towards whom they are targeted. This affects their everyday lives in various ways, but it also shapes the ways migrants understand and perceive Europe. As Laine (2020b) depicts, my research shows how Europe's reaction towards migration actually tells more about Europe itself than about the migrants: by aiming at securing itself, the EU ends up producing insecurities both to itself and to people on the sending and receiving end of migratory patterns by acting against its own proclaimed values. Changing this course would benefit both Europe and Africa in the future. Ending in the words of Tickner (1992), security means nothing if it is built on others' insecurity.

Acknowledgement

This work was supported by the Academy of Finland funded Centre of Excellence in Law, Identity and the European Narratives (funding decision number 312431).

References

Appia-Nyamekye Sanny, J., Rocca, C., and Schultes, I. (2019) "'Updata-ing' the narrative about African migration". MIF Joint Research Paper. Afrobarometre. (online) Available at: afrobarometer.org/sites/default/files/publications/Publications%20 conjointes/partenaires/afrobarometer-moibrahim-updata-ing-the-narrative-about-african-migration.pdf (Accessed 6 Mar. 2020).

Beneduce, R. (2015) The moral economy of lying: Subjectcraft, narrative capital, and uncertainty in the politics of asylum. *Medical Anthropology, 34*(6), pp. 551–71.

Bigo, D. (2002) Security and immigration: Toward a critique of the governmentality of unease. *Alternatives, 27*(1), pp. 63–92.

Bohmer C. and Shuman A. (2018) *Political Asylum Deceptions: The Culture of Suspicion.* Cham: Palgrave Macmillan.

Crawford, A. and Hutchinson, S. (2015) Mapping the contours of "everyday security": Time, space and emotion. *The British Journal of Criminology,* 56(6), pp. 1184–202.

De Genova N. (2018) The "migrant crisis" as racial crisis: Do Black lives matter in Europe? *Ethnic and Racial Studies,* 41(10), pp. 1765–82.

De Genova, N. (2019) Detention, deportation, and waiting: Toward a theory of migrant detainability. *Gender a Výzkum,* 20(1), pp. 92–104.

Del Gaudio, E. and Phillips, S. (2018) Detention of child asylum seekers in the pursuit of state interests: A comparison of the Australian and EU approaches. *Nordic Journal of Human Rights,* 36(1), pp. 1–18.

European Commission. (2018) Standard Eurobarometer 89. Spring 2018. (online) Available at: ec.europa.eu/commfrontoffice/publicopinion/index.cfm/ResultDoc/download/DocumentKy/83548 (Accessed 17 Jan. 2020).

Fierke, K. M. (2007) *Critical Approaches to International Security.* Cambridge: Polity.

FitzGerald, D. S. (2020) Remote control of migration: Theorising territoriality, shared coercion, and deterrence. *Journal of Ethnic and Migration Studies,* 46(1), pp. 4–22.

Giddens, A. (1991) *Modernity and Self-Identity: Self and Society in the Late Modern Age.* Cambridge: Polity Press.

Huysmans, J. (2002) Defining social constructivism in security studies: The normative dilemma of writing security. *Alternatives: Global, Local, Political,* 27(1_suppl), pp. 41–62.

Kent, J., Norman, K. P., and Tennis, K. H. (2019) Changing motivations or capabilities? Migration deterrence in the global context. *International Studies Review,* viz050, pp. 1–26.

Khosravi, S. (2011) *"Laiton" matkaaja": Paperittomuus ja rajojen valta,* trans. A. Sadinmaa. Gaudeamus: Helsinki.

Khosravi, S. (2018) Introduction. In: S. Khosravi, ed., *After Deportation: Ethnographic Perspectives.* Cham: Palgrave Macmillan, pp. 1–14.

Kmak, M. (2020) The right to have rights of undocumented migrants: Inadequacy and rigidity of legal categories of migrants and minorities in international law of human rights. *The International Journal of Human Rights,* pp. 1–17, DOI: 10.1080/13642987.2020.1716740.

Könönen, J. T. (2014) *Tilapäinen elämä, joustava työ: Rajat maahanmuuton ja työvoiman prekarisaation mekanismina.* Joensuu: University of Eastern Finland.

Laine, J. P. (2016) The multiscalar production of borders. *Geopolitics,* 21(3), pp. 465–82.

Laine, J. P. (2020a) Reframing African migration to Europe: An alternative narrative. In: I. Moyo, C. C. Nshimbi and J. P. Laine, eds. *Migration Conundrums, Regional Integration and Development: Africa-Europe Relations in a Changing Global Order.* London: Palgrave Macmillan, pp. 93–116.

Laine, J. P. (2020b) Ambiguous bordering practices at the EU's edges. In: A. Bissonnette and É. Vallet, eds., *Borders and Border Walls: In-Security, Symbolism, Vulnerabilities.* London: Routledge, pp. 69–87.

Nail, T. (2016) *Theory of the Border.* New York: Oxford University Press.

Pallister-Wilkins, P. (2016) How walls do work: Security barriers as devices of interruption and data capture. *Security Dialogue,* 47(2), pp. 151–64.

Rumford, C. (2008) Introduction: Citizens and borderwork in Europe. *Space and Polity,* 12(1), pp. 1–12.

Rumford, C. (2012) Towards a multiperspectival study of borders. *Geopolitics,* 17(4), pp. 887–902.

Spiro, D. E. (2009) Criminalizing immigration: The social construction of borders and national security. *SSRN Electronic Journal.* (November 29, 2009). (online) Available at: ssrn.com/abstract=1515466 (Accessed 13 May 2020).

Squire, V. (2017) Governing migration through death in Europe and the US: Identification, burial and the crisis of modern humanism. *European Journal of International Relations, 23*(3), pp. 513–32.

Stevens, D. and Vaughan-Williams, N. (2016) *Everyday Security Threats: Perceptions, Experiences, and Consequences.* Manchester: Manchester University Press.

Sumari, L. (2016) *Turvassa maailmalla? Suomalaisten vaihto-opiskelijoiden käsityksiä ja kokemuksia turvallisuudesta.* Faculty of Arts, University of Helsinki.

Tickner, J. A. (1992) *Gender in International Relations: Feminist Perspectives on Achieving Global Security.* New York: Columbia University Press.

UNDP. (2019) Scaling fences: Voices of irregular African migrants to Europe. (online) Available at: www.undp.org/content/dam/rba/docs/Reports/UNDP-Scaling-Fences-EN-2019.pdf (Accessed 20 Mar. 2020).

Wæver, O. (1993) Societal security: The concept. In O. Waever, B. Buzan, M. Kelstrup and P. Lemaitre eds., *Identity, Migration and the New Security Agenda in Europe.* London: Pinter, pp. 17–40.

Wæver, O. (1995) Securitization and desecuritization, In R. Lipschutz ed., *On Security.* New York: Columbia University Press, pp. 46–86.

Walker, N. (2004) *Europe's Area of Freedom, Security and Justice.* New York: Oxford University Press.

Walters, W. (2010) Migration and security. In J. P. Burgess ed., *The Routledge Handbook of New Security Studies.* New York: Routledge, pp. 217–28.

World Bank. (2020) Forced displacement. refugees, internally displaced and host communities. (online) Available at: www.worldbank.org/en/topic/forced-displacement (Accessed 14 May 2020).

13 Safe European home – Where did you go? On immigration, the b/ordered self, and the territorial home

Jussi P. Laine

The Clash's (1978) account of the "Safe European Home" provides a captivating narrative about the feelings of displacement and anxiety commonly felt in encountering otherness. The lyrics point to a painful reality in which the freedom of movement of the wealthy and powerful extends further than that of the poor and powerless. They go on to describe how the mere right to move does not necessarily lead to belongingness and acceptance. The song provided inspiration for the argumentation here because of its unblemished articulation of the anxiety caused by unfamiliarity, as well as the yearning for wholeness and the safety of home. As Bourdieu (2000, p. 142) expressed it, whereas the unfamiliar is "out of place", home is the place "to be". It is in acknowledging the highly ambivalent and paradoxical effects of the thick, historically rooted, idea of "home" (Duyvendak, 2011, p. 102) reflected in our self-image and used to block immigrant integration that this chapter underlines the need for introspection, for only by looking inwards first may we see outwards clearly and build an honest base for Europe–Africa relations.

In Europe, as well as generally throughout the global north, there has been a consistent drive for ever stricter border and migration policies. However, the persistent attempts to keep immigrants out is at odds with the continent's increasing need to bring immigrants in (Carr, 2012). Irregular migration has become a field in which estimations often prevail over researched actualities, and hearsay and myths over concrete evidence. The situation has become increasingly paradoxical: what was branded as a "refugee crisis" has become increasingly about filtering between the welcomed and the unwanted rather than a question of mere numbers (Laine, 2020a). European borders have become increasingly unevenly transparent, bringing into question humanitarian pretensions (Harding, 2012) and the ethical premise (Laine, 2018a) of stricter policies. As Finne (2018) expresses it, "[i]mmigration is, literally, the poor man knocking on the rich man's door, and the enforcement of borders is slamming the door shut".

In contrast with the mere attempt to close state spaces, support for more deterrent policies stems from the common narratives that posit borders as hard lines and defences against all kinds of "ill" affecting the body of *our* "national" societies. While much of the recent discussion has quite justifiably

DOI: 10.4324/9781003083726-14

been entangled with the resultant reinforcement of "us" versus "them" divisions, the definition of "them" in this equation requires more attention. The interpretation of the recent events that this chapter seeks to advance with evidence is that the question of migration has indeed become an existential challenge for the European Union (EU). Yet, rather than the people on the move being the ones constituting the perceived threat, the challenge the EU faces is equally, if not more, homegrown. Migration has become an issue that sharply divides the European and national political arenas, whereby "they" can no longer be automatically assumed to be found only on the other side of the border. Consequently, the sense of anxiety and insecurity many ordinary Europeans may feel about migration cannot be solved by borders. Both the cause and the solution lie elsewhere.

As scholars of European security have noted, the levels of fear, anxiety, and threat felt by many seem to drastically exceed the actual levels of physical risk to contemporary EU citizens (Kinnvall, Manners, and Mitzen, 2018, p. 149). This chapter relies on the notion of ontological (in)security to explain how widespread anxiety about migration can be seen as stemming from the strains caused by preserving a continuous positive version of the self amidst the perceived crisis. It is argued that in resorting to exceptional measures in coping with the exceptional situation the recent migration pressures have inflicted, the EU and its member states and citizens have deviated from the fundamental value basis which has traditionally held them together. While migration plays a key role in this conundrum, the actual cause of insecurity stems from the European population becoming increasingly divided. This chapter utilises recent Eurobarometer survey data to examine EU citizens' feelings about and reactions to immigration and the EU's future, providing a theoretically and philosophically grounded analysis of the lack of stability of the European identity and the bordered conception of the self.

This chapter shifts the discussion of migration as a phenomenon in its own right and with its own dynamics to its broader societal implications. I claim the widespread less-than-welcoming mindset towards immigration throughout Europe cannot be taken explicitly to indicate an anti-migrant attitude. Rather, it is a symptom of the much broader insecurities many Europeans have felt. These insecurities have only been exacerbated amidst the current COVID-19 pandemic, which has also further reinforced the perception of borders as barriers to *foreign* threats. This is to say that migration from Africa continues to be misconstrued and misrepresented for internal European reasons. It is these reasons we must better understand in seeking to reconstruct future relations on a more balanced footing. Amidst multiple overlapping crises, migrants have been used as convenient scapegoats in a strategy to combat anxieties and insecurities caused by other kinds of societal change in search of stability and continuity (Laine, 2020b). With a mounting democratic deficit, growing debt, a struggling labour market, related social security concerns, unfavourable demographics stemming from an ageing population, declining birth rates, and a cumulative brain drain, the resilience of European societies has already been considerably weakened. It is this backdrop with which I wish to begin.

Challenges for the EU as post-national political project

In seeking to understand how and why the rational accounts of migration as Europe's saviour became so swiftly overshadowed by more emotional perspectives of migration as threat, the bigger picture needs consideration. What *Spear's* (2019), a niche British bimonthly for high-net-worth individuals, termed the "doom-loop" of Europe will not be overcome by solving the migration "problem". While "the death of Europe" is hardly as evident as *Spear's* analysis would lead us to believe, it must be given credit for going against the grain and not even mentioning migration in their extensive take on the European vicious cycle of economic decline and the potential break-up of the EU. Should their logic be taken further, the "migration crisis" may have been the last nail in the EU's coffin, yet it is hardly the reason to consider the need to put the EU in that coffin in the first place – contrary to the then (2018) president of the European Parliament Antonio Tajani's straightforward speculation that "[t]he migration crisis could spell the end of the European project" (Tajani, 2018).

Tajani's thinking may have been influenced by the substantial – yet often rather lopsided – coverage of migration that hijacked much of the European mediascape following what many referred to misleadingly as a refugee or even more broadly a migration crisis (see Laine, 2019). Interestingly, two years before Tajani made his statement – very soon after the tipping point of asylum seeker arrivals in Europe had passed – the European Commission President Jean-Claude Juncker admitted in his State of the Union address before the European Parliament in 2016 that the EU itself was in "an existential crisis". Mentioning migration only in passing in his 6,000-word speech, Juncker's core concern (2016) was the lack of solidarity that has been taken by default to be the glue that keeps the Union together. Juncker confessed he had never seen such a lack of common ground between the member states, heard so many leaders speak only of their domestic problems, and seen national governments so weakened by the forces of populism. He continued that he had never seen representatives of the EU institutions setting very different priorities, sometimes in direct opposition to national governments and parliaments.

Juncker was not alone in his concern. His desperation about what was to come was widely echoed throughout the EU executive, not to mention by the growing number of statesmen and political commentators across the continent. Issuing a stern word of caution against falling into the trap of identity politics, Frans Timmermans (in Lefranc, 2016), the First Vice-President of the European Commission, stated that for the first time in thirty years he had really come to "believe that the European project [could] fail". It was not migration as such but the lack of solidarity and unity, as well as compliance with one's own rule of law, that would be needed, in contrast to the observed regression into state-centric thinking, to manage the general situation to which the sudden increase of migrant arrivals had contributed.

The EU has been duly criticised for securitising migration through its bordering regime and exclusionary practices, which more than anything else have jeopardised its proclaimed ideals and hollowed out its core values (Cuttitta and Last, 2020; Laine, 2020b; van Houtum and Bueno Lacy, 2020). Machiavelli (1966[1532], p. 56) famously wrote that the way many people live "is so far removed from the way they ought to live that anyone who abandons what is for what should be pursues his downfall rather than his preservation". Given his self-proclaimed intention "to write something useful to whoever understands it", Machiavelli (1998[1532], p. 61) considered it "more fitting to go directly to the effectual truth of the thing than to the imagination of it".[1] In discussing what modes of government a prince should assume towards his "subjects and friends", Machiavelli (1998[1532], p. 61) claimed that many had "imagined republics and principalities that have never been seen or known to exist in truth". While it seems safe to assume that his remarks may more have concerned Plato's *Republic* than providing a prediction of the future contractions between the European idea(l) and practice, the underlying logic of Machiavelli's argument seems to hold true today, as evidenced by the recent surge of political realism.

To keep its promise to act as a "force for good in the world", as the common self-depiction of the 2000s went, and work proactively to create a world "offering justice and opportunity for everyone" (European Security Strategy, 2003), it may be necessary for the EU to stand for its own values and act accordingly. It is certainly worth striving for the Laeken Declaration's aspiration for the EU (Bulletin of the European Union, 2001) to play a leading and stabilising role in a new world order. It has been frequently repeated and fine-tuned, but its attainment is unmistakably receding ever further:

> Europe as the continent of humane values, the Magna Carta, the Bill of Rights, the French Revolution, and the fall of the Berlin Wall; the continent of liberty, solidarity, and above all diversity, meaning respect for others' languages, cultures, and traditions. The European Union's one boundary is democracy and human rights. The Union is open only to countries which uphold basic values such as free elections, respect for minorities, and respect for the rule of law.
>
> (Bulletin of the European Union, 2001)

Instead of simply striving to make the world a better place, the logic of the 2003 strategy already revealed a vested interest: to seek to resolve problems before they reached the EU: that is, to aim for a better world because it would be "more secure for the European Union and its citizens". This logic has evolved increasingly into a chicken and egg situation. Which should come first: a secure Europe or a better world? Instead of being a win-win situation as it was depicted close to two decades ago, the persistent conundrum now appears to be closer to a zero-sum game in which the security of the EU is sought at the expense of others. To play a stabilising role worldwide and claim to act convincingly as a force for good for everyone, it must get its internal act together. It must be ontologically secure to give meaning to the space and polity it has been formed to govern (Mitzen, 2018; Kinnvall, Manners and Mitzen, 2018).

A homogenous home and the irruptions of enjoyment

The logic of this chapter's argumentation relies on the notion of ontological security: the security of being that Laing (1960) and later Giddens (e.g. 1991) considered the fundamental need of humans to feel whole, continuous, and stable over time, and especially during a crisis which threatens their wellbeing. The concept was later introduced in the field of International Relations (IR) to improve the understanding of how and why states, much like individuals, are concerned with maintaining a consistent notion of the self to enhance their ontological security in relations with other states (Kinnvall, 2004; Steele, 2008; Mitzen, 2006). This notion has also been extended to the supranational level. The EU, facing many crises and risks to its security and existence, also seeks ontological security in securing its identity and gives meaning to the space and polity it has been formed to govern (Rumelili, 2015; Kinnvall, Manners, and Mitzen, 2018).

This approach suggests that ontological security can be threatened by rapid political change and manipulated by threat scenarios targeting the specific organisation of groups. The potential threat of a perceived negative difference between peoples, cultures, and states therefore needs to be emphasised (Rumelili, 2015). Partly as a result of long-term migration pressures and the more immediate refugee crisis in Europe, threat scenarios have proliferated in which asylum seekers and migrants are seen as challenging the political foundations of the EU and those of European civilisation itself. More recently, the notion has also been applied to the EU, with the aim of better understanding contemporary fears and anxieties among Europeans, and the consequences of this approach for European security (Della Sala, 2017; Kinnvall, Manners, and Mitzen, 2018; Mitzen, 2018).

Ontological security largely concerns the identity, values, and points of common reference that create a sense of group belonging (Mitzen, 2006). On the flipside of the search for stability and continuity is a cognitive-affective resistance to any disruption it may entail. The experience of ontological security is contingent on routinised personal, social, and political orders that hold hard uncertainties at bay, and a socio-spatial environment – home – that embodies a feeling of being (Mitzen, 2018, p. 1374). Home, she continues, is psychologically central to subjectivity, regardless of how it is construed. From the phenomenological perspective, often stressed by environmental psychologists, home is a safe and familiar space where people feel "at ease" (Duyvendak, 2011, p. 27).

Attachment to a home has been conceptualised as "a positive place-bound affection by which people maintain closeness to a place" (Hidalgo and Hernández, 2001, p. 274). However, it is also created by familiar daily routines and the regular settings of activities and interactions (Fried, 2000). This is to say the familiarity of a place is not derived from that particular place alone but from strong social, psychological, and emotional attachments (Easthope, 2004, p. 136). As long as home is considered a bordered container, as the traditional Westphalian notion of territoriality has etched it in our minds, the psychological comfort that borders can be seen to produce remains strong – inflicting in so doing an impression of borders as protective yet vulnerable walls, safeguarding the inside from a perceived external threat (Laine, 2018a). This is demonstrated perhaps most palpably in the concept and practical applications of homeland security and the related reverberation of the narrative, which conveys an effective image of our homelands on the verge of conquest and of being overrun by foreign elements (Laine, 2020a).

These ideas echo Douglas's (1991, p. 289) work on the material, located aspect of home: "home starts by bringing some space under control". Following Massey (1994), space ought not however be viewed as an inert platform, as a territorial homeland within which stability and coherence would spring out of a mythical sense of unity between a bounded land and "its" people, but rather constitutive of and inseparable from social relations with others and the outside. Surely, as Hollifield (2004) points out, international mobility creates a tension between liberalism's universalist free-movement aspirations and the state project's particularism of bounded security communities. As recent events have shown, this tension manifests itself expressly at the borders and is reflected in migration governance built on the rhetoric of "longing for a homogenous national home" (Duyvendak, 2011, p. 1). The current widespread populist and nationalist appeals to homeland discourses of closure and fear, Mitzen (2018, p. 1383) argues, stem from this mythic sense of the Westphalian home as a comfortable refuge in a threatening world. Offers of a strong and familiar nation state as a solution to perceived uncertainly and chaos have resonated well with the public discourse in many EU member states, yet at the same time effectively watered down the credibility of the EU's own ideas of a security community.

Given that the European project is grounded in the ambition to create unity not only among its states but among its people, it has become of great importance to assume a more interdisciplinary reading of ontological security. While most agree that ontological security is a security of identity, in much International Relations (IR) scholarship the strong association of identity and belonging with the state has overlooked the significance of society in identity formation. As Chernobrov (2016, p. 582) suggests, "ontological security is not about state per se but about society and its need for a stable and continuous self-concept when faced with a crisis". The same inner motivations, he continues, lead societies to (mis)recognise the unexpected as anticipated and familiar, to self-populate the other, spilling into supportive or devaluing narratives about major international crises – and it is this (mis) recognition that enables agents to (re)act as the event becomes explainable, recognisable, and more controllable (ibid., p. 596).

Interpreting societal reactions to uncertainty reveals that we are anxious to preserve a stable identity and transform uncertainty and discontinuity into a recognised routine, even if the latter contradicts rationality or escalates the crisis (Chernobrov, 2016, p. 596). That is, for the sake of ontological security, rationality may be pushed aside and overridden in the search for continuity, even if this compromises values and norms otherwise held dear (Laine, 2018b, p. 233). The failure to measure up to our own ideals surfaces in our psychosocial behaviour in the form of anxiety and insecurity. Questioning one's self-worth easily leads to a defensiveness that tends to be manifested in hostility to others, the glorification of nationalist narratives and radicalisation, and misrepresentations – if not smearing – of migrants. As Chernobrov (2016, p. 596) asserts, a "drawing self" is constantly present behind its portraits of others. The more negative the qualities attributed to the "them" group, the more positive "we" seem in comparison (Laine, 2020a), and these representations seldom seek accuracy. On the contrary, Figlio (2012, p. 11) states that self-love "lives in a world of fantasy, which contact with reality can only contaminate".

Fantasy, Žižek (1997) explains, maintains and masks divisions within society, often by attributing to reviled others the causes of one's own lack of satisfaction, or *jouissance*, or that of the group to which we assume we belong. By extracting coherence from confusion and reducing multiplicity to singularity, fantasy "enables individuals and groups to give themselves histories" (Scott, 2001, p. 289). Yet fantasy is not the *object* of desire but its *setting*, Laplanche and Pontalis (1986, p. 26) maintain. They continue that, in fantasy, the subject "forms no representation of the desired object, but is himself represented as participating in the scene". Contrary to the common understanding, fantasy is not antagonistic to social reality. As Rose (1996, p. 3) asserts, "it is its precondition or psychic glue".

Whether the determinants of the group-based "we-feeling" and the conventional, often inflexible, social-spatial imaginaries and demarcations that maintain it are factual or fictional becomes secondary to their ability to influence socio-spatial behaviours and attitudes – how we perceive different people and places, and how we perceive and interpret our own place and actions. As the question is ultimately about the fundamentals of one's being and the security of the self, these determinants cannot easily be challenged even if proved deceitful or wrong. Fear especially stands out in this conjunction as a factor that cannot be overlooked. While it has been harnessed recently to the advancing of political goals and deliberately politicised by feeding xenophobic readings of the migration situation, fear is a psychological, not a political, phenomenon (Laine, 2020a). It cannot simply be made to go away with a political decision.

To get to the bottom of this, we must dig more deeply into our hearts and minds. The old saying that "home is where the heart is" continues to hold true in underlining the importance of the emotional bond to a place and the safety it brings. In privileging "factual" knowledge we tend to disregard that it is often our emotional response rather than any scientifically proven fact that helps us deal with reality. Tangibly, new brain imaging research shows that imagining a threat lights up similar regions as its actual experiencing (Reddan, Wager, and Schiller, 2018). Emotions, Aizenberg and Geffen (2013) explain, are closely linked to perception. As recent discoveries about human psychology also indicate, facts seldom change our minds, but reason has its limitations (Gorman and Gorman, 2016; Mercier and Sperber, 2017; Sloman and Fernbach, 2017). While the malleability of public sentiment has been heightened during this era of alternative facts, fake news post-truths, and other deceptive or misleading information (Laine, 2020b), it can be seen to reflect a longstanding human behaviour pattern from the hunter-gatherer era: there was little advantage in reasoning clearly when much was to be gained from winning arguments (Mercier and Sperber, 2017).

However, we know already from the classic study by Ross, Lepper, and Hubbard (1975, p. 880) that both self- and social perceptions may persevere even after the initial basis for such perceptions has been completely refuted: "once formed", they discovered, "impressions are remarkably perseverant and unresponsive to new input". Thus, the tendency to embrace information that supports one's beliefs, and the unwillingness to make appropriate revisions to them and reject information that contradicts them, has come to be widely known as "confirmation bias". Such bias, Cunningham (2019, p. 9) explains, is especially common when security is considered. Much of this is connected to resistance to change, which, Kanter (2012) explicates, manifests itself in many ways. Kanter lists loss of control as the most common. Change, she posits, can make people feel they have lost control over their territory. It may also have less to do with a particular space *per se* and more with a deeply rooted attachment to it, and the customary b/ordered identity that this territory is seen to confine and nourish. The question is thus not only political but psychological – as is the second factor on her list: excess uncertainty (ibid.), which, Chernobrov (2016, p. 596) avers, the human mind understands as self-doubt – the key determinant of ontological insecurity.

It is also important in this respect to differentiate between fear and anxiety. To Alleviate them, we must first understand what they actually are, and how they are formed. While both are triggered in response to threat, fear – generally considered a reaction to something immediate and known that threatens one's security or safety – tends to be easier to respond to than anxiety – a more general state of distress, nervousness, or dread, the source of which may be more difficult to pinpoint (see e.g. Lang, Davis, and Öhman, 2000). Fear of the unknown is therefore actually anxiety. While the strategies to alleviate these emotions differ, Öhman (2008) clarifies that both can be transformed into defence mechanisms and irrational behaviours that may obscure the recognition of reality. The idea of defence mechanisms, unconscious strategies whereby people protect themselves from anxiety, is rooted in Freud's (1923) theory of personality, which – at risk of oversimplification – posits that the mind has three duelling forces (the id, the ego, and the superego). To mitigate the tension emerging in the form of anxiety between the unconscious and primitive urges of the id and the partly conscious drive towards the superego's moral and social values, the ego deploys strategies of self-deception to avoid discomfort (ibid.). This may lead to deleterious thoughts or emotions being projected onto someone else, even without provocation, for the sake of one's own comfort and security.

Money well spent? The value of border security

"The land should be large enough to support a certain number of people living moderately and no more", Plato proclaimed in his last dialogue, the *Laws* (Book V, para. 737). He also insisted that in addition to determining the appropriate total number of citizens, it was necessary to agree about their distribution. While Plato's endeavour to seek a balance between the competing aspirations for monarchy and democracy far preceded the now almost natural Westphalian confines, the underlying issue at hand has remained largely the same: how many, and in particular, who to let in? In pursuing the debate with the anonymous Athenian stranger (representing an ideal version of himself, perhaps), Plato eventually points to the unity of the virtues, the noble, and the good as the b/ordering criteria to be applied and the necessary condition for the long-term success of the sought-after political project. In assuming a position of the other, the stranger within, Plato distances himself from his earlier works on more clear-cut political theory (the *Statesman* and the *Republic*) by involving extensive deliberations on ethics, psychology, theology, epistemology, and metaphysics.

The current era of multiple and constant crises, with the various elements of uncertainty they create, has underlined – perhaps more lucidly than ever – the role borders play in the constitution of difference or bringing order amidst the perceived dangers of chaos. Far from mere markers of sovereignty, the approach taken on borders here accentuates their constitutive role as a fundamental social need. I do not, however, intend to devalue the continued and even increasing prominence of borders as something concrete and fixed. Indeed, our world – and Europe is an excellent example – has become more fenced than ever. In addition to various other measures aimed at controlling and restricting movement, almost a thousand kilometres of physical walls, Benedicto and Brunet (2018) detail, have been constructed along the EU and the Schengen borders since the nineties to prevent displaced people migrating into Europe. Furthermore, thirty-five years since the Schengen agreement dismantled most internal border checks in the EU, and more than three decades since the Berlin Wall was torn down – the key moments in materialising the very *idea* of European integration and unity – new walls have been constructed not only along the external borders of the European space but within it. Whether physical, virtual, or even mental, these walls and the mindset they create – and of which they are also a symptom – effectively overshadow perhaps the greatest achievement of the European project – the freedom of movement.

Much has been written about Europe turning itself into a fortress excluding those outside and fostering the division between us and them (e.g. Carr, 2012; Jünemann, Scherer, and Fromm, 2017; van Houtum and Bueno Lacy, 2020). The extent to which boosted border security actually makes people feel safer therefore remains debatable. An increasing number of scholars has suggested that this heavy investment has actually backfired. Despite the stated goals of increasing security against a supposed threat, the amplified securitisation has pushed migrants into more treacherous waters (Squire, 2017; Benedicto and Brunet, 2018; Cuttita and Last, 2020; Laine, 2020a) and endangered the lives and rights of people inside the Union. Stricter border controls do little to stop irregular migration. The answers must be sought elsewhere, yet they certainly make it more dangerous – and frankly, fatal (Figure 13.1). This is especially evident in the statistics exposing that the mortality rate increased despite a drastic decrease in the number of arrivals in 2015. Although these official figures are disquieting, those provided by various human rights groups make the situation even more disheartening. For example, according to the "List of Deaths", collected by UNITED[2] between 1993 and 2019, at least

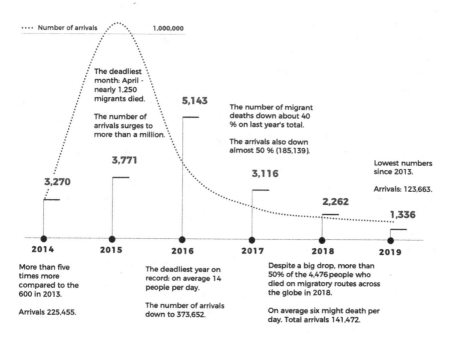

Figure 13.1 Development of the number of migrant arrivals and deaths.

Data source: International Organization for Migration (IOM). Illustration by the author.

36,570 refugee deaths can be attributed to the "fatal policies of Fortress Europe", including border militarisation, asylum laws, detention policies, and deportations – in addition to which "most probably thousands more are never found" (UNITED, 2019). More than forty thousand people died trying to cross international borders in the last decade, no less than half of them at the borders of the EU (Jones, 2016).

Investment in border security has also increased. While straightforward development curves are somewhat difficult to produce because of different calculation methods and the reshuffling of instruments and initiatives, it nevertheless seems safe to say the money spent on border security has grown progressively. The budget of the European Border and Coast Guard Agency (Frontex) has soared from an initial €6.2 million in 2005 to €333 million in 2019[3], and it is expected to increase by another 34.6 percent to €420.6m in 2020 (EUobserver, 2019). Furthermore, companies that provide technology and services that accompany border walls have received significant EU funding, especially from the External Borders Fund (€1.7 billion during the 2007–2013 budgetary period) and as much as €2.76 billion (2014–2020) from the Internal Security Fund (Akkerman, 2019). The budget for the next EU seven-year period, geared towards addressing the key challenges of today and tomorrow and matching aspirations with action, significantly boosts spending on border protection. For example, the increase includes €8.02 billion for the Integrated Border Management Fund and €11.27 billion to Frontex (ibid.).

Having acknowledged in 2018 that "migration and border management will remain a challenge in the future", the Commission proposed to almost triple funding for migration and border management to €34.9 billion during the 2021–2027 EU budgetary period (European Commission, 2018). This would be funded by two instruments, the Asylum and Migration Fund (AMF) and the Integrated Border Management Fund (IBMF), as well as the activities of relevant decentralised EU agencies like the European Border and Coast Guard Agency and the European Asylum Support Office. This was to be granted in addition to a separate allocation or more than €24 billion for security and defence. However, the Juncker Commission's 2018 overall budgetary proposal for the upcoming Multiannual Financial Framework (MFF) was cut, largely because of Brexit. In the more recent proposal by the current president of the European Council, Charles Michel, the share allocated for migration and border management was cut by almost a third, which in practice would have meant a proportional cut far greater than for any other budget item in what was "already modest" (Koerner, 2020) expenditure, representing a small share of the EU budget (D'Alfonso, 2020). However, having received fierce criticism for his proposal from members of the European Parliament (MEPs), who called it a "scandalous" proposal that would make the EU "irrelevant" – especially in light of the challenges to arriving at a common EU response to the migration situation at the Greek–Turkish border and the current COVID-19 emergency (European Parliament, 2020), Michel (2020) acknowledged his failure. The border budget is therefore likely to be clawed back.

Mere numbers aside, it is noteworthy that border security investment continued to increase, despite the fact that the number of irregular migrant arrivals decreased (Figure 13.1), suggesting that the walling of borders has created a momentum – and business – of its own – that is, separate from the actual "problem" it is supposed to be addressing. While the current (2020) COVID-19 pandemic may explain some of the most recent demands for increased border expenditure, most related decisions were made before the outbreak. Moreover, even in the current circumstances, the extent to which further investment in border security will actually help to alleviate the impact of the coronavirus – apart from enhancing the psychological conformity borders tend to bring and reinforcing the perception that the threat is, as usual, foreign – remains unclear.

United we stand, divided we fall

While it cannot be denied that, during recent events, borders have come to foster binary social orders and categories between the internal "us" and the external foreign "them", this has often translated in practice into European and non-European migratory pressures that have also increasingly ruptured the inside group. I argue that it is mounting polarisation and internal estrangement that challenges European societies' resilience and the EU's very future as a coherent actor and unified space. We have witnessed a rise of strongly polarised narratives across the continent that is fed by various actors with competing ideological interests and rival claims to the truth. Efforts to agree to a common European migration policy have gotten nowhere, as charismatic leaders with strong populist anti-migration platforms have swept to victory in recent elections, most notably in Italy, Hungary, and Austria, and effectively manufactured a crisis to support their own agendas and domestic political objectives to the detriment of the core values on which the European project has relied. As the Hungarian case distressingly illustrates, with similar tendencies having emerged elsewhere, the siege mentality has reached levels whereby solidarity with migrants and refugees has been constitutionally criminalised.

One poll after another has indicated that migration[1] has become a key concern for many Europeans. According to the Standard Eurobarometer data[4], immigration has topped the rankings, with 30-plus percent support since the inception of what was branded the "refugee crisis" (Figure 13.2). Between 2015 and 2018, terrorism was ranked the second biggest concern after immigration – and as can be deduced from myriad media reports, these two concepts have often been associated with one another in the minds of many. In all but two EU member states (climate change was ranked ahead of immigration in Sweden and Ireland), immigration was ranked the number one concern for the EU, the highest proportions being in Malta (66 percent) and Cyprus (60 percent), and the lowest in Romania (24 percent), Portugal, and the UK (both 26 percent). Although it was the key concern facing the EU for approximately a third of Europeans, it cannot be understated that the

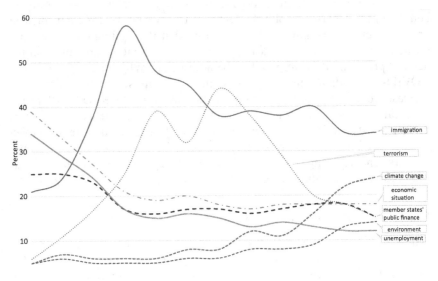

Figure 13.2 Immigration has become EU citizens' main concern facing the EU over the last years.
Data source: Standard Eurobarometer 92 (autumn 2019).

obvious – yet seldom heard – interpretation of the poll figures is that immigration is not the greatest concern of close to 70 percent. Yet almost seven in ten (68 percent) are in favour of the reinforcement of external EU borders with more European border guards and coastguards, support being strongest in Cyprus and Greece (both 91 percent) and Bulgaria (85 percent), and lowest in the United Kingdom (55 percent) and Sweden (57 percent).

At the national level, the concerns hit closer to home and become more personal, yet the overall situation seems more balanced because several issues are now receiving more equal weight in the assessment than ever (Figure 13.3). In the autumn 2019 figures, even before the current COVID-19 pandemic, health and social security was perceived to be the most important national issue, with the highest proportions in Finland (48 percent), Slovakia (45 percent), and Portugal (44 percent). Immigration ranks fourth – as important as inflation and the cost of living. The category of environment, climate, and energy has moved up to second position, while unemployment ranks third, following a long and steady decline of twenty-eight points since its high in the spring of 2014. Terrorism comes last, at an average of 5 percent (France being the outlier, with 14 percent). Immigration is cited as the most worrying national issue only in Malta (61 percent), Greece (54 percent), and Belgium (25 percent). Mere rankings aside, only 18 percent of Europeans consider

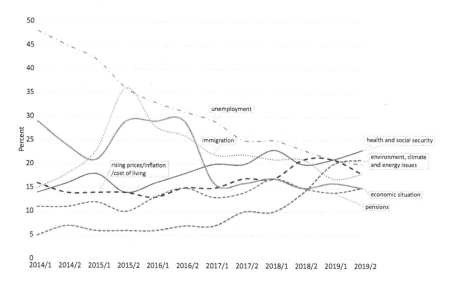

Figure 13.3 Concerns at the national level – the seven most-mentioned items.
Data source: Standard Eurobarometer 92 (autumn 2019).

immigration the main national concern, in contrast to the 34 percent who saw immigration as a broader European challenge.

When views on immigration are closely examined, it becomes evident that European public opinion largely continues to perceive immigration from other EU member states much more positively than that from outside the Union. A comparison with earlier surveys reveals that the distinction between the two has only increased: views on intra-EU migration have become increasingly positive; those on immigration from elsewhere have become more negative. The most negative impressions of immigration from outside the EU can be found in Czechia (82 percent), and Latvia and Estonia (both 74 percent). Non-EU migration is perceived positively in only eight countries: Ireland (72 percent), Spain (64 percent), Luxembourg (63 percent), Sweden (61 percent), the UK (57 percent), Portugal (56 percent), Croatia (49 percent), and Romania (45 percent).

Positive impressions of immigration from other EU member states dominate all socio-demographic categories of the population, yet are most prevalent among younger age groups and middle or higher social categories. However, immigration from outside the EU creates more pronounced divisions among Europeans (Figure 13.4); although there are differences between member states, they also exist within states. Students and young people in general see non-EU immigration most positively. They are joined by people in managerial positions. It generates the most negative response among the elderly, poorly educated, unemployed, and those who consider themselves working

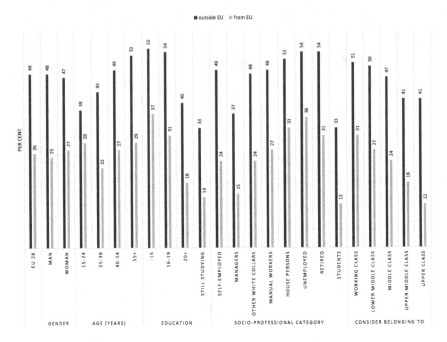

Figure 13.4 Negative view on immigration.
Data source: Standard Eurobarometer 91 – Wave EB91.5 – Kantar (spring 2019).

class. In short, negative views of immigration from outside the EU increase in line with respondents' age and decrease in line with their level of education. This supports the notion that the fundamental premise of the widespread anti-migrant narrative stems from the alleged struggle to secure Europe's welfare state. A majority (82 percent) of Europeans wants more to be done to combat irregular immigration from non-EU countries. Most are of the opinion that these measures should be taken at EU rather than national level. Yet very broad support throughout the EU remains for the principle of the free movement of EU citizens.

At the same time, the EU's positive image had lost some ground by the autumn of 2019, standing at 42 percent (down 3 percent from the spring of 2019), yet remained higher than at any point in the previous decade (Figure 13.5). Although the figures have increased, they also indicate that 58 percent, close to 300 million Europeans, do not view the EU overly positively. Similarly, the level of trust in the EU, which was at an all-time low before the "refugee crisis", has since improved (from 31 percent to 44 percent). The highest proportions of respondents trusting the EU were in Lithuania (72 percent) and Denmark (68 percent); the lowest in the autumn of 2019 were in the United Kingdom (29 percent), Greece (32 percent), and France (33 percent).

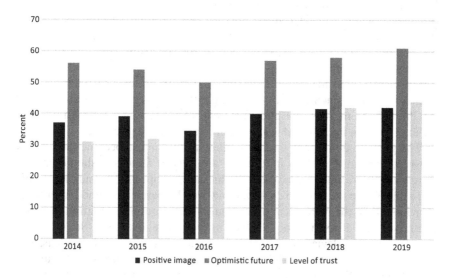

Figure 13.5 Views on the EU, %.
Data source: Standard Eurobarometer 91 – Wave EB91.5 – Kantar (spring 2019).

The level of trust in the EU is higher than in national governments, and its increase is an indication that the harsh action the EU has taken in attempting to manage the situation has gained support among citizens. More than six in ten Europeans are optimistic about the EU's future. The most optimistic perspective is held by the Irish (85 percent), Danish (79 percent), and Lithuanians (76 percent), while optimism (in 2019) was less pronounced, unsurprisingly, among the British (47 percent) and the French (50 percent).

While the average trends are interesting in themselves, they also obscure more than they illuminate in not showing the spread of results and their uneven distribution. A closer assessment of the socio-demographic categories, supported by a general observation made on the ongoing public and political debate, seems to suggest that Europe is more divided than a cursory statistical overview would suggest. There are differences in perspectives between different EU member states, yet there are also major differences of opinion within them. It is considerably more accurate to conclude that half the population does not trust the EU and half does than to claim average trust levels are approaching 50 percent.

Conclusion: A broken home, a broken heart

Migration has become an issue that sharply divides today's European and national political arenas. This chapter claims it is these divisions over migration rather than the immigrants themselves that have tested the unity, and hence resilience, of the EU and European societies. These divisions are real, but they not only divide Europe into various national agendas as is often depicted; the "nations" – to the extent they actually even exist – have also become increasingly torn. At either end of the spectrum, reactions to immigration have become, above all, emotional. While emotions should certainly not be dismissed as meaningless, misinterpretation can occur if their wisdom creates its own momentum, contradicting rather than complementing reason. As thinkers from Aristotle and Nietzsche to C. S. Lewis have all argued, feelings must be intertwined with reason to achieve the good life.

The gruesome fact that the EU's external border has become the world's most lethal border is telling in terms of a variety of factors. It should urge us to rethink the value of *border* security as such, as opposed to making *people* feel safer. While the road to dystopia may well be paved with good intentions (Davies, 2016), the mere silent toleration of the "troubling situation whereby death becomes a norm through which migration is governed" (Squire, 2017, p. 514) suggests a deviation from the conventional collective values, ideas, and ethical concerns for which Europe has stood and which has held its various parts together. While it indeed seems that "one may smile, and smile, and be a villain",[5] the attempts to manage migration by setting aside Europe's core values, to follow Machiavelli, are paving the way to its own downfall, with considerable social and political repercussions.

The accentuation of the perceived difference between states, cultures, and people becomes a major security risk, which increases within contexts of socioeconomic stress and geopolitical instability. The feeling of ontological insecurity has led to the defence of actions that have manifested themselves in antagonism towards others, fuelling misrepresentations of immigration. At times of crisis especially, the extent of association and interests to be cared for tends to shrink. As crisis deepens, the definition of "us" tightens. The national and sometimes regional interest tends to be prioritised above broader European ones to the extent that they differ, and under increased pressure, most people seek to seize the interest of their own family – if not of themselves personally – first. As these closer-to-personal interests are improperly mingled with the state's interests and are not necessarily aligned, the common interest – the voice of the people that serves as the basis of the state's unity – tends to become increasingly polyphonic.

The anxieties stemming from the dissolving of the invisible social glue and the self's resulting rebordering, it is argued, create a sense of ontological insecurity that in turn triggers antagonistic perceptions of difference and anti-immigrant attitudes. Instead of accuracy, to follow Chernobrov (2016, p. 596), the self becomes motivated by the avoidance of anxiety. From this perspective, the securitisation of the immigration agenda can be seen to be facilitated by a profound fear of the loss of one's own b/ordered identity and the meaning of home as a result of mixing with others. Feeling at home is thus a discriminating and differentiating phenomenon: "it necessarily divides those with whom we feel at home from the rest. If home is everywhere and we feel at home with everyone, 'home' tends to lose its meaning" (Duyvendak, 2011, p. 106).

However, by combining these various perspectives and reflecting them onto the empirical evidence, the situation comes to resemble homesickness more closely, even if you are already at home. It is a lingering feeling of acute isolation and being sorely disconnected from a self or time that no longer exists. It is a painful feeling of losing touch with reality, however utopian that may be, whereby our actions come to be guided by our imagination. Ideas of nations as "gated communities" or the EU as a "fortress" are fantasies in which there is no place for inconvenient facts. As Marcus (1979) summarised his review of *The Clash's* "Safe European Home", "home is a crueler joke than paradise". Even if it is imperfect, home is still where the heart is – and as so often in life, we tend to construct walls and barriers not so much against others but because of our own fears and the desire to safeguard what is internally fragile.

Notes

1 Machiavelli talks about *verità effettuale*. I have chosen to use a more recent translation "effectual truth" here instead of the 1966 translation of "practical truth" for clarity.
2 UNITED for Intercultural Action is the European network against nationalism, racism, fascism, and in support of migrants and refugees, consisting of more than 550 organisations from a wide variety of backgrounds, from forty-eight European countries, working together on a voluntary basis. See: unitedagainstrefugeedeaths. eu.
3 Compiled from Frontex's annual budgets (frontex.europa.eu/about-frontex/key-documents/?category=budget).
4 The Standard Eurobarometer surveys, conducted at the request of the European Commission, consist of approximately a thousand face-to-face interviews per country. All the data in this part of the chapter is derived from Standard Eurobarometer surveys 91 (spring 2019) and 92 (autumn 2019) unless otherwise specified.
5 Shakespeare, W., Hamlet: Act I, Scene V.

References

Aizenberg, M. and Geffen, M. N. (2013) Bidirectional Effects of Aversive Learning on Perceptual Acuity are Mediated by the Sensory Cortex. *Nature Neuroscience*, 16(8), pp. 994–6.
Akkerman, M. (2019) *The business of building walls*. Amsterdam: Transnational Institute.
Benedicto, A. R. and Brunet, P. (2018) *Building walls: fear and securitization in the European Union*. Barcelona: Centre Delàs d'Estudis per la Pau.
Bourdieu, P. (2000) *Pascalian meditations*, trans. R. Nice. Cambridge: Polity Press.
Bulletin of the European Union. (2001) Presidency Conclusions of the Laeken European Council (14–15 Dec. 2001), No 12. Luxembourg: Office for Official Publications of the European Communities.

Carr, M. (2012) *Fortress Europe: dispatches from a gated continent.* New York, NY: The New Press.

Chernobrov, D. (2016) Ontological Security and Public (Mis)recognition of International Crises: Uncertainty, Political Imagining, and the Self. *Political Psychology*, 37(5), pp. 581–96.

Cunningham, M. (2019) *Thinking about Thinking: Exploring Bias in Cybersecurity with Insights from Cognitive Science.* Forcepoint X-Labs whitepaper. (online) Available at: www.forcepoint.com/form/ (Accessed 9 Mar. 2020).

Cuttita P. and Last T. (2020) *Border deaths: causes, dynamics and consequences of migration-related mortality.* Amsterdam: Amsterdam University Press.

D'Alfonso, A. (2020) Migration and Border Management: Heading 4 of the 2021–2027 MFF. *European Parliamentary Research Service Blog*, 14 Feb. 2020.

Davies, J. (2016) Fear & Loathing in the EU. *The Perspective*, 28 Apr. 2016.

Della Sala, V. (2017) Homeland Security: Territorial Myths and Ontological Security in the EU. *Journal of European Integration*, 39(5), pp. 545–58.

Douglas, M. (1991) The Idea of a Home: A Kind of Space. *Social Research*, 58(1), pp. 287–307.

Duyvendak, J. W. (2011) *The politics of home belonging and nostalgia in Europe and the United States.* London: Palgrave Macmillan.

Easthope, H. (2004) A Place called Home. *Housing, Theory and Society*, 21(3), pp. 128–38.

EUobserver. (2019) *EU's Frontex border agency set for 34% budget increase.* (online) Available at: euobserver.com/tickers/145089 (Accessed 7 Apr. 2020).

European Commission. (2018) Press release IP/18/4106: EU budget: Commission proposes major funding increase for stronger borders and migration. Brussels: European Commission.

European Parliament. (2020) Press Release. Long-term EU budget: It is not possible to do more with less, say MEPs. 10 Mar. 2020.

European Security Strategy. (2003) *A Secure Europe in a Better World.* 12 Dec. 2003. (online) Available at: ue.eu.int/uedocs/cmsUpload/78367.pdf (Accessed 2 Feb. 2020).

Figlio, K. (2012) The dread of sameness. In: L. Auestad, ed., *Psychoanalysis and politics: exclusion and the politics of representation.* London: Karnac, pp. 7–24.

Finne, E. (2018) *The ethics of borders: A philosophical look at immigration.* (online) Available at: arcdigital.media/the-ethics-of-borders-e004b690e14b (Accessed 7 Apr. 2020).

Freud, S. (1923) The ego and the Id, trans. J. Strachey et al., *The Standard Edition of the Complete Psychological Works of Sigmund Freud*, Volume XIX. London: Hogarth Press.

Fried, M. (2000) Continuities and Discontinuities of Place. *Journal of Environmental Psychology*, 20(3), pp. 193–205.

Giddens, A. (1991) *Modernity and self-identity: self and society in the late modern age.* Palo Alto: Stanford University Press.

Gorman, S. E. and Gorman, J. M. (2016) *Denying to the grave: why we ignore the facts that will save us.* Oxford: Oxford University Press.

Harding, J. (2012) *Border vigils: keeping migrants out of the rich world.* London: Verso.

Hidalgo, M. C. and Hernández, B. (2001) Place Attachment: Conceptual and Empirical Questions. *Journal of Environmental Psychology*, 21(3), pp. 273–81.

Hollifield, J. (2004) The Emerging Migration State. *International Migration Review*, 38(3), pp. 885–912.

Jones, R. (2016) *Violent borders: refugees and the right to move*. London: Verso.

Juncker, J-C. (2016) State of the Union Address 2016: Towards a Better Europe – a Europe that Protects, Empowers and Defends Strasbourg, 14 September 2016. European Commission – SPEECH/16/3043.

Jünemann, A., Scherer, N., and Fromm, N., eds. (2017) *Fortress Europe? Challenges and failures of migration and asylum policies*. Cham: Springer.

Kanter, R. M. (2012) Ten Reasons People Resist Change. *Harvard Business Review*, September 25, 2012.

Kinnvall, C. (2004) Globalization and Religious Nationalism: Self, Identity, and the Search for Ontological Security. *Political psychology*, 25(5), pp. 741–67.

Kinnvall, C., Manners, I., and Mitzen, J. (2018) Ontological (In)security in the European Union. *European* Security, 27(3), pp. 249–65.

Koerner, K. (2020) *EU budget 2021–2027: Europe's future sacrificed to the status quo? Deutsche Bank Research, Talking Point 25 Feb. 2020*. Frankfurt am Main: Deutsche Bank.

Laine, J. P. (2018a) The ethics of bordering: a critical reading of the refugee "crisis". In: G. Besier and K. Stoklosa, eds., *How to deal with refugees? Europe as a continent of dreams*. Berlin: LIT Verlag, pp. 278–301.

Laine, J. P. (2018b) Conditional Welcome and the Ambivalent Self – Commentary to Gill. *Fennia*, 196(2), pp. 230–35.

Laine, J. P. (2019) Tabloid Media and the Dubious Terrain of Migration Reporting. *Ethical Space*, 16(1), pp. 34–40.

Laine, J. P. (2020a) Ambiguous bordering practices at the EU's edges. In: A. Bissonnette and É. Vallet, eds., *Borders and border walls: In-security, symbolism, vulnerabilities*. London: Routledge, pp. 69–87.

Laine, J. P. (2020b) Reframing African migration to Europe: an alternative narrative. In: I. Moyo, C. C. Nshimbi and J. P. Laine, eds., *Migration conundrums, regional integration and development: Africa-Europe relations in a changing global order*. London: Palgrave Macmillan, pp. 93–116.

Laing, R. D. (1960) *The divided self: an existential study in sanity and madness*. London: Penguin.

Lang, P., Davis, M., & Öhman, A. (2000) Fear and anxiety: Animal Models and Human Cognitive Psychophysiology. *Journal of Affective Disorders*, 61(3), pp. 137–59.

Laplanche, J. and Pontalis, J-B. (1986) Fantasy and the origins of sexuality. In: V. Burgin, J. Donald, and C. Kaplan, eds., *Formations of Fantasy*, London: Methuen, pp. 5–34.

Lefranc, F-X. (2016) Frans Timmermans: "The European project can fail". EURACTIV, 7 Nov 2016. (online) Available at: www.euractiv.com/section/euro-finance/interview/frans-timmermans-the-european-project-can-fail/ (Accessed 7 Apr. 2020).

Machiavelli, N. (1998 [1532]) *Il Principe – The Prince*, 2nd Edit, trans. H. Mansfield. Chicago: University of Chicago Press / (1966 [1532]). The Prince, trans. D. Donno. New York: Bantam Books.

Marcus, G. (1979) Review of the Clash's "Give 'Em Enough Rope". *Rolling Stone*, Jan 25, 1979.

Massey, D. B. (1994) *Space, place, and gender*. Minneapolis: University of Minnesota Press.

Mercier, H. and Sperber, D. (2017) *The enigma of reason*. Cambridge: Harvard University Press.

Michel, C. (2020) Plenary Address, the European Parliament, 10 Mar. 2020. (online) Available at: www.europarl.europa.eu/plenary/en/debate-details.html?date=20200310&detailBy=date (Accessed 27 Apr. 2020).

Mitzen, J. (2006) Ontological Security in World Politics: State Identity and the Security Dilemma. *European Journal of International Relations*, 12(6), pp. 341–70.

Mitzen, J. (2018) Feeling at Home in Europe: Migration, Ontological Security, and the Political Psychology of EU Bordering. *Political Psychology*, 39(6): pp. 1373–87.

Öhman, A. (2008) Fear and anxiety: overlaps and dissociations. In: M. Lewis, J. M. Haviland-Jones and L. F. Barrett, eds., *Handbook of emotions*. 3rd edit. New York: The Guilford Press, pp. 709–29.

Reddan, M. C., Wager, T. D., and Schiller, D. (2018) Attenuating Neural Threat Expression with Imagination. *Neuron*, 100(4), pp. 994–1005.

Rose, J. (1996) *States of fantasy*. Oxford: Oxford University Press.

Ross, L., Lepper, M. R., and Hubbard, M. (1975) Perseverance in Self-perception and Social Perception: Biased Attributional Processes in the Debriefing Paradigm. *Journal of Personality and Social Psychology*, 32(5), pp. 880–92.

Rumelili, B. (2015) Identity and Desecuritisation: The Pitfalls of Conflating Ontological and Physical Security. *Journal of International Relations and Development*, 18(1), pp. 52–74.

Scott, J. W. (2001) Fantasy Echo: History and the Construction of Identity. *Critical Inquiry*, 27(2), pp. 284–304.

Sloman, S. and Fernbach, P. (2017) *The knowledge illusion: why we never think alone*. New York: Riverhead Books.

Spear's. (2019) *The death of Europe?* Sept/Oct Issue, pp. 40–4.

Squire, V. (2017) Governing Migration through Death in Europe and the US: Identification, Burial, and the Crisis of Modern Humanism. *European Journal of International Relations*, 23(3), pp. 513–32.

Steele, B. (2008) *Ontological security in international relations*. New York: Routledge.

Tajani, A. (2018) The Migration Crisis Threatens to Destroy the EU. We Must Not Let It. *The Guardian*, 27 Jun 2018.

The Clash. (1978) *Safe European Home*. CBC Records.

UNITED. (2019) The Fatal Policies of Fortress Europe. (online) Available at: unitedagainstrefugeedeaths.eu (Accessed 20 Apr. 2020).

van Houtum, H. and Bueno Lacy, R. (2020) The Autoimmunity of the EU's Deadly B/ordering Regime; Overcoming its Paradoxical Paper, Iron and Camp Borders. *Geopolitics*, DOI: 10.1080/14650045.2020.1728743.

Žižek, S. (1997) *The plague of fantasies*. London: Verso.

14 Climate change and the migration conundrum

Addressing the elephant in the room

Felix Kwabena Donkor and Kevin Mearns

Introduction

The need to reflect on the relations between Africa and Europe is now more important than ever. While there is an apparent requirement to move beyond migration as the dominant factor defining relations and work towards more multisectoral collaboration on an equal footing, there is no denying that migration remains a matter of great concern that cannot be ignored (Laine, 2020). However, migration is a phenomenon with many bearings. With this in mind, this chapter argues that if current migration pressures are to be better understood, attention must be paid to its various root causes, one of the most important of which is climate change. We raise climate change with its many consequences as a pressing global challenge that provides an opportunity to recalibrate Africa–Europe migration patterns and the consequences for their mutual economies and societies.

Social mobility in periods of environmental flux is a common adaptation strategy (Herbeck and Flitner, 2010; Arnall and Kothari, 2015). While there have been major climatic factors in the dynamics of human settlement since ancient times, the scale and nature of this phenomenon have seen significant change over the years. An increasingly conspicuous factor in this complex dynamic is anthropogenic climate change. Human activity has led to the recorded atmospheric concentrations of greenhouse gases, especially carbon dioxide, in the atmosphere being significantly higher than their pre-industrial levels (Höök and Tang, 2013). The debate about climate change migrants – often referred to as the "human face of climate change" (Gemenne, 2011, p. 225) – has therefore gained a global research and policy focus (Klepp, 2016). Since its evolution in the 1980s, discussion of the climate–migration nexus has attracted heated debate, reflecting the competing interests and polarised topics it animates, such as northern–southern hemisphere relationships, environmental justice, and international solidarity (White, 2011; Bettini, 2014; Klepp and Herbeck, 2016).

Although the understanding of the scientific underpinnings of climate change is improving, its implications for migration remain unclear and unpredictable. Given the interplay of several socioeconomic, cultural, political,

DOI: 10.4324/9781003083726-15

and environmental influences, the formation of a linear causative association between anthropogenic climate change and migration becomes convoluted (Brown, 2008; Klepp, 2016). The World Bank's projections indicate that three regions (Latin America, Sub-Saharan Africa, and Southeast Asia) will account for 143 million more climate migrants by 2050 (Rigeau et al., 2018). The Red Cross and Red Crescent Societies' World Disasters Report indicates that there are twenty-five million "environmental refugees" who have been forced to leave their homes because of dire environmental challenges or natural disasters – a figure higher than the total recorded refugees from war and political persecution combined (Ahmed, 2018). This has implications for realising the United Nation's 2030 Agenda for Sustainable Development commitment to leave no one behind as already vulnerable communities are further compromised in their development aspirations. As the number of displaced persons according to UNHCR statistics[1] has grown to a distressing new record of more than seventy million, the Sustainable Development Goals (SDGs) of decent work and economic growth, as well as sustainable cities and communities (SDGS 8 and 11), seem increasingly unattainable.

According to the Intergovernmental Panel on Climate Change (IPCC), an intergovernmental body of the United Nations, the various agro-environmental challenges caused by climate change are likely to result in mass displacements, reaching 200 million by 2050 (IPCC, 2007). These challenges concern both time (the rapidity of change) and scale (the total of affected people), and disproportionately affect countries with different resources and capacities in adapting to external shocks. Forced migration compromises development in several ways, from placing undue pressure on infrastructure services, decline in economic development, and heightened incidences of conflict and poor health in the educational and social challenges migrant communities face (Brown, 2008; Bassett and Fogelman, 2013). Even if much of climate migration tends to be temporary (Baldwin, 2014), the question of an adaptive reaction which requires resources (monetary and social) remains. The individuals most prone to the impact of climate change are often constrained to the point that they are unable to realise their migration aspirations (Brown, 2008; Abu, Codjoe, and Sward, 2013).

This study discusses the interface of climate change and migration in the context of the EU–Africa migration conundrum. It does so by focusing on the region of Darfur (Map 14.1), which provides an illustrative case study for discussing the conundrum's fundamentals. Darfur forms a vast plateau in the west of Sudan in North Africa, with a multi-ethnic population of more than nine million and a local economy based on agriculture. It is home to some eighty tribes and ethnic groups, divided between nomads and sedentary communities. This remote region of Sudan has become internationally known largely because of the grave conflict, which has endured since 2003. Although the conflict has many dimensions, its crux comes down to environmental factors – such as encroaching desertification – which have led to considerable tension between nomadic tribes and the more established sedentary population

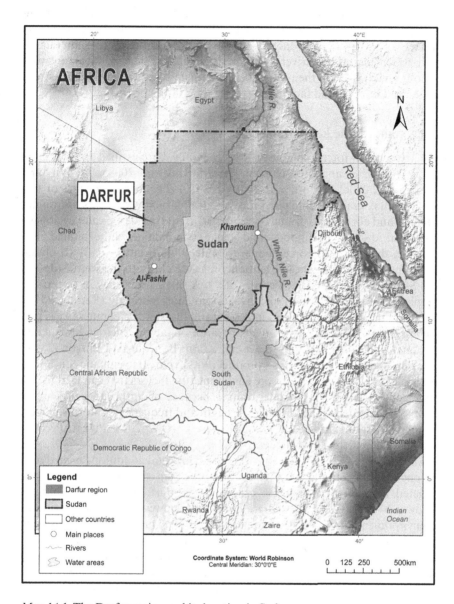

Map 14.1 The Darfur region and its location in Sudan.

over resource and land allocation. Many of Darfur's tribal groups are also known to reside elsewhere in Sudan and in bordering countries, including South Sudan, Chad, Libya, Egypt, and the Central African Republic.

This analysis examines how non-climatic factors amplify community vulnerability and migration. It situates climate change and migration in the context of key underlying factors and consequences for vulnerable communities, with implications for sustainable development goals. By illuminating impacts of environmental factors on migration and the mutual interaction with other migration drivers, the study indicates that political answers, although vital, will of themselves be inadequate to address migration's root causes and background factors.

Understanding the key variables

The triggers of forced migration can generally be classified in two main groups: climate and non-climate drivers (Brown, 2008; de Wit and Stankiewicz, 2006; Bedford and Bedford, 2010). The former consists of two components: gradual climatic processes (rain, biodiversity loss, drought, famine); and abrupt and dramatic individual events (e.g. floods and cyclones). Both can destroy livelihoods and make communities inhospitable. For example, drought may force people to walk long distances daily to obtain water, making it expedient to eventually relocate closer to the source (de Wit and Stankiewicz, 2006; Black et al., 2011). A single event may in turn cause people to leave their homes and livelihoods more abruptly (Bettini, 2014). A natural hazard only develops into a natural disaster if a community is predominantly susceptible to its effects because of factors such as low-quality buildings and poor information dissemination (Boncour and Burson, 2010). A society's susceptibility is thus a product of its *exposure* to climatic conditions and its *adaptive capacity*. The core environmental factors that can lead to displacement are increasingly deteriorating because of anthropogenic climate change. This explains the amplified strength and frequency of storms, floods, droughts, desertification, and rising sea levels (IOM, 2014; Piguet, Pécoud, and de Guchteniere, 2011; Piguet, 2013).

Successful migration to escape dire environmental conditions is mediated by one's social and financial resources, including support systems in the targeted location and financial capital to support the migration process (Brown, 2008; Castles, 2011). Migration cannot, however, be simply attributed to environmental triggers; non-climatic drivers are equally important (Brown, 2008; Donkor et al., 2019). These include land degradation, pollution, escalating population growth and urbanisation, income, and various policies, all of which influence migration patterns. This buttresses the argument that a society's susceptibility to climate impacts is not predetermined, but can be compromised or reinforced by factors not directly linked to the environment (Crate, 2011; Dietz and Garrelts, 2014). It is thus the non-climatic triggers that ensnare the vulnerable in dire conditions that can be significant causes of the challenge, even as the impact of the climate stimulus itself is felt (Donner and Webber, 2014).

The confluence of climate and socioeconomic pressures significantly accentuates the likelihood of displacement from rural environs (Hunter et al., 2012). Environmental degradation is embedded in social and spatial contexts.

This demands a structural approach to the environment in the wider political and cultural setting of an area to appreciate its influence in the dynamics of population displacement (Joarder and Miller, 2013; Marino and Lazrus, 2015). The decision to migrate is often taken at the household level and is determined by an individual's assessment of supporting resources. It is also important to understand that migration is seldom the first and preferred coping strategy for those facing climatic pressures (Brown, 2008; McKune et al., 2015). However, it is adopted in the face of limited options that may be insufficient to satisfy basic needs when external aid is not forthcoming.

Migration, particularly in reaction to slow climate processes, demands financial and social capital in the target destination (McLeman, Schade, and Faist, 2016). It has been observed that even in some of the worst unforeseen events, migrants choose to journey along pre-existing routes to locales where they have kinship ties, support systems, and historical connections, among others (Bhugra and Becker, 2005; Piguet et al., 2011). Following displacement, individuals often seek refuge within their local areas with family and friends as a first resort. In the event of failing to find refuge in their local regions, people resort to areas with pre-existing cultural or ethnic ties (Armstrong, 2007; IOM, 2014). Migration from Africa tends to occur along established routes and colonial ties; people from the Anglophone nations gravitate towards the United Kingdom, while those from Francophone countries prefer France.

Charting a path in the context of climate change

To address crucial issues of common concern, a new relationship should be built on a premise that embraces Europe and Africa, with their respective nations, as equal partners. The United Nations 2030 Agenda for Sustainable Development builds on the earlier Millennium Development Goals (MDGs) by acknowledging migration as part of sustainable development. Migration and mobility have become a cross-cutting theme that can be found in eleven out of seventeen Sustainable Development Goals. The Agenda's key theme, "leave no one behind", also necessitates addressing migrants in vulnerable situations. This makes it imperative to address core non-climatic drivers too, including government policy, population explosion, and community-level vulnerability to natural disasters which affect migrants' vulnerability.

Forced climate migrants are largely unaccounted for in international refugee and immigration policy (Brown, 2008; Hakim, 2011). There is little traction in including climate "refugees" in the general description of refugees, and mass migration is seldom addressed in national adaptation frameworks. This complicates the effective tackling of the problem. Although no global policy addresses climate migration directly, in the African context, the African Union's Agenda 2063: "The Africa We Want" equally fails in this direction. However, given that Africa is a region that is bearing the brunt of climate change impacts, the need for the continent to lead the climate–migration discussion cannot be exaggerated. This is even more the case because climate change is implicated in some of its worst conflict and displacement scenarios.

This is not, however, to deny the role of socioeconomic and political factors. A typical example is the Darfur crisis which, since its inception in 2003, has translated into catastrophic loss of life and human displacement, with climate change playing an underlying factor (Hakim, 2011). Climate change has created a platform for a number of factors to work simultaneously, exacerbating the crisis. A consequence of such a scenario for the Africa–EU migration conundrum is that the highly skilled are more likely to seek asylum or migrate to EU nations where their skills can be harnessed. This exacerbates the brain-drain phenomenon, denying the affected countries scarce skilled human resources to drive much needed development. However, the unskilled are likely to become refugees in neighbouring countries, further straining socioeconomic resources. Host nations are therefore likely to turn to the EU for further assistance, perpetuating the cycle of dependence. This suggests that the issue of climate migration must be mainstreamed in African–EU migration policies, and interventions must be made to help address the elephant in the room.

As the former UN Secretary-General Ban Ki-moon has said, human-induced climate change was a significant agent in the dynamics of the Darfur conflict. The UK's Special Representative for Climate Change prior to the UN Security Council discussion on climate change and security reported that the security implications of climate change had become more palpable (Mazo, 2009). However, given the increasing impact of climate change on our global migration dynamics, it has become imperative to go beyond rhetoric to policy action. In addressing global or cross-border challenges, terminologies are critical points of reference in guiding the requisite action.

In the climate–migration conundrum there is a heated debate about whether those engaged in climate-induced migration should be denoted as "climate refugees" or "climate migrants". The choice of an accepted definition comes with responsibilities for the global community under international law. The assigning of human rights demands both rights and obligations. The requirement to protect obligates states to safeguard persons and communities against human rights abuses. The obligation to fulfil this indicates that states need to initiate the requisite measures that secure the realisation of basic human rights. This came into play as allegations of gross human rights abuses preceded the Darfur crisis, with herdsmen, allegedly supported by the state, abusing settler farmers. The climate change–migration interface presents an interesting challenge in the African context, given that several communities are spread across national borders because of colonial history. People crossing borders may therefore not be considered *refugees* or *migrants* by their relatives and their host communities across the borders.

Some activists have advocated the use of the term *environmental refugee* or *climate refugee* to portray the pressing nature of the issue (Brown, 2008; Ahmed, 2018). They contend that such individuals must secure refuge from the consequences of climate change, whereas other terminologies dilute the urgency of victims' circumstances. The term *refugee* also echoes with the general public and elicits widespread sympathy. Others note that such a term comes with less negative undertones than *migrant*, which denotes a progression towards an enhanced lifestyle (Brown, 2008). The increase in migration flows has exposed some of the weaknesses of the EU's asylum system and has shown that the obligation to grant asylum has become increasingly conditional (Betts, 2015; Laine, 2018). Yet the Darfur crisis shows that African countries cannot afford to be conditional in dealing with the horizontal displacement that comes from climate-induced migration. This is even more the case because there are increasing calls for the decolonisation of borders (Moyo, 2020). This necessitates the addressing of cross-border migration in a way that does not affect the basic fabric of social cohesion and compromise unity as immigrants move to share and/or occupy living spaces with locals. The various stakeholders in Africa – governments, researchers, and civic society organisations, among others – have a unique opportunity to develop a local policy framework that can inform global discourse.

Others, however, consider that the term *refugee* is inappropriate to refer to people escaping environmental challenges, because it is imprecise in international law (Marino and Lazrus, 2015). This is because the UN protocol on the status of refugees indicates this should imply those escaping persecution for reasons of race, religion, nationality, membership of a particular social group, or political opinion. Another semantic complexity is that the use of the term *refugee* denotes the crossing of international frontiers. However, an individual who experiences displacement in their home country is denoted an *internally displaced person* (IDP). Since a large number of climate-induced displacement occurs within national frontiers, limiting the classification to crossing international frontiers belittles the challenge's gravity (Piguet et al., 2011). Furthermore, the notion of the term *refugee* surmises that an individual who flees can return to their home nation once the conditions that triggered their flight are normalised (Brown, 2008; Piguet et al., 2011). This is impractical in the case of climate-induced challenges such as rising sea levels. Furthermore, an expansion in the description of a refugee to embrace environmental pressures compromises the frameworks and solidarity that address refugees.

In the absence of a specific policy definition in the context of international law, affected individuals are invisible in international frameworks; no institution is tasked with garnering information on their circumstances or supplying fundamental services. The inability to authenticate political persecution in home countries results in their being unaccounted for in asylum law. The climate–migration interface presents a unique opportunity for the African continent to reconsider the issues of borders towards continental integration in accordance with the African Union's Vision 2063. Here it can also draw on the experiences and lessons of the EU that have been successful in this respect, introducing a new dynamic in their mutual collaboration.

Community-level resilience

Climate change will worsen prevailing vulnerabilities, especially in the global south, in the areas of food security, health, and freshwater provision (Donkor et al., 2019). Climate change will thus compromise the adaptive capacities of several communities and *inter alia* devastate some deteriorating prevailing challenges of food and water security. Land resources thus become unable to support livelihoods, and individuals will be impelled to move to places that offer better opportunities. This is made vivid in the context of the Darfur crisis, where nomads and resident farmers were competing for arable land to sustain their agricultural activities. The scenario in Darfur allows us to extrapolate the condition of informal traders who cross the borders of the African continent to conduct their business. These people contribute to regional integration from the grassroots, but with the erosion of livelihoods by climate impacts, their operating scope becomes crowded, pushing more people into the margins of society and compromising the SDG of decent work and community resilience, especially because the activities of these traders enhance grassroots economies.

The relatively young age of such traders (Nshimbi, 2017) is a cause of concern, because they are vulnerable to extremism. It is important that African–EU migration interventions integrate measures that enhance climate resilience at the grassroots to mitigate the impact of climate change on vulnerable livelihoods. Research collaborations and the exchange of best practices in climate adaptation will also need more focus. Africa has one of the world's youngest populations, with immense potential for development and the growth of democracy, but also conflict, all of which will directly affect Europe. The need to reflect on Africa–EU relations is now more important than ever if a new relationship that embraces EU and African nations as partners on crucial issues like combating climate change and its consequences is to be fostered.

Climate change will induce migration by causing some regions to become less habitable, disrupting the provisioning of food and water resources, and exacerbating the incidences of natural disasters like droughts and flooding. The percentage of areas experiencing constant drought is projected to rise from 2 to 10 percent by 2050 (Boyd and Roach, 2006), whilst the share of land experiencing extreme drought is forecast to escalate from the current 1 percent to 30 percent towards the turn of the twenty-first century (Burke, Brown, and Christidis, 2006). In Darfur, where sedentary farmers and nomadic groups had coexisted peacefully since antiquity (Hakim, 2011), a prolonged drought in the early nineties accentuated tensions between different groups and their competing modes of farming.

The sedentary tribes such as the Fur were landowners, while nomadic groups were given permission to graze the land. It is noteworthy that this arrangement also saw some minor clashes in the past, which were addressed by tribal leaders (Hakim, 2011). Historic accounts concur that the different livelihoods coexisted symbiotically. The complicated ethnic make-up of Darfur is of less consequence than the distinction between agriculturalists and pastoralists. The association between the two is mediated by contestation over land and water resources exacerbated by climate change. Furthermore, population growth coupled with the declining productivity of agricultural land because of poor precipitation and significant pest predation required the extension of cultivated land (Mazo, 2009). Early 2020 saw Africa's worst locust plague in decades, as billions of desert locusts (the most destructive species) unprecedentedly threatened vast areas. Climate change has been implicated as a contributing factor because it has created the environmental conditions conducive to locust infestation. The simultaneous deterioration of grazing land has resulted in nomads seeking larger pastures to sustain escalating livestock numbers. Fluctuations in the Sahel's aridity rates distort ecological zones, which affects the contestation between an area's pastoralism and agriculture. These scenarios make a case for promoting alternative livelihoods in vulnerable communities. While African nations must encourage skills training and assist people in vulnerable communities to build sustainable livelihoods, their EU partners can assist with funding and expertise.

With the increasingly palpable impact of climate change, especially seen in drought, clashes in Darfur have become more intense because of the scarcity of natural resources such as grazing land and water (Nimir, 2008). Food and water are recognised as basic physiological needs in both Maslow's hierarchy of needs (1943) and Manfred Max-Neef's taxonomy of fundamental human needs (1991), and the inability to adequately meet them leads to deprivation and desperation that are exacerbated in situations in which there are limited options, as in the context of an environmentally sensitive livelihood like farming. This complex scenario is animated in the context of the Darfur crisis, because the area has recorded a reduction in rainfall of 30 percent over an eighty-year period. The drought coincided with the escalation of the livestock and human populations. More than two million individuals experienced forced displacement, several fleeing across neighbouring borders, with the UN recording between two and five hundred thousand dead and injured people. The ensuing mass migration was unprecedented.

However, it is important to note that climate change will make previously less hospitable areas more habitable and accommodate larger populations. For example, increased temperatures will prolong planting seasons, and increased levels of CO_2 in the atmosphere are projected to improve crop yields and vegetation. In addition, fluctuation in rainfall patterns may cause increased precipitation in places that hitherto experienced water stress. This will be accentuated in the context of a warming north Atlantic, which will create more precipitation for the Sahel. Such scenarios create conducive conditions for migration. Furthermore, fluctuating climate and land use will fuel geographic range alterations in wildlife, resulting in the accumulation of novel species and opportunities for viral spread between hitherto isolated species. This will exacerbate the potential spill-over into humans – a likely connection between climate change and emerging zoonotic disease. Changing mammalian species are forecast to converge at areas with high elevations in biodiversity hotspots and in places with dense human populations, like Africa. The outbreak of the COVID-19 pandemic and shutdowns across the globe demonstrates that although external aid is important, recipient nations in Africa will also need to build the requisite policy frameworks and infrastructure to cope by themselves in its absence. The continent must thus proactively develop tailored measures that address its peculiar needs in this direction and that can inform its deliberations with external partners. Similarly, the African Union should have shown greater leadership in stemming the Darfur conflict in its early days before it escalated into a humanitarian crisis of global proportions.

Political instability and ethnic conflict

The rise in radicalism can be seen to have exacerbated the Darfur crisis. Alleged right-wing groups like the Janjaweed, a militia comprised of Sudanese Arab tribes, have been one of the main players in the Darfur conflict. While at the beginning of the crisis they were at odds with Darfur's sedentary population over natural grazing land and farmland, as rainfall dwindled and water became scarce, they have more recently battled against Darfur rebel groups, the Sudan Liberation Movement/Army, and the Justice and Equality Movement.

The conflict testifies to the increased horizontal displacement of people, which necessitates the continent's introduction of the required frameworks to address a potential upsurge in right-wing activities as the continent seeks regional integration. Mass population migrations place disparate groups in close proximity and contestation for the same resources. This can become highly volatile when there is a convergence of poor governance and deprivation, and a proliferation of arms. Additionally, increasing desertification forces farmers and herdsmen to move to areas of limited habitability or congested urban areas. This is against the backdrop of the Darfur conflict's roots in the prolonged drought that caused pastoralists and farmers to compete fiercely for scarce resources.

The UN acknowledges mass population displacements as a risk to global peace and security, particularly because they exacerbate fault lines in ethnic and social tensions. Such mass displacements in the arid or semi-arid areas where more than a third of the global populace lives will transform fragile states into failed states and heighten the pressure on surrounding nations. Darfur highlighted the fault lines in the Sudanese state and catalysed the formation of the breakaway state of South Sudan. This climate–migration nexus therefore needs to be taken seriously. Although industrialised nations will probably mitigate challenges through technological innovation and institutional redesign, poor countries are compromised in their capacity to address such challenges, given their dearth of resources and expertise. In the face of dire environmental challenges, people in poor nations will be forced to abandon affected regions, instigating conflict in host areas because of several factors. The government of Sudan might have supported the suffering farmers with agricultural inputs and subsidies in the period of the prolonged drought to assuage its debilitating effects. However, it is faulted for siding with opposing farming groups, exacerbating the conflict in the process. This poor governance resulted in intense conflict and mass migration.

The United Nations Environmental Programme (UNEP) stated that twenty-nine of the forty violent local conflicts in Darfur following independence in 1956 were associated with contestation over natural resources such as grazing and water rights. Additional empirical studies embracing the whole of Sub-Saharan Africa between 1980 and 2002 have indicated a strong correlation between annual temperature differences and the occurrence of civil war, including the associated mass migrations. The 1970–1980 drought is thus implicated in the Tuareg Rebellion in northern Mali between 1990 and 1995, in which migrating youth were radicalised in neighbouring Algeria and Libya. Africa is often erroneously depicted as a "continent on the move", with excessive African migration increasingly moving towards Europe, fuelled by poverty and violence (Laine, 2020). However, the Darfur crisis demonstrates there is more internal migration, with climate migration driving the regular emigration of Africa's skilled human resources to Europe. Africa–Europe relations need to be critically recalibrated with the times for the opportunities to be grasped.

Conclusions

Africa is home to some of the world's youngest populations, with immense potential for development and the growth of democracy. However, it is a continent of many enduring conflicts, which collectively also have a bearing on its relationship with Europe. With the palpable impact of climate change affecting all segments of global interactions, it has become necessary to reflect on Africa–EU relations to develop a new relationship in which EU and African nations are partners in critical issues like climate change and its implications for their partnership. This is animated in the complex of the Darfur crisis, with key implications for global migration policy and sustainable development. Climate change is recognised as a core challenge to realising global sustainable development, affecting present models of growth and poverty alleviation, while exacerbating injustice and vulnerability.

This study demonstrates that the climate interacts with contingent social and political factors to amplify their consequences in the dynamics of Africa–EU population migration. While other variables like poor governance and institutions are also important, giving focus to the increasing influence of climate change in the migration conundrum is key to rolling out appropriate measures that will effectively address the associated challenges. An apt terminology and description of climate-induced migrants is a key step in this scenario to address climate migration, both inside and outside the continent.

A key takeaway from the COVID-19 pandemic outbreak and shutdowns across the globe is the need for locally tailored and resilient policy framework and infrastructure.

Africa's acknowledgement as a region bearing the brunt of climate change makes it imperative for a more comprehensive approach to addressing the multidimensional impacts of climate change on all facets of the continent's sustainable development, including migration. However, the lack of policy direction is a major hurdle to tackling the climate-induced migration conundrum, even as evidence points to worsening impacts. A political solution to this complex problem, although crucial, does not eliminate the underlying factors amplified by climate change. This indicates that other related factors such as good governance, communal resilience, and robust conflict resolution mechanisms need to act in concert in effectively addressing the complexity of climate-induced migration. Countries in Africa need to prioritise climate mitigation interventions in vulnerable areas where climate sensitive livelihoods predominate, while creating more opportunities for its skilled resource in a framework of public–private partnerships. This can be complemented with EU support as well as the exchange of expertise and best practice.

Note

1 UNHCR Figures at a Glance, www.unhcr.org/figures-at-a-glance.html.

References

Abu, M., Codjoe, S. N. A., and Sward, J. (2013) Climate change and internal migration intentions in the forest-savannah transition zone of Ghana. *Population and Environment*, 35(4), pp. 341–64.

Ahmed, B. (2018) Who takes responsibility for the climate refugees? *International Journal of Climate Change Strategies and Management*, 10(1), pp. 5–26.

Armstrong, H. (2007) Making the unfamiliar familiar: Research journeys towards understanding migration and place. *Landscape Research*, 29(3), pp. 237–60.

Arnall, A. and Kothari, U. (2015) Challenging climate change and migration discourse: Different understandings of timescale and temporality in the Maldives. *Global Environmental Change*, 31, pp. 199–206.

Baldwin, A. (2014) Pluralising climate change and migration: An argument in favour of open futures. *Geography Compass*, 8(8), pp. 516–28.

Bassett, T. J. and Fogelman, C. (2013) Déjà vu or something new? The adaptation concept in the climate change literature. *Geoforum*, 48, pp. 42–53.

Bedford, R. and Bedford, C. (2010) International migration and climate change: A post-Copenhagen perspective on options for Kiribati and Tuvalu. In P. Boncour and B. Burson (eds.), Climate Change and Migration: South Pacific Perspectives. Wellington, NZ: Institute of Policy Studies, Victoria University, pp. 89–135.

Bettini, G. (2014) Climate migration as an adaption strategy: De-securitizing climate-induced migration or making the unruly governable? *Critical Studies on Security*, 2(2), pp. 180–95.

Betts, A. (2015) The normative terrain of the global refugee regime. *Ethics & International Affairs,* 29(4), pp. 363–75.

Black, R., Adger, W. N., Arnell, N. W., Dercon, S., Geddes, A., and Thomas, D. S. G. (2011) The effect of environmental change on human migration. *Global Environmental Change,* 21(1), pp. 3–11.

Boncour, P. and Burson, B. (2010) Climate change and migration in the South Pacific Region: Policy perspectives. In: B. Burson (ed.), *Climate Change and Migration: South Pacific Perspectives.* Wellington: Institute of Policy Studies, pp. 5–29.

Boyd, S. and Roach, R. (2006) *Feeling the Heat: Why Governments Must Act to Tackle the Impact of Climate Change on Global Water Supplies and Avert Mass Movement of Climate Change Refugees.* London: Tearfund.

Brown, O. (2008) Migration and climate change. IOM Migration Research Series Nos. 31.

Bhugra, D. and Becker, M. A. (2005) Migration, cultural bereavement and cultural identity. *World Psychiatry,* 4(1), pp. 18–24.

Burke, E. J., Brown, S. J., and Christidis, N. (2006) Modelling the recent evolution of global drought and projections for the twenty-first century with the Hadley Centre climate model, *Journal of Hydrometeorology,* 7, pp. 15–30.

Castles, S. (2011) Concluding remarks on the climate change–migration nexus. In: E. Piguet, A. Pécoud, and P. de Guchteneire, eds, *Migration and Climate Change.* Cambridge: Cambridge University Press, 415–27.

Crate, S. (2011) Climate and culture: Anthropology in the era of contemporary climate change. *Annual Review of Anthropology,* 40(1), 175–94.

de Wit, M. and J. Stankiewicz. (2006) Changes in surface water supply across Africa with predicted climate change. *Science,* 311(5769), pp. 1917–21.

Dietz, M. and Garrelts, H., eds. (2014) *Routledge Handbook of the Climate Change Movement.* London & New York: Routledge.

Donkor, F. K., Howarth, C., Ebhuoma, E., Daly, M., Vaughan, C., Pretorius, L., Mambo, J., MacLeod, D., Kythreotis, A., Jones, L., Grainger, S., Golding, N., and Anderson, J. A. (2019) Climate services and communication for development: The role of early career researchers in advancing the debate. *Environmental Communication,* 13(5), pp. 561–66.

Donner, S. D. and Webber, S. (2014) Obstacles to climate change adaptation decisions: A case study of sea-level rise and coastal protection measures in Kiribati. *Sustainability Science,* 9(3), pp. 331–45.

Gemenne, F. (2011) How they became the human face of climate change. Research and policy interactions in the birth of the "environmental migration" concept. In: E. Piguet, A. Pecoud and P. De Guchteneire, eds, *Migration and Climate Change.* Cambridge and Paris: Cambridge University Press/UNESCO, pp. 225–60.

Hakim S. (2011) The role of climate change in the Darfur crisis. In: W. Leal Filho, ed., *The Economic, Social and Political Elements of Climate Change.* Berlin, Heidelberg: Springer, pp. 815–23.

Höök, M. and Tang, X. (2013) Depletion of fossil fuels and anthropogenic climate change: A review. *Energy Policy,* 52 (C), 797–809.

Herbeck, J. and Flitner, M. (2010) "A new enemy out there"? Der Klimawandel als Sicherheitsproblem. *Geographica Helvetica,* 65(3), pp. 198–206.

Hunter, L., Leyk, S., Maclaurin, G., Nawrotzki, R., Twine, W., Collinson, M., and Erasmus, B. (2012) *Variation by geographic scale in the migration–environment association: Evidence from rural South Africa.* Institute of Behavioral Science Working Paper. Boulder, CO: University of Colorado.

IOM. (2014) *IOM outlook on migration, environment and climate change.* Geneva: International Organization for Migration.

IPCC. (2007) *Working group II contribution to the intergovernmental panel on climate change fourth assessment report climate change 2007.* (online) Available at: www.ipcc. ch/site/assets/uploads/2018/03/ar4_wg2_full_report.pdf (Accessed 9 Feb. 2020).

Joarder, M. A. M. and Miller, P. W. (2013) Factors affecting whether environmental migration is temporary or permanent: Evidence from Bangladesh. *Migration and Global Environmental Change – Review of Drivers of Migration*, 23(6), pp. 1511–24.

Klepp, S. (2016) *Climate Change and Migration. Oxford Research Encyclopedias, Climate Science.* Oxford: Oxford University Press.

Klepp, S. and Herbeck, J. (2016) The politics of environmental migration and climate justice in the Pacific region. *Journal of Human Rights and the Environment*, 7(1), pp. 54–73.

Laine, J. (2018) The ethics of bordering: a critical reading of the refugee "crisis". In: G. Besier and K. Stokłosa, eds, *How to Deal with Refugees? Europe as a Continent of Dreams.* Berlin: LIT Verlag, pp. 278–301.

Laine, J. (2020) Reframing African migration to Europe: An alternative narrative. In: I. Moyo, C. C. Nshimbi, and J. P. Laine, eds, *Migration Conundrums, Regional Integration and Development: Africa–Europe Relations in a Changing Global Order.* London: Palgrave Macmillan, pp. 93–116.

Maslow, A. H. (1943) A theory of human motivation. *Psychological Review*, 50(4), pp. 370–96.

Marino, E. and Lazrus, H. (2015) Migration or forced displacement? The complex choices of climate change and disaster migrants in Shishmaref, Alaska, and Nanumea, Tuvalu. *Human Organization*, 74(4), pp. 341–50.

Max-Neef, M. A. (1991) *Human Scale Development: Conception, Application and Further Reflections.* New York: Apex Press.

Mazo, J. (2009) Chapter three: Darfur: The first modern climate-change conflict. *The Adelphi Papers*, 49(409), pp. 73–86.

McKune, S. L., Borresen, E. C., Young, A. G., Ryley, T. D. A., Russo, S. L., Camara, A. D., Coleman, M., and Ryan, E. P. (2015) Climate change through a gendered lens: Examining livestock holder food security. *Global Food Security*, 6, pp. 1–8.

McLeman, R., Schade J., and Faist T., eds (2016) *Environmental Migration and Social Inequality.* New York: Springer.

Moyo, I. (2020) On decolonising borders and regional integration in the Southern African Development Community (SADC) region. *Social Sciences, MDPI, Open Access Journal*, 9(4), 1–12.

Nshimbi, C. C. (2017) The human side of regions: Informal cross-border traders in the Zambia–Malawi–Mozambique growth triangle and prospects for integrating Southern Africa, *Journal of Borderlands Studies*, 35(1), pp. 75–97.

Nimir, M. (2008) The environmental roots of Darfur problem. In: N. Najmeldeen, ed., *Issues of Nomads and Peace.* Khartoum, Sudan: Amal Center, Khartoum, pp. 29–37.

Piguet, E. (2013) From "primitive migration" to "climate refugees": The curious fate of the natural environment in migration studies. *Annals of the Association of American Geographers*, 103(1), pp. 148–62.

Piguet, E., Pécoud, A., and de Guchteneire, P. (2011) Introduction: migration and climate change. In: E. Piguet, A. Pécoud, and P. de Guchteneire, eds, *Migration and Climate Change*. Cambridge: Cambridge University Press, pp. 225–59.

Rigeau, K. K., de Sherbinin, A., Jones, B, Bergmann, J., Clement, V., Ober, K., Schewe, J., Adamo, S., McCusker, B., Heuser, S., and Midgley, A. (2018) Groundswell: Preparing for internal climate migration. The World Bank. (online) Available at: openknowledge.worldbank.org/handle/10986/29461 (Accessed 9 April 2020).

White, G. (2011) *Climate Change and Migration: Security and Borders in a Warming World*. Oxford and New York: Oxford University Press.

15 Unveiling the Afro-European common geo-cultural space

Olukayode A. Faleye

Introduction

The notion of disruption, the structural dislocation of a population, is central to the securitisation of transborder migration in world history. Environmental, socioeconomic, and political disruptions stimulate international migration, yet immigration has been linked to environmental, socioeconomic, and political disruptions in receiving countries. The cornerstone of anti-immigration movements affirms that immigration disrupts labour markets by harrowing employment opportunities and emoluments, pressurises public infrastructure and services, distorts cultural and racial homogeneity, and depletes limited environmental endowments (Baker and Tsuda, 2015). These myths of "otherness" engendered by identity insecurity and endangerment, promote "damaging metaphors" that securitise migrant and rationalise injustice and human rights abuses, as well as obliterating human dignity (Laine, 2020). In the context of European Union (EU)–Africa relations, this is particularly complicated, given the biological and cultural "otherness" of interregional migrants. Interregional migration between Africa and the EU has followed a racial pathology that projects the mythology of foreign invasion and security breach. However, studies have shown that disruptions are not determined by the nature of migrants but by the resilience of the host communities in embracing social flexibility and accommodating innovation as engines of development in an interconnected world (Baker and Tsuda, 2015; Laine, 2018a).

The unpleasant implications of the securitisation of immigration, restrictive border control against irregular migrants, and related human rights violations have been well articulated in the literature (de Haas, 2008; Pradella and Taghdisi Rad, 2017; Gammeltoft-Hansen and Tan, 2017; Faleye, 2019a; Laine, 2018b). Migration as an engine of interregional mutual development within the framework of EU–Africa relations has, however, remained under-studied. It is the aim of this chapter to plug this gap in our knowledge. The argumentation presented here stems from the premise that interregional relations are inevitable in a world characterised by resource scarcity and inequality. However, the contestation of human and material resources

DOI: 10.4324/9781003083726-16

across socially constructed state-centric boundaries has led to theoretical multiplicity in explaining the operationalisation of the international system (Faleye, 2020). This chapter draws insights from the social construction of international relations as enlightened by the systemic processes of a multi-cultural global world system in which humanity, and by extension migration, constitutes the most dynamic resource in interregional development. The study is based on the content and context analysis of government records, newspaper reports, ethnographic surveys, and the extant literature on migration and international development.

Conceptual clarifications

Borders are social constructs that define "otherness" in the distribution of socioeconomic and political resources in society (Baud and Van Schendel, 1997), whereas borderlands are areas under the influence of borders. Thus, the construction of borders facilitates changes ingrained in the conduit of opportunities for state and non-state actors in border regions (Nugent, 2002). While immigration regulations construct borders at the margin of the state, immigration policy enforces boundaries at the centre of sovereign territory. In essence, international migration, that is, human movement across international borders, is shaped by socially constructed identities within national territories. Identity formation in national territories and regions thus evolves from normative and material structures which inform regulations on the nature of international relations in a structural world system.

Indeed, state policies are the product of socialisation derived from the negotiation of social norms by human agencies. Borders, like anti-virus software, serve as a filtering tool, configured to eliminate unwanted malicious identities across socio-spatial networks. This is particularly true of the EU's migration policy, in which the fallacy of identity contamination and spoliation reinforces border securitisation. This scenario has engendered a growing consensus among some politicians and electorates that unwanted migrants, tagged as intruders, impurities, vagabonds, and fresh-from-the-boat, deserve elimination, irrespective of the EU's supposed fundamental values and rapidly eroding grand narratives of human rights, freedom, and justice (Laine, 2020). This explains why international migration policies, rather than being ethical, have been rationally political, deriving their core from domestic politics and international economics, as conceived by actors in international society.

The notion of "development" is often associated with demand and supply, and, by implication, production and market. However, the localisation of production and markets produces inequality, as exemplified by the widening gap in economic growth between the "developed" and "developing" world, "First" and "Third" worlds, "global north" and "global south" (Rist, 2008). Thus, rooting the idea of development in these traditional elements suggests development studies legitimise poverty, underdevelopment, and inequality in the global world system. This explains why the economic and political tool of migration control has been used to negate human rights and obstruct economic empowerment in the world. The uneven development in the global world system means that the developmental paradigm should be restructured to embrace inclusive and complementary development within and between geo-cultures. According to Wendt (1992, p. 406), "it is through reciprocal interaction, in other words, that we create and instantiate the relatively enduring social structures in terms of which we define our identities and interests". A space of "anarchy" emerges from "competitive institutions" rather than in "cooperative ones", where interests evolve in a mutually benevolent manner. Thus, migration flow and regulations between Africa and Europe provide an insight into the nature of identity formation, interregional developmental trajectories, and the prospects of EU–Africa relations in the global system.

The material and ideological benefits of migration in sending and receiving countries depict the nexus between migration and development (de Haas, 2005; Adams and Page, 2005; Beauchemin, 2018). In this vein, borders serve as social constructs, built on identities and often sanctioned to utter the natural sequence of the world's circulatory system, which create scarcity or surplus values. In a globalising world, the shift of migration pattern in tandem with the geo-cultural transition in socioeconomic and political structure is inevitable. These circuitous patterns of migration emphasise the importance of international wage disparities, labour conditions, the cost of migration, the market, and social networks as determinants of trans-border migration flows (Taylor, 1986; Todaro, 1989).

In line with world system theory, "migration is a natural outgrowth of disruptions and dislocations that inevitably occur in the process of capitalist development" (Massey et al., 1993, p. 445). The expansion of western capitalism has incorporated different parts of the world into the world market economy, yet, as Wallerstein (2004) observes, the peripheral regions of the global world system assume a somewhat static and subservient role in their relations with core areas. The interconnectivity of African development with the development and processes of the global political economy is well articulated in the literature (Prestholdt, 2008; Moyo, 2009; Taylor, 2009). Rather than constituting a peripheral position in the global system, African nations are important actors and agencies in the currency of the global economy and politics (Falola and Achberger, 2013).

For example, the African developmental catastrophe offers financial and business opportunities for brave investors that somehow meet local social needs at the micro level. Africa has been adjudged the last frontier of capitalism, ingrained with a distinct socioeconomic environment and business dynamism. This appears to have bred an emerging crop of "Africapitalists" – local entrepreneurs who struggle to surmount the poor business environment engendered by political bankruptcy in providing the required business infrastructure and employment opportunities, alleviating poverty, and thus contributing to African development (Amaeshi, Okupe, and Idemudia, 2018). The contributions of the emerging Africapitalists to the provision of new wage streams may help reduce the exodus of youthful African labour resources from the region.

The African diaspora in the EU constitutes an important pool of Africapitalists, empowered by exposure to innovations for development in Africa. Hence, the evolution of Africapitalism is a form of "glo-capitalism", that is, the adaptation of a global capitalism with distinct qualities to the local business environment. However, the extent to which the emerging movement of glo-capitalism can redirect the lever of development in Africa, given the fragility of governance and the political economy of development in the global world system, remains to be seen in the long run.

World system theory provides a systemic explanation for international migration based on the transition to structured productive capacity in a globalising world. In contrast to Wallerstein's definition of a periphery, peripheries or margins are here conceived as the geo-cultural borderlands that are symptomatic of the advances and transitory waves of world systems. In this vein, whereas the "core", otherwise presented here as the "inner core", of the global world system refers to the several areas of power with the strongest regulatory influence on the world production and distribution network, the "peripheries" or "margins" are adapted as the "outer core", that is, the many volatile regions or zones where differential valuation has found expression in multiple socioeconomic and political forms, as well as migration networks that often provoke transitory change in the global world system. The scientific study of the fluid mechanics of the solar system affirms the differential role of the outer and inner cores of the planetary centre in engendering the earth's magnetic field (Le Bars and Lecoanet, 2020). This scientific principle is adapted here to illuminate the geo-cultural dynamics of the global system. Thus, as the outer core at the planetary centre is distinct from the solid inner core and responsible for generating the earth's magnetic field, the outer cores affect transition in the global world system.

While the EU is currently an inner core space, Africa represents one of the transitory and dynamic outer cores – a master key of the emerging global system. The regulation of nature and culture with respect to natural and human resources in the global world system gravitates towards the production of surplus values at the inner core. This has implications for the international migration flow from the outer core. In essence, borders and migration are resources in the global world system. Borders reinforce otherness, and by extension, the interregional developmental divide. Hence, bordering has endured as a vital resource in the hands of nationalist groups seeking to sustain the global world system's socioeconomic and political disequilibrium. Historically, migration serves as a resource that bridges trans-border disparities for cooperation or discord. Hence, the impact of the border–migration nexus on geo-cultural development depends on the social construction of interregional identities.

Reframing borders in the global world system

The policy framework for immigration control is built on limited micro perspectives, thereby tilting towards restrictive state-centric approaches in a globalising world. However, the pattern of international migration exemplifies the nature of geo-cultures and their systemic functioning over time. Indeed, the world has changed in line with alterations to inter-social networks involving migration, trade, warfare, intercultural encounter, and information dispersal (Chase-Dunn and Hall, 1997; Chase-Dunn and Manning, 2002). The history of the world is a history of the emergence, advances, and transition of geo-cultures of production and distribution, as well as the socio-spatial shift in the inner and outer cores of the world system and the expansion of geo-cultures through the incorporation of new areas. Migration was central to the functionality and transition of these systems from the pre-capitalist to the modern capitalist era. Thus, the macro-analysis of the modus operandi of migration in the developmental processes of the global world system provides a rich historical basis for the evaluation of the migration–development nexus in EU–Africa relations.

The emergence of the earliest world system in the Neolithic Age, marking the onset of the domestication of plants and animals, witnessed the evolution of early states, which served as the most popular units of interconnected societies' socioeconomic and political organisation. The evolution of the state followed systemic waves of expansion through incorporation and mergers (Wilkinson, 1995, 2000; Chase-Dunn and Hall, 1997; Zinkina et al., 2019). As Amin (2011, p. 12) observes, "societies prior to the sixteenth century were in no way isolated from one another but were competitive partners within at least regional systems (and perhaps even a world system). Overlooking their interaction, one can hardly understand the dynamics of their evolution". Using the world map of 1530 as an example, Rosenberg (2016) illustrates the cohabitation of distinct societies in the world system based on different regional civilisations, histories, cultural worldviews, and politics, as well as structures ranging from proto-states, states, empires, and nomadism to hunter-gatherer societies. The interaction of these different societies resulted in the exchange of technologies and ideas from China and the Middle East to Europe, stimulating the Renaissance, for example. Further, the European age of discovery and the subsequent European exodus led to the conquest of America in the sixteenth century, thereby empowering Europe through the wealth accrued from the exploitation of America's substantial solid mineral deposits and labour resources.

This transboundary migration scenario advanced the European conquest of other geo-cultures because it facilitated an unprecedented European encroachment into Asia and Africa, and the rise of western civilisation. As Trotsky (1930) notes, the law of "unevenness" in the "historic process" is most obvious in the developmental disparity in the global world system. This assertion is informed by the political economy of uneven international development, which led the Soviet Union to experiment with several developmental frameworks in the first half of the twentieth century. Indeed, uneven development, uneven resources, and scarcity within geo-cultural spaces necessitated an unprecedented drive of "external necessity" encouraged by the privileges of historical inequality, advances in communications technology, and migration impulses which conceived the modern era alongside global capitalism (Chase-Dunn and Hall, 1997; Hall, 2018).

The interaction between geo-cultures, as well as the communities, ethnic groups, and races within them, creates stereotypical images that, over time, constitute identities nurturing the social pathologies of relations. Of vital importance to this discourse is the transition of the African and European imagery in the world system due to Afro–European relations. The image here constitutes the core of interracial identities in EU–Africa relations. As Lasisi (2011, p. 4) observes, the image or identity of a people is a "creation of man arising from his perception of people and things ... a product of where the perceiver lives ... the environment and the nature of his or her conquest of it". While societies and groups of people evolved in distinct spaces with different paces of development engendered by their eco-technological and eco-social transition, the relations along this landscape of uneven development were inevitable. Thus, intergroup, interracial, and interregional relations bred social pathologies based on the perception of identities. The attendant cultural conflict often led to coercion and the expansion of geo-cultures through the incorporation of new areas afforded by uneven technological evolution.

The earliest Afro–European relations were the interactions between Egyptian and Greco-Roman societies. Afro–European relations by the sixteenth century were such that technological evolution in Europe was not superior to what was obtainable in Africa. In the area of architectural technology, European travellers around the sixteenth century reportedly observed that the handsomeness of the buildings in the city of Kilwa in western Sudan was comparable to what existed in Portuguese cities. Benin in the Niger Delta was considered a great city with advanced infrastructure beyond that in the Dutch cities of late Medieval Europe. The concept of Africa in Europe as a "land of great civilisation", "sunny", "full of fruits", and "free from cold and horror" showcases a positive African identity at the onset of Afro–European relations (Lasisi, 2011). The continuum of European relations with Africa is inevitable due to the contiguity of the two continents. However, European exploration of the wider world and its resulting labour extraction from Africa through the transatlantic slave trade by the seventeenth century opened a new chapter of dehumanised African imagery and identity. The partnership between African political elites and European slave merchants ensured the remoulding of the African identity as synonymous with slavery and stupidity, marked by the rape, murder, and captivity of a significant portion of the continent's labour force. Subsequently, Euro–African relations became synonymous with master–slave relations. Indeed, by the turn of the nineteenth century, Afro–European relations had culminated in a disaster for African identity and a developmental trajectory that set in motion the colonisation of the continent and its incorporation into the Eurocentric world empire.

While nationalism, and most importantly, the transition from the Age of Empire to a global world market system, liquidated colonialism in the aftermath of World War II, at independence the African political elites returned shockingly to primitive accumulation through reckless corruption in public service, constituting nothing less than the proxies of the new Eurocentric empire built on the global market economy. In essence, Africa has been funding European development for more than three hundred years. As Tafirenyika (2013) observes, "between $1.2 trillion and $1.4 trillion has left Africa in illicit financial flows between 1980 and 2009". The UN Economic Commission on Africa reported that capital flight through the illicit conduit of financial flows costs Africa about $150 billion per year "compared with the $57 billion it receives in aid" (UNECA, 2018).

The EU is the top destination of funds stolen from the African treasury. In 2016, the chairperson of the African Union Commission (AUC), Nkosazana Dlamini Zuma, lamented that "there are illicit funds from Africa in European banks. We started discussions with the European Union some years ago to bring back these funds. We find it morally and economically good for the banks to send the funds back" (*Business Daily*, 2016). This exemplifies the continuous gravitation of African resources towards the inner core of the global world system in spite of the outer core's political independence. The outcome of European imperial exploitation and the self-inflicted injury of resource misappropriation by African elites is widespread poverty, insecurity, political instability, and the rising informal dimension of south–north migration waves. Metaphorically, it appears "irregular" migrants from Africa, although constituting a minority group of immigrants in Europe, are increasingly moving into Europe in search of their stolen developmental funds.

The incorporation of Africa into the Eurocentric post-colonial world structure found expression in the economic shock to the continent following the capitalist recession of the 1970s. This marked a major turn towards Eurocentric capitalist institutionalised coercion. This has been particularly true since the 1980s, when the International Monetary Fund (IMF), World Bank, and the Paris Club, among others, ensured the gatekeeping of African economies through loan conditionalities and externally supervised Eurocentric fiscal policies. The passive acceptance of a peripheral position offered by the capitalist inner core would ensure the endurance of Africa's underdevelopment in the world system, because "active intervention of the market alienation" lies "behind the capital accumulation that governs" the market economy (Amin, 2010, p. 113).

Unfortunately, Amin's call for a "delinking" from the Eurocentric geocultural space is undermined by African political elites, who have demonstrated a lack of goodwill towards development, seeking instead to assimilate into the Eurocentric world system from an advantageous position of political elitism and the opportunistic privileges it confers (Faleye, 2019b). At the same time, the African political elite class continues to maintain a stranglehold on regional structures through political landlordship. An internal response to the crisis of the state in Africa is the Africapitalism that seeks to cushion the effect of misgovernance, thus filling the vacuum of internal political development machinery. Interregional migration between Africa and the EU is significant in this regard, because the bulk of educated migrant returnees may constitute the heart of this new glocal form of capitalism – "glo-capitalism". However, the Africapitalists, the drivers of glo-capitalism in Africa, contend with the internal political cancer that has found expression in poor governance and global structural imperialism.

Irregular migration in the south–north flow is a product of uneven places, spaces, and, by extension, development between Europe and Africa. The EU's draconian approach to trans-border migration from Africa, illustrated by its external border policy, reveals the EU's identity and its traditional perception of African identity. The informal migration of Africans to Europe is seen as a burden. The contending narratives in the literature focus on the resolution of this mythological international challenge as propounded by the deterrence and humanitarian schools of thought (De Haas, 2008; Gammeltoft-Hansen, 2011; del Valle, 2016; Gammeltoft-Hansen and Tan, 2017; Faleye, 2019a). Indeed, the "nature of migration control in the international system is pre-determined by the global hierarchies of knowledge and power" (Faleye, 2019a, p. 61). In essence, the conceptualisation of the categories of migration in international law projects the coloniality of European imperialism into the global world system. Thus, migration categories such as refugees fleeing war and irregular migrants illegally traversing international borders serve as Eurocentric instruments of bordering in which unwanted migrants are excluded without consideration of their human rights.

Whereas the EU discourages the free interregional movement of people between western Europe and Africa, it desperately clamours for the free movement of goods across the two regions. This is contradictory. It reveals the endurance of economic imperialism in the EU's Africa policy. For example, the history of the European joint strategy in Africa can be traced to the European Economic Community's (EEC) Articles 131, 132, and 133 of the Treaty of Rome (1957), which emphasised the need to cement relationships between the European colonisers, especially France, and their ex-colonies, based on the principle of a preferential free trade system (Treaty of Rome (1957), Articles 131–133, 46–48). These principles were reiterated and reviewed in subsequent treaties. This metamorphosed into the Yaoundé I and II Conventions of 1963 and 1969, which sought economic and technological cooperation between the EEC and some African states. The machinations of the Treaties of Rome and Yaoundé are seen as a French project to perpetually keep its ex-colonies under control through multilateral institutionalism in the name of the EEC (Zartman, 1976; Grilli, 1996; Arts and Dickson, 2004; Brown, 2017). This is an ideology embraced in principle by Britain under the European Community (EC), marking the incorporation of "Associate"

Anglophone African countries in the Community since 1975 (Grilli, 1996; Arts and Dickson, 2004).

The United Kingdom's membership of the European Economic Community in 1973 set the pace for the inclusion of British ex-colonies in Africa and the Caribbean in the EEC framework for interregional economic cooperation, consummated in the Lomé Convention of 1975. The convention was built on five fundamental but interwoven principles. The principle of non-reciprocity in trade commitments entailed a deliberate imbalance between the obligations undertaken by the European Economic Community (EEC) and the African, Caribbean, and Pacific Group of States (ACP). Second, it affirmed that goods from the ACP could be admitted into the EEC duty-free and in unlimited quantities, while EEC-manufactured goods were subject to tariffs in the ACP region. Third, the Lomé Convention stipulated freedom of international trading policies for the ACP countries, provided the policies were indiscriminate. Fourth, it created an institutional framework based on the provision of a bilateral forum of ACP/EEC countries to resolve problems of commercial policy. Finally, the convention encouraged trade promotion between member states through liaison bodies.

The Lomé I Convention provided financial assistantship through the instrument of the Système de Stabilisation des Recettes d'Exportation (STABEX), which aimed to stabilise the export earnings of the ACP countries through grants from the EEC in the event of fluctuation in the price of primary commodities in the international market. As Paterson and Virk (2014) note, ACP–EEC cooperation ultimately showcased an unequal partnership because the dependence of the ACP on the European Development Fund (EDF) had undermined the former's negotiating power in trade policies by the 1980s. In essence, the ACP–EEC relationship was built on colonial connection and unequal endowments, which metamorphosed into a neo-colonial framework of interregional economic relations.

The aid-focused agenda ingrained in the Lomé II Convention of 1980 gave way to human rights concerns and governance in Africa by 1985, when the Lomé III Convention was consummated. The end of the Cold War in 1990 marked the inauguration of the Lomé IV Convention. However, the need for western Europe to look towards its eastern neighbours in the ex-Soviet sphere of influence undermined African partnership with the EEC in the early 1990s. Hence, structural adjustment programmes, human rights, and democratic values became conditions for the sustenance of African association with the EU (Crawford, 1996, Whiteman, 1998; Lister, 1998). The onset of the twenty-first century witnessed a framework for the Economic Partnership Agreements (EPA) based on the 2000 Cotonou agreement (Arts and Dickson, 2004). It appears the rise of China and its south–south economic diplomacy informed the EU's push for a common market with Africa.

Moving forward, whereas the density of intraregional migration within Africa supersedes the migration pattern between the EU and Africa, the rising tide of nationalist parties within the EU has engendered restrictive immigration policies in Europe. This restrictive approach is arguably "harmful" and creates "perverse" effects by reducing the formality of migration, boosting the business of human trafficking, increasing the numbers of undocumented migrants, encouraging xenophobia and human rights abuses, fostering the desire for permanent residence, and obstructing the natural sequence of circular migration (de Haas, 2005; de Haas, Castles, and Miller, 2019). Indeed, the oral testimonies of repatriated Nigerian migrants show that the migration wave from Sub-Saharan Africa to Europe is mainly influenced by economic factors – the need to improve personal and family economic power through legitimate employment in a foreign territory that is perceived to be flourishing.

The significance of the migration–development nexus has been anchored by its implications for development in migrant-sending regions by the effect of migrant remittances and their impact on production and labour productivity in migrants' receiving countries. In this vein, the increase in south–north migration has followed an increase in the money remitted by migrants to the developing countries. The estimates and projections of the migrant remittance flow to Sub-Saharan Africa stood at USD 32 billion in 2010, USD 43 billion (2015), USD 46 billion (2018), and USD 48 billion (2019) (World Bank 2019). While studies have shown the considerable impact of migrant remittances in poverty alleviation in migrant-sending countries, their effects are often micro, at household levels (de Haas, 2005; Adams and Page, 2005; Mohapatra, Ratha, and Scheja, 2010). Besides migrant remittances as an engine of development in the countries of origin, migration ensures the adequate supply of labour in the destination countries required for industrial production and innovation. It also provides scarce social services such as adult care and childcare, thereby improving welfare and labour productivity (Ortega and Peri, 2009; Peri and Spaber, 2009).

The demographic, political, and economic changes and the social disparity between the EU and Africa, as well as the geostrategic contingency of the two regions, stir the cycles of interregional migration. Thus, in harnessing migration for development, understanding the multiple interactions of these factors at the interregional level is important for the reconstruction of a mutually benevolent Afro–European identity and geo-culture. In contrast to the rapid growth rate of the African population following political independence in the 1960s, the EU has experienced a declining rate in population growth. The EU is the world's most rapidly ageing region after Japan. While this phenomenon may indicate a growing standard of living and increasing life expectancy, it also reveals an increasingly low fertility rate and declining labour resources. The EU is projected to experience a declining population trend, with the number of deaths outnumbering the number of births; by 2050 the number of people older than sixty-five is expected to be more than those younger than twenty-five (United Nations, 2019). However, this figure does not take the demographic effect of the COVID-19 pandemic into account.

Meanwhile, Africa is experiencing a rapid population growth. For example, demographic changes in Sub-Saharan Africa reveal an increase in population from 186 million people in 1950 to 670 million in 2000. While the population estimate for Africa stood at 1,308,064,000 in 2019, this figure is expected to increase rapidly to 2,489,275,000 in 2050. Sub-Saharan Africa is expected to add 1.1 billion people to its population between 2019 and 2050. This will account for more than 50 percent of the global population growth rate between 2019 and 2050 (United Nations 2019).

The age structure of population growth is an important indicator of population-driven development. For example, 53 percent of Africa's population was between fifteen and sixty-four in 2010 (Canning, Raja, and Yazbeck, 2015). The working population between twenty-five and sixty-four is growing faster than other age groups – a phenomenon that may culminate in a demographic dividend in the region (United Nations, 2019). Indeed, this indicates a growing young African labour force. The rising level of educational attainment, especially among women, will result in a lower fertility rate and an increase in skilled labour participation in Africa. Infant mortality is also declining in Africa, thanks to improved health services. How can Europe mentor the emerging army of African workers for mutual development through technological transfer within the Euro–African geo-cultural space?

The labour market integration of migrants at their destination and their economic reintegration in their countries of origin are significant in measuring the migration impact on development. Most African immigrants in Europe are educated and come from families with an average standard of living – an indication that such migrants will sooner or later return to their countries of origin. Utilising African migrants' human capital, such as their level of educational attainment in job placements, could further economic growth in Europe. However, although African migrants are often educated, they are downgraded in the European market through preposterous job placements (Beauchemin, 2018), which in itself can be seen as a bordering method. Yet African diaspora migrants constitute an important intellectual labour resource that could be tapped by the countries of origin to pilot innovation and, by extension, development in the home economies.

Despite low fertility and the ageing EU population, increasing education levels and intergender labour participation may mitigate the effect of the declining pool of the EU's labour resources (Lutz et al., 2019). This postulation implies that immigrants from outside Europe, especially regions like Africa, are not technically needed. However, such studies often fail to consider the effect of disruptions such as the current COVID-19 pandemic and its deleterious impact on the EU's population, and by extension its labour resources. The virulent pattern of the COVID-19 outbreak in Europe exposes the facade of Eurocentric high-tech and state-centric mythology. This appears to be the onset of a series of zoonotic diseases in a rapidly changing global environment. With climate change, environmental transition, and emerging infectious diseases, fluidity in interregional transborder migration flows may become the most sustainable survival strategy in the emerging and changing global disease environment. Europeans may be compelled by nature to seek refuge in Africa sooner than imagined.

The rise of the alternative Chinese model of economic diplomacy in Africa suggests that the Eurocentric strategy towards Africa makes for a detrimental footing for EU–Africa relations. Perhaps in the long run, the Eurocentric purview will facilitate the EU's marginality in the emerging world system. In essence, the future of EU–Africa relations lies in the consummation of an Afro–European geo-culture built on mutual benefit – technological transfer, high labour mobility, the utilisation of the rich natural resource base, and a sustainable vibrant local market. While the Afro–European geo-cultural model promises a potential inner core of the emerging global world system, the Sino–African alternative may make Africa a Chinese economic satellite in Europe's backyard. Besides the Sino-African framework, the African diaspora in the EU may drive glo-capitalism within Africa as an alternative path for African development. This scenario projects the death of national and racial boundaries as control instruments in international economics and politics, and compels the strategic reframing of borders in line with transitions in the socioeconomic and political functional regions in the global world system.

Concluding remarks

Despite the contrasting narratives of Afro–European relations common in the literature, this chapter – using the migration–development nexus as a focus – unveils the complementarity of the EU and African geo-cultural space within the global world system. It showcases the potential to reconstruct Afro–European identities for mutual development. The chapter reflects on the alternative path of geo-cultural incorporation and merger in the global world system. It shows that the ongoing informal but structural externalisation of Chinese boundaries towards the Atlantic will, sooner or later, be consolidated if the EU maintains its path of Eurocentrism. Alternatively, reconstructing an interregional network based on fluid transnational migration and technological transfer will facilitate mutual developmental trajectories in the Euro–African zone. An internal response to the development dilemma in Africa is glo-capitalism, a glocal form of capitalism by Africapitalists. While glo-capitalism draws on the continent's emerging class of entrepreneurs, the African EU diaspora may serve as a vital driving force of this development. Considering the emerging trend of climate change and the interregional spatiality of natural resources, labour, and technological expertise, south–north migration could metamorphose into north–south migration. The reconstruction of Afro–European identities for mutual development offers an alternative that may engender a geo-cultural space at the inner core of the emerging global world system. By adopting an interregional framework built on the reality of global citizenry, the EU could right the wrong of European imperialism in African history by constructing a new identity based on mentorship and a mutual developmental journey towards an EU–Africa geo-cultural economic union.

References

Adams, R. and Page. J. (2005) Do international migration and remittances reduce poverty in developing countries? *World Development*, 33(10), pp. 1645–69.

Amaeshi, K., Okupe A., and Idemudia, U., eds. (2018) *Africapitalism: Rethinking the Role of Business in Africa*. Cambridge: Cambridge University Press.

Amin, S. (2010) *The Law of Worldwide Value*. New York: Monthly Review Press.

Amin, S. (2011) *Global History: A View from the South*. Cape Town: Pambazuka Press.

Arts, K. and Dickson, A., eds. (2004) *EU Development Cooperation: From Model to Symbol*. Manchester: Manchester University Press.

Baker, J. B. and Tsuda, T., eds. (2015) *Migration and Disruptions: Towards a Unifying Theory of Ancient and Contemporary Migrations*. Miami: University Press of Florida.

Baud, M. and Van Schendel, W. (1997) Toward a comparative history of borderlands. *Journal of World History*, 8(2), pp. 211–42.

Beauchemin, C. (ed.) (2018) *Migration between Africa and Europe*. Cham: Springer.

Brown, M. (2017) Drawing Algeria into Europe: Shifting French Policy and the Treaty of Rome (1951–1964). *Modern & Contemporary France*, 25(2), pp. 191–208.

Business Daily. (2016) Africa urges Europe to return stolen funds. (online) Available at www.businessdailyafrica.com/economy/Africa-urges-Europe-to-return-stolen-funds/3946234-3151366-jht25rz/index.html (Accessed 12 September 2019).

Canning, D., Raja, S., and Yazbeck, A. S., eds. (2015) *Africa's Demographic Transition: Dividend or Disaster?* Washington DC: World Bank.

Chase-Dunn, C. and Hall, T. (1997) *Rise and Demise: Comparing World-Systems*. Boulder: Westview Press.

Chase-Dunn, C. and Manning, E. (2002) City systems and world-systems: Four millennia of city growth and decline. *Cross-Cultural Research*, 36(4), pp. 379–98.

Crawford, G. (1996) Whither Lomé? The mid-term review and decline of partnership. *The Journal of Modern African Studies,* 34(3), pp. 503–18.

de Haas, H. (2005) Internal migration remittances and development: Myths and Facts. *Third World Quarterly*, 26(8), pp. 1269–84.

de Haas, H. (2008) The myth of invasion: The inconvenient realities of African migration to Europe. *Third World Quarterly*, 29(7), pp. 1305–22.

de Haas, H., Castles, S., and Miller, M. J. (2019) *The Age of Migration: International Population Movements in the Modern World*. New York: The Guilford Press.

del Valle, H. (2016) Search and rescue in the Mediterranean Sea: Negotiating political differences. *Refugee Survey Quarterly*, 35(2), pp. 22–40.

Faleye, O. (2019a) Irregular migration and the EU-external Border Policy in Africa: Historical and philosophical insights. *Filosofia Theoretica*, 8(3), pp. 59–75.

Faleye, O. (2019b) Border securitisation and politics of state policy in Nigeria, 2014–2017. *Insight on Africa*, 11(1), pp. 78–93.

Faleye, O. (2020) IR Theory: Comparative reflections on EU–Africa relations. In: T. Haastrup, L. Mah, and N. Duggan, eds. *The Routledge Handbook on EU–Africa Relations*. London: Routledge.

Falola, T. and Achberger, J., (eds). (2013) *The Political Economy of Development and Underdevelopment in Africa*. New York: Routledge.

Gammeltoft-Hansen, T. (2011) *Access to Asylum: International Refugee Law and the Globalization of Migration Control*. Cambridge: Cambridge University Press.

Gammeltoft-Hansen, T. and Tan, N. (2017) The end of the deterrence paradigm? Future directions for Global Refugee Policy. *Journal of Migration and Human Security*, 5(1), pp. 28–56.

Grilli, E. (1996) *The European Community and the Developing Countries*. Cambridge: Cambridge University Press.

Hall, T. (ed.). (2018) *Comparing Globalizations: Historical and World Systems Approaches*. Cham: Springer.

Laine, J. P. (2018a) Conditional welcome and the ambivalent self – Commentary to Gill. *Fennia* 196(2), pp. 230–35.

Laine, J. P. (2018b) The ethics of bordering: A critical reading of the refugee "crisis". In: G. Besier, and K. Stoklosa, eds. *How to Deal with Refugees? Europe as a Continent of Dreams*, LIT Verlag: Berlin, pp. 278–301.

Laine, J. P. (2020) Ambiguous bordering practices at the EU's edges. In: A. Bissonnette and É. Vallet, eds., *Borders and Border Walls: In-Security, Symbolism, Vulnerabilities*. London: Routledge, pp. 69–87.

Lasisi, R. O. (2011) *The Image of Africa: Rhetoric and Reality of Afro–European Relations*. The ninety-sixth Inaugural Lecture, University of Ilorin, 4 August.

Le Bars, M. and Lecoanet, D., eds. (2020) *Fluid Mechanics of Planets and Stars*. Cham: Springer.

Lister, M. (ed.) (1998) *European Union Development Policy*. London: Macmillan Press Ltd.

Lutz, W., Amran, G., Belanger, A., Conte, A., Gailey, N., Ghio, D., Grapsa, E., Jensen, K., Loichinger, E., Marois, G., Muttarak, R., Potancokova, M., Sabourin, P., and Stonawski, M. (2019) *Demographic Scenarios for the EU, EUR 29739 EN*. Luxembourg: Publications Office of the European Union.

Massey, D., Arango, J., Hugo, G., Kouaouci, A., Pellegrino, A., and Taylor, E. (1993) Theories of international migration: A review and appraisal. *Population and Development Review*, 19(3), pp. 431–66.

Mohapatra, S., Ratha, D., and Scheja, E. (2010) Impact of migration on economic and social development: A review of evidence and emerging issues. *Background Paper*, Migration and Remittances Unit for the Civil Society Days of the Global Forum on migration and Development. The World Bank.

Moyo, D. (2009) *Dead Aid: Why Aid Is Not Working and How There Is a Better Way for Africa*. New York: Farrar, Straus and Giroux.

Nugent, P. (2002) *Smugglers, Secessionists and Loyal Citizens on the Ghana–Togo Frontier: The Life of the Borderlands since 1914*. Athens, OH: Ohio University Press.

Ortega, F. and Peri, G. (2009) The causes and effects of international labor mobility: Evidence from OECD countries 1980–2005. *Human Development Research Paper*, No. 6, United Nations Development Program, New York.

Paterson, M. and Virk, K. (2014) The ACP/EU historical and trade relationship. *The African Caribbean and Pacific (ACP) Group and the European Union (EU)*: 9–12. Center for Conflict Resolution.

Peri, G. and Spaber, C. (2009) Task specialization, immigration and wages. *American Economic Journal: Applied Economics*, 1(3), pp. 135–69.

Pradella, L. and Taghdisi Rad, S. (2017) Libya and Europe: Imperialism, crisis and migration. *Third World Quarterly*, 38(11), pp. 2411–27.

Prestholdt, J. (2008) *Domesticating the World: African Consumerism and the Genealogies of Globalization*. Berkeley: University of California Press.

Rist, G. (2008) *The History of Development: From Western Origins to Global Faith*. New York: Zed Book.

Rosenberg, J. (2016) International relations in the prison of political science. *International Relations*, 30(2), 127–53.

Tafirenyika, M. (2013) Illicit financial flows from Africa: Track it, stop it, get it. *Africa Renewal*. (online) Available at www.un.org/africarenewal/magazine/december-2013/illicit-financial-flows-africa-track-it-stop-it-get-it (Accessed 12 February 2020).

Taylor, E. (1986) *Differential Migration, Networks, Information and Risk. Research in Human Capital and Development: Migration, Human Capital, and Development*. ODED Stark, Greenwich, Con.: JAI Press, pp. 147–71.

Taylor, I. (2009) *China's New Role in Africa*. Boulder: Lynne Rienner.

Todaro, M. (1989) *Economic Development in the Third World*. New York: Longman.

Trotsky, L. (1930) *The History of the Russian Revolution*. New York: Pathfinder.

United Nations Economic Commission for Africa (UNECA). (2018) Obliterating corruption for development: How the UN plans to support Africa. (online) Available at www.uneca.org/stories/obliterating-corruption-development-how-un-plans-support-africa (Accessed 4 February 2020).

United Nations. (2019) *World Population Prospects 2019: Data Booklet* (ST/ESA/SER.A/424). United Nations Department of Economic and Social Affairs.

Wallerstein, I. (2004) *World Systems Analysis: An Introduction*. Durham: Duke University Press.

Wendt, A. (1992) Anarchy is what states make of it: The social construction of power politics. *International Organization*, 46(2), pp. 391–425.

Whiteman, K. (1998) Africa, the ACP and Europe: The lessons of 25 years. *Development Policy Review*, 16(1), pp. 29–37.

Wilkinson, D. (1995) Central civilization In: S. Sanderson, ed., *Civilizations and World-Systems: Two Approaches to the Study of World-Historical Change*. Walnut Creek, CA: Altamira Press, pp. 32–60.

Wilkinson, D. (2000) Civilizations, world systems and hegemonies In: A. Robert, R. Denemark, J. Friedman, B. Gills, and G. Modelski, eds. World *System History: The Social Science of Long-Term Change*, London: Routledge, pp. 54–84.

World Bank. (2019) Migration and remittances (online). Available at: https://www.worldbank.org/en/topic/labormarkets/brief/migration-and-remittances (Accessed 7 March 2020).

Zartman, W. (1976) Europe and Africa: Decolonization or dependency? *Foreign Affairs,* 54(2), pp. 325–43.

Zinkina, J., Christian, D., Grinin, L., Ilyin, I., Andreev, A. Aleshkovski, I., Shulgin, S., and Korotayev, A. (2019) *A Big History of Globalization: The Emergence of a Global World System*. Cham: Springer Nature.

Closing remarks

Expanding the boundaries of Euro–Africa relations

Jussi P. Laine, Christopher Changwe Nshimbi, and Inocent Moyo

Migration is a much broader phenomenon than the common descriptions would have us believe. Its very complexity creates the demand for simplistic and simplifying explanations and descriptions. Various offers of easy answers to the many open questions have gained wide support – despite their inaccuracy. Yet they have seldom been enough to thoroughly comprehend the witnessed course of events. The success of the often unresearched and unattested accounts highlights the affectual character of the migration debate, in which rational arguments – even if acknowledged and recognised – tend to be pushed aside when the fundamental requirements of both the individual and society are being challenged.

In its response to migration pressure, the EU especially has shown its inability to address the situation in all its complexity. In struggling with many successive and simultaneous crises, the Union's resilience had undoubtedly already been severely weakened before the events that became labelled the "refugee crisis". In this context, migrants have been used as convenient scapegoats and as yet another burden to be endured and funded (Laine, 2020). While the European actions deserve criticism, thorough attention needs to be paid to the development on the African side. Borders not only separate Africa from Europe – both Africa and Europe are increasingly divided by internal borders. Following the European example of rebordering, state spaces seem especially detrimental for Africa, a continent that has historically thrived on mobility and migration, despite the colonially imposed boundaries.

This volume has sought to underline two fundamental notions: that European–African relations cannot be reduced to migration matters alone, and that, while there is no denying that migration constitutes a major challenge both continents on their own and together must address, it cannot be isolated from the broader challenges and phenomena to which it is inherently linked. It has been argued that specific migration or border policies will only have a limited effect because they often fail to address the reasons people are on the move in the first place. Although this volume has drawn attention to the roles of borders, from their management and the regimes that maintain them to their politicised functions and symbolic roles, borders are offered here neither as a clear-cut cause of, nor as a solution to, the challenge migration poses.

DOI: 10.4324/9781003083726-17

Rather, borders have been used here as a prism through which to view broader phenomena from which migration cannot be analysed separately.

Migration between the continents also needs to be reframed and recontextualised. As the chapters in this volume have shown, understanding the complexity of the shifting relations between a Europe in decline and an Africa on the rise will be essential. The narrow framing of African migrants, especially refugees and asylum seekers, as overwhelming Europe and challenging its resilience hides the undeniable fact that most African migrants never leave the continent. Many African states, despite their lack of resources, host far greater numbers of refugees than any European state. While the EU as a whole and its various member states have pushed for increasingly deterrent border and migration policies that have effectively suppressed welcome, developing countries – many of them African – disproportionally host the vast majority (some 85 percent) of the world's refugees (UNHCR, 2019). Some, like Ethiopia and Uganda, are praised for being open to receiving and welcoming those in need.

The widespread unwelcoming attitudes in Europe can be seen as reflecting the lack of political will to address the matter properly and manage the European project amidst the increased uncertainly and anxiety caused by this era's turbulent and unpredictable environment, in which constant, multiple crises have become the new normal, challenging European societies' response capacity and resilience (Laine, 2018). Certainly, speaking of Europe – just as of Africa – as a cohesive bloc obscures more than it illuminates. As the chapters in this volume have indicated, the analytical lens needs to be more specific to allow regional nuances and alternative framings to be brought to light. It is important to remember that there are many in Europe who oppose the populist capitalisation of the fabricated external threat, the dominant securitisation rhetoric, and the simplistic depiction of borders as solutions to the purported invasion.

Despite the peak in asylum seekers' arrivals in 2015, the challenge that ensued cannot be seen as having stemmed from numbers alone. While the arrival of more than a million people is significant, it fades in comparison to many other human flows – be they of tourists or more regular migrants. This illustrates the apparent bordering between those who are wanted and those who are not. Numbers alone do little to explain why a continent in desperate need of more people is fighting so hard to keep migrants out instead of seeking to offer legal and safe ways for borders to be crossed and migration patterns to be managed in order for the demand and supply to be met without discrimination on the basis of where a person was born. Nor do numbers alone explain why the richest continent in the world is struggling to host refugees, while much higher numbers are being welcomed by individual developing countries with challenges of their own. The drivers of antagonistic attitudes and deterrent politics stem from something much deeper; as this volume has suggested, it is likely to be caused by internal insecurities than any external threat.

Building on previous works (see Laine, 2018; 2020; Moyo, Nshimbi, and Laine, 2020), this volume collectively sees that a key part of this is to break away from the dominant migration–security nexus by pointing to the opportunities that welcoming migrants can bring and elucidating them as valuable resources, instead of as a burden or even a threat. Given the realities of today's interconnected world, short-term isolation and exclusionary politics are bound to backfire in the long run. The centrality of migrants in the social, cultural, and economic fabric of our globalised world suggests that only inclusive approaches help protect and promote everybody's rights and well-being, allow communities and societies to respond more effectively to the ongoing crisis, and reduce the risk of future crises (Guadagno, 2020, p. 14).

A key part of the conundrum is derived from the lack of proper information, which is only exacerbated by the wealth of misinformation. The misconstructions of the migration patterns between Africa and Europe that follow have had a negative effect on the entire relations between the continents, thwarting positive advances in other areas. Migration remains the key challenge to relations, yet at the same time it holds the greatest potential. This volume has sought to challenge some of the most prominent taken-for-grantedness and debunk tenacious false narratives about migration from Africa to Europe. It has offered alternative framings that may enable us to take proper action in addressing mutual challenges. Building on the notion that migration has the potential to contribute to the development of both sending and receiving countries (Garcés-Mascareñas and Penninx, 2016), it has highlighted that the marginalisation of migrants seems both unjust and counterproductive. Rather than endangering socioeconomic well-being in Europe, migrants contribute to it. The role of European-based African migrants in the socioeconomic and even political developments of their home countries should be paid more attention, because it is these factors that form the key driver of migration in the first place.

Another layer adding to the complexity of the matter at hand has been introduced by the COVID-19 pandemic. Although it has overshadowed much of the existing migration debates and related concerns, the debate that has ensued has also exposed telling similarities in the underlining thinking about mobilities and movements, and the perceived role of borders in their management. In both cases, the threat is commonly depicted as something foreign, external to "us", whereby borders are posited as protective structures insulating the inside and keeping it safe, secure, and healthy. The lack of proper crisis management has become evident in the uncoordinated approaches to managing borders and balancing solidarity. Throughout Europe, the initial response to both challenges has been to regress to state-centric thinking and nationalist agendas and revert to ad-hoc border closures. In addition to their apparent short-sightedness, rallying around the flag and emphasising national solutions to what are fundamentally international challenges seems inherently ineffective. They are likely also to have more long-term consequences: the commonplace each-to-their-own approach is effectively pulling the rug from under the vision of a borderless cohesive Europe, a hollowing out of the value base on which the very European *idea* has been built.

A matter which would have deserved to have been addressed in more detail in this volume is related to the impact of the COVID-19 pandemic on migrants, and particularly on refugees or irregular migrants, who are in especially vulnerable and precarious positions. As the outbreak of what became the pandemic that now dominates much of societal discussion occurred after much of the groundwork for this volume had been conducted, the topic is not given the prominence it arguably would have gained later. Crossing borders has clearly become more challenging for everyone than it used to be, yet it seems safe to argue that its consequences fall most heavily on those seeking protection, yet lacking the means not only to avoid the infection but to navigate around the travel restrictions. As the UN Refugee Agency has stated, COVID-19 is a "situation unlike anything we've faced before" (UNHCR, 2020), and it is already evident that further closures have forced larger numbers to wait in limbo for extended periods in camps and temporary settlements outside Europe in harsh conditions (see e.g. Liem et al., 2020; Sanderson, 2020; Sobecki, 2020).

Of course, the influence of the COVID-19 pandemic is not limited to people on the move. As Guadagno (2020, p. 2) underlines, the presence of migrants is fundamental for the demographic, social, cultural, and economic dynamics shaping the specific local context in societies and communities throughout the world. The role of migrants ought thus to be paid proper attention not only in responding to COVID-19 but in contemplating recovery efforts. It will be crucial to include migrants not only in effectively containing and mitigating the outbreak, but in reducing the overall number of people affected and shortening the duration of the emergency situation (Berger et al., 2020). Where Europe is concerned, this volume has sought to highlight, in contrast with the common unwelcoming rhetoric, that greying European societies need migrants to survive and prosper. Short-sighted exclusionary decisions made now may prove costly in the long term. Mitigating the economic, social, and even psychological impacts of the outbreak on all affected persons will allow for swifter recovery (Guadagno, 2020, p. 2).

In many countries affected by COVID-19, migrants have been among the frontline workers fighting the pandemic and bearing the cost by getting infected, in some cases lethally (Siddique, 2020). As Guadagno (2020, p. 13) argues, by threatening migrants' permanence and living conditions in receiving countries, COVID-19 is posing systemic risks that governments, employers, and service providers need to manage. Solutions proposed or adopted, including the simplified entry and processing of visa applications (Kucharczyk and Pazura, 2020), fast-track recognition of foreign education and qualifications (Batalova and Fix, 2020), dialogue with and engagement of (irregular) migrant representatives, and economic incentives to motivate citizens and other migrants for specific jobs (Davies, 2020) also serve as a reminder of the economic, social, and political marginalisation migrants were enduring before the outbreak (Guadagno, 2020). Although at the time of writing, COVID-19 dominates the public and political debates, it does not provide a way out of the challenges stemming from the inherent injustices and imbalances that have characterised broader Euro–African relations for decades.

Historical evidence suggests migration between the two regions will continue to be entrenched into the future. People have always migrated and will continue to do so in a post-COVID-19 world. Rather than a threat, migration between Europe and Africa presents an opportunity for the refinement of policy on how these two continents can engage on issues of future common concern. Quite understandably, given their different historical premises, the European Union and the African Union adopt different approaches to the management of migration. While both sides have repeatedly expressed their willingness to work together, they have struggled to understand the concerns, perspectives, and actions of the other. The fact that we simply do not know each other can only be alleviated by encouraging more interaction and engagement, especially at the people-to-people level, not by restricting it.

Here, like the nocturnal drunkard searching for his lost keys under a streetlight because it is where they are easiest to see, solutions for the encountered challenges have been sought in the areas illuminated by their past perspectives and practices. Clearly, as Marchetti (2020, pp. 3–4) argues, Africa and Europe are mutually dependent: Africa needs Europe; Europe needs Africa. Yet the post-COVID-19 world may be ripe for the two to go beyond a relationship of mere dependency and intricately redraw the boundaries of their relations by focusing on networks, flows, and crossroads rather than on borders. The fundamental impact of COVID-19 on all sectors of society may also offer an unforeseen and unique opportunity for the partners to reframe their relations, seek a completely new basis for them, and draft a common proactive strategic vision for the future – not by ignoring the remaining past and persistent hierarchies of scale, wealth, and power but by moving forward by allowing the prime focus of the partnership to be on common future challenges, interests, and synergies. Although we may not be able to change yesterday, we can do something today that may change tomorrow.

References

Batalova, J. and Fix, M. (2020) *As U.S. Health-Care System Buckles under Pandemic, Immigrant & Refugee Professionals Could Represent a Critical Resource.* Washington, DC: Migration Policy Institute.

Berger, Z. D., Evans, N. G., Phelan, A. L., and Silverman, R. D. (2020) Covid-19: Control measures must be equitable and inclusive. *BMJ* 2020; 368:m1141, doi: doi.org/10.1136/bmj.m1141.

Davies, S. (2020) Spain asks illegal migrants and jobless to pick fruit as coronavirus bites. *Reuters*, 8 April. (online) Available at: www.reuters.com/article/us-health-coronavirus-spain-agriculture/spain-asks-illegal-migrants-and-jobless-to-pick-fruit-as-coronavirus-bites-idUSKCN21Q2MX (Accessed 18 Apr. 2020).

Garcés-Mascareñas, B. and Penninx, R., eds. (2016) *Integration Processes and Policies in Europe: Contexts, Levels and Actors*. Cham: Springer.

Guadagno, L. (2020) Migrants and the COVID-19 pandemic: An initial analysis. Migration Research Series, No. 60. Geneva: International Organization for Migration.

Kucharczyk, M. and Pazura, N. (2020) Polish farmers push to keep Ukrainians in agriculture after border closure. *Euractiv*, 20 March.

Laine, J. P. (2018) The ethics of bordering: a critical reading of the refugee "crisis". In: G. Besier and K. Stoklosa, eds., *How to Deal with Refugees? Europe as a Continent of Dreams*. Berlin: LIT Verlag, pp. 278–301.

Laine, J. P. (2020) Reframing African migration to Europe: an alternative narrative. In: I. Moyo, C. C. Nshimbi and J. P. Laine, eds., *Migration Conundrums, Regional Integration and Development: Africa-Europe Relations in a Changing Global Order*. London: Palgrave Macmillan, pp. 93–116.

Liem, A., Wang, C. Wariyanti, Y., Latkin, C. A. and Hall, B. J. (2020) The neglected health of international migrant workers in the COVID-19 epidemic. *The Lancet*, 7(4).

Marchetti, R. (2020) A more encompassing understanding of the African-European relationship. In: R. Marchetti, eds. *Africa–Europe Relationships: A Multistakeholder Perspective*. London: Routledge, pp. 3–13.

Moyo, I., Nshimbi, C. C. and Laine, J. P., eds. (2020) *Migration Conundrums, Regional Integration and Development: Africa-Europe Relations in a Changing Global Order*. London: Palgrave Macmillan.

Sanderson, D. (2020) Coronavirus: Having fled crisis before, displaced people living in Africa's cities are especially at risk. Sydney: Kaldor Centre for International Refugee Law, 7 Apr 2020. (online) Available at: www.kaldorcentre.unsw.edu.au/publication/coronavirus-having-fled-crisis-displaced-people-living-africa%E2%80%99s-cities-are-especially (Accessed 22 May 2020).

Siddique, H. (2020) UK Government urged to investigate coronavirus deaths of BAME doctors. *The Guardian*, 10 April.

Sobecki, N. (2020) In Nairobi, quarantine is a luxury few can afford. *National Geographic*, 10 April.

UNHCR. (2019) Global trends. (online) Available at: www.unhcr.org/globaltrends2018/ (Accessed 18 Apr. 2020).

UNHCR. (2020) Urgent appeal for Coronavirus (COVID-19). (online) Available at: www.unhcr.org/g-5049ea0d6 (Accessed 18 May. 2020).

Index

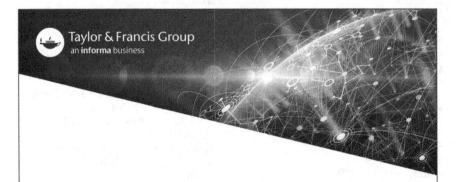

Printed in the United States
by Baker & Taylor Publisher Services